DATE DUE

DE 10 97			
MY 10 0L			
NO 15 11			
OC 22 02			

DEMCO 38-296

IMAGES FROM THE UNDERWORLD

Images from the Underworld

NAJ TUNICH AND THE TRADITION OF MAYA CAVE PAINTING

Andrea J. Stone

♦ UNIVERSITY OF TEXAS PRESS

AUSTIN

Published with the assistance of the Getty Grant Program

Copyright © 1995 by the University of Texas Press

All rights reserved

Printed in the United States of America

First edition, 1995

Requests for permission to reproduce material from this work should be sent to Permissions, University of Texas Press, Box 7819, Austin, TX 78713-7819.

∞ The paper used in this publication meets the minimum requirements of American National Standard for Information Sciences—Permanence of Paper for Printed Library Materials, ANSI Z39.1984.

Library of Congress Cataloging-in-Publication Data

Stone, Andrea J.
    Images from the underworld : Naj Tunich and the tradition of Maya cave painting / Andrea J. Stone — 1st ed.
        p.   cm.
    Includes bibliographical references (p.   ) and index.
    ISBN 0-292-75552-X (acid-free paper)
    1. Naj Tunich Site (Guatemala) 2. Maya art—Guatemala. 3. Maya painting—Guatemala. 4. Cave paintings—Guatemala. 5. Mayas—Antiquities.
    F1435.1.N35S76   1995
    972.81—dc20   94-11145

Dedicated to the memory of Michael DeVine,

who played a key role in the discovery and exploration of Naj Tunich

Contents

Acknowledgments

A study of this kind, involving research in three countries and evolving over more than a decade, could not have materialized without the support of many individuals and institutions to whom I am deeply grateful. I am most indebted to my colleagues who worked alongside me in the field, above all James and Sandra Brady, who in some sense inspired this study by inviting me to work at Naj Tunich in 1981. I am fortunate for having had the opportunity to collaborate "underground" with George Veni, who has over the years shared his vast knowledge of caves with me. Chip and Jennifer Clark also made a major contribution to this study with their superb photographs of the Naj Tunich paintings, taken, I might add, under extremely difficult conditions, such as the fifteen-hour workdays they endured with never a grumble. Others with whom I worked at Naj Tunich include Bernabé Pop, who was especially helpful in the early days of exploration. I immensely enjoyed working alongside Vivian Broman de Morales, Miguel Orrego, and John Pitzer in 1981, and Dacio Castellano and Tito Sandoval Segura were welcome additions to our 1988 expedition. Others who donated their time and energy in the field include Patty Mothes, Roy Jameson, Thomas Miller, Mark Johnson, Elizabeth Williamson, José Aban Campos, Allan Cobb, and Karl Taube. I apologize to Ron Jameson for permit problems in 1987 that botched a planned photographic project.

In the early days of Naj Tunich exploration we often stayed on Emilio Pop's farm, known as La Compuerta. Emilio filled us every morning with greasy eggs and every evening with his homespun humor. I am grateful for having had the privilege to know him.

Matthias Strecker, one of the most generous scholars I have ever known, played a pivotal role in this study by offering me, unsolicited, much of his unpublished research on Maya caves. He continues to be my window onto the world of Latin American rock art. Gary Rex Walters was kind enough to host me at his Laguna Village camp and give me free access to his data. Veronique Breuil also did not hesitate to share her survey data from Yucatan and Campeche.

The first draft of this manuscript was written in 1986–1987 at that oasis of pre-Columbian studies, Dumbarton Oaks. I was fortunate to have spent my fellowship year with co-Mesoamericanists Janet Berlo, Flora Clancy, Karl Taube, and Bruce Love, all of whom freely shared their ideas and friendship. A grant from the Graduate School of the University of Wisconsin–Milwaukee made possible additional time for writing. Grants for fieldwork were provided by the National Geographic Society, the Tinker Foundation, and the Center for Latin America of the University of Wisconsin–Milwaukee. I am especially grateful to the Center for its constant, generous support. I would also like to thank George Stuart of the National Geographic Society for his unflagging interest in cave research.

The cooperation of the Instituto de Antropología e Historia de Guatemala was essential to this project, and I thank the two directors with whom I dealt, Leopoldo Colom Molina and Francis Polo Sifantes. Many other staff members of the IDEAH generously worked on my behalf. I was also assisted by various members of the Centro Regional de Yucatán del Instituto Nacional de Antropología e Historia. Their successive directors, Rubén Maldonado Cárdenas and Alfredo Barrera Rubio, are owed special thanks. I am also grateful to the Middle American Research Institute at Tulane University for use of its archives.

Several individuals commented on various draft chapters of the manuscript. For this, I would like to thank Paul Bahn, Nikolai Grube, Stephen Houston, Virginia Miller, Dorie Reents-Budet, Karl Taube, James Brady, and any others whom I have unwittingly forgotten. Alison Tartt, of the University of Texas Press, did an admirable job of editing the end product. Clemency Coggins wrote what may have seemed like an endless stream of letters in support of this project to granting agencies. David Pendergast and Linda Schele also wrote supporting letters. Rosa Morales Carroll helped with the translation of Catalán.

I am grateful to a number of individuals who supplied photographs: Alfredo Barrera Rubio, Pierre Becquelin, Nicholas Hellmuth, Allan Cobb, Eldon Leiter, Margot Schevill, James Brady, and Matthias Strecker.

Several of my cohorts at the University of Wisconsin–Milwaukee assisted this project in a variety of ways. Donna Schenstrom of the Cartographic Laboratory helped prepare illustrations. Tom Phillip of the Computing Services Division provided hours of cool-headed troubleshooting. Lewis Schultz printed many of the photographic illustrations. My colleague in the Department of Art History, Jane Waldbaum, graciously assisted with Greek as well as many other of my inquiries.

I would like to single out for special thanks two friends who drew me into the world of caves by providing inspiration and opportunities, Thomas Miller and Barbara MacLeod. By letting me tag along on some of his cave expeditions in Belize, Tom guided me through some of the most memorable experiences of my life. Barbara, a phenomenally talented individual and the co-author of Chapter 7, has the most profound understanding of caves in Maya culture of anyone I have ever known. And to my parents, who nursed me back to health on more than one occasion after returning from the field, I express my love and gratitude, as always.

Finally, I want to acknowledge Michael and Carole DeVine, whose marvelous farm, Finca Ixobel, was the perennial starting point of our Naj Tunich expeditions. I have many wonderful memories of Mike, Carole, and their children María and Conrad, from playing croquet with their pet macaws flying overhead to riding around with Carole in her beat-up station wagon. The tragic murder of Mike DeVine in 1990 was a shock to all who knew and cared for him. It will always be difficult for me to comprehend this event, which hangs like a black cloud over the history of Naj Tunich, as Mike was one of the discoverers of the cave.

IMAGES FROM THE UNDERWORLD

Introduction

The paintings and drawings found in Maya caves, the subject of this book, form an intriguing chapter in the history of Mesoamerican art that has yet to be written. Cave art may well be one of the last great frontiers of Maya studies; and, in spite of a recent flurry of books, films, and popular articles on the ancient Maya, their cave art still remains little known to professional archaeologists and the public alike. Yet, owing to the perplexing nature of this art, it is not all that surprising to find it coming to light two hundred years after the dawn of research into Maya civilization. This diverse collection of figures, symbols, and even hieroglyphic writing, found in caverns from the southern highlands of Mexico to the remote Maya Mountains of Belize, was produced by individuals working by firelight with varying levels of skill and different motivations. Moreover, like their Paleolithic counterparts, they did not just decorate rock shelters and shallow caves but also created extraordinary works of art on the walls of deep caves, the kind with vast tunnels and spectacular geological formations.

Cave painting is extremely rare in the world, and the Maya area and western Europe are two of the few places on earth where paintings have ever been found in deep caves. Comparatively speaking, Paleolithic cave painting is far more extensive than the Maya corpus, perhaps on the order of eight times. Obviously it is also much better known. In fact, as it is the only cave art about which most people know anything at all, cave art in its totality tends to be viewed as an exclusive phenomenon of late Paleolithic European culture. This abiding linkage between cave art and some usually fuzzy notion of "cavemen" has not just served to enhance the mystique of cave art, which is already weighty owing to its rarity and exotic location, but also to situate it squarely in the camp of the "primitive." In the popular imagination, cave art evokes scenes of grunting, fur-clad hunters with little on their minds save the next meal. Such un-informed stereotypes (e.g., see Bahn 1992) have fueled the misconception that the making of cave art could only interest "uncivilized" people, like the "caveman" artists and audiences parodied in cartoons (fig. 1-1). Cave art has also become part of an evolutionary paradigm where it alludes to dredging up deep layers of the psyche: to paint on a cave wall is to tap primitive instincts and relive primordial experiences. Cave art is the art of our evolutionary ancestors.

Fortunately, the ancient Maya offer an alternative view to all of this, for, at the same time that they were exploring caves and decorating their walls, they were also building cities, inaugurating kings, waging war, writing in books, practicing astronomy—essentially getting on with the business of civilization (fig. 1-2). Hardly the enigma of the people we typically associate with what might be called "deep-cave art," the Maya offer an unusual opportunity to gain concrete insights into the motivation of this rare, little-understood art form. But beyond this, the paintings and drawings left by the Maya in the earth's deepest recesses, what they viewed as a sacred underworld, reveal in unexpected ways how the natural environment shaped thought and action in aboriginal American culture.

This book discusses twenty-five painted caves found in the Maya area and attempts to assemble under one cover all that is currently known about Maya cave painting. Owing to the relative novelty of this subject in Maya literature, this study has had to contend with a number of unwelcome difficulties. Foremost is a lack of literature, as the cave art presented here has had little previous publication. It also comes from places few readers of this book will ever have a chance to see: caves that are either closed to the public or too remote to visit casually. This, too, is unfortu-nate, as the experience of viewing cave art in situ is well beyond the scope of any book. But even more disturbing is the fact that some of these paintings have already been destroyed and will never again be seen in their original state.

The only published work prior to my own (e.g., Stone 1987a, 1989b) to deal systematically with Maya cave painting is J. Eric S. Thompson's introduction to the reprint of Henry Mercer's *Hill Caves of Yucatan*. In this classic study of Maya cave utilization, Thompson (1975: xxxvi) summarized what was known in 1975 about Maya cave art, proclaiming: "The best Maya cave art is painted, is quite rare, and on present evidence appears to be confined to Chiapas." He managed to describe the entire corpus of Maya cave painting in two pages, testimony to how little was known about the subject. But when Thompson penned his remarks, few painted caves had been discovered in the Maya area. Those reported from Chiapas (Joloniel and Yaleltsemen) and Yucatan (Loltun) were sketchily published, at best, and did little to bring Maya cave art out of obscurity. Certainly, cave painting paled in comparison with the splendid sculptures and paintings left by the Maya in dozens of architectural centers. The few anomalous cave paintings known at that time were of little interest in the face of the archaeological treasures at Maya surface sites.

The status of Maya cave art dramatically changed in 1980 with the discovery of Naj Tunich, a cave located in remote hill country of southeastern Peten, Guatemala. Naj Tunich revealed something unknown in the archaeological record: a corpus of fine Late Classic paintings, including dozens of human figures and hieroglyphic texts. This unprecedented find, reported with much fanfare initially in the Guatemalan press (Rodas 1980) and later in a cover story in *National Geographic*

"I adore your place. Did you do it yourselves?"

FIG. 1-2. Temple I, Tikal.

(G. Stuart 1981), showed beyond any doubt that cave art was part of the ancient Maya's artistic legacy.

Living in Guatemala in 1980, I was able to visit Naj Tunich shortly after it was discovered. I was immediately struck upon arrival by an uncanny juxtaposition of art and environment, one in which delicate paintings, clearly the product of a refined mindset, covered the labyrinthine tunnels of a rugged, three-kilometer-long cave. Not only was this something splendid to see, but it also raised a question: why would the Maya leave paintings of this caliber in a forbidding wilderness? It was a question that drew me to learn more about Naj Tunich and ultimately led to a comprehensive study of Maya cave painting.

The discovery of Naj Tunich seemed to open a floodgate of new cave art finds in the Maya area. In actuality, this was an outgrowth of two earlier trends. One was a revived interest in cave studies by a new generation of Maya archaeologists working on a foundation built by such pioneers as Carlos Navarrete and David Pendergast. Since the late 1970s James Brady, Matthias Strecker, Veronique Breuil, Gary Rex Walters, Juan Luis

Bonor, and others have undertaken cave-centered archaeological projects that contributed to a burgeoning corpus of Maya caves and cave art. But an even greater impact on the discovery of painted caves was the expanding human presence in the jungle wilderness that once formed the backdrop of Classic Maya civilization. And as this process accelerates—something which I think is inevitable—the corpus of Maya cave art will grow in the coming decades, and the ideas presented below will be amended and enriched with every new discovery. I hope this book will serve as a stepping-stone for future studies of new painted Maya caves that will eventually come to light.

History of Fieldwork

My introduction to Maya cave archaeology came by way of two individuals extremely knowledgeable about Belizean caves, my fellow graduate students at the University of Texas at Austin, Barbara MacLeod and Dorie Reents-Budet. In the late 1970s they both worked at Petroglyph Cave in Belize, and under their aegis in 1977 I visited Petroglyph Cave and Footprint Cave. Both caves are extremely large, geologically complex, and remote, and I relished exploring them, even though I was a complete novice.

To my great fortune, an opportunity to work at Naj Tunich arose in 1981. I first visited Naj Tunich in April of that year with Michael DeVine, owner of Finca Ixobel and one of the original discoverers of the cave, along with several other friends. Shortly after our trip, James Brady extended an invitation to study the cave's collection of paintings as part of the first official archaeological expedition to Naj Tunich, along with Sandra Villagrán de Brady and archaeologists Miguel Orrego and Vivian Broman de Morales. Our team worked in Naj Tunich for two weeks in June and July of 1981.

Armed with a permit from the Instituto de Antropología e Historia, I returned to Naj Tunich for a week in September of 1981, this time with archaeologist Mark Johnson and our Australian assistant, Elizabeth Williamson. On this expedition we mapped every painting known at that time in plan and elevation. That was my last work at Naj Tunich for about five years, as I finished my dissertation and began a new academic appointment.

In 1986 I returned to Naj Tunich in an unofficial capacity and sadly noted more damage to the paintings. It became obvious that careful photographic documentation was needed before more destruction ensued. With financial assistance from the National Geographic Society and the expertise of cave photographer Chip Clark and his assistant, Jennifer Clark, both on staff at the Natural History Museum of the Smithsonian Institution, we carried out a photographic project in July of 1988. As we now know, this was none too soon, as the paintings were badly vandalized in 1989. A mapping project was also initiated during the 1988 expedition, supervised by George Veni, the staff karst-geomorphologist. To our delight, a new section of Naj Tunich with an important hieroglyphic inscription was discovered. My final work at Naj Tunich came in June of 1989, when I participated in part of a field season directed by James Brady. All told, I made six trips to Naj Tunich and spent over a month in the cave.

Work in Yucatan began with the encouragement of Matthias Strecker, a German archaeologist now residing in Bolivia. Strecker gave me much of his unpublished research on Yucatecan cave art. Between 1984 and 1990 I made several trips to Yucatan, following leads by Strecker and others, and managed to augment my corpus of decorated caves. I visited five painted caves in Yucatan: Actun Ch'on, Loltun, Tixkuytun, Dzi-

bichen, and Caactun. In 1989 I visited Actun Dzib and Roberto's Cave in the Toledo District of Belize, then under investigation by Gary Rex Walters.

One other field experience important to the formation of my ideas was a three-week expedition in 1984 into the remote Vaca Plateau of central Belize; led by Thomas Miller, it enabled me to participate in the discovery of the largest caves now known in the Maya area. I was deeply impressed with the awesome beauty and size of these caverns, which have passage *widths* of one hundred meters! I was also able to see Maya cave archaeology in its pristine state, for this part of Belize has been virtually intruder-free since pre-Columbian times. The tremendous size and remoteness of these caverns, most of which had been explored by the ancient Maya, gave me a new appreciation of their spelunking abilities.

These excursions into the field not only brought me to Maya cave art but also expanded my awareness of spatial constructs in ancient Maya thought and ritual life. My previous research on Maya art, a dissertation on the Quirigua zoomorphs, also dealt with space, but space figurated in visual metaphors as part of sculpted compositions (Stone 1983a; 1985a). It was obvious even at that time that these sculpted images alluded to the natural, spatial, specifically topographic environment as a means of constituting sacred space; but the caves—with their spectacular terrain and archaeological contents—added a new dimension to what I had known only as symbols manipulated in a pictorial system: the caves themselves, I realized, were the targeted references in the Maya symbolization of sacred space and entailed a distinct set of human experiences. Caves were an unexplored context for the study of Maya art, but at the same time they resonated with symbolic representations of sacred space in the built environment.

Place and Time

In this study "Maya caves" are understood as those found in the area occupied by Maya-speaking people before the conquest, omitting the territory of the Huastec Maya of Veracruz, who were isolated at an early date from their linguistic cousins. The core Maya area roughly includes all of Belize and Guatemala, that part of Honduras west of the Ulua River, and the area west of the Lempa River in El Salvador (fig. 1-3). Maya territory in Mexico encompasses all of the Yucatan Peninsula, Tabasco as far west as the site of Comalcalco and highland Chiapas, where Maya languages have a border with Mixe-Zoquean.

The largest subregion of the Maya area is the Lowlands, which lie below an elevation of 3,000 feet. The Lowlands constitute the most important sector of the Maya area for this study. Geologically they comprise a vast tract of limestone that provided not only an excellent construction material, but also an environment in which caves and other karstic features abound. The Lowlands formed the core area of Classic Maya civilization; they are also the location of most of the known cave painting sites. The Lowlands are flanked to the south by the volcanic *cordillera* that shall be loosely referred to as highland Guatemala and to the west by highland Chiapas. Both of these areas have major limestone deposits and large numbers of caves. The Maya Mountains in southwestern Belize form an upland zone which, as a noncarbonate geological formation, strongly shaped cave development in adjacent limestone regions (see Appendix A). That caves proliferate in

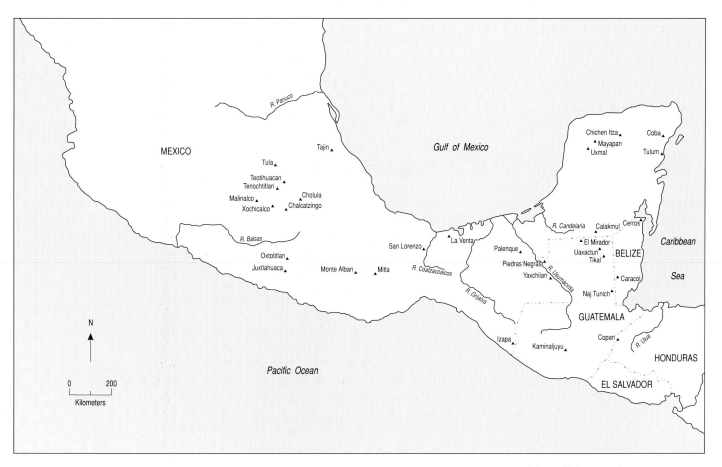

FIG. 1-3. Map of Mesoamerica.

the land inhabited by Maya peoples accounts in no small measure for their cultural importance. And lest there be any doubt that caves are prolific in Maya country, consider the fact that around one Yucatecan town there are reported to be no less than two hundred caves!

The Maya area forms the southern boundary of Mesoamerica; its northern limit is generally placed just north of the Panuco River in Veracruz. Though this book focuses on cave painting in the Maya area, it is set within a broader Mesoamerican framework, and references will be made to cave and surface sites across the region. Material covered in this book spans the greater part of the Mesoamerican culture sequence. Table 1 provides a general chronology for time periods mentioned in the text.

Orthography

The spelling of Maya words in recent scholarly writing has shown considerable inconsistency owing to the use of both Colonial and modern (linguistic) orthographies in spelling native-language terms. Though the linguistic orthography is gradually becoming the norm, it is still common practice to employ Colonial spellings for certain often-used Maya words, such as *katun* (rather than *k'atun*), *kan* (rather than *k'an*), *kin* (rather than *k'in*), and so forth, while simultaneously employing a modern orthography for other words, such as *ahaw* (rather than Colonial *ahau*). Though I attempted to eliminate such spelling inconsistencies, they proved to be unavoidable in that I have preserved original spellings from published sources of many foreign words. In addition, modern Nahuatl orthography has stayed closer to Colonial conventions, and I found it especially unappealing, as a nonlinguist, to change conventional Nahuatl or Mixtec spellings to the system I employ for Maya words. For final clarification the reader

must turn, with my apologies, to native-language dictionaries. It can be assumed, however, that the following spellings represent identical sounds in Mesoamerican languages:

COLONIAL	MODERN
/hu/ (in Nahuatl and Mixtec)	= /w/
/c/ (except before /e/ and /i/ in Nahuatl and Mixtec)	= /k/
/c/ (before /e/ and /i/ in Nahuatl and Mixtec)	= /s/
/k/ (for Maya words)	= /k'/*
/tz/ (for Maya words)	= /ts/
/dz/ (for Maya words)	= /ts'/ = /tz'/
/x/ (for all Meso-american languages)	= /sh/

* /'/ represents glottalization

Scope of Study

The present study is largely concerned with paintings and drawings found in Maya caves and does not consider the production of petroglyphs in any comprehensive fashion; this omission was deliberate. One of my goals was to amass a complete corpus of cave images for systematic analysis, a task that needed some reasonable delimitations. Second, petroglyphs found in Maya caves, with some notable exceptions, are crudely executed and extremely difficult to interpret; many consist of roughly carved human or skull-like heads (e.g., see Bonor 1987:fig. 4; Siffre 1979; Strecker 1984b). A study of Maya cave petroglyphs would not have appreciably advanced my ideas, and their documentation would have been cumbersome. Though Maya cave graphic art has a comparable folk-art component, some of it shares the visual language of the art of surface sites, about which we have a great deal of information. It would appear that overlap between the professional arts and cave art among the Maya was minimal in the medium of sculpture. It also seemed appropriate to focus on painting in light of the emphasis this study places on the art of Naj Tunich. In fact, the discovery of Naj Tunich makes one of Thompson's observations, quoted earlier, seem almost prophetic: the best Maya cave art, indeed, is painted.

Maya cave painting is as much about the received ideas informing spatial categories as it is about the interpretation of isolated images. This study attempts to understand how a spatial environment lends meaning to the content of art and also influences its formal characteristics, shaping it not just through physical determinants but also cultural ones. Though the meaning of art is always contingent upon spatial context, this relationship has not been given due consideration in historical studies of Mesoamerican art. First of all, certain facts need to be at hand, such as knowledge about the original setting of a work of art. Yet this seemingly basic information is often lacking for a variety of reasons, one of which is prehispanic disturbance and the other, unfortunately, is modern pillaging. The issue of art and environment has also been taken for granted to some extent, as it has an anticipated range of possibilities centering on elite architectural complexes.

Clancy (1985) is one art historian who has given some thought to the relationship between environment and the monumental sculpture of the Maya. She divides Maya sculpture into three categories based on its setting: plaza sculpture, architectural sculpture, and buried sculpture. Each class of sculpture has certain thematic and stylistic genres associated with it, often depending on the degree to which this setting is private or public. Caves, however, provide an essentially different kind of setting from the architectural ones typically dealt with in art historical studies. One of the main tasks I have set out for myself is to articulate how this is so.

TABLE I. Mesoamerican Chronology (Maya and Central Mexican Area)

	Archaic	7000–1500 B.C.		
	Early Preclassic	1500–1000 B.C.		
	Middle Preclassic	1000–400 B.C.		
Maya			*Central Mexico*	
Late Preclassic	400 B.C.–A.D. 250		Late Preclassic	400–1 B.C.
Protoclassic	50 B.C.–A.D. 250			
Early Classic	A.D. 250–600		Classic	A.D. 1–750
Late Classic	A.D. 600–800			
Terminal Classic	A.D. 800–900		Epiclassic	A.D. 750–900
	Early Postclassic	A.D. 900–1200		
	Late Postclassic	A.D. 1200–1521		
	Colonial	A.D. 1521–1821		
	Modern	A.D. 1821–present		

The significant difference between these environments rests on the fact that caves hold a special place in Mesoamerican culture; this idea, well known to Mesoamericanists, will be expanded upon in succeeding chapters. Suffice it to say for the moment that caves play a pivotal role in Mesoamericans' conceptions of space and are associated with a number of different ritual practices. These beliefs and rituals will be referred to collectively as a "cave cult"; we should remember, however, that unique constellations of beliefs and rites vary across ethnic boundaries.

The Mesoamerican cave cult is so widespread in time and space that it seems to reflect some fundamental impulse in Mesoamericans' perception of the universe, occupying a central position in what Coe (1981:161) calls the "pan-Mesoamerican religious system with roots in the distant past." The cave cult can be traced through several thousand years of Mesoamerican prehistory. It survived zealous attempts at eradication after the conquest and may have even played a role in the native assertion of ethnic identity, as Broda (1989:145) suggests. Native Mesoamericans who persisted in their ritual use of caves were often mercilessly tortured or in some cases killed. A sixteenth-century Tlaxcalan manuscript details the wretched end met by one native *cacique* caught performing pagan rites at the mouth of a cave (fig. 1-4). Brutally hanged under the stern gaze of a Spanish cleric, the fate of the *cacique* is a warning to onlookers who might harbor any thought of reverting to their "heathen" customs. This kind of scenario was played out in all corners of colonized Mesoamerica on more occasions than we care to imagine.[1] In spite of such repressive measures, Mesoamericans worshipped in caves throughout the Colonial period and continue to do so to this day.

This book is deeply concerned with the context of a particular form of visual expression and, therefore, expends great effort in trying to flesh out all of the nuances of that context. Chapter 2 offers an approach to the perplexing issues posed by art in the landscape, better known as rock art, and introduces the idea of topographic context as a way of reconstituting its meaning. Topographic context is then developed with respect to Mesoamerica and its own special brand of "sacred geography." My understanding of sacred geography

FIG. 1-4. Illustration in Muñoz Camargo's *Descripción de la ciudad y provincia de Tlaxcala*, c. 1585. MS. Hunter 242, fol. 241v, Hunterian Collection, Glasgow University Library. Courtesy of the Librarian, Glasgow University Library.

hinges on a proposed cognitive model of space in which "community" and "wilderness" form binary, but interrelated, poles. Chapter 3 fleshes out context in greater detail by looking at the symbolic role of the cave and its complement, the mountain, in Mesoamerica.

Chapter 4 surveys the archaeological evidence for cave painting, first in Mesoamerica and then in a systematic fashion for the Maya area. The next four chapters, Chapters 5, 6, 7, and 8, discuss the greatest of all Maya cave painting sites, Naj Tunich. Chapter 9 attempts to develop the idea of Maya cave painting as a tradition with regional and chronological variants and with a coher-

ent subject matter. It also attempts to wed the issue of topographic context with the visual evidence.

Interests expressed in this book are admittedly wide-ranging. They encompass such broad issues as rock art in general and sacred geography in Mesoamerica as well as the very specialized subject of Maya hieroglyphic writing. I have taken an eclectic approach to the issue of Maya cave art, culling evidence from all sources that I deemed worthy. My apologies to the reader who might find the technical language in Chapter 7 troublesome, but a serious discussion of Maya hieroglyphic writing, especially texts as difficult as those of Naj Tunich, demands this kind of idiom.

2

The Topographic Context of
Maya Cave Painting

Context and the Study of Rock Art

Cave painting is a type of "rock art" or "parietal art" (i.e., wall art). These conventional terms encompass all manner of human markings on natural rock supports. Rock art can be technically subdivided into rock paintings, also called pictographs, and rock engravings or rock carvings, also called petroglyphs (Grant 1967:12; Meighan 1981:68; Schaafsma 1985:237). "Rock painting" and "rock carving" (or "engraving") are currently the favored terminology; however, in this study I will use "rock painting" and "petroglyph" to distinguish the two primary techniques of making parietal art. The term "pictograph" is the most unsatisfactory, as its usage is the most inconsistent; to some authors pictographs are also carved![1]

Rock art clings to the walls of what to the outside observer is an unmediated natural environment: boulders, rock shelters, caves, and similar kinds of natural settings. Like no other class of cultural artifact, rock art is defined by its setting. Schaafsma (1985:244) characterizes rock art as "seemingly inexplicable graphic imagery often spatially separated from other cultural material." Isolated as such, rock art resides in an environment that often precludes direct archaeological associations. As Davis (1984:10), addressing himself to prehistoric African rock art, puts it, "the context of the rock picture is something other than its position in the archaeological assemblage; the picture *is* the assemblage, *is* the site."[2]

In light of these constraints, how can rock pictures be resituated in a meaningful analytical context? There are as many answers to this question as there are collections of rock art that differ in their fundamental makeup. For instance, Sundstrom (1990), working with a heterogeneous collection of rock art from the southern Black Hills, has developed a two-pronged analytical paradigm centering on style, which is "the basis on which the data are initially ordered into culturally meaningful categories" (p. 7) and context, which has spatial, temporal, functional, and symbolic parameters. Davis (1984), on the other hand, proposes three rather broad avenues of inquiry that lead to a "reconstitution of context" in rock art: art historical, the ethnography of artistic production, and what he terms "establishing a visual grammar." This approach, more in keeping with the tenor of the present study, will be discussed briefly below.

The Art Historical Context

Rock art cultures may also have flourishing arts in other media. Ceramic and textile motifs, sculpture, painting, and the like can provide comparative data with which to identify the style, date, and content of rock art. This kind of comparison is useful not just in finding points of similarity but also in discovering *differences* between rock art and "regular" art. These differences entail their own set of issues: for instance, private versus public art, sacred versus profane space, and professional versus non-professional artists.

While the art historical context of African rock art has shown little promise (Davis 1984:10), that of Mesoamerican rock art is most productive, but only when the rock art in question belongs to a well-known high-art style, such as Olmec, Maya, Teotihuacan, and Aztec. Here we have many avenues of art historical interpretation open, including, for the Maya, hieroglyphic writing, something rarely found among rock art cultures. Indeed, the art historical context for Mesoamerican rock art is so good that the kinds of relational studies that compare rock art and "regular" art are entirely feasible. It is important to point out, however, that most Mesoamerican rock art does not fall into one of these high-art styles, and here the art historical context weakens considerably.

The Ethnographic Context

The actual production of rock art sometimes, though rarely, has been observed as part of a living tradition, as in Africa. We know, for instance, that the Dogon of Mali paint rock shelters with key symbols which permeate their ritual life and art. These paintings play a role in the initiation of male youth and seem to function as mnemonic devices during their instruction (Griaule 1934). Contemporary ethnographic accounts treat the production of rock art for certain areas of western North America. Among the Salish of the Columbia–Fraser River plateau, some rock painting is associated with puberty and initiation rites, the images often being derived from the initiates' visions and dreams. Among the Luiseño of California, rock painting is associated with the girl's puberty ceremony (Grant 1967: 29–30; Wellmann 1979:44, 72).

To have such direct insights into the impetus of rock art requires an observer's close contact with those who produce it. Yet eye witness accounts of this type are rare and are obviously absent in a prehistoric setting. However, ethnography has another role to play, and that is in aiding the reconstruction of past motivations and meanings through analogy. Ethnographic analogy has been used, for instance, by J. David Lewis-Williams (1981) to reconstitute the meaning of cryptic rock paintings made by a now-extinct branch of San (Bushmen), referred to as the southern San. The paintings are found across southern Africa at nearly four thousand sites (ibid.:ix). Based on ethnographic models derived from contact-period and modern San peoples (the !Kung), Lewis-Williams has shown that southern San rock art is very much concerned with ritual behavior—the ecstatic trances experienced by medicine men, for instance. His work shows, too, that southern San rock painting is not only internally coherent, but it may also be the most complex narrative painting style known from pre-modern sub-Saharan Africa.

Ethnographic models have contributed greatly to our understanding of native North American rock art (e.g., see Sundstrom 1990:Ch. 7). One of the more innovative studies is that of Young (1988), who elicited from modern Zunis their interpretation of ancient rock paintings and carvings surrounding Zuni Pueblo. Their responses are obviously more pertinent to contemporary beliefs, but they do point toward possible meanings and functions of rock art made by their distant ancestors.

Another interesting study based on ethnographic models is Sundstrom's (1990:289–292) view of one style of southern Black Hills rock art, the Pecked Abstract style, as "phosphene art." Phosphenes are phantom images seen under certain stressful conditions, mainly from light deprivation or during a hallucinatory state. In lowland South America phosphene art has been linked to ritual drug use by shamans. Sundstrom invokes the South American analogy based on a presumption of shamanic ritual practices, including drug use, in native North American cultures.

Ethnographic Analogy as a Tool in the Study of Mesoamerican Rock Art

Ethnographic analogy is an important tool in the study of Mesoamerican rock art, not just to interpret isolated images, but also to understand the topographic support of parietal art. In the present study that topographic support is the cave. As will be seen in Chapter 3, ethnographic data from many areas and time periods in Mesoamerica have been culled to paint a broad picture of the role of caves in Maya culture. It is an unabashedly pan-Mesoamerican approach that makes liberal use of ethnographic data from all corners of Meso-

america past and present and so may require some justification.

Ethnographic analogy takes as an assumption the continuity of particular forms or behaviors so that the better-documented appearance of that form, whether earlier, contemporary, or later (which is usually the case), can explain the more poorly documented one. Naturally, such comparisons are invalid if discontinuities among seemingly like forms have occurred, whether due to synchronic or diachronic cultural differences.

The debate over the validity of ethnographic analogy as a method of reconstructing the meaning of ancient symbols has been long and fierce, particularly with regard to prehistoric Mesoamerica. Frequently cited are the views expressed by George Kubler and Gordon Willey in *The Iconology of Middle American Sculpture* (1973). Kubler, on the one hand, is skeptical of relying on ethnographic models, just as he is skeptical of the notion of a unitary Mesoamerican ethos and the assumption of continuity, especially if forms are separated by many centuries. Willey (1973:157), on the other hand, supports what has proven to be the more mainstream view—that there is a "fundamental conservatism of all Mesoamerican cultures," making temporal and areal continuity at least a reasonable possibility. Nicholson (1976:159–163) has joined the fray with his own rebuttal to Kubler. I agree with Nicholson that the question of continuity is a "mixed bag," "depending on what aspects of Mesoamerican culture history one selects and emphasizes in support of one's position."

Kubler is closely identified with the so-called "principle of disjunction" (e.g., Kubler 1972; 1973; 1984a), an idea derived from Erwin Panofsky's (1960:84) work on the survival of classical forms in medieval European art. It is important to remember that Panofsky

framed his discussion of this principle in historically precise terms, concluding that, in the visual arts of the high and later Middle Ages, a disjunction of form and meaning had occurred when classical forms became invested with non-classical, contemporary (usually Christian) meaning, while classical content appeared only in medieval form. Panofsky's observation was later extended by Kubler to the more general thesis that form and meaning do not coexist in a timeless, unchanging universe, that, over time, forms become invested with new meanings while old meanings assume new forms. If we take this principle as axiomatic, then it would be unwise to rely on evidence from later cultures to explain similar forms appearing in earlier ones, as the meaning of any form is likely to change with the passage of time. The principle of disjunction constitutes Kubler's main objection to the use of ethnographic models when they attempt to account for temporally distant cultural forms or behaviors.

As Panofsky (ibid.:106) suggested, though, the principle of disjunction must be accounted for by a "fundamental tendency or idiosyncrasy"; it is not a given but rather a result of profound changes in cultural attitudes. He noted, for instance, that in the Carolingian period classical forms retained much of their original meaning; in other words, in this case disjunction did *not* occur (ibid.:82). Kubler (1984a:352) himself acknowledges that coherence of form and meaning over time is possible when he states that "useful objects and everyday expressions usually display a greater conjunction of form and meaning through time than do the more fragile expressions of religious symbolic systems."

Many factors influence the coherence of form and meaning over time, making it difficult to determine precisely which spheres of symbolic expression are most susceptible to disjunction; certainly, historical perturbations are central to the process. But symbols may evolve in such a way that new layers of meaning are added onto old forms, leaving at least a residue of continuity. Likewise, analogous symbols from distant periods or areas may share certain structural similarities, even if their meanings are not completely coextensive. In any case, it seems unlikely that tendencies to retain the coherence of form and meaning are somehow restricted to mundane aspects of culture. Religious symbols embedded in relatively stable phenomena, I would argue, are also likely to have integrity of form and meaning over long periods of time. In Mesoamerica these would be religious symbols that pertain to observations of nature and enduring relationships to the natural environment. Broda (1989:145) also sees continuity in these aspects of Mesoamerican culture: "If there exists a striking continuity of certain elements of Indian cosmovision throughout Colonial times up to the present day, this is due to the fact that this cosmovision continues to correspond to the material conditions of existence of Mesoamerican Indian peasant communities. Observation of nature with respect to geography, climate, astronomy, agricultural cycles and curing practices continues to have validity today."

Though Broda addresses her remarks to the period separating the Colonial and modern native Mesoamerican, her rationale for continuity can be extended back into preconquest times. I would argue that the Mesoamerican cave cult, arising from human interaction with the natural environment, is a likely candidate for cultural continuity. I also believe that the cave cult was widely shared in its essential features and rationale, that it is basic to the common traditions of the Mesoamerican area. Cave symbolism can rightfully be viewed, then, in a pan-Mesoamerican

context. Moreover, by examining the larger picture, the role of the cave in Maya culture can be seen as part of a greater whole.

I want to emphasize, though, that by seeking common threads in Mesoamerican culture, I am not trying to depict Mesoamerica as a "timeless" and therefore "primitive" aggregation of peoples (Price 1989: Chs. 2, 4). Rather, culture can be approached in terms of general and persistent patterns, something that is found in all cultures, even technologically advanced ones like our own. Research problems that aim to describe general phenomena can benefit from casting a wide net. This approach also provides one option when historical texts are limited or absent (Berlo 1983). In the final analysis, however, the validity of a pan-Mesoamerican rationale must be judged on a case-by-case basis.

The Internal Evidence

Davis's third approach to the reconstitution of meaning in rock art is to establish a visual "grammar," which in a narrow sense looks toward a linguistic model to consider relationships among parts of images or groups of images, such that they create "sentences" or a "syntax." More broadly speaking, this method seeks answers in the *internal evidence*, the forms themselves. Since studies of this kind often concern typological, quantitative, and distributional data, they usually require a sizable corpus of images to have any validity (e.g., Lynch and Donahue 1980). This approach may be the only option when cultural context of any sort is lacking, and therefore it is not surprising that it has enjoyed considerable popularity among students of Upper Paleolithic cave art. Indeed one of Leroi-Gourhan's (1982) books on Ice Age painting is a model in the examination of internal evidence; he provides typological studies of form and technique as well as

quantitative and distributional analyses of animal species.

But even in more auspicious circumstances, much can be learned from an examination of the internal evidence. Style—in and of itself, divorced from cultural context—can play a role in the analytical process (Sundstrom 1990). Superimpositions can provide a framework for relative dating. Counting the number of occurrences of a particular motif can also lend important insights, as Lewis-Williams (1981:19–20) has demonstrated in his study of southern San rock painting. Quantitative analysis revealed a disproportionately large number of eland (a type of antelope) and their more consistently elaborate coloration. In an ethnographic context such raw data can be given cultural meaning. For instance, among the !Kung, the eland is not an important food animal but one with pervasive symbolic and religious significance. These quantitative analyses, then, can at least signal motivated choices; their deeper meaning must be sought within the culture itself.

The examination of internal evidence may be most useful in the study of Mesoamerican rock art which does not fall within a high-art style category—that is, the art historical context is poor. Noting the number and distribution of motifs offers some clue as to whether forms have a serious purpose or are mere doodling. The recurrence of a particular form within one site or over a wider area suggests an important purpose. Similarly, if one animal were repeated in far greater numbers, it would be wise to consider the cultural ramifications of this choice.

Topographic Context

A fourth approach to the reconstitution of meaning in rock art is its *topographic context*. Davis (1984:11) mentions topography but mainly in the sense of an armature for the distribution of images, whereas topographic context should also include the culturally mediated perception of landforms that act as a support for parietal art. Cultural mediation of the cave is implicit, for instance, in Leroi-Gourhan's (1982:58) proposal that Franco-Cantabrian caves in Upper Paleolithic times may have played the role of a female symbol. The Easthams (1979) also emphasize the importance of the cave in reading Paleolithic art. They conclude that for some groups of paintings the cave wall with its crags and layered planes represents the surrounding landscape in miniature across which the painted and incised animals appear to run. That the cave must be understood as an integral part of Ice Age painting and engraving is also implicit in Kehoe's (1990) suggestion that some paintings represent animals driven into corrals. Not only are the corrals depicted as small rectangular enclosures, but the cave itself is also to be thought of as a kind of grand corral with animals stampeding across the walls. Finally, Bahn (1978) notes the likelihood that the location of some Paleolithic cave art was determined by the presence of water—for instance, streams and springs—which most likely played a role in the contemporary religion. All of these authors consider the idea that the cave and associated physiographic features had their own symbolic life in late Upper Paleolithic times.

As the immediate physical setting, topography is the most palpable context of rock art, replacing the absent archaeological context not just as a physical surrounding but also as a milieu of ideas. Topographic context has both ideational and behavioral components that include received ideas about the landscape and also actions directed toward it. These actions usually take the form of religious rituals. In many traditional societies landforms, such as caves, mountaintops, springs, and the like, serve in this kind of ritual capacity, or

as what I call a "topographic shrine."

Topography thus serves the dual function of structuring rock art in a landscape and also distributing places of worship considered sacred to a population. Quite often these two functions coincide. This is especially evident in the Americas, where prehistoric and modern rock art sites still serve as active shrines (Schaafsma 1985:261–262). To take one example, the modern Zuni conduct rituals at prehistoric rock art sites. The importance of these places in Zuni religion is often linked with the role topography plays in traditional lore (Young 1988:170, 175). That the original makers of this art were also attuned to the cultural significance of topography is suggested by the fact that certain Zuni petroglyphs actually depict the topographic locale in which they are found (ibid.:175–176). The convergence of rock art with active shrines appears to be a widespread cultural pattern among Pueblo people (Schaafsma 1980:293–294). This convergence is again present in a modern setting in Cochambamba, Bolivia, where Quechua peasants hurl clay and masticated coca on prehispanic rock paintings as part of an elaborate ritual (Querejazu Lewis 1987). What is more difficult to prove, although it has often been proposed, is that the original makers of prehistoric rock art engaged in similar kinds of activities. For example, Heizer and Baumhoff (1962:13) suggest that Great Basin petroglyphs were created by shamans as part of hunting rituals. Rock art of North America has frequently been interpreted as a function of shamanic activities (Schaafsma 1985:260–261; Sundstrom 1990:291; Grant 1967:29; Wellmann 1979:20).

The same rock walls and caverns that draw people to them to make rock pictures also attract them for deeper reasons stemming from religious thought and ceremonial life. This is a compelling reason for people to place rock pictures in some stunningly remote and dangerous places. While rock art may appear to be a search for convenience, taking advantage of easily available wall surfaces, this is less often the case. Producing rock art may require heroic efforts just to reach the site and then to work in the most trying of circumstances. This is especially true of cave art. Consider for a moment an Ice Age cave painter pressing through narrow confines by the flickering light of a torch. In Magdalenian times (ca. 15,000–10,000 B.C.) these artists worked nearly a mile and a quarter from the cave entrance (Ruspoli 1986: 17), an arduous trek by any standards and hardly an exercise in convenience.

The Maya cave painter demonstrates equally amazing feats of daring. We know that the ancient Maya made their way through vast caverns only with the light of torches, sometimes held in ceramic tube holders (fig. 2-1). Prehispanic torch holders and the remains of torches have been found in caves in Belize (Graham et al. 1980: 169) as well as at Naj Tunich (Brady 1989: 257–258).

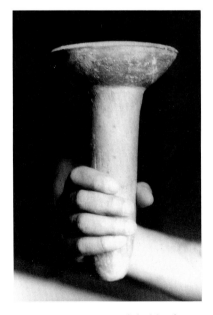

FIG. 2-1. Ceramic torch holder from a cave in Belize.

It is also likely that the Maya explored caves in bare feet, a sobering thought to the heavily booted modern cave explorer. No doubt bare feet provided better traction than wet leather sandals. Footprints preserved in mud at several Maya caves always show bare feet (e.g., Footprint Cave and Naj Tunich). With this simple caving toolkit the Maya explored caverns up to a depth of one mile (MacLeod and Puleston 1980). Maya artists penetrated up to half a mile from the cave entrance to decorate walls. One journey to a painted chamber entails a sheer twenty-foot rope descent exposed to a potentially fatal drop (fig. 2-2). In this case the Maya definitely used ropes in their cave exploration; and to scale steep walls, they would sometimes excavate shallow hand- and footholds.

The Maya made remarkable efforts to reach remote parts of caves, as seen at Hokeb Ha (also known as Blue Creek Cave) in Belize. To reach a remote upper-level chamber, the Maya probably scaled a sheer rock face one hundred feet above the raging waters of Blue Creek, using the trunk and branches of a tree to make the highest part of the ascent. There they left dozens of vessels, including the beautiful polychrome Hokeb Ha Vase, around a stone altar (Palacio 1977). Furthermore, the Maya, like their counterparts in other regions of Mesoamerica, were village and urban dwellers who had a variety of artistic media at their disposal. Yet they chose to explore inhospitable territory to worship in caves and decorate their walls. Among the Maya it was certainly not the case that individuals used cave walls for their convenience in venting artistic urges.

Topographic Context and Sacred Geography

In searching for meaning in Mesoamerican cave art in general and Maya cave painting in particular, we must inevitably turn to the issue of topographic context, for the Mesoamerican landscape had a rich symbolic life of its own. It is widely known that Mesoamericans held, and many continue to hold, certain features of the landscape to be sacred and incorporated them into their ceremonial life (see Vogt 1969: 375–391; Thompson 1959; 1975; Heyden 1975; 1976; 1981). On the one hand, these practices reflect global attitudes. They express "a special complex of relations between man and nature," which Yi-Fu Tuan (1975:11)—borrowing from another cultural geographer, John K. Wright—calls "geopiety." Geopiety, reverence for the earth found in all human cultures, is motivated by the obligation that people feel toward the natural world which sustains them. It also entails the notion of reciprocity; respect for the earth will yield prosperity and harmony in kind.

The Mesoamerican version of geopiety generally goes by the name "sacred geography," defined by Vogt (1981:119) as prominent topographic features "visited and prayed to in the rituals of the people." Turner (1974: 184) also speaks of "ritual topography," which is "a distribution in space of permanent sacred sites." Vogt (1981:120) lists five classes of topography in the modern Tzotzil Maya community of Zinacantan, Chiapas, giving a fair idea of the landforms constituting Mesoamerican sacred geography: *vits* "mountain," *ch'en* "hole in the ground" (such as a cave, well, or ravine), *hap 'osil* "mountain pass," *ton* "rock," and *te'* "tree," with caves and mountains assuming the most prominent roles. These, as well as springs, lakes, and *cenotes* (a type of sinkhole reaching the watertable found in Yucatan), were the places utilized as topographic shrines in Mesoamerica.[3]

FIG. 2-2. Negotiating a shaft in Naj Tunich. The ancient Maya must have descended by a rope or ladder. Photograph by Allan Cobb.

Kaah versus *K'aax:* The Community versus the Wilderness

As stated earlier, sacred geography comprises a set of received ideas as well as corresponding ritual actions. They arise from a cognitive model of space about which we have the greatest detail from Mesoamerican ethnographic studies, albeit a limited number, mainly from the Maya area; but fragmentary evidence of this spatial model also exists in the ethnohistoric and archaeological record. Together they describe a model of socially constructed space that cleaves along the lines of two polar spatial categories: the domestic center or community and what might be termed the wilderness, forest, or bush.

Gossen (1974:Ch. 11, fig. 5) describes such a binary spatial model for the Tzotzil Maya of San Juan de Chamula, in which the realm of the forest and the domestic center paradigmatically align with distinct spheres of cultural phenomena. Spatial proximity to the familiar domain of everyday life, the community, aligns in the Tzotzil model of space and time with nonformal discourse, ordered, mundane life, historical specificity, and recent time. Greater distance or movement toward the unfamiliar domain of the wilderness enters deeper into the mythological past, chaos, and a higher level of symbolic encoding and formalized speech patterns. It is in these distant, obscure places where major deities live, as well as malevolent witches and demons.

Vogt observed a similar socio-spatial dichotomy among the neighbors of the Chamula, the Tzotzil Maya of Zinacantan. He notes the spatial category *te'tik* "forest," which is "an undomesticated domain populated by wild plants, wild animals, and demons" (Vogt 1976:33). The *te'tik* "trees" stand in opposition to *naetik* "houses," protected under the watchful eyes of the ancestors, the Totilme'iletik.

Taggart's (1983:557–567) proposed cleavage of socially constructed space for present-day Nahuat peoples invokes the much-used terms "center" and "periphery":

The center (*centro*) is represented with words standing for the human community-house (-*čan*), community (*pueblo*), or place where one finds Christians from the earth (*tlaltikpak cristianos*). The center represents the moral order and stands for safety guaranteed by that order. It is juxtaposed against the periphery, which the Nahuat regard as filled with creative and dangerous forces. The Nahuat identify the periphery with the word forest (*kwowta*), or with terms for geographical features of the forest that connote danger—a mountain (*tepet*), a canyon (*atawit*), an abyss (*tepekonko*) or a dangerous and ugly place (*owikan*).

As Taggart suggests, wilderness is represented by its most dramatic and dangerous topographic extensions: mountains and caves. These places have inverse qualities of mundane existence. They are associated with chaos in the sense of lacking internal order and spatial divisions. In Gossen's structuralist paradigm, chaos is also drawn into the equation by the fact that the remote and dangerous places in the forest are

also temporally distant and predate the creation of the world when order in its most fundamental sense was established. Interestingly, the ancient Greeks drew a similar analogy, as chaos (χάος) could also indicate a chasm or "passage into the underworld darkness" (Fontenrose 1959:418); in Greek, as in English, "chaos" and "chasm" have a shared etymology.

Burkhart's (1989:Ch. 3) discussion of this spatial cleavage among the Nahua, again couched in the language of a center-periphery dichotomy, also emphasizes the importance of the periphery's lack of spatial order, which parallels its lack of social and moral authority. This is picked up again by Hanks (1990:306) when working among the Yucatec Maya of Oxkutzcab. Their binary spatial categories are *kaah* "town, inhabited space" and *k'aax* "forest." Disorder is likewise inherent to the Yucatec forest: "It is a dangerous place outside the realm of the guardian spirits posted at the cardinal corners of inhabited and cultivated space. It lacks the many internal divisions and marked perimeter of all socially defined spaces" (Hanks 1990:306).

In Yucatan the binary relationship between *kaah* and *k'aax* is also realized in contrasting linguistic (prepositional) forms: *yook'ol* "over" and *yaanal* "under." Domestic life in Yucatan is carried out upon or over the earth, which can be seen in the expression for "world," *u yook'ol kaab* "upon this earth" (Sosa 1985:404). However, one is said to walk under (*yaanal*) the bush (Hanks 1984:133; 1990:306).

This binary spatial model should not be seen, however, as inflexible, as there were gradations and blendings of "community" and "wilderness" space. Hanks (1990:307) mentions that agricultural land in Oxkutzcab is a kind of intermediate space, associated both with the bush and socially ordered space. What seems more likely is that community

and forest space had intermediate forms or could symbolically interpenetrate. Such interpenetration is suggested by the use of plants as ritual offerings at Zinacanteco cross shrines, located in the "forest" zone. Vogt (1976:47) sees a nature-culture opposition between the wild pine tree, present as pine boughs tied to the crosses and a carpet of pine needles, and red geraniums laid on the altar. The pine trees are invariably placed toward the "forest" (*te'tik*) side of the altar and the red geraniums toward the "houses" (*naetik*). Thus, domestic space can have a symbolic presence at the topographic shrine.

The Cave as *K'aax*

It could be argued that caves epitomize wilderness in Mesoamerica, for it is essentially defined by its physical distinctiveness from the community. I can imagine no type of environment that breaks so strongly with customary experience as the cave. It is a dim, bone-chilling world, with dazzling geological formations and curious inhabitants, such as bats, blind, pigmentless crabs and fish, and extraordinarily delicate insects. Cave entrances have their own breathtaking beauty (fig. 2-3). The cave interior is the antithesis of an ordered environment, articulated by a bizarre stone landscape (fig. 2-4). With meandering tunnels difficult to perceive in poor light, the cave defies physical assessment and is in a sense unmeasurable. Cave interiors present a given set of conditions to which the intruder responds rather than controls. Since the sun's motion cannot be seen in a cave, socially ordered space, as established by the path of the sun (Gossen 1974), is inoperable.

While the forest is dangerous, it is also seen as closer to the supernatural powers of the earth—indeed, it is their dwelling place—and that is why the topographic shrine must be visited: to establish a line of communication with

FIG. 2-3. Entrance to Actun Kabal, Belize. Photograph by Steve Knutson.

divine forces which can benefit the human petitioner. Vogt (1969:375) sees the wooden Latin crosses which mark Zinacateco altars at mountain shrines as symbolic doorways to the world of deities and ancestors who are petitioned there; offerings at cross shrines are called in Tzotzil "visits to the gods" (Vogt 1976:44).

Indeed, the spatial gulf that distances the topographic shrine from everyday affairs is coveted insofar as it opens up this line of communication with the sacred.[4] Conversely, to have ready access dissipates qualities of sacredness. It is stated by both Las Casas writing on the people of Verapaz (Thompson 1959: 122) and Ximénez (1857:180) on the Quiche that Indians would hide their idols in dark places because it was believed that, if they were seen too frequently, the people would lose respect for them. We also know that the Aztecs shrouded their cult statue of Cihuacoatl in utter seclusion (Durán 1971:211), perhaps for the same reason. Indeed, there were prohibitions against looking directly at the Aztec *tlatoani* (ruler), perhaps to preserve respect by not gazing upon him too frequently (Todorov 1984:71–72).

That physical remoteness sanctifies space is also seen in the Maya concept of *suhuy*, usually translated as "virgin." In expanding upon the meaning of *suhuy*, Redfield and Villa Rojas (1934: 131) show that it is attributed to things unsullied by the human presence, often because of spatial remoteness: "The water, drawn for the ch'a-chaac from covered cenotes where men seldom or never come, is zuhuy ha [virgin water]. The animals of the zip, the deer that are kept by their supernatural owners in secluded spots in the woods, are zuhuy alakob. A hammock or tablecloth that has never been used is zuhuy. The high bush, distant from the homes of men, is zuhuy."

FIG. 2-4. The stone landscape of Actun Kabal, Belize. Photograph by Thomas E. Miller.

Large caves and, even more so, remote parts of large caves were among the most distant and unsullied (*suhuy*) places in the Maya universe.[5] Thompson (1959; 1975) first proposed that the Maya sought *suhuy ha* "virgin water" in caves, providing an explanation for the vast number of water-collection vessels found in them.

The most stunning example of such water collection I have seen in a prehispanic setting is from the Actun Kabal cave system in the Vaca Plateau of Belize, utilized in the Late to Terminal Classic period. Near one entrance into the cave system the Maya had ascended a narrow, precipitous slope that was exposed to a one-hundred-foot drop, passed through a spacious terraced chamber, and climbed up a steep fifteen-foot wall of friable rock where we observed crude hand- and footholds. Having scaled the wall, they continued up a narrow, winding passage, finally stopping to deposit several *ollas* on bases of broken pottery and stalactites. One of the *ollas* had clearly been left to collect water, as it was sitting under an active drip. Coated in a thick layer of calcite and bearing the weight of a growing stalagmite, the pot was brimming with water (fig. 2-5). Since a river flows through a more accessible part of the cave, it is certain that the Maya were seeking this remote water source for ritual purposes.

The Origins of Sacred Geography

Sacred geography can be presumed to be very ancient precisely because it is so widely shared among Mesoamerican societies, suggesting that some form of it was part of the belief system of the "mother culture." Little is known about the ceremonial life of Mesoamerica's nomadic Archaic populations, but we do know that caves were used for burial rites during the Archaic. Three caves in the Tehuacan Valley (Coxcatlan, Purron, and El Riego) have burials in El Riego phase levels, ca. 7000–5000 B.C. (Anderson 1967:96). Late El Riego phase (ca. 5500–5000 B.C.) burials in the Coxcatlan Cave revealed especially elaborate ritual treatment of the dead (Drennan 1976:350–351). In one case the bodies of a young woman, an elderly man, and a child were placed in a grass-lined pit. Baskets, netting, and cloth were found near each body. Red paint had been sprinkled on the female, and the male skeleton was charred black. The child, whose skull had been smashed, had probably been sacrificed. In another multiple burial, a six-month-old infant was interred over a five-year-old child. Both children had been decapitated and their skulls exchanged (Anderson 1967:94–95). One of the skulls was found in a basket along with beads and some vertebrae. These finds have been touted by MacNeish (1972: 71) as "the beginning of the ritual activities that became so prevalent in Mesoamerica." Drennan (1976:351) remarks, "What the El Riego phase burials do show is that even preceramic Mesoamerica probably had a substantial body of ritual out of which the great ceremonialism of the Formative could evolve."

These elaborate burials are significant not just in their ritual treatment of the dead; they also show that caves served as ritual settings in Mesoamerica as early as the Archaic period. Some of these caves, utilized both as Archaic base camps and places of burial and sacrificial rites, and possibly other rituals unknown to us today, may have evolved into permanent sacred sites. Loltun Cave in Yucatan, for example, was visited by Archaic hunters; stone tools have been found there in association with skeletons of extinct megafauna (MacNeish 1983:127; Velázquez 1980). Loltun was also an important ritual cave in the Preclassic, and in the Proto- and Late Classic its walls were painted and carved. It is possible that the beginnings of ritual activity at Loltun go back to the Archaic, though conclusive evidence of this is lacking. Certainly the use of natural landforms as ritual sites must have been more widespread during this "architecture-less" Archaic period than the archaeology suggests. This tradition may have sown the seeds of Mesoamerican sacred geography. Though caves alone have preserved the remains of Archaic "ritual

FIG. 2-5. Late Classic Maya collected drip-water in the ceramic vessel with a stalagmite on the edge, Actun Kabal, Belize. Photograph by George Veni.

in the landscape," other topographic features may have served a similar function.

Yet it would seem only logical that the wilderness-community dichotomy, an essential ingredient of Mesoamerican sacred geography in its later form, evolved after the advent of settled village life, when such a view of space had meaning in human spatial experience. It has been noted in Africa, too, that nomadic and seminomadic peoples—hunters and gatherers and pastoralists—have a different relationship to the land than those who live in permanent communities and who cleave space along a

village-wilderness model (Anderson and Kreamer 1989:23–24).

In any event, sacred geography, fully developed, does seem to be present in Mesoamerica by the earliest appearance of high culture. It is discernible in the earliest phase of Olmec art, seen for instance in the mutilated Monument 20 from San Lorenzo (fig. 2-6), which dates no later than the San Lorenzo phase, ca. 1150–900 B.C. (Coe and Diehl 1980:330). Tabletop altars feature a three-dimensional carved figure seated in a niche, here badly effaced. Altar 4 from La Venta (see fig. 4-5) is a better-preserved example of this type of monument. Middle Preclassic works of art, such as Altar 4 and a mural found over a cave entrance at Oxtotitlan, Guerrero (see fig. 4-4), show beyond doubt that the niche represents a cave entrance (Grove 1973). These works of art demonstrate that the earliest Olmec imbued caves with at least some of the supernatural qualities that are better known among later Mesoamerican cultures (e.g., Thompson 1959; 1975; Heyden 1975; 1981). That the Olmec inherited a notion of the cave's sanctity from an earlier population or phase of development is suggested by the fact that major Olmec sites are located in a swampy, coastal plain, not near caves. Cave ideology probably had its beginnings in an area where caves had a stronger presence in the immediate environment. The role that the Tuxtla Mountains played in Olmec sacred geography is obscure, but the Tuxtla Mountains contain caves that today serve as topographic shrines (Olavarrieta 1977:133). Whether they also served the Olmec in this capacity is not known, though it seems highly likely.

Sacred Geography and Art

Sacred geography played a major role in the development of Mesoamerican ceremonial architecture, and it also forms the basis of much Mesoamerican iconography (Carlson 1981; Stone 1992). One can find analogous concepts in other art traditions. For instance, a recent monograph on African art shows that a village-wilderness spatial paradigm informs a rich tradition of west African sculpture (Anderson and Kreamer 1989). The spatial categories are remarkably similar in their symbolic associations with their Mesoamerican counterparts. In west Africa, as in Mesoamerica, the forest is considered dangerous but also a locus of supernatural forces that must be addressed.

Cave art's placement in wilderness makes it distinct, and even more so in light of the fact that caves also served as topographic shrines. The topographic shrine is remote from the community in both a physical and psychological sense. The private and personal character of the topographic shrine will be seen to influence Maya cave painting, its content, and its rules of decorum. The reconstitution of meaning in Maya cave painting inevitably returns to topography, mute only to those who are unacculturated. The context of Maya cave painting is nothing less than the sacred earth perforated by an enormous cavity that established a meeting ground between the human and the divine.

FIG. 2-6. One of the earliest surviving depictions of a cave in Mesoamerica, Monument 20, San Lorenzo. From Coe and Diehl 1980: fig. 451.

Images from the Underworld

3

A Further Exploration of Topographic Context:
The Mesoamerican Landscape and the Cave

The Mesoamerican Landscape

Vivification of the Landscape
and Its Representation

Topography was a critical concept in prehispanic Mesoamerican religion, as the earth and all of its topographical extensions were considered to be alive and, as living beings, to interact in human affairs. Topographic features were often personified (Hunt 1977:95; López Austin 1980:396). For instance, in one well-known Aztec creation myth, preserved in the *Histoyre du Mechique*, the earth appears as a saurian monster, called Tlaltecuhtli (earth lord), floating on the dark seas of the pre-creation universe. The story relates that two gods in the guise of great serpents, Quetzalcoatl and Tezcatlipoca, suddenly descend upon the earth monster and cleave her body into two parts. One half rises up to become the sky. The other becomes the earth and is transformed into a lush carpet of verdure, punctuated by major topographical features: "they made

from her hair, trees and flowers and meadows; from her skin, the very delicate grass and tiny flowers; from her eyes, pools and springs and small caves; from her mouth, large rivers and caverns; from her nose, valleys and mountains" (Garibay 1965:108; my translation). This story encapsulates a view of terrestrial topography present in all Mesoamerican cultures: that it *is* the body of a divine being. The concept of a personified earth also informs the linguistic classification of *oztotl* "cave" and *tepetl* "mountain" as animate nouns in Classical Nahuatl.[1]

Anthropomorphic metaphors for the earth are especially prevalent in the art of central Mexico. Laden with death and sacrificial accoutrements, a hocker figure—part human, part clawed beast—portrays the earth as the devourer of human blood and body parts, which she perpetually craves (fig. 3-1). The earth monster takes on many guises. On the one hand, the aforementioned Tlaltecuhtli is conceived as a toad or saurian with knifelike fangs and joints formed from snapping jaws, ever ready to consume humans sacrificed for the earth's sustenance (Nicholson 1971:406). The Aztec earth monster also took the form of such goddesses as Cihuacoatl, Coatlicue, and Coyolxauhqui, who, like the earth in the Aztec origin myth mentioned above, were also slain and dismembered (Klein 1988).[2] The zoomorphic features of these earth monsters—fangs, claws, and eyes—were inset into a band that functioned as a terrestrial platform, not just identifying the ground, but the animate, sacred earth (fig. 3-2). These earth monsters have knees and elbows transformed into eery faces with exaggerated teeth, emphasizing the earth's lust for blood and hearts, as well as its identification with the dangerous beasts of the forest, the seat of supernatural power.

While at times assuming a human countenance, the earth was also conceived in Mesoamerica as a theriomorph, having features of a crocodilian, toad, or turtle, or any combination of these creatures. What they all have in common is their shape: low and flat like the surface of the earth. They are also creatures of the water, the medium in which the earth was seen to float. One such being was called Cipactli by the Aztecs, and it represented the plane of the earth or at times an entrance into the earth in the guise of a gaping jaw (fig. 3-3). In the *Historia de los mexicanos por sus pinturas*, Cipactli is also described as a big fish and is identified with the earth lord Tlaltecuhtli (Garibay 1965:25–26).

Perhaps the most ancient zoomorphic model of the earth in Mesoamerica is saurian. This is certainly one aspect of the "Olmec Dragon," a pervasive supernatural in Middle Preclassic Mesoamerican iconography (Joralemon 1976). The Late Preclassic Stela 25 from Izapa shows the tail of an upended caiman blooming into a tree (fig. 3-4). In Classic Maya art the top of Altar T from Copan represents a caiman as the plane of the earth (fig. 3-5; Thompson 1970a: 220). The benign Maya crocodilian usually floats among water lilies with fish nibbling at the blossoms. The saurian was also incorporated into complex compositions by giving theriomorphic creatures scaled limbs and belly plates; Zoomorph B from Quirigua is configured in this fashion (fig. 3-6). Here the creature's saurian-terrestrial attributes are integrated with other cosmic symbols (Stone 1985a). In Postclassic Yucatan saurian earth monsters took on an even more prominent role in the guise of Itzam Cab Ain, an avatar of Itzam Na (Taube 1989b).

The Maya also envisioned the earth as a large disk that could take the form of a turtle's back (fig. 3-7). The shell of the turtle made it a particularly appropriate terrestrial image when the Maya wished to show the earth as a platform support (fig. 3-8) or integrate space with cyclical concepts of time. Taube (1988a) has shown, for example, that the turtle-earth disk was often combined with hieroglyphic references to the twenty-year *k'atun* cycle.

Caves and mountains are other topographic features incorporated into Mesoamerican iconography. The earliest representation of a cave in Mesoamerican art occurs at the end of the Early Preclassic period at the Olmec site of San Lorenzo. Just as sculpture in the round predominates in this period, the cave is rendered three-dimensionally, as a niche sculpted into a tabletop altar (fig. 2-6). As the symbol system matured in the Middle Preclassic, conventional signs for caves appear, one being the quatrefoil. This four-lobed version of a cave entrance comprises a Middle Preclassic sculpture from Chalcatzingo, Monument 9 (fig. 3-9; Grove 1968:489–490). Eyes and a nose turn the quatrefoil into the open mouth of a zoomorph, figuring the cave as a living extension

FIG. 3-1. Aztec anthropomorphic earth monster. Adapted from Seler 1963: vol. 3, fig. 267.

of the earth. The creature's terrestrial identity is signaled by plants sprouting from the corners of the quatrefoil. The quatrefoil cave entrance is a standard fixture of Mesoamerican pictorial systems, though the quatrefoil represents not just a cave entrance but any kind of sacred aperture.

Cave entrances are also pictured as the open mouth of some wild beast, such as a serpent, saurian, or jaguar, a device also favored in architectural renditions of caves (figs. 3-10, 3-11; Gendrop 1980; Schávelzon 1980). Animals selected to represent the cave were metonyms signifying "wilderness"; that is, a jaguar or serpent could stand in a general way for "forest space," and their open mouth alluded to the penetration of this sacred zone. Indeed, the open maw of a beast, a common motif in Mesoamerican art, essentially represented a portal into sacred space. For the Maya the mouth-doorway analogy also has a linguistic correlate in that any opening, whether a mouth or doorway, could be expressed by the same term or a closely related one.[3] In Yucatan today the Maya of Yalcoba still view the cave entrance as the open mouth of a wild beast (Sosa 1985: 414).

FIG. 3-2. Aztec earth band is composed of mouth parts and eyes, Dedication Stone. Adapted from Pasztory 1983: pl. 95

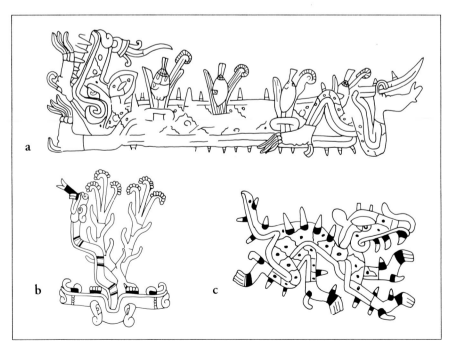

FIG. 3-3. Central Mexican earth crocodiles: *a,* Borgia 27, adapted from Puleston 1977: fig. 6; *b,* Fejervary-Mayer, adapted from Seler 1963: vol. 2, fig. 104; *c,* Borgia 21, adapted from Seler 1963: vol. 1, fig. 1.

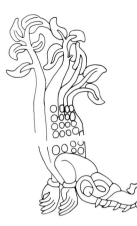

FIG. 3-4. Preclassic earth crocodile, Stela 25, Izapa. Adapted from Cortez 1986: fig. 56.

FIG. 3-5. Maya earth crocodile, Altar T, Copan. Adapted from Puleston 1977: fig. 4.

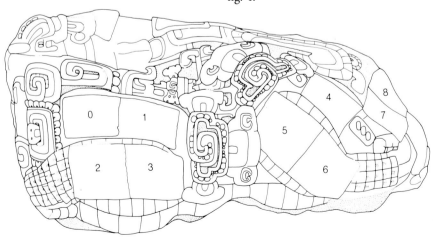

FIG. 3-6. Maya earth crocodile combined with diverse symbols, Zoomorph B, Quirigua.

The earliest representations of mountains in Mesoamerican art are also three-dimensional; they are the large mounds dominating many Preclassic sites (fig. 3-12). Conventional signs for mountains appear in the Classic period. At Teotihuacan one such sign is a cluster of rounded cones (see fig. 3-29). Images of the Great Goddess of Teotihuacan, whose body at times is penetrated by cavities, may be the anthropomorphic embodiment of mountains.[4]

Thanks to hieroglyphic detective work by David Stuart (1987), we now know that the Maya also had their conventional sign for mountains in the guise of the Cauac Monster (also called the Wits Monster). This zoomorphic creature, always appearing as one or multiple heads, has a long, down-curved snout, stepped forehead (usually in the form of a half-quatrefoil), and pendant vegetal motifs often referring to maize (fig. 3-13a–c). Circlet clusters (the so-called "bunch of grapes"), curved dotted lines, and crosshatched semicircles are symbols that identify the Cauac Monster and the related glyph T528. The Cauac Monster gets its name from the day called Cauac in Yucatec (fig. 3-14a), a word meaning "lightning" (Kaufman and Norman 1984:89) but related as well to rain and storms. "Cauac" markings can also signify "stone" and in a cartouche can represent individual stones (fig. 3-14b). They also mark spear points and other objects made of stone (fig. 3-14c). In glyphic contexts this symbol, with the addition of a phonetic complement (T116), is one version of the "*tun*" glyph, which means both "stone" and the 360-day period known as the "*tun*."

Images from the Underworld

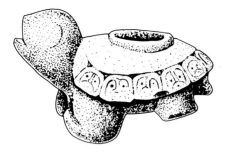

FIG. 3-7. Stone censer from Mayapan. Back of turtle represents terrestrial space, and 13 "Ahau" glyphs rim the shell. From Taube 1988a: fig. 2a.

FIG. 3-8. Deceased figure rides on turtle-earth platform, Madrid 71b. Adapted from Lee 1985.

FIG. 3-9. Entrance into the sacred earth through a zoomorphic quatrefoil portal, Monument 9, Chalcatzingo. Adapted from Grove 1987.

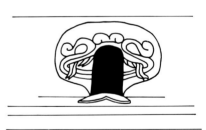

FIG. 3-10. Zoomorphic mouth portal, Temple 1, Malinalco. Adapted from Schávelzon 1980: fig. 14.

FIG. 3-11. Zoomorphic mouth portal, Building 1, Tabasqueño. Adapted from Gendrop 1980: fig. 8.

FIG. 3-12. Architectural mountain in Complex C, La Venta. Adapted from Miller 1986: fig. 8.

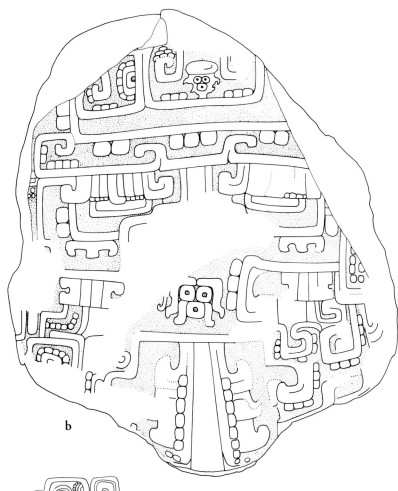

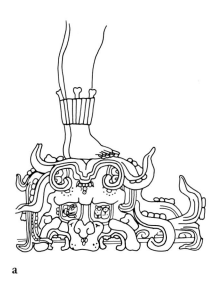

a

b

c

FIG. 3-13. Cauac Monsters: *a,* Temple of the Foliated Cross, Palenque, adapted from drawing by Linda Schele; *b,* top of Zoomorph O, Quirigua; *c,* detail of Stela 1, Bonampak, adapted from Mathews 1980: fig. 3.

Images from the Underworld

The Cauac Monster forms enclosures in which figures sit or from which they emerge (e.g., fig. 3-31). These shelters have long been identified as caves (Taylor 1980; Tate 1982). As Stuart (1987) has shown, some Cauac Monsters are tagged glyphically by the word *wits*, which means "mountain" in many Mayan languages (in fig. 3-13a, the glyph in the right eye reads *wits nal* "maize mountain"). Thus, the Cauac Monster as an external structure can represent a mountain, but, as an enclosure, it can also represent a cave.

Tikal Altar 4 shows the marvelous visage of a Cauac Monster, eyes draped in foliage and the edge of the upper lip marked by reptilian scales that ally this creature with wild animals of the forest (fig. 3-15). The open mouth takes the expected form of a quatrefoil, and within it sits the old God N, wearing his turtle carapace. In his right hand he raises a dish holding some ritual object: a torch or cigar and a sharp bloodletting instrument. Here the Cauac Monster surely alludes to a topographic (cave) shrine wherein a quadripartite version of God N performs ritual acts.

One conventional sign for mountains in central Mexican iconography also seems to have developed in the context of the writing system, specifically in its use as a toponym. Perhaps the earliest version of this glyph occurs in Zapotec writing, a stepped form that represents a hill or mountain (fig. 3-16; Caso 1946:124). This sign is antecedent to the toponym for "hill," appearing later in the Mixtec codices (fig. 3-17). The Mixtec version includes a basal cavity filled with water, as though acknowledging that mountains are often penetrated by water-filled caves. The Mixtec codices preserve some of the most complex landscape scenes in all of Mesoamerican art. They have conventional signs to show cliff faces, caves, springs, hills, and plains (Smith 1973:charts 3 and 4) and often combine these in

FIG. 3-14. Use of "Cauac" symbols: *a,* as Cauac day sign; *b,* as individual stones, Madrid 70b, adapted from Lee 1985; *c,* on stone axe, Dumbarton Oaks Tablet, adapted from drawing by Linda Schele.

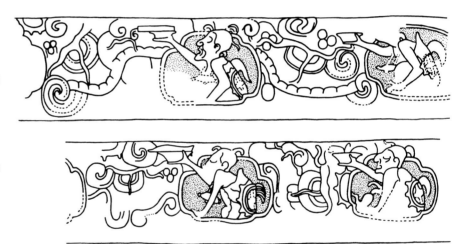

FIG. 3-15. God N, holding various ritual objects, in four cave shrines, Altar 4, Tikal. Adapted from Jones and Satterthwaite 1982: fig. 58b.

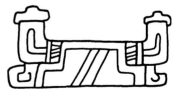

FIG. 3-16. Zapotec mountain symbol, Mound J, Monte Alban. Adapted from Caso 1946.

FIG. 3-17. Mountain symbol in Post-classic central Mexican art. Adapted from Nuttall 1975.

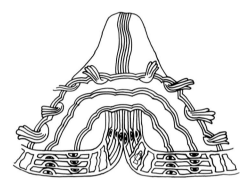

FIG. 3-18. Mountain and gushing spring from the Tlalocan mural, Tepantitla, Teotihuacan. Adapted from Taube 1983: fig. 41c.

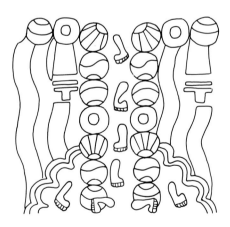

FIG. 3-19. Spring shown as shells gushing from scalloped orifice, Palace of the Jaguars, Mural 4, Teotihuacan. Adapted from Miller 1973: fig. 33.

elaborate scenes to represent known geographical locales (e.g., Byland and Pohl 1987).

Regional Topography and Ecology

While regional styles of Mesoamerican art generally access the same topographic inventory—the earth, caves, and mountains—they can also reflect local ecological conditions. For example, springs appear in the art of Teotihuacan. The volcanic mountains surrounding the site are the source of permanent springs that contributed to the area's viability for human habitation. Springs, represented by wavy bands of water or rows of seashells, gush out of scalloped orifices (figs. 3-18, 3-19). In general, springs are more prominent in the art of central Mexico, appearing also in the Mixtec codices (fig. 3-20).

On the other hand, in the Maya Lowlands the water lily, taking what seems to be an endless variety of forms, is the most important aquatic metaphor (fig. 3-21; Rands 1953; Bowles 1974). The water lily can be identified by its blossom, from which derives the form of the "Imix" glyph (Thompson 1960: 72). The large, scalloped water lily pad bears a diamond pattern with central dot, which has a wide distribution in Mesoamerican art, associated with various terrestrial images, such as crocodiles, turtles, and mountains (e.g., figs. 3-3, 3-30). This conventional form for the water lily pad apparently derives from the Olmec, as suggested by carved pottery motifs on San Lorenzo phase ceramics (ca. 1150–900 B.C.), which depict the characteristic scalloped contour and dotted diamond pattern of the pad (Coe and Diehl 1980: vol. 1: fig. 140b, f). As the Olmec inhabited a swampy coastal plain, their use of the water lily as an aquatic symbol comes as no surprise. Puleston (1977) showed that the water lily in Maya art has agrarian references, alluding to the seasonally

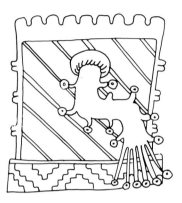

FIG. 3-20. Spring gushing out of a rock wall, Nuttall 53. Adapted from Nuttall 1975.

inundated *bajos* covering large portions of the central Lowlands and, by extension, to the fecundity of raised-field agriculture.

Certain topographic symbols used in Maya art and writing are even more regionally specific than the water lily. A U-shaped enclosure filled with parallel lines and marked by disks (fig. 3-22) is believed to represent a *cenote* (Thompson 1962:219), a physiographic feature limited mainly to the northern Yucatan Peninsula. Needless to say, the *cenote* glyph (T591) and its pictorial variants are largely restricted to the art of Yucatan.

The Pictorial Codification of the Landscape

In prehispanic Mesoamerican art landforms and the sky (here considered an extension of the landscape) are personified or highly conventionalized. They function more as encoded symbols than iconic representations of landscape features. The sky usually appears as a band identified by a string of celestial symbols (fig. 3-23a). The predictable motion of the heavens to which Mesoamericans attached great importance is especially evident in the form of the Maya skyband whose rectilinear contours and predictable segmentation evoke a sense of logical precision (fig. 3-23b). The rectilinear form of the skyband with its underlying sense of regularity stands in marked contrast to the form of the Cauac Monster, whose eccentric contours and unpartitioned interior echo the disordered terrain of wilderness (fig. 3-13).

In Mesoamerican art bodies of water are sometimes contained within a border that isolates them from their surroundings (fig. 3-24). Well-defined borders around topographic depictions make them "portable," allowing them to be inserted anywhere in a composition. Other features of the iconographic system, which might be termed expan-

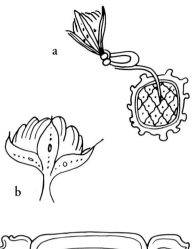

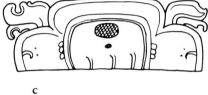

FIG. 3-21. Examples of Maya water lily: *a,* adapted from Robicsek and Hales 1981: Vessel 47; *b,* adapted from Robicsek and Hales 1981: Vessel 30; *c,* adapted from Graham 1967: fig. 51.

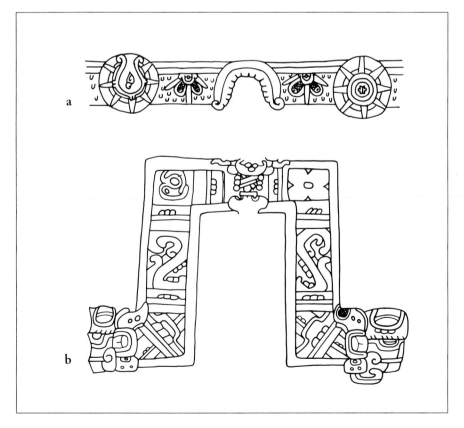

FIG. 3-22. Cenote glyph (T591). Adapted from Thompson 1962:219.

FIG. 3-23. Skybands: *a,* Nuttall 19, adapted from Seler 1963: vol. 2, fig. 295k; *b,* Stela I, east, Quirigua.

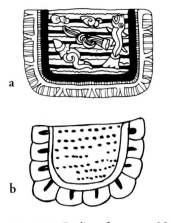

FIG. 3-24. Bodies of water: *a,* Nuttall 96, adapted from Nuttall 1975; *b,* Dresden 34c, adapted from Villacorta and Villacorta 1976.

sion and compression, allow flexibility in adapting potentially cumbersome landscape imagery. Hence, while an overarching skyband allows a figure to be framed by the sky and injects some degree of accurate spatial relationships, the sky can be shown shorthand in limited space by the presence of a single glyph. In the Dresden Codex Chac is shown seated on a Maya sky glyph (T561), an economical and highly conceptual rendering of Chac in the sky (fig. 3-25a). In the Madrid Codex God D, Itzamna, smokes a cigar while reclining on a platform bearing several signs that look like query marks (fig. 3-25b). This symbol comprises the day sign called Caban in Yucatec, a word that contains the root *kab,* having "earth" or "world" among its meanings (Thompson 1960:89). Hence, Itzamna reclines upon an earth rendered within limited space but with unmistakable clarity. In another scene from the Madrid Codex the earth, appearing as a "*kab*"-marked platform, sprouts a bean vine (*Phaseolus* sp.) supported by a pole (fig. 3-25c).

This conceptual approach to topographic representation emphasizes the associative qualities of individual features of the landscape, while precise

boundaries make for their easy recognition. The objectification of topographic features also suits their use as metaphor and symbol in a codified pictorial system with enormous conceptual latitude. Conventional landscape signs evoke multilevel "readings" that parallel the landscape's multivocal symbolism.

The Mountain
Spatial and Temporal Benchmarks

Bridging the earth and distant heavens, mountains function as *axes mundi* in Mesoamerica, articulating the boundaries of culturally defined space and time (Eliade 1959:38). Mountains may be seen as the physical limits of a community. Tedlock (1982:82) observes that in Momostenango Quiche Maya make ceremonial circuits marking the four quarters by visiting four mountain shrines that also define the boundaries of the town. In the Maya area, mountains are closely connected with gods of temporal and spatial benchmarks, such as gods of the four corners and gods of the New Year, who go under a variety of names: Mam, Pahuatun, Bacab, and so on (Thompson 1970b; Taube 1988b). As parameters of cosmic space, these deities often manifest a fourfold nature. Tlaloc, the great rain god of central Mexico, is also affiliated with spatial boundaries, usually as the fourfold Tlaloque (fig. 3-26).[5] As seen in a sixteenth-century illustration, the Tlaloc-associated *tepictoton,* which explicitly represent mountains (discussed below), are arranged at the four sides of a ritual arena to demarcate sacred space (fig. 3-27).

Anthropomorphic Mountains

Mountains take on human attributes in Mesoamerica. They are often identified with specific deities or ancestors whose names they frequently bear (Hunt 1977:96–99). As anthropomorphic beings, mountains are sometimes given human social roles and are placed in so-

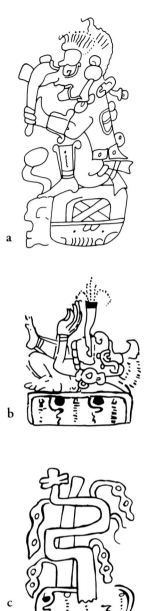

FIG. 3-25. Symbolic spatial references: *a,* Chac in the sky, Dresden 34c, adapted from Villacorta and Villacorta 1976; *b,* Itzamna reclining on the earth, Madrid 79b, adapted from Lee 1985; *c,* bean plants growing out of the earth, Madrid 25b, adapted from Lee 1985.

cial hierarchical relationships. They may be classified by kinship terms, such as husband, wife, mother, father, child, or simply "chief." For example, the mountain known today as Cerro Gordo, which frames the northern boundary of Teotihuacan, was known in Late Postclassic central Mexico as Tenan, meaning "Stone Mother" in Nahuatl (Nuttall 1926:53). The Florentine Codex records the names of two mountains in the Valley of Mexico as Tonan, "Our Mother" (Sahagún 1950–1982: 11:259). Among the Maya, some sacred mountains are given the names of saints (Holland 1963:107).

The imposition of the human social order on mountains is also seen in Muñoz Camargo's statement that Popocatepetl and Iztaccihuatl were envisioned by the indigenous population as husband and wife.[6] In this regard it is interesting to note that Sahagún's illustration of five important mountains of central Mexico differentiates "female" and "male" mountains by costume. The female mountains wear a paper skirt daubed with rubber (fig. 3-28a). Gender is revealed in their names. Female mountains include Iztactepetl (White Mountain, another name for Iztaccihuatl, or White Lady), Matlalcueye (Green Skirt), and Chalchiuhtlicue (Jade Skirt). The male mountains include Popocatepetl (Smoking Mountain) and Quetzaltepetl (Quetzal Mountain). Unlike the skirted female mountains, the male mountains have curious *olla*-like bodies (fig. 3-28b). Gender distinction of mountains by the Aztecs is also seen in the fact that during the feast of Tepeilhuitl (Mountain Celebration), women were sacrificed on what were considered to be female mountains (Hunt 1977:96). In a modern variant of this theme, Nahua-speaking people of Puyecaco conceive of hills as individual entities, some of which are believed to be the "boss" of others (Sandstrom 1975:141, 171–173).

FIG. 3-26. Fourfold Tlaloque painted on inside cover of stone box. Adapted from Pijoán 1946:vol. 10, pl. 1.

The imposition of a social hierarchy on anthropomorphic mountains can also be found in the Maya area. Among the Kekchi, the two most important mountains are called "Our Lord Shukaneb'" and "Our Mother Itz'am,"[7] and the rest of the mountains are thought to be their offspring (Carlson and Eachus 1977:41). In Zinacantan the Tzotzil word for "sacred mountain," *vits*, alternates with *totilme'iletik*, the expression for ancestral gods meaning "father-mother" (Vogt 1969:298). Six male-female pairs of ancestors live in the sacred mountains delimiting the ceremonial precinct of Zincantan. Two of the mountains have names that utilize the terms *bankilal* and *its'inal*, which Vogt translates as "senior" and "junior," kinship terms that mean, respectively, "male's elder brother" and "male's younger brother."[8] Mountains in Zinacantan have a corresponding waterhole with which they share a designated gender (Hunt 1977:97). Furthermore, in the Tzotzil-Tzeltal area lineage patro-

FIG. 3-27. Mountaintop shrine with four *tepictoton*; one is hidden by a child who has undergone heart sacrifice. Illustration for Cuauitleua ceremony in *Primeros Memoriales*. Adapted from Jiménez Moreno 1974.

nyms are sometimes identical to the names of sacred mountains (Nash 1970:19 n. 6). Holland (1963:105) mentions that the Tzotzil use the word *chie'bal* and the Quiche *chipal* to refer to certain important mountains; these terms are cognate with Yucatec *ch'ibal*, which refers to one's patrilineage. Thus, mountains symbolically encode social order by structuring space, time, and social relations. This tendency to see

FIG. 3-28. *Tepictoton: a, "Iztac tepetl. La sierra nevada,"* adapted from Sahagún 1979: fol. 20; *b, "Pupuca tepetl. La sierra de tlalmanalco que humea,"* adapted from ibid.; *c, "Rain"* from *Primeros Memoriales*, after Sahagún 1950–1982:7: fig. 22.

mountains in a kind of parallel society to our own is perhaps due to their vertical orientation, which matches human orientation to the plane of the earth. Vertically oriented features of the landscape are often seen to have greater individual personality than horizontal features (Tuan 1974).[9]

The Tepictoton

One of the most interesting anthropomorphic transformations of mountains in ancient Mesoamerica is the Aztec practice of making *tepictoton* (also *tepicme* or *tepictli*) "little molded ones" (Sahagún 1950–1982:1:47). Conceived as mountain deities, the *tepictoton* were figurated amaranth and maize dough images with dough faces animated by gourd-seed teeth and eyes of black beans. They are typically illustrated in the Florentine Codex as a head resting upon a paper skirt, decorated with daubs of rubber (fig. 3-28a). The skirt represents actual costuming added to the dough images by priests; Sahagún's illustration, then, is a personification of their ritual attire. The skirted figure is sometimes set upon the conventional mountain sign to invoke the basic association of *tepictoton* with mountains (Sahagún 1979:1:40).

The *tepictoton* make appearances in the Aztec feast cycle, particularly when rain gods are being invoked. The *tepictoton* were closely affiliated with the major rain deity complex involving the Tlaloque, deities closely connected with mountains and with shrines on mountain crests (Broda 1971:254–255). In Sahagún's illustration for the feast of Cuauitleua, which petitions gods of wind, rain, and water, the Tlaloque depicted as *tepictoton* can be seen in a precinct on a mountain shrine where a child has just been sacrificed (fig. 3-27; Jiménez Moreno 1974:21–22). The practice of making these mountain images appears to have been widespread among the peasant class. As stated by an informant of Sahagún, "And the common folk (*populares*) made vows to fashion the images of the mountains, which are called *tepictli*, because they are dedicated [to] those gods of rain" (Sahagún 1950–1982:2:29).

The dough images were featured in the thirteenth feast of the annual calendar, Tepeilhuitl. Durán (1971:453) states that the images represent "principal mountains of the land," with Popocateptl and Iztaccihuatl placed at the center and surrounded by hills representing pilgrimage shrines of important water deities, such as Tlaloc and Matlalcueye (ibid.:256). During both Atemoztli and Tepeilhuitl, the dough images were revered through arrayment in paper garments, presentation of offerings, and prayer vigil. Later they would be sacrificed in a manner identical to human deity impersonators, making their anthropomorphic identification most obvious. The *tepictoton* undergo heart excision and decapitation, their dough bodies are eaten, and the paper raiment is burned. The *tepictoton* encapsulate the association of mountains with rain deities and with human forms among the Aztecs. The confluence of these ideas again emerges in Sahagún's illustration for "rain" as the image of a mountain wearing the attributes of Tlaloc (fig. 3-28c).

A variant of this theme is seen in Durán's description of Tlaloc worship at his shrine atop Mount Tlaloc southwest of Coatlinchan (Wicke and Horcasitas 1957). The shrine housed a stone image of Tlaloc around which sat a number of small idols, most likely of clay or stone. Durán states (1971:156): "These little idols represented the other hills and cliffs which surrounded this great mountain [Mount Tlaloc]. Each one of them was named according to the hill he stood for."

Caves and Mountains

In their physical form, mountains and caves have little in common. Illumi-

Images from the Underworld

FIG. 3-29. Vase decorated with mountain and cave motifs, Teotihuacan. Adapted from von Winning 1949: fig. 1.

FIG. 3-30. Mountain and cave symbol on a carved block from Huitzuco, Guerrero. Adapted from Seler 1963: vol. 2, fig. 287.

nated by day, mountains teem with plant and animal life; they boldly punctuate the landscape and in this way structure space in the visible environment. Caves, on the other hand, are dark, hollow, and secretive. Yet in the minds of Mesoamericans, mountains and caves are linked like opposite sides of a coin, a view fostered, no doubt, by their frequent geographic coincidence. Caves often penetrate mountains, and this image became the basis of the toponym specifying "hill" or "mountain" in the central Mexican codical tradition (fig. 3-17). As a toponym, this sign, which features a mountain and a water-filled cave, neatly encapsulates the Nahuatl compound word for "city": *altepetl* "water-mountain" (Siméon 1981: 21).

As opposite sides of a coin, caves and mountains can be conceived in terms of a binary opposition. Indeed, Vogt (1981: 120–122) sees the mountain and cave heading a chain of dyads including mountain-cave, up-down, ancestor god–earth lord, and hot-cold. A similar binary and complementary sense to mountain and cave is seen in the directional glyphs of the Mixtec codices in which south, the Temple of Skulls, is a cave, and north, Checkerboard Hill, is a mountain (Jansen 1982: 1: 230–231). Modern Mixtec preserves the underlying sense of this nomenclature in the words for "south" and "north"— *huahi cahi* "large house" (cave) for "south" and *yucu naa* "dark hill" for "north" (ibid.).

The complementary relationship between the mountain and cave is also

evident in prehispanic art. A design on a vase from Teotihuacan juxtaposes a conventional mountain sign, consisting of multiple peaks sprouting plants (von Winning 1949), with a scalloped water-filled chamber, possibly alluding to a cavern (fig. 3-29). One face of a carved stone block from Huitzuco, Guerrero, probably of Late Postclassic date, pairs a conventional sign for a cave with that for a mountain (fig. 3-30). Both the cave and mountain have the dotted diamond pattern associated with terrestrial iconography in Mesoamerica. The identification of the upper image, featuring a fanged quatrefoil mouth, as a cave is quite clear, as the same form appears in postconquest manuscripts when the word *oztotl* "cave" is used in compound place-names (Heyden 1975: fig. 4).

Though mountains and caves can be seen in a relationship of opposition, they can also share metaphorical roles, so that, in a sense, the two sides of the coin are seen as a single entity. Many Mesoamerican deities, particularly rain gods, are identified simultaneously with mountains and caves. In Late Postclassic central Mexico, Tlaloc is thought to have lived inside a cave located on a mountaintop. Sullivan (1974:217) suggests that Tlaloc may have originally been an earth god who resided in a cave and later evolved into a rain god with a primary sacred location on mountaintops. It seems, however, that Tlaloc never lost his identification with caves. Youths sacrificed to Tlaloc were deposited in a cave (Motolinía 1951:119), most likely representing his home, and vessels decorated with Tlaloc's goggle-eyed visage have been found in caves in diverse regions of Mesoamerica.[10] Taggart (1983:60) explains the dual association of mountaintops and caves as a home for meteorological deities in terms of a mediating role—that of uniting terrestrial and celestial forces.

In Classic Maya iconography and writing, mountains and caves semantically overlap through the Cauac Monster, which, as stated earlier, can represent both a mountain and a cave (fig. 3-13). And like the central Mexican sign for "hill," the Cauac Monster contains water, seen in clusters and strings of dots, and vegetal eyelids that characterize the water-associated Water-Lily Monster.

In Mesoamerica mountains and caves also share the role of home to ancestors. When we hear that a particular ancestor or deity lives inside a mountain or that an event took place there, it is probable that the interior mountain locale is a cave.[11] As portals of communication with the supernatural, mountain-tops and caves constitute the most important classes of topographic shrines in Mesoamerica.

The Cave

Cave

It is narrow, penetrating, perforated, dark. It is spacious, enlarged. It is extensive, profound, deep. It is the home of wild beasts, of the coyote, of the ser-

pent—a frightful place, made into a hole: perforated.

(Sahagún 1950–1982:11:262)

This description of a cave by one of Sahagún's native informants conveys a sense of wonderment; but his circuitous language hints at the difficulty of defining caves by any simple formula. Here the cave is narrow and confining; yet at the same time it is spacious. It is a frightening home of wild beasts; and yet it is only a hole. In Mesoamerica cave symbolism likewise cannot be defined by some neat formula. The cave is a fluid, polysemic, sometimes contradictory concept; it is, in Victor Turner's parlance, a "dominant symbol" in that it encodes and interconnects a variety of referents. Dominant symbols have the property of multivocality, which "allows for the economic representation of key aspects of a culture and beliefs" (Turner 1967:50).

Mesoamerican cave symbolism can be understood as a constellation of distinct but related themes, each encoding a chain of symbolic associations. The theme has as its starting point some empirical observation, which Turner (1970:13) calls the "substantial basis of symbolic meaning." Turner (1967:52–54) traces such a chain among the Ndembu with the *mudyi* tree, whose white sap links it with breast milk, female breasts in general, girls' puberty rites, matrilineage, and so forth. In the case of caves, the empirical basis of an associational chain might be that caves are dark and hollow, they contain water, and so forth. Each of these primary attributes links by analogy with other concepts, as with the white sap of the *mudyi* tree. A dominant symbol possesses many of these associational chains, and they connect and diverge in complex patterns, sometimes of a contradictory nature. Indeed, Mesoamerican cave symbolism is rife with apparent internal contradictions. Through

FIG. 3-31. Chac in a stone cave house, detail of painted vase. Adapted from Coe 1978: no. 11.

this capacity to encode multiple themes simultaneously, the Mesoamerican cave condenses an enormous amount of cultural information, making it an extremely potent symbol.

The remainder of this chapter outlines the themes comprising Mesoamerican cave symbolism, though making no claim to cover all. Some themes, not treated here, have been discussed by others. The contributions of J. Eric S. Thompson (1959; 1975) and Doris Heyden (1975; 1976; 1981), writing respectively on the Maya and central Mexican culture, are particularly important. Together their work charts most of the well-known patterns of Mesoamerican cave ritual and symbolism. Other contributions have been made by, among others, MacLeod and Puleston (1980), Brady (1988; 1989), Taube (1986),

Strecker (1987), Bonor (1989), Bassie-Sweet (1991), and Stone (1989b).

The Cave as a House

Differences in the symbolic role of caves versus mountains can be traced to their striking morphological differences. Caves are hollow, dark, and of a character alien to the everyday world. Whereas mountains are envisioned as corporeal beings, caves are thought of as the inside of such beings or more often as containers. Their identification with the human container, a house, is well attested across Mesoamerica and is seen in Mesoamerican art as the representation of a cave as a houselike structure (fig. 3-31).

In the Maya area the view of the cave as a house is seen in the expression "stone house" for cave, found in Mo-

pan, *nah tunich*,[12] Jacaltec, *na' ch'en* (La Farge and Beyers 1931:243), and Kekchi, *ochoch pek* (Sedat 1955:201). A Colonial Yucatec dictionary defines *casa de piedra* "stone house" as *aktun* "cave" (*Diccionario de San Francisco* 1976: 531). The names of Maya caves frequently incorporate the word "house," as in the Yucatecan cave Dzab Na (Rattle House; Strömsvik 1956), the Tzeltal cave Muk' Naj (Large House; Hermitte 1970:33), the Kanjobal cave Yalan Na' (Under the House; La Farge 1947:127), and the Chol cave Ak'abalnaj (Dark House; Reents Budet and MacLeod 1986:100). And recall that in the Popol Vuh, Xibalba contains a number of "houses": House of Knives, House of Cold, House of Darkness, and so forth (Edmonson 1971:71–73), each characterizing some typical quality of caves.[13] The idea of the cave as a container is also affirmed in the Yucatec numeral classifier for caves, which is *ak*, forming part of the word *aktun* "cave." This numeral classifier is for canoes, boats, houses, lots, chairs, containers, churches, altars, holes, pits, towns, and milpas (Beltrán de Santa Rosa María 1746:160), items that serve as containers of people or objects, such as maize.

In the Aztec *tonalpohualli* (260-day count) the equivalent of the Maya day sign Akbal, which is associated with darkness, night, and caves (Thompson 1960:73), is Calli, a word meaning "house" in Nahuatl; its glyphic notation is a house.[14] This may be the "cave house" in the earth's interior, thereby revealing a common thread of meaning linking Calli and Akbal. And we might recall that in Mixtec "south," associated with caves, is called *huahi cahi* "large house" (Jansen 1982:1:230).

The idea of the cave as a stone house suggests the analogy between caves and temple superstructures in Mesoamerica. Temples were also thought of as houses, but houses of the gods, as in the Nahuatl *teocalli* or Yucatec *k'u na*, both expressions for a pyramid-temple meaning "god house" or "divine house." The quality of an enclosed, dark space shared by temples and caves may also be reflected in the fact that in Yucatec the words *k'u* "temple" and *aktun* "cave" both have secondary meanings of an animal burrow or nest (Barrera Vásquez 1980:7, 416).

Shrines set atop terraced platforms are architectural expressions of the mountain-cave complex. There can be no doubt that the Mesoamerican pyramid was viewed as a symbolic mountain. The terraced pyramid is referred to as "an artificial mountain, with levels, with steps" by an informant of Sahagún (1950–1982:11:269), and the great pyramid of Cholula acquired the epithet *tlachihualtepetl* "man-made mountain" (ibid.:10:192). The cave was also replicated in Mesoamerican architecture. Townsend (1982) has suggested that the circular rock-cut temple at Malinalco represents a cave, and Taube (1986) has found more persistent associations of circular temples with caves in Mesoamerica. Furthermore, shrines surmounting pyramids were intentionally kept dark, for windows rarely pierced their walls, and in this sense they emulated the enclosed black space of a cave. We certainly sense this in Durán's (1971:211) description of the temple of Cihuacoatl: "This room was always pitch-black. It had no small openings, no windows, no main door save for a small one through which one could barely crawl. This door was always kept hidden by a sort of lid so that no one would see it and enter the chamber except for the priests who served the goddess. These were elders who performed the usual ceremonies. This room was called Tlillan, which means Place of Blackness. . . ."

The Cave as a Hole

The idea of the cave as a conduit or hole is one of surprising richness, as seen in John Sosa's (1985) ethnographic study of Yalcoba, Yucatan. Caves function in Yalcoba as entry and exit points at the eastern and western horizons for celestial bodies, winds, and even human souls that move over the face of the earth during the course of the day (ibid.:423 and fig. 11). Even God himself, *halal dios*, circulates over the earth by passing through the cave-holes at the eastern and western horizon.[15] By their emptiness, then, caves direct the movement of natural forces seen to circulate above the earth.

The cave as a hole provides a mechanism of removing the ill-desired from the mundane world. Sosa states (p. 447) that the *hmeen* "shaman" disposes of *taankas* "illness" by sweeping it into a cave at the western horizon. It is then sent off with the sun in the west, disappearing via the cave into the underworld. By the same logic, cleansing rituals in Yalcoba are associated with sunset and ritual disposal through the western cave-hole.

In visiting the cave Dzibichen, located in central Yucatan, quite close to Yalcoba, Karl Taube and I noticed a pile of small rocks and an upright cross resting on a boulder by the cave entrance (fig. 4-66). According to our guide, the rocks were to sweep away fatigue.[16] The rocks functioned as tributary payment to the deity; branches could then be switched across the legs to remove weariness. The location of this shrine next to a cave entrance can be understood in light of Sosa's observations from Yalcoba—that is, fatigue can be "swept" into the underworld and disposed of through the cave-hole.

As Sosa (p. 423) suggests, ritual "disposals" can occur through a natural hole, such as a cave, or a ritually constructed one, such as a hole for ceremonial deposition or ritual burial.[17] We see this, for instance, in the *k'ex* "exchange" ceremony intended to remove harmful winds that may be causing illness (Redfield and Villa Rojas 1934: 174). In one documented performance near Coba, a banana flower representing a sick child, along with "payment" of coins and candles, were buried in a hole on a trail leading away from the house (Bruce Love, personal communication, 1987). Thus, the winds, satisfied with their booty, would remove illness from the child. A similar ceremony is found among the Tzeltal Maya. When illness strikes a child, a square hole is dug and filled with a live chicken, liquor, bread, and chocolate. All of this forms a meal for the spirit of the house, who, appeased, is expected to intercede as a protector (Nash 1970:17).

The placement of these offerings in a hole follows the same logic as sending *taankas* into a cave. It is a way of dispatching something into another realm, which could have several beneficial results: removing something unwanted or transferring a gift to a deity. In either case, this process illustrates the strong operational overlap between caves (natural holes) and cache holes (ritually constructed holes). A Late Classic Maya vase shows a rare depiction of a cache hole containing *ollas*, two-part cache vessels, a cylindrical vase, and other typical ceramics found in Maya caches (fig. 3-32). The hole is configured as a quatrefoil (only half is seen here), a form usually marking an entrance into the sacred earth. Indeed, this scene may portray a cache of artifacts in a cave.

This also raises the possibility that altars and ballcourt markers that feature quatrefoils on their upper surface may represent holes connecting the plane of the earth with the underworld, an idea also suggested by Miller and Houston (1988:fig. 10). We see quatrefoils on ballcourt markers from Copan (Schele and Miller 1986:figs. 6.10, 6.11 and pl. 102) and Altars Q and R from Quirigua (fig. 3-33). In a study of the central Mexican ballgame, Seler (1960:3: 308) argued that the ball moving over

Images from the Underworld

the ballcourt and passing through rings represented the sun and moon in their diurnal journey. In this regard we might note that the two markers from Quirigua feature an individual attached to a large lunar glyph. Another cave-hole–ballcourt connection is seen in the use of the word *hom* in Yucatec to mean a cave or deep cavity (Barrera Vásquez 1980:228–229), while *hom* means "ballcourt" in Quiche (Edmonson 1965:41), and in the Popol Vuh the ballcourt is called "Great Abyss at Carchah" (Tedlock 1985:109).

As we will see presently, the cave-hole is the path by which cosmic strata are transitted. The hole was conceived in Olmec and Maya art as a quatrefoil (fig. 3-9), whereas at Teotihuacan cosmic apertures appear as a scalloped orifice (figs. 3-18, 3-19, 3-29). In central Mexican codices the sacred cave-hole might be represented by an aperture with a wavy lining (fig. 3-20), which also characterizes female reproductive anatomy, such as the vagina and umbilical cord (Milbrath 1987).

Thus, according to Mesoamerican beliefs, cosmic strata could be transitted through a hole that was identified with the empty space of a cave passage. In Yalcoba, Yucatan, a hole (*hol*), *u hol gloryah* "the hole of heaven," is conceived as penetrating the center of the sky and functions as a conduit of cosmic entry and exit (Sosa 1985:Ch. 7 and fig. 11). Similarly, in the Popol Vuh, when Xquiq, the mother of the twins Hunahpu and Xbalanque, is sent up from the underworld to the earth, she is transitting two cosmic strata. The Popol Vuh says that she makes this journey "through a hole," *chi hul* in Quiche (Edmonson 1971:80, l. 2419). A Maya vase shows a figure transitting cosmic strata through such a hole, in this case entering the underworld through a "Cauac"-marked quatrefoil opening (fig. 3-34).

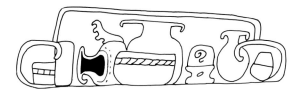

FIG. 3-32. Detail of painted vase showing a pottery cache in a sacred hole, possibly a cave. Adapted from Robicsek and Hales 1982: no. 1.

FIG. 3-33. Ballcourt marker with quatrefoil frame and figure with attached lunar glyph, Altar Q, Quirigua.

The Cave and Transformation

Material objects, such as wind, lightning bolts, clouds, and water, pass inside and outside of caves. Indeed, caves channel elements of the upper atmosphere as often as those of the earth. Because of the special quality of caves, however, what passes through is recognized as having undergone a profound transformation. A myth from the Tojolobal region of southern Chiapas illustrates this point. A cave passage leads to a land abundant with fruit, but upon attempting to bring it out, the fruit evaporates (MacLeod and Puleston 1980: 73). Here objects brought out of a cave are subject to this law of transformation.

FIG. 3-34. Detail of painted vase showing a hunter penetrating a cosmic aperture. Adapted from Coe 1978: no. 16.

The transformational property of caves is pertinent to their role in rites of passage, for caves provide the perfect setting for separating, spatially and psychologically, the individual from his or her former social existence (Heyden 1976; MacLeod and Puleston 1980). In 1911 Van Gennep (1960) proposed his theory of the rite of passage and a mechanism for it that proceeded in three major stages: separation, transition, and incorporation. Physical separation from mundane reality is one way psychological separation is achieved. Thus, rites of separation are often staged in a remote area where ordinary social rules are suspended. Caves provide the ideal "Far Place" (V. Turner 1972:211) for such liminal rites. Not surprisingly, caves have always been favored places of pilgrimage in Mesoamerica. Kubler's (1985) survey of Mesoamerican pilgrimage centers includes many caves, which usually serve as shrines for water deities. The cave's transformative powers facilitate the pilgrim's desire to undergo a spiritual transformation.

The cave's perceived ability to alter the human psyche becomes an explanatory model for all events within the physical world, so inanimate objects are also subject to the cave's transformative powers. We can understand, then, how a cave operates as a receptacle for offerings. Objects placed in a cave, having been removed from the everyday world, pass into the world of the sacred.

In the view of Mesoamericans (in this instance, in accord with modern science) changes in physical state can also be achieved through burning and decomposition. A well-known Aztec legend treating the birth of the sun and the moon states that one deity jumped into a fire to become the sun, while another entered a cave to become the moon (Mendieta 1945:87). Here fire and the act of entering a cave are seen as parallel forms of producing physical change. The tradition of buried caches in Mesoamerica also underscores the function of holes as a means of transferring material goods to the sacred realm. As we have seen, burial in holes is analogous to placement in a cave.

In Mesoamerica periodicity of natural phenomena was also explained in terms of the anthropomorphic model of human rites of passage. The disappearance of celestial bodies into their nightly passage through the underworld and their reappearance at dawn was equated with the process of death and birth. As Sosa (1985:423) puts it, celestial gods are seen to dive in their diurnal circuit through a cave and emerge through one at dawn. One cave in the Maya area, Dzibichen, has prehispanic paintings that show a diving feline (figs. 4-69c, 4-70d), forming a visual counterpart to Sosa's description of celestial deities diving into the cave-hole at sunset. Furthermore, birthing images in Mesoamerica show the child diving out of the birth canal, paralleling the diving motion of celestial bodies as they move through cosmic strata. As a transit path for celestial death and birth, the cave can assure that physical transformation has taken place, given its inherent association with this process. The cave acts as mediator and rationale for the daytime and nighttime duality of celestial beings across Mesoamerica.

Effecting a change in physical state, epitomized by birth and death, is fundamental to the role of the cave in the sacred geography of Mesoamerica. Caves in Mesoamerica have a well-attested association with both human and divine birth and death. Heyden (1976) has summarized this for central Mexico. This association explains the importance of the cave as a receptacle of offerings, as a conduit for the passage of celestial bodies, and as a site for human rites of passage, which may have included the additional trauma of ritual bloodletting (MacLeod and Puleston 1980).

The point of interface between the interior and exterior of the cave is, of course, the cave entrance. Points of interface between two qualitatively different worlds are of special importance, as they highlight the very existence of differences. In Zinacantan, for example, it is not rivers themselves that are considered sacred but rather their point of emergence, which may be a cave (Vogt 1981:131). Cave entrances are often the site of ritual, not merely for the convenience of light filtering in but because of their own special significance. That Mesoamerican art depicts the cave entrance rather than the tunnel system reflects the importance of transitional zones.

The Cave as a Source of Fertility and Material Wealth

The cave is also thought of as a kind of magical source of material wealth and objects prized for their ritual value. Reports in the literature of finding riches in caves or the bush are frequent.[18] In Zinacantan a silver cross was reportedly found in a cave (Vogt 1981:128), and Tzotzil myths tell of saints being found in the woods (Vogt 1969:307). No doubt valued objects are occasionally found in caves, some left by accident and others intentionally left by worshippers.[19] To most individuals, discoveries of this kind, whether real or apocryphal, reinforce the view of caves as treasure houses.

The association of caves with wealth is also observable in the fact that many cave-dwelling gods, particularly a class of gods who control meteorological phenomena, are conceived of as wealthy. We can document a complex of wealthy, cave-dwelling gods whose manifestation throughout Mesoamerica is remarkably consistent. The deities in question usually control not just water and weather, but the most coveted fruits of nature, including land, game, and agricultural products. With this storehouse of natu-

ral riches at their disposal, it is no wonder that they are thought of as having achieved success in a material sense. If you are rich in nature's bounty, then you must be rich in the broader sense of the word, and so these "owners" of water, land, and game are envisioned as living in a state of almost obscene luxury. In the Maya area these gods are sometimes pictured as looking like and living in the style of successful ladinos. Supplication of these gods usually entails a petition that they share their great bounty. Petitions sometimes take the form of apologizing for killing game or requests for rain, a successful crop, or good health. Such petitions often take place in caves. Suffice it to say that these cave-dwelling deities hold enormous power over human life in a material sense and must be appeased.

One prime example of such a cave-dwelling god is the Zincanteco earth lord, Yahval Balamil. Pictured as a fat ladino, he is believed to possess piles of money and herds of domesticated animals (ibid.:302). He recalls the Tojolobal earth lord Niwan Pukuh, who also lives in a cave and is pictured as a tall, light-complexioned man who wears a large hat and has silver spurs on his boots (Ruz 1982, cited in Spero 1987:173). Yahval Balamil has complete dominion over rain, clouds, and lightning in addition to the land and all that is upon it. Indeed, propitiatory rites give Zincantecos access to his material wealth, which is essential to their survival. The earth lord is not considered a "good guy" by the Zincantecos and is especially feared for his desire to steal souls (Guiteras-Holmes 1961:116). Soul loss is commonly seen in conjunction with this cave-dwelling god across Mesoamerica.[20]

A closely related character is found in the Tzeltal area. Called Chauc (Lightning), he lives in a luxurious house in the deepest part of the caves around Pinola, Chiapas (Hermitte 1970:7, 39).

Like the earth lord, he is a possessor of great wealth. His extravagant house is modeled after that of a ladino and is cared for by his many servants. The persona of the earth lord is more finely divided in the Tzeltal area, so another cave-dwelling deity, called Sombreron, is directly responsible for granting wealth and health. In this regard, the caves around Pinola have achieved a level of specialization. As Hermitte observes (1970:40): "In the caves surrounding the town diverse things can be petitioned. The cave of the Marimba, for example, is where the marimba players go to ask that their marimbas play well and do not get damaged. In the cave of Ch'en one goes to petition for good cattle and other animals. At the cave Campanaton one goes to petition for money and good tools" (my translation).

Tzultaca, the Kekchi mountain-valley god, is a highland Guatemalan manifestation of this deity complex (Dieseldorff 1926; Thompson 1970a: 272–276). He inhabits caves and is also the "owner" of rain, weather, and the products of nature, including the land and wild animals. The latter are thought to be his "servants" (Carlson and Eachus 1977:41), conjuring up the notion of a wealthy overlord, as in the Chiapas examples. He is petitioned for game, rain, and abundant maize crops and is the most important deity worshipped among the Kekchi (Sapper 1897:267–295).

The Tzultaca complex echoes across highland Guatemala (with one Lowland example in the Mopan area) under the names of deities who are also called "mountain-valley" in their respective languages:

Tzultaca (*tsul-tak'a*)—Kekchi
Uitzailic (*wits-ailik*)—Chuh (Thompson 1970a:275)
Huyub-Takah (*huyub-tak'ah*)— Quiche (Dieseldorff 1926:380; Schultze-Jena 1946:23–24)

Yut-Kixkab—Pokomchi (Dieseldorff
1926:380)

Hyub-Ta'ah—Achi (Neuenswander
1981:146)

Huitz-Hok (*wits-hook*)—Mopan
(Thompson 1930:57)

Another Quiche deity, Saki C'oxol, a divine, dwarflike being associated with lightning and the acquisition of material rewards (Tedlock 1983), also seems to be a manifestation of this cave-dwelling entity. In the Soconusco region of Chiapas what may be an analogous deity named Uotan was revered as the "heart of the people." In a treatise of 1702 Francisco Nuñez de la Vega stated that Uotan lived in a temple inside a cave near the town of Huehuetan, where he possessed a treasure guarded by a priestess and her assistants (Thompson 1960:73; Seler 1963:2:175–176; Carmen Leon Cázares and Ruz 1988:275).

Gusi (Lightning) is an example of this deity complex among the Zapotecs (Parsons 1936:211). A parallel can also be seen in the Mixteca Alta in the demonic El Gachupin, or Ja Uhu (He Who Hurts), a god believed to inhabit caves around Chalcatongo. Local people visit these caves to petition El Gachupin for riches, in return for which they offer their soul (Jansen 1982:255).

Because of the demonic nature of this cave-dwelling earth lord and some obvious parallels with Old World ideas about caves as treasure houses,[21] we must consider to what extent this feature of modern Mesoamerican cave ideology is a product of European ideas. At times, this god is suggestive of a devil-like being, to whom, for instance, one sells one's soul. We know that Colonial priests viewed caves as loathsome dens of idolatry and in many cases equated them with hell. One of Sahagún's sermons composed in Nahuatl could not be more explicit on this point: "Indeed it [hell] is a very great cave, there in the

middle of the earth. It is a very gloomy place, a very dark place, it is filled with fire" (Burkhart 1989:56).

Furthermore, it is difficult to find in prehispanic sources precise parallels for this cave-dwelling mountain deity, who controlled the fruits of the earth. However, Tlaloc may provide one such example. As a rain, lightning, and mountain god, Tlaloc fits the profile of this deity, and he, too, is associated with material wealth. The principal idol of Tlaloc, which stood atop Mount Tlaloc, was bedecked with greenstone beads and gold. Klein (1980:168–170) has brought other evidence to bear on the idea that Tlaloc was considered to be a rich and bejewelled god among the Aztecs. Tlalocan (Place of Tlaloc; Sullivan 1974:213) was a paradisiacal afterworld where those who died under the auspices of the rain god spent a pleasant eternity. One of Sahagún's (1950–1982:10:188) native informants reveals that Tlalocan had the general connotations of a "place of wealth."

Among the Classic Maya the role of this mountain-valley god seems to have been split among several deities. In his guise as the Mam, God N is one good candidate (Taube 1988b:112). God N appears in scenes with an avatar of the Maya deity GI, now thought to be the rain god Chac; this may allude to God N's association with rain and lightning (Taube 1989a:357). Taube believes that Chac and God N are related, the former being an axe-wielding lightning god and the latter an aged god of thunder. The quadripartite Pahuatuns, a Yucatecan variant of God N, was identified with wind and rain in early contact times (Tozzer 1941:note 638), suggesting that God N did have some rainmaking functions. On Classic vases God N displays self-indulgent behavior—lechery and intoxication (Taube 1989a)—and is sometimes shown receiving jewelry (Coe 1975:18–19 and no. 10; Robicsek and Hales 1981:

fig. 48b), traits suggestive of the wealthy mountain-valley god we have been discussing. Dwarves depicted in Maya cave art at Naj Tunich may also represent one of these cave-dwelling beings (fig. 6-51). Given this evidence and the fact that European ideas cannot account for many aspects of the deity in question, I believe we are dealing with a fundamentally prehispanic, pan-Mesoamerican concept. This "owner" of the earth seems to have accrued new characteristics in accord with changing views of self-indulgent behavior and material wealth, so associations with the devil and ladinos emerged later.[22]

Caves, Water, and Maize

Caves also provide materials of practical use. Among the Maya, soils and minerals were mined from caves, perhaps for use in pigments and pottery-making (Hatt et al. 1953:16, 23), and calcite obtained from speleothems (geological formations from precipitated calcite) was crushed for pottery temper (Reddell 1977:225; Arnold 1971). In Belize minerals were extracted from deep, remote caves by the ancient Maya in what looks like a ritual context (MacLeod and Puleston 1980:72). Saltpeter extracted from lava tube caves around Teotihuacan was used by the Spanish to manufacture gunpowder (Nuttall 1926:76–77).

Most important, caves appear to produce that precious substance water; they contain rivers and lakes, and water drips from the ceiling. In Campeche and Yucatan, cave water sometimes played a critical role in getting through the dry season, as at Bolonchen (Thompson 1975:x) and the Gruta de Chac (Andrews 1975). The fact that water is found in caves makes sense not only geologically but also within the scheme of Mesoamerican cosmology whereby the world is surrounded by primordial waters. Among the Tzeltal Maya of Pinola the proof of this is that if a hole is dug deep enough, water is eventually struck (Hermitte 1970:32). Caves, penetrating deep into the earth, could easily tap this primordial source of water. The Yucatec Maya believe that underground rivers, observed in caves and *cenotes,* actually support the earth's crust (Hanks 1990:305–306). Classic Maya art offers abundant evidence that the underworld was viewed as a watery environment, another aspect of the cave's association with water.

This affiliation with water gives caves a position of importance in Mesoamerican sacred geography. Since water is found in caves, by extension they are a source of rain and storms. In the Tzotzil-Tzeltal area of Chiapas these latter beliefs may be encouraged by the fact that storm clouds appear to emanate from the mountains where caves are found (MacLeod and Puleston 1980). Zincantecos believe that lightning shoots out of cave entrances (Vogt 1969:387). The quintessentially Mesoamerican notion that rain gods live in caves has already been mentioned. This belief is so widespread[23] and the character of the rain gods so consistent that the rain god–cave complex must have great antiquity. Certainly, this one aspect of Mesoamerican ideology has shown resistance to "disjunction" in Kubler's sense.

The cave as a source of water places it squarely in a fertility complex, a fact with far-reaching implications. One of these has to do with the cave as a giver of life, a theme no doubt also stemming from the womblike character of the cave. As a dark, secretive, enclosed space, the cave achieves a natural identification as a source of biological life (Tuan 1974:28). Identified with biological regeneration and fruitfulness, caves are usually classified in a structural sense with things female. In the hot-cold system of Yucatan, caves fall into the cold-wet-female category. Cave water, for example, might be used to cool the "hot" *sastun* crystals used in divina-tion (William Hanks, personal communication, 1986). Brady (1988) has documented a pervasive association of caves in Mesoamerica with female sexuality.

The association of caves with fertility also extends to agricultural fertility, which, after all, receives the benefit of water. Hence caves are associated with maize, often in the context of origin myths, as noted by Taube (1986). In one well-known story of the origin of maize, Quetzalcoatl steals maize kernels from inside a mountain called Tonaca-tepetl (Sustenance Mountain; Nichol-son 1971:401). As we have seen, the interior of a mountain is an indirect reference to caves. In the Popol Vuh the corn from which man was made was found inside a mountain (Tedlock 1985:47), probably a cave. Even today, caves are thought by some indigenous people to house the maize god.[24] Cave archaeology throughout the Maya area affirms this association with maize: implements of maize processing, such as manos and metates, are often found in great abundance in Maya caves (see Brady [1989:304] for a summary). At Balankanche, Yucatan, 232 miniature manos and metates were found in a heap associated with Tlaloc effigy jars (Andrews 1970:11). James Brady (personal communication, 1991) reports that manos and metates are common in the caves of the Dos Pilas region. In Ak-tun Kabal, Belize, I observed that the votive offerings littering the floor of a highly inaccessible chamber included at least twenty full-size broken metates.

Witches and Ghouls of Mictlan/Xibalba

That caves represent a rupture with everyday space also makes them alien. Though they offer wealth and material benefits, they are feared, especially for their malevolent inhabitants. Such frightening creatures are often native to any unprotected place in the distant forest. Among the Maya of Chamula, remote forest lands are inhabited by the most unsavory assortment of characters who exhibit deviant behavior and morphological ambiguity. They embody the asocial and evil as well as those practicing sorcery in Chamula society, such as monkeys, demons, witches, and Jews.

Caves fit squarely into this ambivalent and treacherous zone, which Mesoamericanists often refer to as the "underworld." As the name implies, the underworld was located beneath the earth's surface. The Aztecs called this nether land Mictlan (Place of Death), a nine-level subterranean region where the dead came to spend an eternity. In Colonial and Late Postclassic Yucatan the underworld went by the name Metnal, a corruption of Mictlan, and among the Quiche Maya it was Xibalba, a name made famous in the Popol Vuh.[25] MacLeod and Puleston (1980) have masterfully treated the issue of the cave's identification with this eery but supernaturally charged underworld zone.

The Maya cave-underworld was much more than a spooky place filled with weird, malevolent beings, but at the same time it *was* conceived in just that way. Caves are inhabited by such anomalous animals as bats (Blaffer 1972:76–77, 80; Hunt 1977:64–65) and are often believed to house evil spirits.[26] For example, in Yalcoba, Yucatan, the mischievous *alux* are believed to live in dry sinkholes or caves (Sosa 1985:411). Gann (1926:93) reported that his Maya guides were afraid to enter Loltun cave, as they feared the *pixan* "spirits of the ancient inhabitants." The Popol Vuh also offers a grim picture of the lords of Xibalba. Their chilling names place them among the ghouls and goblins of the Maya pantheon: One Death, Seven Death, Pus Master, Jaundice Master, Trash Master, Stab Master, and so forth (Tedlock 1985:106–107).

Even the cave-dwelling Zinacanteco earth lord, who controls water, rain, lightning, and clouds, is viewed with mistrust and apprehension. Many cave denizens, like the earth lord, exhibit socially reprehensible behavior that ranges from outlandish to outright dangerous. Bad behavior may take the form of unseemly sexual conduct. Sexual deviance may also manifest itself in the possession of oversized genitals. The Blackman of Zinacantan, identified with caves, has an enormous penis and a voracious sexual appetite. He is universally loathed as a creature of wanton violence, including rape and murder (Blaffer 1972). The intersection of sexual excess with caves also appears in a Ch'ol tale in which the antisocial flavor of the cave-underworld comes across in the repeated themes of rape, adultery, and murder (Whittaker and Warkentin 1965:81–84). Here men and women who dance wildly in caves are said to be foreigners. They wantonly commit adultery and even murder. One of the men entices young girls to his side by claiming that the gods beckon them; then he rapes them. This is an image of caves as foreign, dangerous, and amoral.

The cave as a locus of witchcraft is also well attested. Hanks (1984:134), working in western Yucatan, observes, "Witches wreak havoc on victims from out of the bowels of caves." The cave allows witches to work undetected by blocking the force of *sastun* crystals, which might permit a benign shaman to localize and act upon the source of danger. Similarly Vogt (1969:370) states that in Zinacantan soul loss can occur to "an evil person who performs witchcraft ritual in a cave to 'sell' one or more parts of a victim's soul to the Earth Lord, who uses the victim as a servant." Here we see the cave as the locus of sorcery and the cave-associated earth lord as the enslaver of human souls (see also Collier 1973:114–116). Paul Turner (1972:70–71) reports an incident among the highland Chontal of Oaxaca in which a man seen entering a sacred cave was immediately suspected of witchcraft: "Evidently just entering the cave is enough evidence of witchcraft for some people that they would not listen to any other explanations." In the Kanjobal town of Santa Eulalia curses are uttered in the cave of Yalan Na' (La Farge 1947:128).

The Number Seven

In Mesoamerica caves and their spatial analogues in the forest are often associated with the number seven. This is apparent in the famous expression "Seven Caves," the name of a place of origin in Mesoamerican lore: in Nahuatl, Chicomoztoc, and in Quiche, Vukub Pek. Apparently one name for Chichen Itza (and perhaps its original name) was Uucil-Abnal (Seven Bushy Places/Hollows), which Roys (1966:159) likens to the Quiche *vukub zivan* "seven canyons." The number seven crops up in other contexts that suggest a wild and dangerous setting. For example, Grigsby (1986) reports a group of seven ritual caves around Tlalxictlan in central Mexico.

In the day name–head variant correspondence set (Thompson 1960:140), the number seven aligns with Akbal for the Maya and Calli in central Mexico, which have already been discussed in terms of their cave associations. Moreover, in Maya writing the head variant of the number seven is a personified jaguar deity, the so-called Jaguar God of the Underworld (ibid.:134). Jaguars, archetypal beasts of the forest, are linked with caves. For instance, the Chilam Balam of Chumayel refers to the *balamil aktun* "jaguar of the cave" (Roys 1967:96). Heyden (1983:69) associates jaguars and caves through the jaguar's flowerlike pelage marks. The flower in her estimation also falls into the camp of Mesoamerican cave symbolism. Certainly, the Aztec jaguar deity Tepeyollotl (Heart of the Mountain) provides evidence of a central Mexican jaguar-cave complex. Furthermore,

there are reports, both Colonial and modern, of ritual performances in caves involving jaguar impersonators (Navarrete 1971; Vogt 1981:130).

In Classic Maya art, groups of seven often characterize iconography associated with the wilderness. Zoomorph P from Quirigua illustrates this with the seven ghoulish figures that adorn its sides (fig. 3-35). They are the strange biologically anomalous inhabitants of a Xibalba-like domain. They float in the convolutions of the Cauac Monster, a symbol of the mountains and caves of wilderness. A relief from Structure 22 from Copan has a group of seven small figures crawling through a series of S-shaped scrolls; they seem to parallel the seven figures on Zoomorph P (Stone 1985a:46).

We also find that spirits who inhabit forest space are sometimes associated with the number seven. The *sip* (or *zip*), for instance, are believed in Yucatan to be small forest-dwelling spirits who care for deer and protect them from hunters (Redfield and Villa Rojas 1934:117–118). One *sip*, depicted in the Dresden Codex (fol. 13c) with black and white body stripes, bears the name 7-*sip* (Fox and Justeson 1984:39).

Another interesting use of the number seven in Maya art has been proposed by Bonor (1989:29–30). The celebrated Sarcophagus Lid from Palenque has six half-quatrefoils with emerging figures at either end (Schele and Miller 1986:pl. 111). Each quatrefoil may represent a different cave containing its own tutelary ancestor. The de-

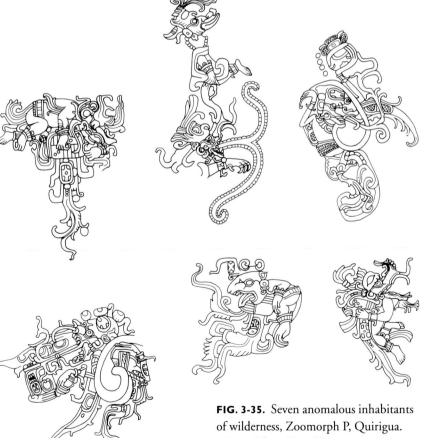

FIG. 3-35. Seven anomalous inhabitants of wilderness, Zoomorph P, Quirigua. Adapted from Maudslay 1889–1902: vol. 2, pl. 60.

ceased Pacal is depicted as falling into a pair of skeletalized jaws, widely recognized as a symbolic entrance into the underworld. If these skeletalized jaws are also counted as one cave, Bonor notes, the total number of caves would add up to seven, recalling the aforementioned mythical "Seven Caves." The Sarcophagus Lid provides some support for the idea that the "Seven Caves" origin myth formed part of Classic Maya religion. Perhaps Pacal in death was destined to be the tutelary ancestor of the seventh cave.

Ancestors and Caves

The above-mentioned Chicomoztoc, or "Seven Caves," was a legendary place from which many Nahua peoples around the Valley of Mexico believed their ancestors had migrated (Heyden 1975). The widespread adoption of this myth is evident in the Quiche Maya epithet for their legendary place of origin, Tulan Zuyua: *vukub pek, vukub zivan* "seven caves, seven canyons" (Tedlock 1985:360; López Austin 1973:56). The cave discovered underneath the Pyramid of the Sun at Teotihuacan has been suggested by Heyden (1975) to be the Classic precursor of Chicomoztoc, pushing back the cave origin myth to the Classic period, an idea also suggested by the iconography of the Palenque Sarcophagus Lid, as noted earlier. There can be no doubt that the ancestor-cave emergence theme has great antiquity and was widespread in Mesoamerica. Some Mesoamericans today still believe their ancestors emerged from a cave (Nash 1970:5), and many more believe that ancestor spirits reside in caves.

Colonial chroniclers speak of ancestor cults centered in caves where human skeletal remains, said to be those of ancestors, were venerated. For example, Nuñez de la Vega's publication of 1702 mentions that certain unspecified Maya groups in highland Chiapas revered the bones of founding ancestors with such

fervor it was "as though they had been saints" (Thompson 1975:xxxiii). Offerings, such as flowers and copal, were left in the cave for these ancestor spirits until Nuñez de la Vega had the bones removed.

Lowland Maya caves utilized in pre-Columbian times sometimes contain human bones. It is often difficult to tell, though, whether the bones are from sacrificed or interred individuals. Caches of bones may be indicative of ancestor cults of the kind described by Nuñez de la Vega. Ancestor worship is suggested by a cache of skulls and "idols" removed by Spanish clerics from a cave in Yucatan in 1562 (Scholes and Adams 1938:24–25). Piles of long bones and skulls were also found in the Gruta de Xcan, Yucatan (Márquez de González, Castillo, and Schmidt 1982). Thompson (1975:xxxi–xxxvi) notes a number of other Maya caves containing piles of human bones.

The use of caves for burial is also well documented in Oaxaca. The remarkable cave of Ejutla in the Mixteca Alta is a Postclassic site with at least forty-five cells built into the cave wall and used as tombs (Moser 1975). Other early sources indicate that the Mixtec held the custom of burying high-status individuals in caves, a practice that potentially might evolve into a cave-centered cult of ancestor worship.

The association of caves with ancestors can be understood in terms of various threads that weave through cave symbolism. Ancestors and caves have a mutual association with the life and death cycle. As archetypal mothers and fathers, ancestors are identified with life-giving concepts like fertility, just as caves are identified with maize, water, and other aspects of fertility. At the same time, ancestors have attained the status of the dead and belong in the underworld realm of the cave. Caves and ancestors are also allied through their mutual association with light-

ning. Armed with data from ethnographic studies across the Maya and Mixe-Zoque area, Spero (1987) has identified a lightning-ancestor-cave complex that was widespread in southern Mesoamerica. Lightning and rain have well-documented connections with caves. Spero has shown that ancestors who are believed to inhabit caves often manifest themselves in the form of lightning.

A number of themes and ritual practices that center on caves have been discussed in the preceding pages. They represent a master inventory, only part of which was realized in any given locale. What is important for the study of cave painting is that those Mesoamericans who entered caves in order to paint on their walls carried some of this weighty cultural baggage with them. In Mesoamerica the cave was an imposing environment from a cultural as well as a physical standpoint. Above all, the cave presented a sharp rupture from everyday life.

4

Maya and Mesoamerican Cave Painting: A Survey of Sites and Images

While Europe can claim 275 caves decorated during the Upper Paleolithic (Bahn and Vertut 1988:191), fewer than 40 caves housing about two thousand painted images are known in Mesoamerica. Given the artistic proclivities of the ancient Mesoamericans and the importance of caves in their environment and religion, this may seem a surprisingly limited number, but, compared with other agricultural societies, which have rarely shown an interest in such matters, it is a relatively abundant collection of cave art.

In addition, what presently remains is surely a paler reflection of what existed in the past. Painted wall art is vulnerable, especially to the destructive effects of water, and roughly two-thirds of Mesoamerica lies within the humid tropical latitudes where monsoon rains trigger spectacular hydrological activity in caves. Vandalism is also a serious problem owing to the proximity of caves to population centers. No doubt more of these paintings would have sur-

vived if they were preserved, like north African rock art, in an uninhabited desert!

One interesting feature of Mesoamerican cave art and, more broadly speaking, all forms of Mesoamerican wall art is that it includes both elite and, for want of a better term, nonelite art styles. Elite styles, associated with such high cultures as the Olmec, Maya, and Aztecs, will be referred to collectively as "Greater Classic." This term has both chronological and stylistic parameters. It spans the period when the great art styles of Mesoamerica prevailed, from roughly 1200 B.C. to A.D. 1500, and has a characteristic figural style with a fair degree of anatomical definition. Its symbols derive from a codified inventory that developed over many centuries. Parietal art in a Greater Classic style suggests interaction with the political upper echelon in the region and may have actually been produced by court artists.

The nonelite component of Meso-american parietal art is not necessarily from a different epoch than Greater Classic art; in fact, in a few cases we can be sure of contemporaneity. What differs significantly is style and content, as this art is characterized by linear, schematic motifs, not seen in Greater Classic art. Given the distinction of formal characteristics, the term "schematic" will refer collectively to this style of Mesoamerican wall art.

Schematic parietal art is far more common than the Greater Classic corpus. In fact, Cera (1977) found that only 7 percent of Mexican rock art could be associated with a known style of Mesoamerican high art. Though it may have limited appeal to our sensibilities, schematic art should not be dismissed as the random doodlings of peasants. No doubt some qualifies as such; a simple face etched onto a stalactite may have been motivated by nothing more profound than to acknowledge one's presence in a cave or the urge to draw. But schematic motifs are often carefully and repetitively painted on rock walls, sometimes in hard-to-reach places, surely a sign of some serious intent. In addition, the pictorial vocabulary (for example, spirals, concentric circles, and linear quadrupeds) is widely shared in the rock art of Mesoamerica and can even be found as far north as the American Southwest. This fact has prompted at least one scholar to suggest that an ancient stratum of art, spread during the Archaic, survived in Meso-american schematic parietal art (Cera 1977).

The History of Cave Painting in Mesoamerica

Archaic Cave Painting

Mesoamerican cave painting probably has its origins in the Archaic period (ca. 7000–1500 B.C.). Archaic rock painting has been found in a reasonably secure stratigraphic context in Mexico,

but north of Mesoamerica proper, at Cueva Ahumada near Monterrey. There rock paintings and petroglyphs were discovered two meters below ground level in association with Archaic artifacts (Clark 1965; Cera 1976:19). As the style of the buried paintings matched what remained on the surface, an Archaic date has been assigned to the entire group. Cave painting has also been found in Mesoamerican caves that have an Archaic occupation: for instance, the Santa Marta Cave in Chiapas (García-Bárcena and Santamaría 1982: fig. V-2). Velázquez (1980:53) proposes a Late Archaic date, around 2000 B.C., for some paintings from Loltun Cave, Yucatan, which he likens to a stick-figure rock art style found among hunting and gathering societies in many parts of the world. In addition, the cave of Espíritú Santo in El Salvador has a collection of stick-figure paintings that may be coeval with a stratified layer of Archaic lithics found in the cave (fig. 4-1; Haberland 1972; Haberland, personal communication, 1991). However, in the final analysis, these archaeological associations are not totally secure, thereby leaving the question of Archaic cave painting in Meso-america, at least for the moment, an open one.

Olmec Cave Painting

Based on present evidence, the earliest Mesoamerican cave paintings that can be stylistically dated pertain to the Middle Preclassic Olmec art style. Olmec paintings, probably produced no earlier than 900 B.C., survive at three caves in the state of Guerrero in southern Mexico: Juxtlahuaca, Oxtotitlan, and Cacahuaziziqui, a fairly recent discovery. Sheltered in remote, arid mountains over one hundred miles south of Mexico City, these caves are distant from the tropical Olmec "heartland" in coastal Veracruz and Tabasco. Indeed, the caves appear to be affiliated with local highland polities of Guerrero and Morelos, such as Chalcatzingo and Teopantecuanitlan (Kent Reilly, personal communication, 1992), though there are hints of contact with Gulf Coast sites, such as La Venta. Hence, the Olmec rubric attached to these paintings in the following discussion refers only to an art style and not to a Gulf Coast Olmec attribution. It has become increasingly clear that the term "Olmec art" is problematical in subsuming objects with a broad geographical distribution in Mesoamerica and manufactured by distinct Preclassic populations (Grove 1989; Reilly 1990).

Olmec cave paintings first came to light in Juxtlahuaca Cave, located about three and one-half miles north of Colotlipa, Guerrero. With the publications of Carlo Gay, beginning in 1966, their presence became widely known, although Mexican officials had known of these paintings at least since the 1930s (Grove 1967:38). Gay (1967: 28) proclaimed that they were "the earliest examples of large-scale paintings ever recorded in the New World." This idea now seems untenable in light of mural paintings from Cerro Sechin, Peru, which may date well before 1000 B.C. (Bonavia 1985: fig. 7; Samaniego, Vergara, and Bischof 1985); but the Juxtlahuaca paintings still rank as the earliest large-scale mural paintings in Mesoamerica.

Juxtlahuaca, a deep cave with almost a mile of passages, has long corridors punctuated intermittently by rooms. The corridors communicate on several different levels (Gay 1967:33, map; Grove 1967:38). The cave is located in dry, secluded country, and the paintings are found toward the back, factors that must have contributed to their preservation for nearly three thousand years. Found 3,400 to 4,000 feet from the entrance in a lower-level passage, the paintings of Juxtlahuaca are among the most deeply sequestered cave paintings

in Mesoamerica (though not the most difficult to reach compared with certain paintings at Naj Tunich). Their remote setting is unquestionably deliberate and strongly suggests a ritual motivation.

Juxtlahuaca's Gallery of Drawings contains Painting 1, in brilliant red, yellow, and black. It features a standing anthropomorphic jaguar who towers over a small, seated figure sporting a beard (Plate 1). The massive, standing figure wears a circular earflare and a plumed device on the front of his headdress, recalling the costumes of the nobility depicted in Olmec monumental sculpture. Indeed, this figure, garbed in a brilliant, multicolored banded tunic, could be a jaguar impersonator. A curious whiplike object that looks something like a jaguar or coyote tail leads from his hand to the crouched figure (appearing as though the feline is taming a human in an odd sort of role reversal!). Judging by posture and size, the small bearded figure would appear to be subordinate to the jaguar, but the relationship is complicated by the fact that the seated figure shows evidence of high rank in his costume. Reilly (personal communication, 1992) has identified the object held by the seated figure as a standard type of Olmec zoomorphic ceremonial bar with an animal head appearing on one side (here to the right). Owing to the presence of the ceremonial bar, Reilly believes that the small figure represents a nobleman who may have been seeking the vision of an ancestor in the cave. Hence, the anthropomorphic jaguar, dressed in elite trappings, may be the specter of his distinguished ancestor.

Across from Painting 1 is Drawing 1 (Griffin 1981: fig. 3), a composition of rectilinear lines that has been described as a temple (Gay 1967:35; Griffin 1982). Farther down the passage in the Gallery of Drawings is Drawing 2, a standing male dressed in a loincloth. To the right is Drawing 3, incomplete

FIG. 4-1. Paintings from Espiritu Santo Cave, El Salvador. Adapted from Haberland 1972.

heads of a serpent and perhaps a jaguar (Gay 1967:31). Grove (1967:39) suspects that these drawings are modern. Deeper still into the Hall of the Serpent are two important paintings. Painting 2 depicts a serpent with a feathered crown, a bifurcated tongue, and a crossed-bands symbol set into the eye (fig. 4-2). Grove (ibid.) notes of the plumed serpent that an underlayer of black paint, forming details of the face, are finely painted, whereas the red paint delineating the body is crudely painted. Based on this observation, he suggests that the red represents later repainting. Painting 3 is a naturalistic rendering of a jaguar with a lolling tongue (fig. 4-3). The juxtaposition of a jaguar and serpent in Paintings 2 and 3 may be significant, as noted by Gay (1967); they are two animals associated with caves in Mesoamerican thought.

Thirteen miles north of Juxtlahuaca, near the town of Chilapa, is Oxtotitlan, investigated by David Grove in 1968 (1969; 1970). The entrance hall of Oxtotitlan, cut into a hillside, is wide and shallow like a rock shelter, but it leads at the back to two sections of a deeper tunnel (Grottos 1 and 2), each about

FIG. 4-2. Feathered serpent, Painting 3, Juxtlahuaca. Photograph by Eldon Leiter.

FIG. 4-3. Jaguar with lolling tongue, Painting 2, Juxtlahuaca. Adapted from photograph by Eldon Leiter.

FIG. 4-4. Mural 1, Oxtotitlan. Adapted from Grove 1969: fig. 2.

FIG. 4-5. Altar 4, La Venta. Adapted from Grove 1973: 131.

twenty-five meters deep. At least twenty paintings are found along the grotto walls and over the entrance.

Perhaps the best-known Olmec cave painting, Mural 1 from Oxtotitlan, is not found inside the cave but rather sits over the entrance to one of the grottos (fig. 4-4). This painting is brilliantly polychromatic, consisting of red, brown, ocher, and various shades of blue-green (Grove 1970:9; color frontispiece). An individual, shown "x-ray" fashion in bird costume, sits on a stylized zoomorphic band that recalls the upper register of Olmec tabletop altars, such as Altar 4 from La Venta (fig. 4-5). Because of the figure's position, the Oxtotitlan painting shows that the La Venta "altar" was used as a throne (Grove 1973). Altar 4 also demonstrates

Images from the Underworld

that the placement of the zoomorphic mask over the cave entrance in Mural 1 of Oxtotitlan was purposeful: the cave entrance forms the zoomorph's mouth, structurally occupying the position of the tabletop altar's niche.[1] Thus, in Mural 1 and Altar 4 a depiction of a cave in one image is replaced by an actual cave in an analogous image. This substitution confirms beyond doubt that the niche found in all tabletop altars represents a cave.

Like that of Juxtlahuaca, the repertoire of paintings at Oxtotitlan draws on animal imagery. A remarkable painting in black, Painting I-d shows a feline standing next to an ithyphallic man with one arm raised (fig. 4-6). Grove (1970:18; 1973:133) has proposed that the man is copulating with the jaguar, just as some Olmec sculptures are believed to show a were-jaguar copulating with a woman—in Portrero Nuevo Monument 3 and Río Chiquito Monument 1, for instance. According to Stirling (1955:19), this union may have engendered a jaguar race thought by scholars as recently as the early 1970s to be the patron gods of the Olmec. How-

ever, to use the sculptures (which may or may not depict a jaguar and woman copulating) as a model for interpreting the cave painting seems unfounded. In the sculpted "copulation" scenes the male partner is the jaguar. Indeed, jaguars seem to fulfill largely masculine roles in Olmec art, so Painting I-d would be out of character if the jaguar is placed in a receptive female role. If a connection were intended between these figures, it may have been to draw a parallel between the human being and the jaguar. But what seems more likely is that the jaguar represents later repainting, as suggested by the fact that the two figures do not form a coherent composition. And in other respects they are out of character with each other. For example, the jaguar is more ornate than the rigid human figure. Grove (1970: 17) mentions that the jaguar is difficult to see. Perhaps it was painted with a different recipe, a less dense or adherent paint, for instance, than the human figure. In addition, the published drawing shows the tail darkening where it overlaps the human figure, which might be the underlayer of paint.

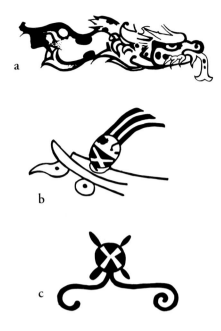

FIG. 4-7. Various plumed serpents, Oxtotitlan: *a*, Painting I-c, Oxtotitlan, adapted from Grove 1970: fig. 12; *b*, Painting I-b, Oxtotitlan, adapted from Grove 1970: fig. 11; *c*, Painting A-I, Oxtotitlan, adapted from Grove 1970: fig. 25.

The theme of the plumed serpent also makes an appearance at Oxtotitlan. The bifurcated tongue, fangs, and thick undulating body are those of a serpent, while a feather ruff encircles the head and neck (fig. 4-7a). A more conceptual rendition of this creature shows the crossed-bands eye, a fang on a stylized upper jaw, and three plumes issuing from the top of the head (fig. 4-7b). In the south grotto is a painting showing the crossed-bands eye attached to two scrolls that may represent a bifurcated tongue (fig. 4-7c).

Another animal portrayed at Oxtotitlan is the owl (Grove 1970: fig. 9). It is noteworthy that another rock art site, Dos Peñas, northeast of Oxtotitlan (but undated), depicts the head of an owl in red paint (Leicht 1972: fig. 5).

Calendrical notations may also be present at Oxtotitlan. Grove (1970:20, fig. 14) suggests that Painting 3 (north

FIG. 4-6. Painting 1-d, Oxtotitlan. Adapted from Grove 1970: fig. 13.

grotto), a zoomorphic head associated with circles, may represent a day sign, which would make it the earliest day sign known in Mesoamerica; however, his identification is highly tentative. Juxtlahuaca Cave also revealed clusters of painted dots that might be numerical notations: three red spots in a niche near the so-called Hall of the Dead (Gay 1967:31) and six red spots to the right of Painting 2, the plumed serpent.

A third cave with paintings in the Olmec style has been reported in Guerrero about thirty miles west of Oxtotitlan and Juxtlahuaca. Cacahuaziziqui, southeast of Tlapa, is a shallow cave, much like a rock shelter. It has over one hundred paintings, most of which are unidentifiable schematic designs and stick figures (Villela 1989: fig. 1). However, Paintings 1 and 2 from Cacahuaziziqui are undeniably Olmec in style. Painting 1, in white, shows the flat silhouette of a partial figure with a helmetlike head covering, typical of Olmec costuming (fig. 4-8a). The raised arm is a gesture common in Olmec rock art and was seen earlier at Oxtotitlan (fig. 4-7).[2] Painting 2 is a larger, incomplete figure wearing a headdress, decorated with what appear to be symbolic motifs (fig. 4-8b). This painting is polychromatic, consisting of yellow, white, and a small amount of red (Villela 1989: fig. 2). If complete, the figure would have been larger than life-size; from head to elbow it measures 1.77 meters (ibid.:39).

Some generalizations can be made about the corpus of Olmec cave painting. First, it shows a love of bright, polychrome colors. The paintings of Juxtlahuaca employ red, yellow ocher, and black, and Oxtotitlan adds several shades of blue-green to the palette of colors used by these cave artists. The Cacahuaziziqui paintings are also polychrome. The gusto with which color is employed in Olmec-style cave art raises the specter of polychrome Olmec sculp-

ture and perhaps mural paintings. Preservation on the Gulf Coast is so poor, reducing pottery to "blobs of fired clay" (Coe and Diehl 1980:131), that paint would not have had much chance of survival. Olmec cave painting provides tantalizing evidence for a now-lost tradition of Preclassic mural painting.

Another feature of Olmec cave painting is its large size. Mural 1 from Oxtotitlan covers an area 2.8 × 3.5 meters (Grove 1970:8). The plumed serpent from Juxtlahuaca measures over two meters in height (Gay 1967:30). One of the Cacahuaziziqui figures is over life-size. With the additional emphasis on flat shapes and color infill, Olmec cave paintings are bold and massive, akin to the style of Olmec sculpture. This style of painting is well suited to the cave environment, where large walls seem to encourage large-scale images. Large, infilled paintings with simple contours also afford better viewing in dim light. With forms expanding to fit available wall space, Olmec cave paintings have a commanding presence. Their harmonious blending with the environment recalls formal solutions found in Upper Paleolithic cave painting.

The paintings of Juxtlahuaca and Oxtotitlan are the work of trained artists, well versed in the themes and pictorial conventions of Olmec art, though the paintings of Cacahuaziziqui have a cruder provincial flavor. Like Olmec sculpture of the ceremonial centers, Olmec cave paintings comfortably alternate between naturalism and symbolic encoding. This sophisticated manipulation of form suggests that the cave painters were court artists and that the caves were used by some local elites. An elite affiliation is also suggested by iconographic parallels between the cave paintings and monumental sculpture in the Olmec style. Angulo V. (1987: 152), for example, compares Painting 1 from Juxtlahuaca (Plate 1) to a stela

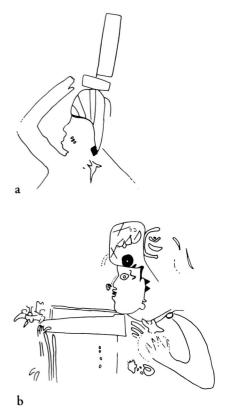

FIG. 4-8. Paintings, Cacahuaziziqui, adapted from Villela 1989: *a,* Painting 1; *b,* Painting 2.

from Chalcatzingo in that both include a standing figure and a seated figure. The comparison between Mural 1 from Oxtotitlan (fig. 4-4) and the La Venta tabletop altars (fig. 4-5) has already been mentioned. The fact that Mural 1 is located over an entrance to one of the grottos rather than in the totally private setting of the cave interior suggests a public-political context for this painting. The most blatant political images associated with caves in Mesoamerica are not found completely out of public view, as in the relief from Loltun Cave (fig. 4-25), which features a stelalike royal portrait carved next to a cave entrance.

Olmec cave paintings show a sensitivity of composition to natural rock forms. For example, as Gay (1967:34) observed of Painting 2 from Juxtlahuaca, the serpent repeats the sinuous contour of the natural wall (fig. 4-2). The graceful curves of the cave wall most likely attracted attention and evoked the image of an undulating serpent, prompting the creation of the painting in that spot. Here cave topography has influenced the artist's choice of subject matter and its formal resolution. Monument 19 from La Venta parallels Painting 2 from Juxtlahuaca in its similarly configured feathered serpent (fig. 4-9). Like the cave wall, the edge of the stela follows the serpent's writhing motion, as though the monument were intentionally evoking the irregular shapes of natural rocks. Generally speaking, Preclassic Mesoamerican art is more literal than that of later periods in the way it relates rock art, monumental art, and the topographic forms constituting the sacred landscape (Stone 1992).

Olmec cave painting takes unusual liberty in depicting male genitalia, something it has in common with Maya cave painting. This is seen in Oxtotitlan Painting I-d, which is the only ithyphallic portrayal of a high-status individual in Olmec art (fig. 4-6).[3] In this brash genital display, Painting I-d might be compared with Naj Tunich Drawing 18 (fig. 6-28). It would appear that in the privacy of the cave customary modesty is more relaxed.

Cave and Rock Painting Sites in Mesoamerica

Though Cera (1977) recorded two hundred rock art sites in Mexico alone, only a fraction of the corpus of Mesoamerican rock art includes cave painting. Therefore, the following discussion broadens to include both rock painting and cave painting sites. The line dividing the two is often very fine (especially

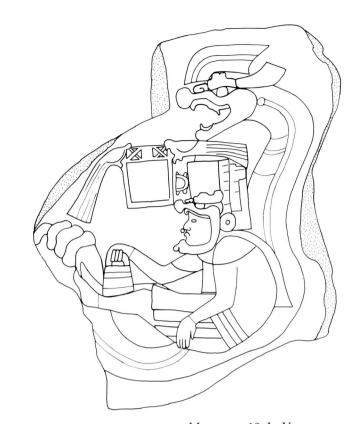

FIG. 4-9. Monument 19, La Venta. Drawing after original in the Museo Nacional de Antropología e Historia, Mexico City.

in the case of rock shelters), and they often access a common pictorial vocabulary.[4]

Western Chiapas

Western Chiapas is home to a number of painted caves and rock shelters that in pre-Columbian times lay in Zoque-speaking territory, just beyond the modern western border with the Maya. These rock art sites were probably affiliated with Zoquean people, though a Maya affiliation is not out of the question.

Lee (1969) found paintings in two caves along the Río La Venta, northwest of Tuxtla Gutiérrez. One, Cuatro Hacha, contains red paintings on the ceiling near the entrance. They consist of roughly painted outlines of an inverted T, somewhat like an inverted Maya "Ik" sign, with four interior dots (fig. 4-10a). The cave took its name from these forms, which resemble an axe. Paintings in the cave of Media Luna, like Cuatro Hacha, are in red and have thick outlines forming simple shapes. Based on

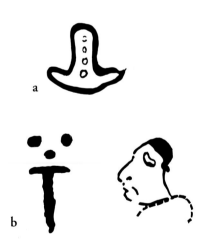

FIG. 4-10. Paintings from caves north of Tuxtla Gutiérrez, Chiapas: *a*, axe form, Cuatro Hacha, adapted from Lee 1969: fig. 3; *b*, T-shape, dots, and human head, Cueva de la Chepa, adapted from Cera 1980.

associated ceramics, Lee (p. 29) dates the Media Luna paintings to Chiapa VII–IX, ca. A.D. 150–650.

Cera (1980) reports twenty-six red paintings from Cueva de la Chepa, located just north of Tuxtla Gutiérrez. Partly effaced by modern graffiti, the paintings are found on the side walls and ceiling of the cave as well as on a large pillar. Counted among the Cueva de la Chepa paintings are positive and negative handprints, schematic human and animal figures, geometrical designs, and a human head (fig. 4-10b). Cera (p. 9) notes that the head looks vaguely Mayan and therefore suggests that all of the paintings may have been made by the Maya, possibly during the Postclassic. Other than this tentative resemblance, however, the date and affiliation of the Cueva de la Chepa paintings remain uncertain.

Some half-dozen paintings are found in the Santa Marta Cave, an important Archaic site in Chiapas (García Bárcena and Santamaría 1982:146–147). With one exception in yellow, the paintings are all red. Three consist of handprints, and the remaining paintings are simple renderings of a fish and a human figure. Navarrete and Martínez (1961) report paintings in a pair of rock shelters east of Tuxtla Gutiérrez that they refer to collectively as the "eagles' nest." On the ceiling of the upper chamber are crude red paintings; the only discernible form is an animal, though exactly what type is unclear (ibid.: fig. 20). The lower rock shelter contains paintings of human figures in orange and appear to be modern (ibid.: figs. 21, 22).

Rock paintings are also found near the village of Chicoasen, about twenty kilometers northwest of Tuxtla Gutiérrez. Juy Juy, a two-meter-high depression in the rock face, is decorated with a painting and is located at the entrance to Sumidero Canyon (Gussinyer 1976). The depression occupies a remote spot on the cliff face but apparently can be seen from quite a distance. The painting represents a schematic but carefully delineated bird in red (fig. 4-11a). The bird stands over two horizontal, parallel lines that resemble a bar and dot notation for the number ten.

About one kilometer farther into the canyon from Juy Juy is another painted rock shelter known as Los Monos (Gussinyer 1980). Here, spread across a vertical wall, are about twenty-seven red paintings, ranging from fifteen to twenty centimeters in height. The paintings are infilled silhouettes, lacking any internal detail, mainly of human figures and animals, the latter including monkeys (fig. 4-11b) and possibly deer or dogs. Some of the human figures have a series of dots over the head (fig. 4-11c). Pigment analysis revealed that iron oxide mixed with a kaolin binder was employed for some of the red paintings (ibid.:150).

About three kilometers west of Chicoasen is the rock shelter known locally as Cueva del Tigre, which has two red paintings: one of a costumed figure with a bird beak (fig. 4-11d) and the other, a pair of concentric circles intersected by four lines (Strecker 1984a). The latter painting has been identified by Strecker as a spiderweb. Four hundred meters below them is a wall with positive and negative handprints in red.

A widely shared trait among these Chiapas rock paintings is the use of red pigment to create either thick outlines or infilled areas. T-shaped designs occur in several Chiapas caves, and they crop up as well in Maya cave painting (e.g., Actun Dzib).

Chalcatzingo

Chalcatzingo, Morelos, best known for its Olmec-style petroglyphs, has an important collection of paintings found in concavities, ranging from shallow niches to small caves, that dot the hills, which form the dramatic backdrop of the site (Gay 1971). A recent survey includes

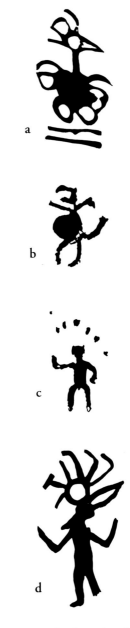

FIG. 4-11. Rock art sites from Chicoasen area: *a,* bird over two bars, Juy Juy, adapted from Gussinyer 1976: fig. 7; *b,* monkey, Los Monos, adapted from Gussinyer 1980; *c,* figure with dots over head, Los Monos, adapted from Gussinyer 1980; *d,* costumed performer, Tigre, adapted from Strecker 1984a.

well over two hundred paintings, predominantly in red and white pigment (fig. 4-12; Apostolides 1987). Since the white paintings sometimes overlap the red and the reverse is never true, it is thought that the white paintings date to a later epoch, possibly Postclassic (ibid.: 197). Most of the paintings are simple schematic figures or unidentifiable rectilinear designs—that is, they are in a style of Mesoamerican rock art about which little is presently known. Apostolides (ibid.: 172–173) divides the paintings into five broad categories: stick figures (anthropomorphic and zoomorphic), triangle and slit, sunburst, plumed, and clockwise and counterclockwise spirals. Many of these forms, as will be seen later, occur in Maya caves. For example, the triangle and slit, commonly called a "vulva," is found in Maya cave paintings and petroglyphs of Yucatan (Strecker 1987; Velázquez Morlet and López de la Rosa 1988: 95). Other simple forms, such as spirals, comblike designs, and **T** shapes, recall paintings from Actun Dzib, Belize.

One group of paintings at Chalcatzingo can be identified with a Mesoamerican high-art style. They are found on the western slope of Cerro Delgado in Cave 19. The climb up to Cave 19 is difficult, underscoring the serious intent of those who made the journey. Three red linear paintings in Cave 19 reflect

the style of Teotihuacan art (Apostolides 1987: 191–193). Chalcatzingo, like other sites in eastern Morelos, was influenced by Teotihuacan during the Classic period (Martín Arana 1987: 387). A Teotihuacan-style ballcourt marker, for example, was also found at Chalcatzingo (Grove and Angulo V. 1987: fig. 9.28). These influences are strongest at Chalcatzingo during Teotihuacan III and IV (Tlamimilolpan-Xolalpan), ca. A.D. 400–600, presumably the period when the Cave 19 paintings were created.

Apostolides proposes that the two lobes in Painting 1 represent hills, possibly Cerro Delgado and Cerro Chalcatzingo themselves (fig. 4-13a). I would further note that on the lobes' interior, the scalloped line and mouthlike opening may represent a sacred orifice, such as a cave entrance, out of which gush streams of water, seen in the painting as two volutes (cf. figs. 3-18, 3-19); this could also refer to a sacred spring. Painting 3 portrays what Baird (1989: 108) calls a "star enclosure," a frame filled with five-pointed stars inset with a circle, typical of Teotihuacan art (fig. 4-13b). The Teotihuacan star motif has varied symbolic associations with water, earth, and warfare (ibid.: 111). Its usage in decorated borders also suggests a relationship with the natural environment, such as water, the sky, or

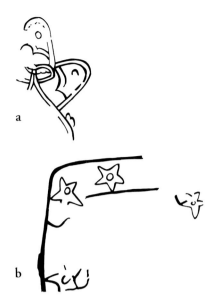

FIG. 4-13. Cave 19 paintings, Chalcatzingo, adapted from Apostolides 1987: fig. 12.45: *a,* Painting 1; *b,* Painting 3.

the underworld. The star enclosure of Painting 3 may complement the natural environment depicted in Painting 1, a conventionalized mountain-spring form. I strongly suspect that these paintings convey ideas about the sacred landscape, as do many Olmec-style petroglyphs at Chalcatzingo.

Teotihuacan

While cave paintings in a Teotihuacan style are found at Chalcatzingo, there are also cave paintings reported from around the site of Teotihuacan itself. Bastante Gutiérrez (1982) notes that Cave 1 and Cave 5 in Group I, located on the south side of Cerro Gordo, have paintings in red, apparently not well preserved. Cave 1 in Group II, in the Otzoyohualco sector, has postcontact drawings in white, including Latin crosses and Roman numerals.

Postclassic Rock Painting

Early Postclassic rock painting (ca. A.D. 900–1200) is reported by Villagra Caleti (1971: 148–151) at a place called Ixtapatongo "Mateo A. Saldaña" in the state of Mexico. The paintings

FIG. 4-12. Various rock paintings, Chalcatzingo. Adapted from Apostolides 1987.

FIG. 4-14. Postclassic rock painting, Ixtapatongo "Mateo A. Saldaña." From Villagra Caleti 1971: fig. 27.

cover a rock abutting the Tilostoc River. The best-preserved of the lot, Group 1, shows affinities with the art of Chichen Itza (fig. 4-14). The upper two-thirds of the scene is populated by "Toltec" warriors carrying *atlatl*s and darts. One, framed by a "sun disk," evokes the murals of the Upper Temple of the Jaguars at Chichen Itza (Miller 1977). Surely this scene refers to some parallel event. A group of "Star Warriors" (Miller 1989) occupies the upper right-hand corner. This painting offers

important evidence of Early Postclassic contact between Chichen Itza and central Mexico.

An interesting collection of cave and rock paintings in the Late Postclassic Mixteca-Puebla style can be found in widely separated areas of Mesoamerica. Two such sites are in the heart of Maya country, both on cliffs overlooking a lake. At Lake Ayarza in the department of Santa Rosa, Guatemala, is a group of paintings on a cliff face fifty meters above the lake (Ricketson 1936). Ex-

cept for a single undatable painting of concentric circles, all appear to be Late Postclassic (fig. 4-15). I might note that rock paintings of concentric circles, sometimes segmented by radiating lines, occur at diverse rock art sites in Meso-america—for example, near Chicoasen, Chiapas (Strecker 1984a), the Sierra de Tamaulipas (Stresser-Pean 1990: fig. 1), Atlihuetzian, Tlaxcala (Mora 1974: unit 21), Chalcatzingo, Morelos (Apostolides 1987: fig. 12.30), Cave of Pusilha, Peten (Siffre 1979: figs. 47–48), and Roberto's Cave in the Toledo District of Belize.

One painting at Lake Ayarza presents a figure with a butterfly nose plaque and seven *chalchihuitl*s (jade disks) standing for the number seven. Another painting appears to be a Cipactli-like earth monster (Ricketson 1936: fig. 2). These paintings utilize three colors: red, yellow, and green. Somewhat comparable is a group of paintings on a cliff face above a lake in Lacandon country (Wonham 1985). One black-line painting of an elaborate serpent head looks Postclassic (fig. 4-16). Nearby are a stick figure and several negative handprints in red, yellow, and white.

About forty kilometers south of Tuxtla Gutiérrez, Chiapas, is the rock shelter Cerro Naranjo (Navarrete 1960: 8–9). Two paintings on the ceiling look as though they could have come out of a Late Postclassic central Mexican codex (fig. 4-17). One depicts a figure with a shield and darts and red paint covering the upper part of his face. The entire painting utilizes red and blue-green paint. As noted by Navarrete, the second painting portrays an earth crocodile with dorsal spines, just as Cipactli is portrayed in the Mixteca-Puebla style of painting. What look like plants and a skull float above the body of Cipactli. This painting is in blue-green.

Another Postclassic codexlike painting occupies an actual cave, called Los

FIG. 4-15. Rock paintings, Lake Ayarza. Adapted from Ricketson 1936: fig. 2.

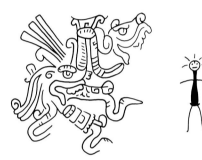

FIG. 4-16. Rock paintings, Lake Petha. Adapted from Wonham 1985: figs. 4, 5.

Tecotines, located in San Cristóbal Ecatepec in the state of Mexico (Du Solier 1939). This cave, 12.5 meters long, has most of its interior walls stuccoed, while a smaller cave directly above is completely stuccoed. These caves were no doubt important shrines in pre-Columbian times. On the east wall of the larger cave, presumably on a stuccoed surface, is a polychrome painting in red, yellow, and black, measuring a little over one meter in height (fig. 4-18). The painting shows a terraced platform surmounted by a temple. Du Solier notes that the roof appears to be conical and is colored yellow, indicating that it may be a conical straw roof seen in some depictions of wind temples. The deity depicted in the temple is completely skeletalized and holds an incense pouch in one hand and what looks like a knife in the other. Most likely he represents the Aztec death deity Mictlantecuhtli (though Du Solier identifies him as Quetzalcoatl). The temple with the conical roof could represent a cave, echoing the painting's actual location.

A rock shelter on the side of Popocatepetl, near Achichipilco, Morelos, is decorated with white paintings in a style comparable to sixteenth-century Aztec illustrated manuscripts (Piho and Hernandez 1972; Piho 1982). Featured are deity impersonators regaled in the manner of well-known Aztec deities.

FIG. 4-17. Postclassic paintings, Cerro Naranjo. Adapted from Navarrete 1960: figs. 8, 9.

One is an Ehecatl-Quetzalcoatl impersonator wearing the *ehecailacacozcatl* pectoral; he poses atop a terraced structure with steps (fig. 4-19). Xipe Totec impersonators carry the *chicahuaztli* "rattle staff." Tlaloc, identified by his crenated headdress, appears at the top. The collection of paintings also includes a sacrificial victim tied to a scaffold, schematic quadrupeds, and a number of geometric designs. Piho (p. 381) suggests that the paintings may be related to the celebration of one of the Aztec monthly feasts, such as Atlcahualo.

A heterogeneous group of paintings is found at Cueva de la Malinche in east-central Hidalgo, close to the border

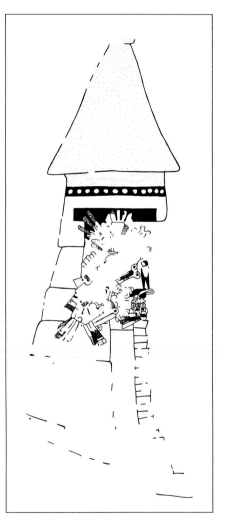

FIG. 4-18. Postclassic cave painting featuring death god and conical temple, Los Tecotines. Adapted from Du Solier 1939.

of Veracruz (Ochoa Salas 1972). The shallow cave, about seven meters deep, has simple schematic paintings—for example, stick figures recalling simple rock paintings from the not-too-distant site of Tulancingo (Villagra Caleti 1971: fig. 26). Other paintings evoke Mesoamerican high-art styles: step frets, a jaguar, and several figures (Ochoa Salas 1972: figs. 4, 12, 16, 17). Based on style, it is difficult to pinpoint their date, though Ochoa Salas (p. 13) suggests that a Postclassic date is likely based on regional archaeology. One cruciform painting with ornamental arabesques looks Colonial (fig. 4-20).

In general these Late Postclassic cave and rock paintings are reminiscent of codex-style painting, particularly in their polychrome palette. As in the codices, they emphasize deities and their ritual paraphernalia.

Cave Painting in the Maya Area

The Maya produced the most extensive collection of cave painting in Mesoamerica and the most abundant, covering the broadest geographical area and spanning the longest period of time (fig. 4-21). I have visited a number of the caves described in the following survey and so was able to draw on first-hand observations. Where I have not had this opportunity, my information derives from publications and also relies heavily on unpublished materials. Hence, the reader may note a lack of uniformity in the treatment of individual caves, and I can only attribute this to the disparate nature of my sources. The names of caves may also follow different spelling conventions, following their published form. Alternate names for caves appear in parentheses. A key to the symbols used on the maps of Actun Ch'on and Dzibichen is found in Appendix B. For an explanation of conventions used in the discussion of hieroglyphic texts, see Chapter 7.

FIG. 4-19. Painted scene with deity impersonators, Popocatepetl. Adapted from Piho and Hernandez 1972.

Loltun (Actun Loltun), Yucatan

It is fitting to begin a survey of Maya cave painting with Loltun Cave, located southwest of Oxkutzcab in the Sierrita de Ticul, the eastern range of the Puuc Hills that begins at Maxcanu and runs southeast into Quintana Roo. In Yucatec *lol-tun* means "stone flower," a phrase alluding to the florid appearance of certain calcite concretions found in the cave. Of longtime interest to archaeologists, Loltun had already been investigated by Henry Mercer (1975), Edward Thompson (1897), and Teobert Maler (Strecker 1981) by the end of the nineteenth century. Thompson's illustrations of two Loltun paintings in 1897 represent the first published account of Maya cave painting. He paid them little notice, remarking, "Upon these walls of a tunnel-like passage with a general trend toward the northwest, we found curious symbols outlined in black pigment, showing re-

FIG. 4-20. Cruciform figure, Cueva de La Malinche. Adapted from Ochoa Salas 1972: fig. 17.

markably clear and distinct against the yellow-white surface of the stone wall" (Thompson 1897:21). More recently, the wall art of Loltun has been investigated by Matthias Strecker (1976; 1982b) and Ricardo Velázquez Valadez.[5] I visited Loltun several times between 1985 and 1986.

Loltun is a large cave with around two kilometers of passageways (fig. 4-22). The main tunnel averages thirty meters in width and twenty-two meters in height; remarkably, the cave has seven entrances (Reddell 1977:274). Some eighty paintings and an equal number of handprints are found throughout the network of passages. Because of the cave's complexity, it might be useful at the outset to review the general distribution of painting groups.[6] The Galeria Principal and the area known as Pak'il K'ab contain mostly negative handprints. Bonanil Aktun and the adjacent Room 7 mainly house large profile faces, which appear to be Late or Terminal Classic. Room 3, Edward Thompson's (1897:7) "Inscription Chamber," contains five groups of paintings on the southeast wall that feature lively stick figures in a brownish-red pigment (Strecker 1976). Thompson's name for Room 3 comes not from the paintings, which he appears to have overlooked, but from the collection of petroglyphs. Room 5 contains four paintings, three of which appear to be Protoclassic, as will be discussed below. Other paintings and petroglyphs are scattered throughout Loltun. The famous bas-relief flanks the Nahkab (also called Hunacab) entrance at the east end.

Paintings in Room 5. The paintings in Room 5 are extremely important as they constitute the oldest stylistically datable cave paintings in the Maya area. They are situated on a calcite column formed from an aggregate of half-columns; each painting occupies one half-column, except in one case where two paintings occupy the same shaft (fig. 4-23). They are located at about the same height on the column, around two or two and one-half meters above the floor—above eye level for the Maya. All of the paintings are linear, rendered in a deep black paint, and have no infilled areas. The left three paintings have firm, broad outlines, some three to five centimeters in width. The right-

hand painting uses a thinner line. It seems highly probable that at least the left three paintings date from the same period.

The central painting shows a human figure lacking a head, feet, and any indication of costume (fig. 4-24). The figure stands about eighty-four centimeters tall. The fluid contours and positioning of the chest, arms, and legs

FIG. 4-21. Location of painted caves in the Maya area.

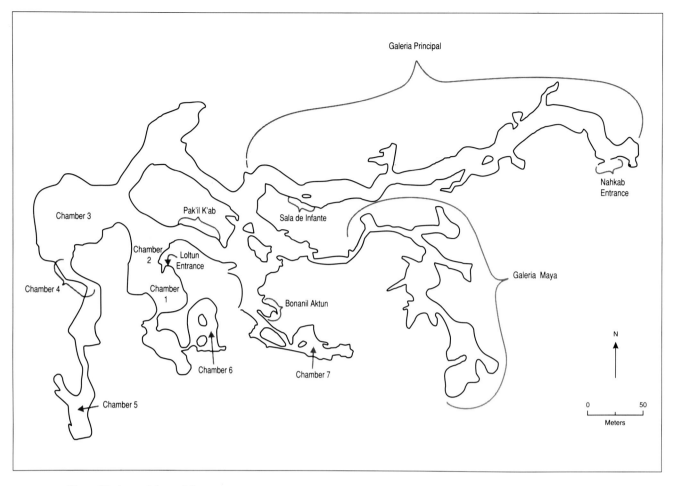

FIG. 4-22. Plan of Loltun. Adapted from Zavala Ruiz et al. 1978.

compare well with the Nahkab entrance relief. In both, the right arm swings forward and the left arm back. The legs do not overlap from the knees down. In addition, the firm line describes strong, simple shapes.

Ever since Proskouriakoff (1950: 154–155) noted affinities between the Nahkab entrance relief and Izapan-style sculpture, a Protoclassic date for the former has been widely accepted (fig. 4-25). The Loltun entrance relief compares closely with the Dumbarton Oaks recarved pectoral (Coe 1966: fig. 7)[7] and Kaminaljuyu Stela 11 (Gallenkamp and Johnson 1985: no. 19). Parsons' (1986:

FIG. 4-23. Composite column with early paintings in Room 5, Loltun.

FIG. 4-24. Figure painted on composite column, Room 5, Loltun.

FIG. 4-25. Relief next to the Nahkab entrance of Loltun showing a ruler portrait and associated text. Adapted from Andrews 1981.

78) dating of the Loltun relief in the period A.D. 50–200 seems reasonable based on current evidence and is the date assigned here to the Room 5 paintings.

Left of the figure is a painting thirty-eight centimeters high, which shows the number eight (a bar and three dots) over a cartouche with a *u*-element infix (fig. 4-26). That this painting represents a date finds support in the first glyph of the entrance relief text, identified by Coe (1976:118) as the *tsolk'in* day 3 Chuen (fig. 4-25). Coe suggests that the date may function as a personal name. However, its position, leading off the text, and larger size indicate a calendrical function; the latter trait is common in early texts (Justeson et al. 1985:40). In both the relief and the cave painting the coefficient is positioned over the day sign, which is contained in a cartouche lacking a pedestal. Again, the placement of the coefficient above the day sign is typical of the earliest-known calendrical inscriptions of Mesoamerica outside of Oaxaca (ibid.).

The *u*-element is an early style marker and appears in some of the earliest renditions of Maya day glyphs—for example, on early forms of Ahau. A series of early day glyphs on a painted cylinder from the Mundo Perdido Complex at Tikal shows one in the form of a *u*-element in a cartouche with two scrolls projecting from the top. Because of the sequence, that glyph should represent Chicchan (Mayer 1988). An argument has been made elsewhere that the *u*-element in the cave painting may substitute for a circle, which could yield a reading of Muluc (Stone 1989b). In any case, both the entrance relief date and the painted day glyph are important as two of the earliest calendrical inscriptions in the Maya area and, clearly, are among the earliest inscriptions known from Yucatan.

About ten centimeters below the day glyph another painting, measuring forty-one centimeters high, depicts an individual with fat cheeks, a prominent nose, and squarish simian lips (fig. 4-27). A volute that looks like a monkey tail is adjacent to the chest. The flabby face and simian features point to the figure's affiliation with the so-called "*pa* character," a grotesque, monkeylike performer who has connections as well to the Maya God N (Taube 1989a). The monkey's rude antics associate him with the iconography of public performance and ritual humour.

Given the three paintings just discussed, some interesting, though admittedly speculative, conclusions can be drawn. If we accept that the *tsolk'in* position of the entrance relief is 3 Chuen, it is noteworthy that the next occurrence of Muluc falls on an 8 Muluc, the proposed date of one of the paintings.

FIG. 4-26. Calendrical inscription, possibly 8 Muluc, Room 5, Loltun.

FIG. 4-27. Simian figure, Room 5, Loltun.

Furthermore, if the New Year ceremony were celebrated at Protoclassic Loltun according to the same system used in Yucatan during Landa's time, then 8 Muluc could designate a Year Bearer—that is, one of the four possible days of the *tsolk'in* on which the New Year could begin.[8]

The presence of the simian "performer" makes sense in the context of a New Year celebration, as renewal ceremonies in the Maya area often feature monkeylike clowns (ibid.). The fact that the glyph and the simian figure are paired on the same half-column may connect them with the same event. Both the simian figure and the striding figure are drawn at approximately the same scale, which further suggests that all three paintings are related. The striding figure probably represents a ritual performer.

Measuring forty-three centimeters high, the profile face to the right of the striding figure is not in character with the three Protoclassic paintings (fig. 4-28): it is drawn at a larger scale with a thinner, less insistent line. The head has more affinities with the large human faces painted in other areas of Loltun.

Large human heads. The paintings of Loltun include seven large human heads, ranging from one-half to over one meter in height. All are painted in black. Four are found in Bonanil Aktun, painted on a weathered limestone surface. Three grouped together on the west wall are each about one meter in height. The leftmost face is decorated with patches of black paint (fig. 4-29a). The eye covered in black paint and the spots on the jaw suggest that this head is a version of God A, the Maya death god. To the right is a face with a disk over the forehead, juxtaposed to a glyphic motif that looks like a jar infixed with crossed bands (fig. 4-29b). Sitting to the right is a head with a solid black area over the eye and a vo-

FIG. 4-28. Large human head, Room 5, Loltun.

lute emerging from the top of the head (fig. 4-29c). Room 7 also contains a painting of a human head that measures sixty-two centimeters high. This one, with a circular earflare and ornate coiffure, also looks to be Late to Terminal Classic (fig. 4-30). Other large human heads can be found in the painted wall art of Loltun. Considered as a group, they show consistencies in size, color, and line quality and probably date to the Late to Terminal Classic.

Small figures in Room 3. In Room 3 are groups of schematic figures, most occupying shallow depressions in the wall (fig. 4-31). Room 3 also contains petroglyphs and thirty-nine *haltun*s, the stone troughs used to collect dripwater in many Yucatecan caves (Strecker 1976). The paintings are in a brownish-red pigment that resembles the color of floor sediments. The figures average twenty to thirty centimeters in height. Some, rather freely drawn, exude considerable energy and appear to be dancing. A nearby larger figure, fifty-one centimeters high, is in a more static style (fig. 4-32). The tight curls on the shoulders and boxlike body give the impression of a drawing from the Colonial era.

Pak'il K'ab. In addition to extensive negative handprints, to be discussed later, the Pak'il K'ab area has one painting worth mentioning, a cartouche framing a human head with a coefficient of seven (fig. 4-33). This painting,

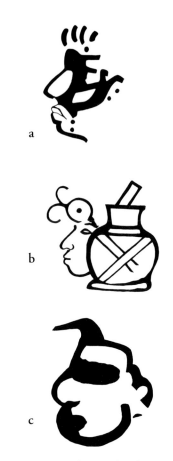

FIG. 4-29. Large human heads, Bonanil Actun, Loltun: *a,* face with black painted over eye and spots on jaw; *b,* face attached to glyphic element; *c,* simple human head, adapted from drawing by Matthias Strecker.

FIG. 4-30. Large human head, Room 7, Loltun. Adapted from photograph by Matthias Strecker.

FIG. 4-31. Dynamic, linear figures, Room 3, Loltun.

FIG. 4-32. Rigid human figure, possibly Colonial, Room 3, Loltun.

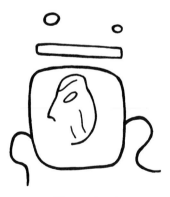

FIG. 4-33. Human head in cartouche associated with the number seven, Pak'il Kab, Loltun. Adapted from drawing by Matthias Strecker.

about eighty centimeters high, appears to be a *tsolk'in* date. The volutes at the sides may be crude versions of the day-sign pedestal. This painting also appears to be Late to Terminal Classic.

Handprints. Loltun has a large collection of handprints, only surpassed by Acum, another cave in the Sierrita de Ticul. According to Strecker (1982b: 49, 51), Loltun houses two positive handprints, eighty-eight negative handprints, and one negative and one positive footprint. All are in black. The bulk of the handprints are found in the areas known as the Sala de Infante and Pak'il K'ab, some clustering in groups of over a dozen. Among the negative handprints are some that make more complicated designs. The most unusual one shows a thin rod attached to the index fingers of a pair of hands (fig. 4-34).

Paintings in the Greater Classic style from Loltun center around two periods, the Protoclassic (apparently the earlier part) and the Late Classic. Excavated ceramics from Loltun are also most abundant from these periods (Velázquez Valadez 1980; 1981; González Licón 1986; 1987: fig. 3). The Classic art of Loltun consists mainly of large human heads, but *tsolk'in* dates are also present.

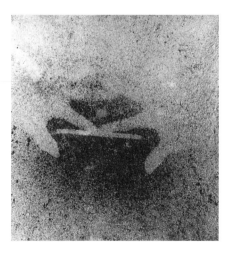

FIG. 4-34. Negative handprint comprised of two hands and rod, Loltun. Photograph by Matthias Strecker.

The group of Protoclassic paintings in Room 5 may have been painted for a specific ritual occasion, such as the New Year. On the whole, Greater Classic paintings are larger than schematic paintings at Loltun. The latter mainly depict small human figures.

Actun Ch'on, Yucatan

Another Puuc cave, Actun Ch'on, is located in some low hills at the southern boundary of the town of Oxkutzcab, near the Hermita Virgen del Pilar. The name of the cave may derive from *ch'om* "vulture" in Yucatec. The modern discovery of Actun Ch'on can be credited to INAH guard Vicente Vázquez Pacho in the 1930s. While some explorations were carried out in the 1970s by Matthias Strecker and Peter Schmidt, Actun Ch'on remained unreported in any detail. I visited this cave in 1985 and 1986 (Stone 1989a).

Actun Ch'on contains a single large chamber about sixty-five meters across, filled with ceiling-collapse rubble (fig. 4-35). This rocky area is not amenable to human activity, and a quick inspection showed no signs of artifacts, except a few broken *haltuns*. The southern perimeter of the cave has two entrances accessing an extensive maze that was only partially surveyed. Space within the maze is fairly restricted; the ceiling height generally stays below two and one-half meters, and the width, some two meters (fig. 4-36). The maze narrows down to a tight crawlway in places. Unlike the entrance chamber, sections of the maze are littered with broken pottery. The easternmost entrance to the maze, which is small and obscured by an overburden of boulders, is not at all obvious. Nonetheless, casual intruders have found it in modern times, evidenced by signatures and smoke stains marring the walls. This entrance leads back to an area with five paintings (fig. 4-37). The upper half of the passage has a curved cross-section

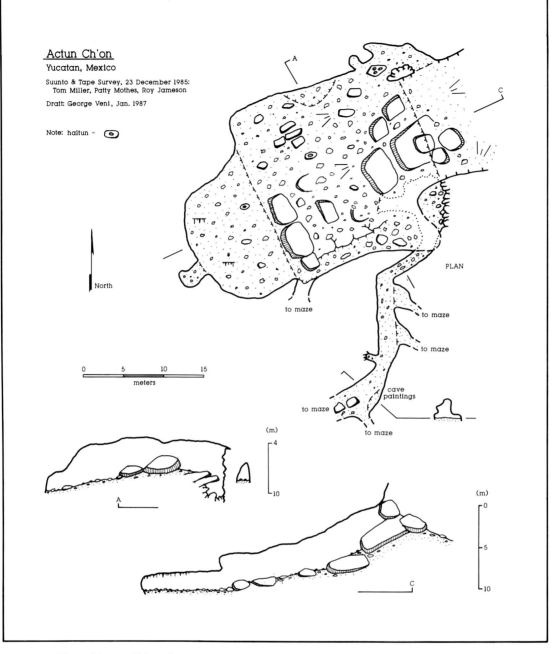

Actun Ch'on
Yucatan, Mexico

Suunto & Tape Survey, 23 December 1985:
Tom Miller, Patty Mothes, Roy Jameson

Draft: George Veni, Jan. 1987

Note: haltun = ⊙

North

0   5   10   15
meters

to maze

PLAN

to maze

to maze

cave
paintings

to maze

to maze

(m)
4
10

A

(m)
0
5
10

C

FIG. 4-35. Plan of Actun Ch'on. Surveyed by Roy Jameson, Thomas Miller, Patty Mothes, and George Veni. Drafted by George Veni.

with a channel running through the center, while the lower half is deeply undercut, so the passage is framed by smooth, eye-level overhangs (fig. 4-36). Four paintings occur on the overhangs and one on the ceiling channel.

Since the five paintings were recorded systematically, discussion will take the form of a catalog. DFGL stands for "Distance from Ground Level" and measures the distance from the top of the painting to the floor directly below.

Drawing 1: height 60 cm, length 1.28 m, DFGL 1.75 m. Drawing 1 is, without doubt, the most important painting from Actun Ch'on (fig. 4-38).

This uncluttered scene presents three figures. Attention is immediately drawn to the central, nude figure; he has an erect penis and his arms are tied behind his back. He displays many typical traits of a Maya captive, especially his contorted posture caused by the restraint of both arms, forcing an arch in the upper torso. His mouth appears to hang open in dread (though the pigment is faint here). Strong facial expressions of this

FIG. 4-36. Maze passage with paintings,
Actun Ch'on.

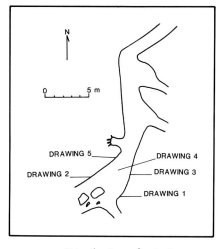

FIG. 4-37. Distribution of paintings,
Actun Ch'on.

FIG. 4-38. Drawing 1, Actun Ch'on.
Drawing by Susan Trammell.

sort are common in depictions of
Maya captives (e.g., Schele and Miller
1986: pl. 94). Traces of paint show
the remains of a circular earflare and a
simple cap.

Behind this figure is another kneeling
figure. His left arm is thrown over his
left shoulder, though this gesture is
more commonly seen with the opposite
arm and shoulder. This figure wears a
cap, possibly with a wide brim, in addition to circular earflares and a beaded
necklace. The loincloth and hipcloth
assemblage have some detail but are not
clearly rendered.

Both figures face a seated person who
seems to have the highest status: he
wears a feathered nose ornament and
the most elaborate cap, with a beaded
headband and feathers. Paint on his
chest and back may represent jewelry or
costuming, though the forms are indis-

tinct. In addition, this figure is the only one not kneeling. However, he exhibits the arm-over-shoulder gesture that is usually seen on subordinate figures: hence its name, "gesture of submission." Virginia Miller (1983) has shown, however, that this gesture can be displayed by high-ranking figures, as it would appear in this instance. Considered in its entirety, the scene seems to concern the presentation of a captive by one nobleman to another of higher rank. Yet it is difficult to know exactly why the central figure is shown with an erect phallus. Genital display was one way that the Maya disgraced captives (e.g., Schele and Miller 1986 : pl. 84), but they usually do not have an erect penis. Owing to this, other avenues of interpretation seem plausible.

Drawing 1 from Actun Ch'on is one of the more technically elaborate Maya cave paintings known and is unusual for its use of polychrome paint and color infill. Infill is sometimes combined with a dark outline. Three colors are used (Plate 2). Black outlines the central and right-hand figures and also infills feathers, jewelry, and headgear. A thick brown pigment decorates portions of the hipcloth of the right-hand figure. A thin wash of reddish-orange creates the skin tone for all the figures. The brown and reddish-orange pigment both seem to derive from the clay on the cave floor, the latter simply being a more dilute version of the former. Since the passage walls have been stained by a dilute mixture of the floor sediment due to the ebbing of floodwater, the walls have broad streaks that match the skin tone of the figures. Unfortunately, this gives the painting poor contrast against the background and makes it extremely difficult to photograph.

Drawing 2: height 25 cm, length 1.52 m, DFGL 1.52 m. It is not clear whether this row of ten hieroglyphs in black was ever completed (fig. 4-39). All that remain are the outlines of glyphs with no trace of internal detail. Glyphs 2 and 3 are preceded by bars that probably represent the number five. Glyph 4 is a human face. The lack of textual detail, however, precludes any meaningful decipherment. A line with vertical and diagonal bars frames the upper perimeter of the text. The height of this supernal band is 6.5 centimeters, while the individual glyphs measure about 15 centimeters high. Both the text and the band fit perfectly into the expanse of the overhang at this point in the cave.

Drawing 3: height 14.5 cm, length 1.22 m, DFGL 1.75 m. Drawing 3 consists of a band of reddish-orange paint from the bottom of which depend seven scrolls (fig. 4-40). It was also painted with a diluted mixture of floor clay and therefore blends in with the orange wall stains. On the first scroll to the left, where there are undissolved lumps of clay, the dark brown floor sediment is visible. Under the painting is the modern inscription "Luis Gonzaloro de Ticul," drawn with undiluted floor sediment.

Drawing 4: height 28 cm, length 19 cm, DFGL 2.26 m. This painting fits into the channel running through the center of the ceiling. All that is left is a cartouche with a number seven affix (a bar and two dots) painted in a broad, firm black line, comparable to the style of glyphs in Drawing 2 (fig. 4-41).

Drawing 5: height 13.5 cm, length 16.5 cm, DFGL 1.63 m. Drawing 5 consists of seven alternating brown and black lines (fig. 4-42). The brown again matches the floor sediment, and the black appears to be charcoal.

Based on style, Drawings 1, 2, and 3 from Actun Ch'on can be assigned a Late to Terminal Classic date, most likely from the eighth century. It is also possible that Drawing 4, the scrolls, dates from the same period, as it compares favorably with Drawings 1 and 2

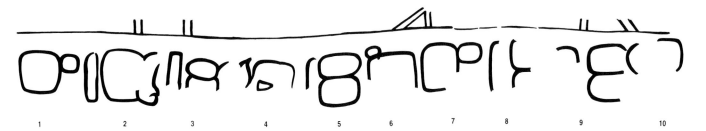

1   2   3   4   5   6   7   8   9   10

FIG. 4-39. Drawing 2, Actun Ch'on.

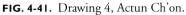

FIG. 4-40. Drawing 3, Actun Ch'on.

in terms of line quality. The date of Drawing 5, the alternating black and brown lines, is not at all clear and could be fairly recent.

The private maze passage was the favored area of ceremonial activity in Actun Ch'on. What some of these activities may have entailed is suggested by Drawing 1: captives may have been brought into the side tunnels for ritual sacrifice. Maya caves are rife with evidence of human sacrifice. It sometimes entailed decapitation, though children were occasionally drowned in pools of water (Reents-Budet and MacLeod 1986). Finally, it might be noted that the number seven crops up on several occasions in the paintings: the seven scrolls of Drawing 2, the seven alternating lines of Drawing 5, and the number seven coefficient in Drawing 3. Seven is a number with cave-underworld associations, as discussed in Chapter 3.

Acum, Yucatan

The cave of Acum is located southwest of Oxkutzcab (Strecker 1984b: fig. 1). As it has a single small entrance, INAH authorities were able to seal off access to the cave in 1960. Given its proximity to a town, blocking off the entrance protected the art of Acum from the graffiti and smoke that have defaced paintings at nearby Loltun and Ch'on. Acum was reopened in 1979, and in 1980 and 1981 Matthias Strecker carried out a preliminary study of the cave paintings; shortly after, the cave entrance was

FIG. 4-41. Drawing 4, Actun Ch'on.

FIG. 4-42. Drawing 5, Actun Ch'on.

again sealed and, at this writing, remains that way. The following discussion is based on information gathered by Strecker.[9]

The single corridor at Acum extends for about five hundred meters until it opens up into an expansive room. The passage drops steeply after the room; consequently, the survey was never extended beyond that point. One of the most interesting features of Acum is a door constructed about one hundred meters from the entrance at a constriction in the tunnel. With an opening of 50 × 60 centimeters, the doorway is constructed of a packed mixture of clay and stone; a single large stone forms the lintel. Strecker suggests that in the past this opening may have held a wooden door that controlled access to the deeper chambers. In a widening of the passage just before the door, a clay and stone structure of 2 × 2 meters was

noted. Only one painting was found before the door, while all other paintings and handprints—there may be as many as two hundred at Acum—lay beyond, suggesting restricted access to the paintings. Strecker's notes also indicate that pottery sherds were found throughout Acum, which were identified by Ernesto González Licón as Late Classic. The Late Classic pottery provides a basis for dating the paintings.

Paintings in the corridor. After the doorway, paintings crowd both sides of the corridor walls approaching the big chamber. The corridor paintings fall into distinct groups. One consists of symbolic forms, such as the "Kan" cross (fig. 4-43; *k'an* has the general connotations of "precious" and "yellow"). A series of "Kan" crosses appears on the north wall immediately after the gate. To the right of one is an inverted **T**, which may be an inverted "Ik" sign. In

FIG. 4-43. Various symbols in the corridor, Acum. Adapted from photographs and drawings by Matthias Strecker.

FIG. 4-44. Skeletalized figure, Acum. Adapted from photograph by Matthias Strecker.

Lowland Mayan languages, *ik'* means "breath," "wind," or "spirit." These symbols are drawn at a large scale, about one-half meter on a side.

Among the most interesting paintings from Acum are representations of skulls and nearly complete skeletons. One, standing about one meter high, shows the skull, right arm, and what may be part of a skeletalized rib cage (fig. 4-44). The shape of the cranium suggests artificial head flattening. On the same wall is an enormous skull measuring 1.10 meters in height (fig. 4-45). The small disk to the right of the jaw looks like an earflare placed low on the head. On the opposite wall, farther toward the entrance, is another, less detailed skull (fig. 4-46). It can be identified as such by the nose socket and rendering of the teeth as triangular segments. Several other heads in the passage may also represent skulls.

Skeletal figures in Maya art can represent one of any number of death deities (fig. 4-47). But simple skulls can also symbolize the earth-underworld. For example the basal register of the relief in Structure 22 at Copan shows a row of skulls, presumably referring to the cave-underworld (Stone 1985a: fig. 16a). The partial skeletal figure at Acum seems to allude to one of the many unsavory demons believed by the Maya to inhabit the underworld. I suspect that the remaining skulls also represent some type of death god. Death gods known from Colonial Yucatan include Cizin (still part of the Lacandon pantheon), Yum Cimil, and Uac Mitun Ahau.

Another interesting group of paintings in the corridor shows two schematic figures to the right of a large, possibly zoomorphic head (fig. 4-48). These swaying figures have an eery, spectral appearance. Positive handprints cover the wall in this area. Another pictorial genre at Acum is the large human head, seen earlier at Loltun (fig. 4-49). One of the Acum heads, with parted lips and a closed eye, probably a deceased person, appears in the center of an alcove.

Still other paintings portray animals, such as a turtle, a long-necked bird, and a long-muzzled animal that may be a deer (fig. 4-50).

Paintings in the chamber. Acum opens up into a low room measuring 40 × 20 meters and containing dozens of paintings that are found on the ceiling and side walls (fig. 4-51). A remarkable painting on the ceiling shows what appears to be another denizen of the underworld (fig. 4-52; Plate 3). Though the head is fleshed and has pronounced fronto-occipital flattening, this figure probably falls into the class of skeletal death gods discussed earlier. The bony jaw may allude to its underlying skeletal (i.e., deathlike) nature. The ghoulish face, animated by an insidious sneer, ex-

FIG. 4-45. Large skull, Acum. Photograph by Matthias Strecker.

FIG. 4-46. Skull with serrated teeth. Adapted from photograph by Matthias Strecker.

Images from the Underworld

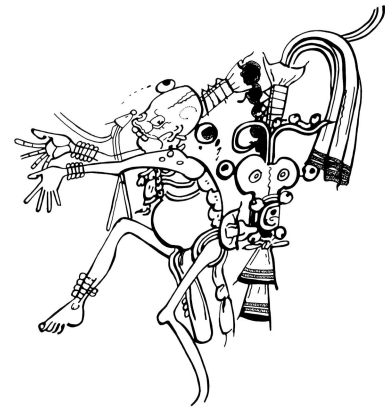

FIG. 4-47. Skeletal death god, detail of the Metropolitan Vase. Adapted from Coe 1973: no. 45.

udes plumes, perhaps of stench. Maya death gods are typically associated with noxious odors. The large round eye and knobby profile add to his grotesque demeanor. The ballooning torso, half of which is solid black, and skinny arm are also indicative of an underworld death god. The Acum demon holds a torch, as though illuminating the dark chamber. To the lower right is the partial outline of a human face.

The chamber is painted with a number of symbolic motifs (fig. 4-53); some are vaguely glyphic in appearance but cannot be identified with known hieroglyphs. One cluster of scrolls may show smoke. Another carefully drawn circle with some internal detail has a number six coefficient. Nearby is another care-

FIG. 4-49. Large human heads, Acum. Adapted from photographs by Matthias Strecker.

FIG. 4-50. Turtle, bird, and long-muzzled animal, possibly a deer, Acum. Adapted from photographs by Matthias Strecker.

FIG. 4-48. Partial figure and head, Acum. Photograph by Matthias Strecker.

A Survey of Sites and Images

fully drawn circle and a cross. Interestingly, a circle and a cross are executed in a negative technique on another part of the ceiling. Other geometrical forms include a step-fret and a U-shaped enclosure with circles and rectangles. One painting forms a weave pattern that may be a "mat" symbol.

Another geometrical design in the chamber cannot be identified but might be singled out for its early stylistic attributes. Unlike other paintings in the chamber, this one uses infill to create a rectangular, stamplike design (fig. 4-54). Both ends of the rectangle are notched. Within the U-shaped enclosure of one notched end is a *u*-element. A *u*-element appears as well in the other end and in the central open area. The rectilinear shape and notched ends of this form, whatever it may ultimately represent, recall certain Middle Preclassic motifs; yet the *u*-element is a style marker of Late Preclassic and Early Classic art. Certainly, this image looks Preclassic, though it cannot be identified.

Handprints. Acum houses the largest collection of handprints of any Maya site. Strecker's (1982b: Table 1) tally includes 79 positive handprints and 56 negative handprints, a grand total of 135 handprints, all in black. The negative handprints are a remarkable achievement, even considered in a global perspective. One or both hands are sometimes used as a stencil to make a number of different designs. The most interesting are negative handprints which, like shadow images, project the shape of an animal head with open mouth, eye, and ear, the latter being an erect little finger (fig. 4-55). There are twelve such handprint animal heads at Acum (ibid.: 50). In another part of the cave are two rows of repetitive designs made by joining several fingers of both hands. Another negative handprint shows a pair of hands with fingers drawn in, while another shows a six-

FIG. 4-51. The Chamber ceiling, Acum. Photograph by Matthias Strecker.

FIG. 4-52. Death god with torch, Acum. Adapted from photographs by Matthias Strecker.

FIG. 4-53. Various symbols in the Chamber, Acum. Adapted from photographs and drawings by Matthias Strecker.

Images from the Underworld

FIG. 4-54. Motif with early style traits, Acum. Adapted from photographs and drawings by Matthias Strecker.

fingered hand. The variety of hand-prints found at Acum is unmatched anywhere in the Maya area.

On stylistic and iconographic grounds, some Acum paintings can be dated to the Classic period. The "Ik" and "mat" symbols and the death demon holding the torch are the most likely candidates for a Late Classic date. The remaining skeletal figures, the scrolls, the glyphlike designs, and most of the human heads are surely Greater Classic. Given the preponderance of Late Classic ceramics, this would be the most likely date. Acum is a remarkable cave, and we can hope it will get the attention it deserves in a future study.

Xcosmil, Yucatan

Eight kilometers south of Oxkutzcab is another Puuc cave with paintings, Xcosmil. It was visited in the nineteenth century by German explorer Teobert Maler but drifted out of the archaeo-logical record until a recent survey by Strecker (1985). Xcosmil is a small cave, consisting of a single room some thirty meters across. The cave has a collection of twelve petroglyphs, consisting largely of simple frontal faces, but also ladder-like designs and arabesques as well as six rudimentary paintings in black that cover an area of 2.40 × .70 meters (ibid.: 17). One painting shows a "Kan" cross, and five depict schematic circular heads (fig. 4-56). The circular faces with circular eyes and mouth echo the carved faces of Xcosmil.

Tixkuytun, Yucatan

Southeast of Oxkutzcab in the Sierrita de Ticul is the town of Tekax; a number of caves with archaeological materials have recently been reported in the vicinity. Tixkuytun is the most interesting of these caves and has a collection of some forty paintings. In June of 1990 archaeologists from INAH's Centro Regional de Yucatán, under the direction of Alfredo Barrera Rubio, carried out a survey and documented the paintings of Tixkuytun. I was also present and have been permitted to discuss some of the highlights of this new collection of Yucatecan cave art.

Tixkuytun has a low entrance chamber that leads into a maze network of tunnels. The main tunnel, where the bulk of the paintings are found, is low and narrow, and the floor, clogged with rocks. The ceiling height often does not exceed one meter, forcing an uncomfortable crawl. Limestone exposed on the ceiling is layered in smooth bedding planes. Many of the paintings appear on these flat ceiling surfaces or on the smoothly planed side walls. Lower-level side passages open up into roomlike spaces where paintings also appear. Most of the paintings from Tixkuytun range between fifteen and thirty centimeters in height.

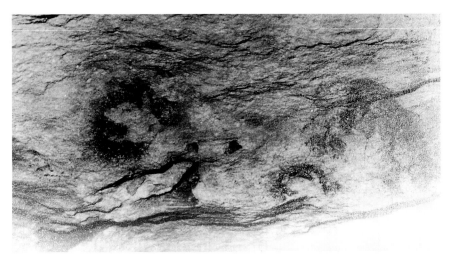

FIG. 4-55. Negative handprint in the form of an animal head, Acum. Photograph by Matthias Strecker.

FIG. 4-56. Charcoal drawings of simple faces, Xcosmil. Adapted from photograph by Matthias Strecker.

The paintings of Tixkuytun utilize three colors. Red, really a reddish-orange, comes from iron-rich clay typical of lateritic tropical soils, called *k'ankab* in Yucatec (Plate 4). Black paintings range from a soft black to deep black. One painting employs Maya blue (Plate 5). The blue resembles the blue used in mural paintings at the nearby site of Chacmultun. This is the first blue pigment reported in painted caves of the Maya Lowlands.

Most of the Tixkuytun paintings are geometrical designs. Two types predominate: circles, sometimes multiple concentric circles, which make the whole look like an eye, and the "Kan" cross. The circles, mostly in black pigment, are carefully painted in a wide, firm line and sometimes appear in groups to form a face. "Kan" crosses also appear as concentric crosses. Perhaps the most novel painting in the cave is a "Kan" cross with bar and dot numerals situated at the end and between the arms (Plate 4). This intriguing red painting is found on the ceiling of a lower-level passage off the main trunk of the maze. Another "Kan" cross with numbers, though only half-finished, is located nearby. The Tixkuytun paintings also include two "mat" symbols, one in black and one in red.

Animals are also found among the paintings of Tixkuytun; some are rudimentary and difficult to identify. However, one painting of the head of a deer follows Classic conventions, albeit with a provincial Yucatecan flavor (Plate 5). A blue line, forked at the end, extends from the deer's nose. The antlers are short, indicative perhaps of a young male deer or a brocket deer.

Anthropomorphic figures are rare at Tixkuytun, though a stick-figure anthropomorph is painted in black. One of the most important paintings in the cave is a part-human, part-zoomorphic head, apparently some kind of deity, located on a low ceiling close to a side

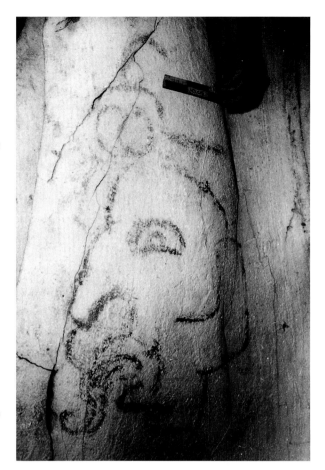

FIG. 4-57. Deity head, Tixkuytun. Photograph by Alfredo Barrera Rubio.

wall (fig. 4-57). This painting can only be viewed in the awkward position of lying on one's back pressed against the wall. The painting seems reasonably dated to the Late to Terminal Classic period.

Tixkuytun contains handprints and footprints. They include positive and negative handprints and negative footprints. The negative imprints are mostly in red. Footprints, especially negative footprints, are rare in the Maya area (Strecker 1982b:51). The most interesting handprints from Tixkuytun are negative handprints in red ringed by a carefully drawn black circle.

Certain paintings, such as the deer head, the "mat" symbol, the deity head, and the "Kan" crosses point toward a Late to Terminal Classic date for the Tixkuytun paintings. They seem to be

contemporaneous, then, with the period of Puuc florescence. There also seem to be Colonial or modern drawings present, as in one crudely drawn Latin cross. Modern graffiti and candle smoke stains are common in the main tunnel.

Another feature of the Tixkuytun paintings is that some seem to have been deliberately placed over entrances to side passages or niches. The circles seem to be marking routes or particular locations in the tunnel system. It is also noteworthy that pottery sherds collected by Carlos Perraza were more plentiful in the entrance and uncommon in the deep tunnels (personal communication, 1990). Thus, broken pottery was found in the cave but not in association with the paintings.

Uxil (Cueva de las Tres Marias), Yucatan

The cave of Uxil, located near Max-canu, is briefly discussed by Bonor (1989:155–156). The cave has an illuminated entrance chamber and a rear chamber. The second chamber revealed a collection of ceramic sherds with a Terminal Classic date. Red paintings appear on the ceiling of the first chamber and represent hieroglyphs (ibid.: fig. 47). One series of three paintings resembles Ahau day signs.

Caactun, Yucatan

In central Yucatan is a remarkable cave with parietal art called Caactun (Two Caves), named after its multiple entrances (though there are three). Caactun is located in the vicinity of Canakam, southeast of San Pedro Yaxcaba, and was brought to my attention by José Aban Campos. We visited the cave together with several of his friends in June of 1986. The entrances of Caactun lead to a small chamber that contains the remains of a low, partly toppled masonry wall. From this chamber a narrow limestone corridor begins and quickly fans out into parallel tunnels that give the cave a mazelike character. These passages continue more or less straight for about four hundred meters and finally reach a pool of water that we could not cross due to the low height of the ceiling.

Caactun has a large collection of handprints in addition to some singularly important petroglyphs. The handprints are found in groups at eye level. There are about fifty-six handprints divided nearly equally between positive and negative. They employ three colors: black, brown, and orange-red. Both the brown and red appear to derive from floor clays that occur in stratified layers in the cave. A hole dug in the cave floor, apparently from a small mining operation, revealed a thin layer of red clay over a thicker layer of brown. Most of the positive handprints employ the orange-red pigment. Fifteen such handprints formed a single line on one section of wall.

The handprints include many using the hand as a stencil. These negative handprints occur in all three colors, though primarily in black and red. While some negative handprints show the full hand or part of one hand, others employ both hands to create patterns, similar to negative handprints at Loltun and Acum. One recurrent form of negative handprint at Caactun was made by joining the index fingers and nearly joining the thumbs of both hands, then painting the resultant triangle as well as a line extending down between the thumbs (fig. 4-58). The design looks something like an arrow or spear. Sometimes the adjacent fingers were stenciled in, but at other times only the "arrow" is visible. Another negative handprint shows several fingers gathered together to make random patterns (fig. 4-59).

On the white limestone walls forming the corridors of Caactun, about fifty meters before reaching the pool, are incised petroglyphs. Three can be dated by style to an early phase of the Early Classic, probably no later than A.D. 400. They are the only Early Classic petroglyphs reported from a Maya cave and therefore merit further discussion.

The most interesting of these petroglyphs is Drawing 1, which is thirty-nine centimeters high (fig. 4-60). Drawing 1 is an abbreviated version of the most prominent of the Maya avian deities. This serpent-winged bird, often called the Principal Bird Deity (Bardawil 1976), is well represented in Late Preclassic Highland sculpture, where it may have originated (Parsons 1983; Cortez 1986). Early Classic Lowland Maya art is replete with depictions of the Principal Bird Deity; the bird seems to have had greater prominence

FIG. 4-58. Negative handprint forming arrowlike design, Caactun.

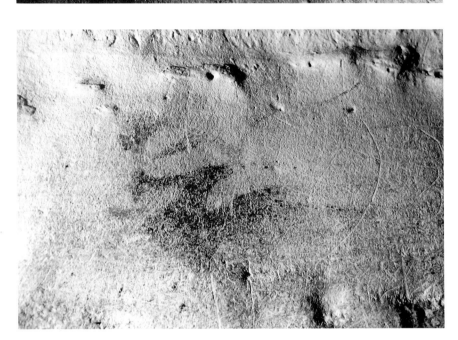

FIG. 4-59. Negative handprint, Caactun.

in the Early Classic than the Late Classic. The Caactun petroglyph accords with the early emphasis of Maya art on this cosmic bird, and it is certainly the first example to be found in a cave.

Drawing 1 amalgamates conventional traits of the Principal Bird Deity's head; one is the extended beak. The attenuated and sharply downturned form of the beak is an early trait found on many Preclassic examples of the bird. An even stronger indicator of an early date is the oversized supraorbital plate (a section of the brow emphasized in Maya art), shown here as two concentric circles with an infixed *u*-element. The placement of a *u*-element in the supraorbital plate of zoomorphic deities occurs on the earliest images from the Lowland Maya area, such as the stucco masks on Preclassic façades at El Mirador and Cerros (e.g., Schele and Miller 1986: fig. 2.1) and the Late Preclassic fuchsite sculpture from Uaxactun (Gallenkamp and Johnson 1985:pl. 17). The Principal Bird Deity in Drawing 1 from

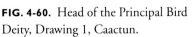

FIG. 4-60. Head of the Principal Bird Deity, Drawing 1, Caactun.

Caactun has a curious eye, shown as a circle infixed with a scroll. The scalloped motif below is a glyph (T23, phonetic **na**), often attached to the lower rim of the eye of zoomorphic monsters in Maya art.

The tabs with ball ends cantilevered over the beak probably depict part of a headdress (the so-called "cantilevered headdress") worn by the Principal Bird Deity. This headdress usually includes a beaded band supporting a medallion with pendant floral forms (fig. 4-61). Oddly the petroglyph includes only these pendant elements and omits the rest of the headdress. The scroll at the top of the head is a water scroll, often seen in this position on Early Classic versions of the Principal Bird Deity on carved pottery.

The scrolls replacing the lower jaw, however, do not fit canonical Principal Bird Deity iconography. The style of the scrolls, one tight and one loose, is typical of Classic Maya depictions of smoke or blood. It has been posited that the Principal Bird Deity may be connected with a character known from the Popol Vuh as Vukub Kakix (Seven Macaw; Stone 1983a:216–217; Cortez 1986). In the Popol Vuh he is shot in the jaw by a pellet from the blowgun of Hunahpu (Tedlock 1985:92). Thus, the scrolls, if they represent blood, could refer to the bird's injured jaw. The lines found under the scrolls (not shown in fig. 4-60) do not seem to be part of the composition and may have been added later.

Drawing 1 overlaps two negative handprints, providing an opportunity for relative dating by superimposition (fig. 4-62). Interestingly, the petroglyph seems to have been incised through the handprints, indicating that these elaborate negative handprints in Caactun should date no later than about A.D. 400.

Drawing 2 from Caactun conforms to the early style date of Drawing 1.

Here we see a profile human head sprouting a vine with bulbous tip, probably a leaf (fig. 4-63). An earflare with a pendant tab is also present. There are many early style indicators here. For one, the face has an unmistakable Olmec cast: short, bulging forehead, flattened nose, and the configuration of the lips, with the upper lip touching the lower edge of the nose. Furthermore, the lips, sealed tightly shut and with downturned corners, give the face a stern demeanor more common in Olmec than Maya art (e.g., Joralemon 1971:figs. 209, 245). The horizontal plane of the eye and its inert, ovoid shape, as well as the lantern jaw, further make the face look like an Olmec portrait. However, one certainly could not

FIG. 4-61. Detail of Kaminaljuyu, Stela 11. Adapted from Schele and Miller 1986: fig. 2.2.

FIG. 4-62. Drawing 1, Caactun.

FIG. 4-63. Human head sprouting a plant, Drawing 2, Caactun.

FIG. 4-64. "*K'in*" glyph, Drawing 3, Caactun.

posit direct Olmec influence at this late date, and, moreover, Olmec influence on Preclassic Yucatecan culture seems to have been slight at best (Joesink-Mandeville and Meluzin 1976).

The squarish planes of the face seen in Drawing 2 recall the style of Late Preclassic sculptures from highland Guatemala, such as Kaminaljuyu Stela 11. In fact, Drawing 2 could easily be contemporary with that sculpture. The plant rising from the head distantly recalls the plant and shell headdress device seen on Kaminaljuyu Stela 11 (fig. 4-61) and the Dumbarton Oaks recarved pectoral. Caactun Drawing 2 also recalls a headdress mask worn by a figure on Stela 1 from Nakbe, which is the oldest carved monument currently known from the Maya Lowlands and which may date as early as the latter part of the Middle Preclassic (Hansen 1991). As with the above-mentioned

Preclassic sculptures, Drawing 2 looks like a transitional work bridging Olmec and early Maya art. This may mean that Drawing 1, the Principal Bird Deity, is a Late Preclassic depiction, making it among the earliest Lowland depictions of that creature as well.

Drawing 3 from Caactun depicts a "*k'in*" glyph six centimeters high, a symbol of the sun (fig. 4-64). The "*k'in*" flower is articulated by short parallel lines on four sides of a cartouche. The "tail" is the typical phonetic complementation (T116) to the spelling of *k'in* "sun" or "day." This form of the "*k'in*" flower appears on the Early Classic Deletaille Vase (Berjonneau and Sonnery 1985: no. 329), which shows stylistic affinities with the Caactun petroglyphs.

The Caactun petroglyphs hold a singular place in the inventory of Maya rock art. They are among a small group of Mesoamerican cave petroglyphs in a Greater Classic style. In addition, Early Classic art and writing, especially prior to A.D. 400, is rare in northern Yucatan (Proskouriakoff 1950: 110). One Early Classic stela, however, comes from the site of Yaxuna, which is less than ten kilometers from Caactun (Brainerd 1958: fig. A). In light of these petroglyphs and the Protoclassic relief and paintings from Loltun, it seems fair to say that some of the earliest art and hieroglyphs from Yucatan are found in caves.

Dzibichen (Dzibih Actun), Yucatan

In May of 1986 my colleague Karl Taube gave me a promising lead on a cave painting site that he had heard about in the village of San Juan de Dios. Several villagers, native to the town of Yalcoba, northeast of Valladolid, knew of a cave they called *ts'ibih aktun* "cave with writing" (Taube 1988a: 200 n. 5). The next month George Veni and I tracked down this cave, which turned out to be within the

boundaries of Yokdzonot Presentado in the municipality of Tizimin. Unknown to us, archaeologists Adriana Velázquez Morlet and Edmundo López de la Rosa (1988) were surveying the cave for the Proyecto Atlas Arqueológico Nacional of Mexico. Unaware of one another's work, we carried out independent research.

Approached by a hunting trail, the cave lies about one and one-half kilometers south of Yokdzonot Presentado, close to the border with Yalcoba (ibid.: 95). In an earlier article I referred to this cave as Dzibih Actun, the name which Taube had heard in San Juan de Dios and an alternate name acknowledged by residents (Stone 1989b: 323). However, the cave is more commonly called *ts'ibih ch'en*. We found the word "*ɔibichen*" inscribed on the cave wall, probably quite a long time ago, given the orthography /ɔ/ for the sound /ts'/ (fig. 4-70h). As the official name in the Proyecto Atlas Arqueológico Nacional of Mexico, Dzibichen is the name that will be used in the discussion below. Both *aktun* and *ch'en* mean "cave" in Yucatec, though *ch'en* refers to a cave or well containing water. Indeed, Dzibichen has a small pool of water, one meter across, resulting from exposure of the water table, so this water source should be fairly reliable.

The cave is entered by way of a sinkhole (fig. 4-65). To the right of the entrance a wooden cross and a pile of small rocks rest on a boulder (fig. 4-66). These rocks were explained by our Maya guide to be "payment" to certain spirits who "sweep away" fatigue from the hunter's legs. We were also told that Dzibichen was still being used by a local shaman for curing ceremonies.

Dzibichen has a single chamber twenty-five meters wide and fifty meters deep (Velázquez Morlet and López de la Rosa 1988: 95). Pottery sherds were not in evidence, but we did observe a stone staircase partly covered in debris. The

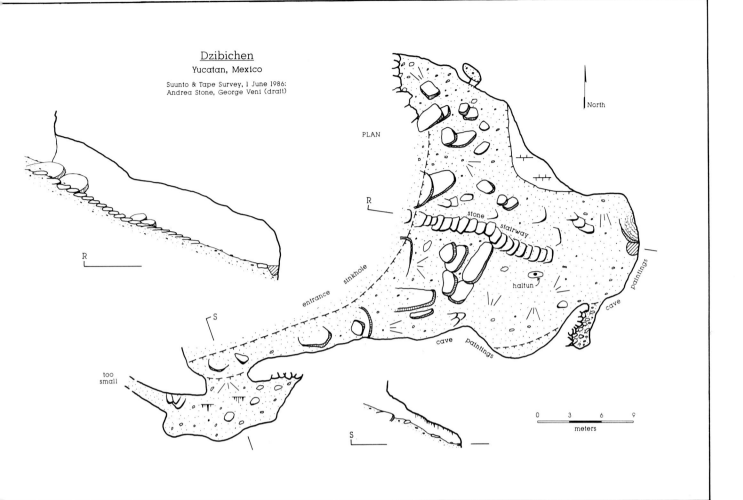

Dzibichen
Yucatan, Mexico

Suunto & Tape Survey, 1 June 1986:
Andrea Stone, George Veni (draft)

North

PLAN

R

R

stone stairway

entrance sinkhole

haltun

cave paintings

cave paintings

S

too small

S

0   3   6   9
meters

FIG. 4-65. Plan of Dzibichen. Survey by
Andrea Stone and George Veni. Drafted
by George Veni.

staircase leads toward the pool of water
and drawings at the back of the cave. To
the side of the staircase is a flat rock
with a cuplike depression, possibly a
haltun.

The art of Dzibichen is most appropriately called cave drawing, as the bulk
of it seems to have been produced with
sticks of charcoal, though some of the
finer drawings may have been painted
with a brush or swab (e.g., Drawing 24). Apart from charcoal black, the
only other pigment noted is a bright red
hematite that covers a bulge in the wall
decorated with a face, and that is also
streaked in other areas.[10] The drawings
are executed on an irregular surface of

redissolved calcite; but a small group, to
the right of the main group, is on limestone (Drawings 40–47). The pigment
appears to be quite stable and smear-
resistant, which I suspect is the result of
having been covered by a fine layer of
calcite, fortunately not thick enough to
obscure the image. Nonetheless, the
drawings have been damaged. In some
cases the outlines have been scratched
over; worse yet, a few appear to have
been battered by a sharp implement.

The drawings begin one and one-half
meters to the left of the pool and sweep
around the rear wall. The greatest concentration is at eye level to the immediate right of the pool (fig. 4-67). In fact,

FIG. 4-66. Cross with pile of small stones
at the base, at entrance of Dzibichen.

A Survey of Sites and Images

FIG. 4-67. Detail of painted wall, Dzibichen.

FIG. 4-68. Diagram of painting location, Dzibichen.

at eye level drawings are superimposed, something generally not found in Maya cave art. This suggests that the act of drawing on a limited wall surface took precedence over the clarity of viewing. To escape the crowd, a number of images were placed at a much higher level, the highest rising over three meters above the floor (fig. 4-68). These drawings, which all date to the Colonial era, undoubtedly required a physical support for the artist, a scaffolding or ladder, and thus involved substantial effort in their production.

Drawing 1: height 16 cm, length 19 cm, DFGL 1.05 m. This collection of lines has a vague glyphic appearance, but no imagery is recognizable (fig. 4-69a). It is one of the few drawings found to the left of the pool.

Drawing 2: height 30 cm, length 24 cm, DFGL 2.5 m. The drawing depicts a house and awkwardly uses perspective to show the end of the house with a door (fig. 4-69b). Such pictorial conventions are unknown in Mesoamerican art. The drawing lies on an overhang directly above the pool of water.

Drawing 3: height 38 cm, length 30.5 cm, DFGL 1.98 m. Just to the right of the pool is a depiction of a diving jaguar (fig. 4-69c). The limbs are splayed, and the tail, marked by parallel lines, swings to the right. The drawing is not very clear but can be compared with Drawing 12. Since the style of Drawing 12 is Late Postclassic, this is probably the date of Drawing 3.

Drawing 4: height 14 cm, length 14 cm, DFGL 2.03 m. A circle with schematic facial features, Drawing 4 is surrounded by short lines and looks like a representation of the sun (fig. 4-69d). It may date from Colonial times.

Drawing 5: height 20 cm, length 15 cm, DFGL 2.15 m. This morass of lines presents hints of a face with a supraorbital plate over the eye (fig. 4-69e). It may show a deity head.

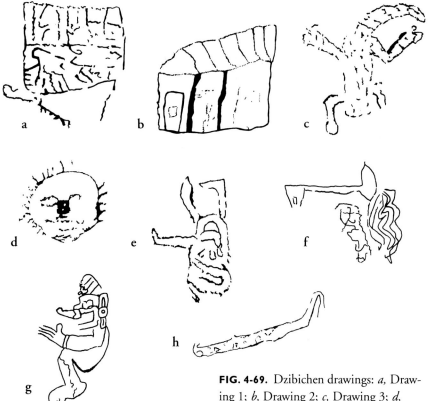

FIG. 4-69. Dzibichen drawings: *a*, Drawing 1; *b*, Drawing 2; *c*, Drawing 3; *d*, Drawing 4; *e*, Drawing 5; *f*, Drawing 6; *g*, Drawing 7; *h*, Drawing 8.

Drawing 6: height 38 cm, length 40 cm, DFGL 2.15 m. With its profusion of sausagelike shapes, Drawing 6 can be compared with Drawing 5. In this case, though, a tube extends to the left and joins a triangular shape with an interior rectangle (fig. 4-69f). This form can be compared with other "vulva" representations at Dzibichen.

Drawing 7: height 35 cm, length 22 cm, DFGL 1.63 m. Drawing 7 depicts a long-nosed god with a tall headdress, a disk earflare, a thin wristlet, but not much else in the way of costuming (fig. 4-69g). Given the codical association of long-nosed gods with God B, it seems reasonable to identify this figure as the Yucatecan rain god Chac. As Taube (1988b:59) notes, God B, or Chac, is the most important and pervasive deity of Postclassic Yucatecan iconography. Chac is often accompanied by serpents, which Taube rightly interprets as lightning, a logical fixture of

a storm god. Appropriately, the Dzibichen Chac is surrounded by serpents (Drawings 8 and 13). To find an image of the rain god in a cave near a pool of water is in perfect harmony with the role of caves in Maya culture. This figure shows affinities with deity figures in the Madrid Codex, as will be discussed below; hence, a Late Postclassic time frame seems reasonable.

Drawing 8: height 25.5 cm, length 53 cm, DFGL 1.45 m. The drawing depicts a rudimentary serpent with some body markings and an abruptly raised tail (fig. 4-69h). It is located immediately below Drawing 7.

Drawing 9: height 60 cm, length 35 cm, DFGL 1.26 m. A schematic figure with triangular patches over the eye raises both arms, giving the impression of a spook (fig. 4-70a). The open mouth with spinelike teeth adds to its grotesque appearance.

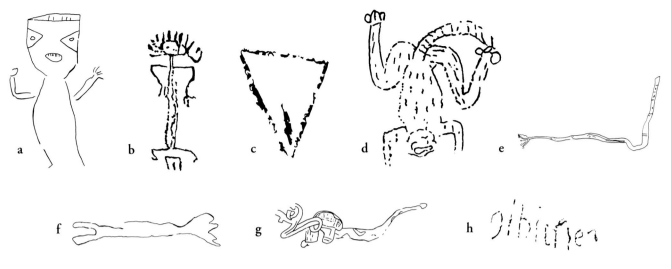

FIG. 4-70. Dzibichen drawings: *a,* Drawing 9; *b,* Drawing 10; *c,* Drawing 11; *d,* Drawing 12; *e,* Drawing 13; *f,* Drawing 14; *g,* Drawing 15; *h,* Drawing 16.

Drawing 10: height 24 cm, length 9 cm, DFGL 1.75 m. Rays surrounding the head of this rigid stick figure represent hair (fig. 4-70b). The three-sided form with central slit at the bottom found between the legs would seem to be another "vulva," in this case strategically placed.

Drawing 11: height 11 cm, length 11 cm, DFGL 1.64 m. A "vulva" is depicted in the drawing (fig. 4-70c).

Drawing 12: height 38 cm, length 27 cm, DFGL 1.74 m. The second diving jaguar at Dzibichen has a striped tail and spots marking the body (fig. 4-70d). The configuration of the feet, as a series of loops, is noteworthy. Similar looped designs occur in other drawings in the cave. Diving felines are uncommon in Maya iconography, but one is painted on Structure A at Xelha (fig. 4-75). In general, diving figures are more common in Postclassic art, such as the "diving gods" over doorways at Tulum or in the codices. This jaguar probably dates to the Late Postclassic.

The presence of a diving jaguar in a cave has interesting implications. The two jaguars could be diving into the underworld, which might have astro-nomical import if the jaguars were intended to represent the night sun (Thompson 1960:134). The jaguar sun may here sink into the underworld through the cave entrance at the western edge of the cosmos.

Drawing 13: height 56 cm, length 1.32 m, DFGL 1.60 m. Slithering across the wall is this crude depiction of a serpent (fig. 4-70e). The tail turns up abruptly, a common feature of Dzibichen serpents.

Drawing 14: height 30 cm, length 60 cm, DFGL 1.35 m. The drawing depicts a serpentlike creature but with a fin tail and no fangs (fig. 4-70f). It may represent some kind of fish.

Drawing 15: height 22 cm, length 89 cm, DFGL 2.01 m. The most unusual of the Dzibichen serpents is Drawing 15 (fig. 4-70g). The neck makes a loop and then joins a segmented area filled with assorted patterns, which joins a more typical serpent body marked with half disks. Again, the tail turns up abruptly.

Drawing 16: height 7 cm, length 8 cm, DFGL 1.9 m. The name of the cave "ɔibichen," is spelled out (fig. 4-70h). The drawing is positioned above the back of the serpent in Drawing 15.

Drawing 17: height 20.5 cm, length 18 cm, DFGL 3 m. A "vulva" drawn over a rounded protuberance in the wall imparts three-dimensionality to the pubic region (fig. 4-71a).

Drawing 18: height 90 cm, length 8 cm, DFGL 1.56 m. The drawing depicts a "vulva" (fig. 4-71b).

Drawing 19: height 90 cm, length 8 cm, DFGL 1.56 m. This serpent has a sausagelike body (fig. 4-71c). A second lower jaw repeats the form of the first.

Drawing 20: average height 20 cm, average length 20 cm, DFGL 1.14– 1.70 m. Drawing 20 includes nine examples of an unusual turtle motif (fig. 4-71d). The body of the turtle consists of a cartouche with circular eyes and mouth. Each eye is sectioned off by a line. This rudimentary face can be identified as the day sign Ahau. It especially resembles late versions of Ahau seen in some Colonial Chilam Balams. Attached to each corner of the "Ahau" glyph is a rectangular or ovoid appendage sectioned off by lines. At the "head" is a pointed form, sometimes divided by diagonal lines. In one case a beaked turtle head fills this position. Velázquez

Images from the Underworld

Morlet and López de la Rosa (1988) and Taube (1988a) identified these curious creatures as turtles. Taube alone, however, has accounted for the presence of the "Ahau" glyph. In his study of prehispanic Maya *k'atun* wheels, Taube shows that the turtle carapace served as a metaphor for the disk-shaped surface of the earth among the preconquest and Colonial Maya. Furthermore, this turtle-earth platform was often combined with references to the *k'atun* ending, thereby integrating concepts of space and time. The *k'atun* is sometimes recorded on these turtle carapaces as the Ahau date marking its completion. One stone *incensario* from Mayapan even shows a turtle with thirteen "Ahau" glyphs encircling the carapace, a summary of the entire *k'atun* round (fig. 3-7). As Taube (1988a: 189) rightly asserts, the Dzibichen "turtle-Ahaus" can be compared to the Mayapan *incensarios* and other turtle-*k'atun* images.

Drawing 21: height 9 cm, length 22 cm, DFGL 1.76 m. A rounded wall protrusion has eyes and mouth added to create a three-dimensional head (fig. 4-71e). Red hematite covers the surface of the rock.

Drawing 22: height 10 cm, length 1.40 m, DFGL 1.75 m. A serpent, facing left, with an open mouth revealing two sharp fangs comprises Drawing 22 (fig. 4-71f). The long body, sweeping in a horizontal direction, is covered with half-disk saddle patterns.

Drawing 23: height 9 cm, length 18 cm, DFGL 1.36 m. The drawing depicts a schematic quadruped (fig. 4-71g).

Drawing 24: height 18 cm, length 10 cm, DFGL 40 cm. The bird in Drawing 24, certainly prehispanic, is rendered with particular care (fig. 4-71h). The painting rests close to ground level; perhaps the artist was searching for some free wall space.

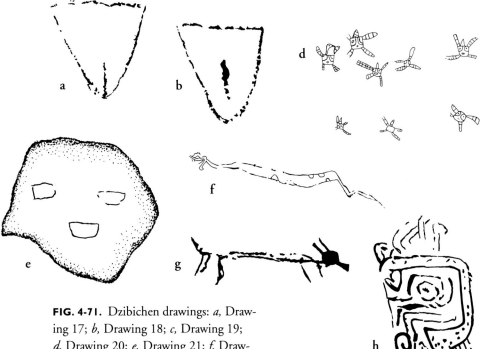

FIG. 4-71. Dzibichen drawings: *a,* Drawing 17; *b,* Drawing 18; *c,* Drawing 19; *d,* Drawing 20; *e,* Drawing 21; *f,* Drawing 22; *g,* Drawing 23; *h,* Drawing 24.

Drawing 25: height 43 cm, length 20 cm, DFGL 1.37 m. This curious head, virtually identical to that seen in Drawing 9, has eyes covered by triangular patches and a mouth that bares sharp teeth (fig. 4-72a). No doubt Drawings 9 and 25 were drawn by the same individual.

Drawing 26: height 10 cm, length 14 cm, DFGL 1.95 m. An animal with a broad tail is depicted in the drawing (fig. 4-72b).

Drawing 27: height 17 cm, length 8 cm, DFGL 1.45 m. The drawing consists of a circle divided by a line (fig. 4-72c). It is not identifiable.

Drawing 28: height 25.5 cm, width 4 cm, DFGL 1.60 m. Wavy or zigzag *atlatl* darts held by the rain god at Teotihuacan have been interpreted as lightning (e.g., Pasztory 1974: figs. 3, 5). The cave's zigzag serpent is similar to those lightning images and therefore can be identified as an ophidian form of lightning (fig. 4-72d). Taube (1988b: 60) has demonstrated a close connection between serpents and lightning in Maya iconography. As lightning, it may be significant that the serpent is positioned vertically, the orientation of lightning when it strikes the earth.

Drawing 29: height 53 cm, length 10 cm, DFGL 1.85 m. A fold with a deep central groove in the cave wall forms the spine of what looks like a caterpillar (fig. 4-72e).

Drawing 30: height 13 cm, length 10 cm, DFGL 2.08 m. This figure, possibly wearing a skirt, has one hand on the hip and raises the right hand, which holds a rectangular object (fig. 4-72f). The imagery compares well with Drawing 39. The arm gestures in both suggest that the figures are dancing.

Drawing 31: height 12 cm, length 37 cm, DFGL 2 m. The drawing is one of two in Dzibichen that show a person riding a horse (fig. 4-72g; cf. Drawing 46). This image is definitely postconquest.

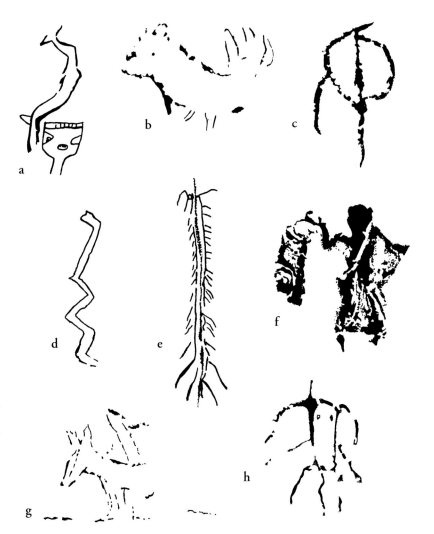

Drawing 32: height 20 cm, length 15 cm, DFGL 1.65 m. A crude drawing depicts a rayed circle with dotlike eyes (fig. 4-72h). This may be another solar face.

Drawing 33: height 22 cm, length 8 cm, DFGL 1.23 m. The rectangle with a central line recalls the "vulva" (fig. 4-73a). To this is added what looks like legs and a looped head.

Drawing 34: height 35 cm, length 30.5 cm, DFGL 3.12 m. Included under the heading of Drawing 34 are two juxtaposed images (fig. 4-73b). Both show simple circle faces. The treatment of the face is consistent: a single line forms the nose and eyebrows, and the mouth has been omitted. The larger of the two circles has an aureole. Looped and zigzag lines are drawn nearby. This

FIG. 4-72. Dzibichen drawings: *a,* Drawing 25; *b,* Drawing 26; *c,* Drawing 27; *d,* Drawing 28; *e,* Drawing 29; *f,* Drawing 30; *g,* Drawing 31; *h,* Drawing 32.

Images from the Underworld

is one of many Colonial circle faces to appear at Dzibichen. Those with rays or aureoles depict the sun.

Drawing 35: height 30 cm, DFGL 2.57 m. Two circle faces are subsumed under Drawing 35 (fig. 4-73c; Plate 6). The larger of the two is surrounded by short, straight, and wavy lines and has linear projections above and below, ending in an asterisk. This image immediately recalls illustrations from the Chilam Balam of Chumayel of the "lord of the *k'atun*" for 13 Ahau (fig. 4-80). As with the cave circle faces, the nose and eyebrows are formed from a continuous line. Instead of two linear projections, the Chumayel version has six, and they end in a cross rather than an asterisk. Nonetheless, the parallels are quite strong. In the Chumayel, this type of head represents the *k'atun* ending for 13 Ahau in two separate illustrations, so the association seems deliberate. As in the Chumayel, the head in Drawing 35 (and Drawing 34) seems to represent the sun, but it is, in ways not clearly understood, also emblematic of the *k'atun*.

Drawing 36: height 5 cm, length 21 cm, DFGL 2.1 m. A bicycle is depicted on a groundline (fig. 4-73d). Obviously this image is fairly recent.

Drawing 37: height 60 cm, length 40 cm, DFGL 3 m. Perhaps the most elaborate drawing at Dzibichen is this Hapsburg eagle (fig. 4-73e). The two heads are shown in conventional fashion as two beaklike projections on either side of a circular head. The short wings are typical of many Colonial Hapsburg eagles, and the triangular body and legs are marked with patterns that may indicate feathers. The oversized talons rest upon a base that may have as its inspiration a bannerlike scroll. The Hapsburg eagle is often seen standing upon such a scroll, which usually bears an inscription. The eagle is surrounded by looped and wavy lines as well as a number of reverse **S** shapes.

Drawing 38: height 30 cm, length 25 cm, DFGL 2.57 m. The drawing in all probability is a single-headed Hapsburg eagle (fig. 4-73f). The style is similar to Drawing 37; the wings are short, and the feet consist of thin lines branching off the leg. No doubt the two drawings date closely in time. Drawing 38 is more carefully composed than Drawing 37, suggesting that they are not the work of the same individual. What looks to be an **S** (or number five?) appears on the eagle's chest.

Drawing 39: height 16.5 cm, length 15 cm, DFGL 1.02 m. Drawing 39 shows a standing figure with one arm on the hip and the other holding a rectangular object (fig. 4-73g). The haunchlike appearance of the legs suggests that this is some kind of animal.

As with Drawing 30, the figure appears to be dancing.

Drawing 40: height 21 cm, length 6.5 cm, DFGL 1.4 m. This enigmatic drawing consists of a series of loops surrounded by a circle and bracketed by linear extensions that end in a cross (fig. 4-73h). Though the meaning of the image is obscure, there can be no doubt that it dates from the Colonial era. The looped, or guilloche, pattern is drawn all over the walls where we see other Colonial drawings, such as the Hapsburg eagle and circular faces. The crosses suggest that the drawing has religious content.

Drawing 41: height 27 cm, length 21 cm, DFGL 73 cm. This drawing is a schematic quadruped (fig. 4-74a). It cannot be identified more precisely.

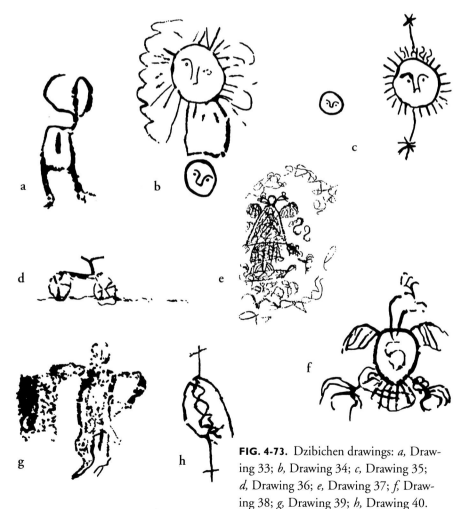

FIG. 4-73. Dzibichen drawings: *a,* Drawing 33; *b,* Drawing 34; *c,* Drawing 35; *d,* Drawing 36; *e,* Drawing 37; *f,* Drawing 38; *g,* Drawing 39; *h,* Drawing 40.

A Survey of Sites and Images

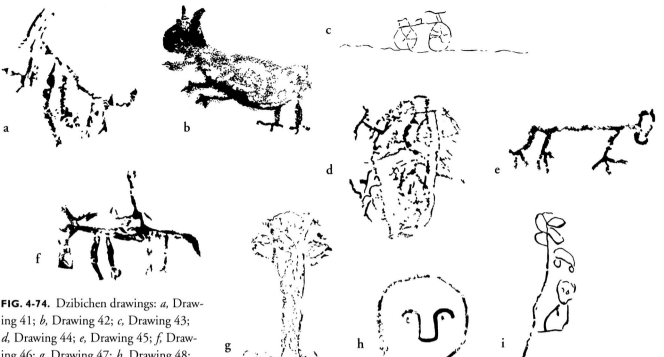

FIG. 4-74. Dzibichen drawings: *a,* Drawing 41; *b,* Drawing 42; *c,* Drawing 43; *d,* Drawing 44; *e,* Drawing 45; *f,* Drawing 46; *g,* Drawing 47; *h,* Drawing 48; *i,* Drawing 49.

Drawing 42: height 16.5 cm, length 28.5 cm, DFGL 89 cm. The drawing consists of another quadruped, but with a fuller body and an indication of ears (fig. 4-74b). Based on its similarity to a number of petroglyphs found in Yucatan and Quintana Roo (e.g., Mercer 1975: fig. 10; Rätsch 1979: illus. 4), it can be identified as a deer.

Drawing 43: height 26 cm, length 28 cm, DFGL 2.50 m. The second bicycle to appear in Dzibichen (fig. 4-74c), Drawing 43 is more carefully rendered than Drawing 36, and it is located out of normal reach, requiring some kind of structural support for its execution.

Drawing 44: height 16 cm, length 13 cm, DFGL 1.42 m. This profusion of lines (fig. 4-74d) cannot be identified.

Drawing 45: height 6 cm, length 15 cm, DFGL 1.43 m. The drawing consists of a rudimentary stick figure that looks like an animal (fig. 4-74e). Only three legs are shown.

Drawing 46: height 17.3 cm, length 32 cm, DFGL 1.88 m. This drawing seems to show a horse and rider (fig. 4-74f). The style of the animal recalls Drawing 41.

Drawing 47: height 31 cm, length 15 cm, DFGL 1.65 m. This curious drawing looks like a tree (fig. 4-74g), but little can be said about it.

Drawing 48: height 11 cm, length 10 cm, DFGL 1.72 m. Another Colonial circle face is located on the wall, only 60 cm to the right of the pool (fig. 4-74h). Unfortunately, it is one of the most badly defaced drawings in the cave.

Drawing 49: measurements not available. Drawing 49 is located just below and to the left of Drawing 37, the Colonial Hapsburg eagle. Drawing 49 may also date from the Colonial period. Three objects appear here (fig. 4-74i). One consists of a long line with loops at the top. To the right of the loops is an object that looks like a wagon. Below that is a figure, the body assuming a squarish shape. The looped

forms seem to be characteristic of Colonial drawings at Dzibichen.

Velázquez Morlet and López de la Rosa (1988) divide the art of Dzibichen into three chronological groups that are also thematically distinct: a prehispanic group with fertility, earth, and water symbolism; a Colonial group; and a modern group that includes beasts of burden and bicycles. They are certainly correct that fertility and water are important themes at Dzibichen. These authors include in the fertility group the drawing of Chac (Drawing 7) and his many accompanying serpents, the many "vulva" images, and the turtles in Drawing 20. While turtles represent the plane of the earth, their symbolism in Drawing 20 also extends to the *k'atun* cycle; that, I believe, is their primary significance here.

Postclassic drawings. Some of the prehispanic drawings at Dzibichen can be assigned a Postclassic date in light of their stylistic affinities with the Madrid Codex. The Madrid Codex is the most

Images from the Underworld

FIG. 4-75. Diving jaguar, Structure A, Mural 6, Xelha. Adapted from Miller 1982:pl. 45.

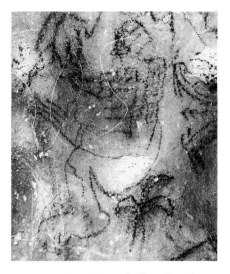

FIG. 4-77. Depiction of Chac, Drawing 7, Dzibichen.

crudely painted of the three Yucatecan codices (fig. 4-76a). Kelley (1976:15) even suggested that the Madrid scribe's frequent inscriptional oddities may have been a result of dyslexia. Apart from the codex itself, there are few representatives of this style, but those that do exist show that the Madrid style is not the lone product of the Madrid scribe or scribes. Room 1 in Structure 44 from Tancah has murals in a style strongly reminiscent of the Madrid Codex (fig. 4-76b). Miller (1982:54) assigns Structure 44 to the Middle Postclassic, ca. A.D. 1350. Two other figures in the Madrid style are incised on jade pendants found in the province of Guanacaste in Costa Rica (fig. 4-76c); however, their authenticity is questionable (Dorie Reents-Budet, personal communication, 1991). Figures in the style of the Madrid Codex also occur in the Río Bec area. Southeast of Xpuhil at the site of Pasión de Cristo graffiti in the style of the Madrid Codex are incised into a stucco wall (Eldon Leiter, personal communication, 1991). These images, along with the Dzibichen drawings, in-

dicate that the Madrid Codex style had a wide distribution in the Yucatan Peninsula. Given its sloppy, degenerate character, it strikes me as being very late. Thompson (1960:26) also saw the Madrid Codex as late, "perhaps as late as the middle of the fifteenth century."

At Dzibichen the best candidate for the Madrid Codex style is Drawing 7 (fig. 4-77). First of all, the posture of the figure, squatting with knees tucked under the arms, is a typical codical posture, but it is especially characteristic of the Madrid Codex (fig. 4-76a). Most telling is the fact that the hand has only three fingers and a thumb, a convention found often in the Madrid Codex but not in the Paris or Dresden codices, which on the whole are more carefully drawn. Finally, the overblown size of the foot and the hump behind the ankle are entirely characteristic of figural conventions in the Madrid Codex.

Other images from Dzibichen recall conventions found in the Madrid Codex—for instance, the diving jaguars and many of the serpents. There are seven depictions of serpents at Dzibichen. At least four have saddle patterns in the form of half-disks alternating from one side of the body to the

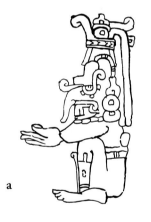

a

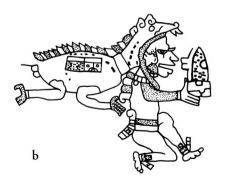

b

c

FIG. 4-76. Madrid Codex figural style: *a*, Madrid 72a, adapted from Lee 1985; *b*, Structure 44, Room 1, Tancah, adapted from Miller 1982: pl. 8; *c*, incised jade found in Costa Rica, adapted from D. Stone 1982: fig. 39.

next (Drawings 8, 13, 15, and 22). Most of the Madrid serpents have similar half-disk markings, though often filled with cross-hatching (fig. 4-78a). The body of one Dzibichen serpent is formed from staggering two wavy lines. A serpent body is formed in identical fashion in Madrid 5b (fig. 4-78b).

The diving jaguars also compare well to figural conventions in the Madrid Codex. The loose rendering of the body and the depiction of jaguar pelt as parallel dashes are found with the cave figures and in the Madrid (fig. 4-79). Given these connections with the Madrid Codex style, it seems reasonable to assign several other prehispanic drawings to this time period. For example, the bird in Drawing 24 has patterned spots recalling conventions found in the Madrid Codex.

It is also possible that the "turtle-Ahaus" in Drawing 20 date from the time of the Madrid Codex. Yet the day signs were also depicted in the Colonial period; the Chilam Balam of Mani, for example, has decadent versions of Ahau (Craine and Reindorp 1979). So the possibility remains that the "turtle-Ahaus" are from the early contact period. Two other images, Drawings 25 and 9, can be tied stylistically to the "turtle-Ahaus" of Drawing 20.

FIG. 4-79. Madrid 49. Note parallel dashes as conventional fur markings on peccary. Adapted from Lee 1985.

Colonial drawings. The Colonial drawings primarily consist of simple frontal faces, which I call "circle faces"; three framed by rays or aureoles seem to represent the sun. As discussed earlier, one rayed face resembles the "lord of the *k'atun*" for 13 Ahau from the Chilam Balam of Chumayel (fig. 4-80; Plate 6). Calendrical ties are also evident in the fact that similar faces are found on Colonial Year Bearer wheels. A Year Bearer wheel from the Chilam Balam of Ixil, for example, places a circle face framed by an aureole in the center of the wheel, representing the sun, while faces associated with numbered Year Bearers form the perimeter (Bowditch 1910:fig. 62). Though the cave's circle faces are not organized in a wheel or table, their iconography is closest to these calendrical diagrams. The circle faces may have an underlying reference to the *k'atun*. This is suggested by the striking resemblance of one in Drawing 35 to a "lord of the *k'atun*" from the Chilam Balam of Chumayel. We might also consider the fact that the "turtle-Ahaus" surely refer to the *k'atun* ending, and they are also scattered over the wall.

It is surprising to find the supreme symbol of Spanish imperial might, the Hapsburg eagle, adorning the wall of a remote ritual cave in the Maya area (figs. 4-81, 4-82). And as the highest drawings on the wall, the two eagles literally dominate the room (fig. 4-68). How the Maya viewed this symbol of

FIG. 4-80. Lord of Katun 13 Ahau, Chilam Balam of Chumayel. Adapted from Roys 1967.

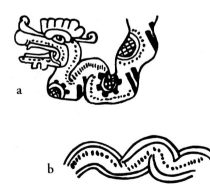

a

b

FIG. 4-78. Madrid serpents: *a,* Madrid 12 (note circular saddle patterns), adapted from Lee 1985; *b,* Madrid 5b, adapted from Lee 1985.

Images from the Underworld

foreign power is difficult to say. A reference in the Chilam Balam of Tizimin to *yemel ahaw kap'el u poli* "the descent of the ruler with two heads" is thought by Roys (1954:18) to refer to the Hapsburg eagle and suggests that the Maya identified it with the Spanish king. Hapsburg eagles occasionally adorned church entrances and windows in Yucatan and, therefore, may have had religious as well as political connotations.[11] The image of a two-headed bird was a form with pre-Columbian precedents and so had the added attraction of familiarity to the native artist. Hapsburg eagles were quickly absorbed into native iconography, appearing commonly in textile designs in highland Guatemala (Schevill 1985). The eagle's presence at Dzibichen is further evidence of its assimilation into the native pictorial vocabulary. The use of such a blatant political symbol also suggests that Dzibichen had some communitywide function and was not just used for private curing or fertility ceremonies.

Pinning down the date of the Colonial drawings is difficult, but my sense is that they are early Colonial, probably from the sixteenth century. I have addressed the problem of chronology elsewhere by focusing on the "lord of the *k'atun*" in Drawing 35 (Stone 1989b). If, as suggested, this image refers to a 13 Ahau *k'atun* ending, then it points to two possible dates: 1539 and 1796. Given the importance of Dzibichen in the Late Postclassic, an early postconquest date may be the more reasonable of the two possibilities.

Schematic drawings. The schematic drawings at Dzibichen are quite interesting and include five examples of "vulvas," more, perhaps, than at any other Mesoamerican site. Two identical forms are painted in red in a rock shelter at Chalcatzingo (fig. 4-12; Apostolides 1987:figs. 12.9, 12.11), and similar designs occur in Olmec clay stamps (Gay 1971:29). Velázquez Mor-

FIG. 4-81. Drawing 37, Dzibichen.

let and López de la Rosa (1988) note that a "vula" appears in Tikal graffiti in the Temple of the Inscriptions. Strecker (1987) discusses "vulva" representations in Maya cave art, but those he illustrates from Loltun are different in that they consist of a painted **U** over a triangular, pecked depression. The Dzibichen examples are more straightforward in what they represent. I suspect that the "vulva" forms at Dzibichen may be Late Postclassic, though this is just a hunch.

Some of the schematic drawings can be chronologically situated by their imagery. For example, the two mounted steeds are certainly postconquest (in spite of the "woman riding deer" motif known on Late Classic Maya vases). Mounted horses are also painted in the cave of Miramar, Campeche (Veronique Breuil, personal communication, 1988) and in caves and rock shelters in the Si-

FIG. 4-82. Drawing 38, Dzibichen.

erra de Tamaulipas (MacNeish 1958: 136, fig. 45; Stresser-Pean 1990). The two bicycles from Dzibichen must be from the twentieth century. One of the bicycles is carefully drawn high on the wall, suggesting some serious intent on the part of its creator.

Other Yucatecan Caves with Handprints

Several other caves in the Sierrita de Ti-cul contain handprints. One of these is Xkukican, a cave in the vicinity of Oxkutzcab that has a collection of positive and negative handprints, many located around the wall above a narrow entrance to a large chamber (Valentine 1965). The cave of Tres Manos near Akil is reported to have three handprints ringed by a circle (Lisa Rock, personal communication, 1990).

The well-known cave near Chichen Itza, Balankanche (Throne of the Jaguar), is reported to contain handprints. Two positive red handprints appear on the massive calcite column at the center of the chamber designated as Group I (Andrews 1970:11, fig. 49a). Handprints were also noted on "the roof of a low tunnel leading to Group II" (ibid.:11).

Strecker (1982b:49) reports a cave in the vicinity of Kaua with red and black handprints. This may be the Actun Kaua mentioned by Pearse (1938:14), who makes the tantalizing, though unsupported, statement that the cave has painted figures that the local inhabitants thought were very ancient. According to Reddell (1977:260), Actun Kaua has at least 7,000 meters of passages, putting it among the longer surveyed caves in Mexico.

Xyatil, Quintana Roo

One cave with a painting was found in the cenote of Xyatil near the village of the same name in Quintana Roo: a black painting of a schematic frontal face, measuring eighty centimeters high (Rätsch 1979).

Miramar (Actun Huachap), Campeche

In the vicinity of Bolonchen is the archaeological site of Miramar. A cave lies about one hundred meters north of its main structure. The cave has been called both Actun Huachap (Reddell 1977:246) and Miramar, after the name of the site. Veronique Breuil (1986) studied the cave of Miramar in a survey of the cave archaeology of Yucatan and Campeche. Miramar contains dozens of black and brownish-red paintings and drawings. All are rudimentary and linear, most consisting of human and animal stick figures. They range from about one meter to twenty centimeters in length. The majority lack diagnostic features for style dating, but several show the vestiges of pre-Columbian pictorial conventions, and several others can be securely dated to the Colonial period.

The most intricate painting that may be prehispanic or early contact is a black-line scene close to one meter in length (fig. 4-83). Breuil (personal communication, 1988) observes that a zoomorphic head and tail, with a distinctly prehispanic flavor, frame a rectangular precinct; the split tail looks piscine. The parallel lines forming the enclosure are suggestive of a plaza surrounded by a stepped platform. A schematic figure in the center can be seen holding a fan. Similar fans are held by ritual performers in Classic Maya art who are usually dancers (Taube 1989a). In light of the fan, it is reasonable to suggest that a dance performance is going on within the enclosure. The dancer in the painting wears a fancy feather headdress, and a number of objects, possibly ritual offerings, fill the plaza. The zoomorph seems to place these events in a cosmic setting. Under the tail are rayed concentric circles.

Other paintings from Miramar represent stick figures in animated poses who may be dancing. Nearby is another zoo-

FIG. 4-83. Plaza scene, Miramar. Adapted from drawing by Veronique Breuil.

FIG. 4-84. Zoomorphic head, Miramar. Adapted from drawing by Veronique Breuil.

Images from the Underworld

morphic head (fig. 4-84). One lizard-like creature may also be prehispanic (fig. 4-85). The cave drawings also include a monkey with curled tail and protruding belly.

Another interesting group of paintings dates from the Colonial period. Two represent Hapsburg eagles curiously configured with a European-style heart forming the body. In the simplest of the two versions straight lines form the legs, wings, and three-part tail, while curved lines form the two heads (fig. 4-86). This image distantly resembles a Hapsburg eagle incised onto the wall of a pre-Columbian structure at Hochob, Campeche (Robina 1956). The second eagle has a face in the center of the heart (fig. 4-87). Apart from subject matter, another Colonial trait is the continuous line forming the brow and nose. Greater definition is given to the legs, wings, and two heads, the latter consisting of crescentic forms attached to a hump atop the heart "body." At least one other circle face uses a continuous line for the eyebrow and nose, and, therefore, would seem to be Colonial. Other figures possibly painted during the Colonial period at the cave of Miramar have boxlike bodies.

The ceramic associations of the cave of Miramar are strongest in the Early Classic, but all the caves surveyed around Bolonchen had a Terminal Classic occupation (Breuil 1986). Breuil comments that the cave of Miramar contains a dense accumulation of pot sherds, indicative of the kind of ceremonial pottery dumps found in many Maya caves (e.g., Thompson 1975:xvii–xx).

Joloniel (Ixtelha), Chiapas

Joloniel Cave is situated along the Ixtelha River about eight kilometers north of Tumbala. Its modern discovery can be credited to linguist Wilbur Aulie and photographer Gertrude Duby

Blom, both of whom visited the cave in 1961 (Nicholson 1962). In the 1970s Carlos Navarrete and Eduardo Martínez carried out an archaeological survey of Joloniel, the results of which are much anticipated. A newspaper interview with Navarrete (Aguilar Zinser 1974) provides a glimmer of information about this important painted cave. We learn that Joloniel is a cave two hundred meters long and that the paintings are predominantly in black, but red and small amounts of yellow are also present. These paintings are, then, rare examples of polychrome Maya cave painting. In 1981 Riese published ink drawings of the Joloniel paintings based on the Blom photographs. The collection of paintings from Joloniel, as can be determined from the Blom photographs, consists of two scenes and seven hieroglyphic texts containing about eighty-five hieroglyphs that are clearly discernible. An examination of the Blom photographs indicates, however, that more faded glyphs are present that have never been drawn.

The Joloniel paintings. The paintings constitute the only collection of Early Classic cave paintings currently known in the Maya area. The main scene is positioned over a horizontal ridge, so the figures appear to stand on a rocky outcropping. The Maya may have reworked the wall to enhance this effect, as the Navarrete interview mentions that the Maya modified some of the painted wall surfaces.

The main scene has been described by Thompson (1975:xxxvi). It features two figures painted entirely in black. Unfortunately, the right-hand figure is obliterated from the waist up (figs. 4-88, 4-89). The left-hand figure has details added by the absence of black paint: light-colored hands, a prominent white nose, a light strip following the skull line, three bars on the cheek, and a feathered headdress. The right-hand figure holds a torch while

FIG. 4-85. Quadruped with tail, Miramar. Adapted from drawing by Veronique Breuil.

FIG. 4-86. Hapsburg eagle, Miramar. Adapted from photograph by Nicholas Hellmuth.

FIG. 4-87. Hapsburg eagle, Miramar (note heart-shaped face as body). Adapted from photograph by Nicholas Hellmuth.

the other looks on passively, arms hanging.[12]

The two figures flank an unusual altar that shows an "Ahau" glyph superfixed by the number nine (fig. 4-90). A comparison with so-called Giant Ahau Altars, known from such sites as Caracol (Beetz and Satterthwaite 1981: figs. 20, 21) and Tikal (Jones and Satterthwaite 1982:fig. 50b), immediately comes to mind. Giant Ahau Altars are drum-shaped stones, like the typical Maya altar, but decorated with the Ahau date of a specific *k'atun* ending

FIG. 4-88. Figurative paintings, Joloniel. Photograph by Gertrude Duby Blom.

FIG. 4-89. Main scene showing two figures standing over 8 Ahau altar, Joloniel. Photograph by Gertrude Duby Blom.

FIG. 4-90. Main scene, Joloniel. Adapted from photograph by Gertrude Duby Blom.

(fig. 4-91). In terms of scale relative to the figures, placement on the ground, and the presence of an Ahau date, the Joloniel painted altar forms a tight comparison with the carved Giant Ahau Altars.

The main scene from Joloniel seems to involve a period-ending ritual, an idea supported by a nearby painting. Below the main scene within a projecting rectangular block of stone is an image that restates the period-ending theme (figs. 4-92, 4-93). A coefficient of nine (four dots and a bar) stands to the right of an object that combines traits of an "Ahau" glyph and the Cauac Monster. The stepped forehead, dots, and loops allude to the Cauac Monster, while the half-rectangular mouth duplicates the mouth form of the "Ahau" glyph, as found in the main scene. Hence, both paintings allude to the idea of a period-ending ritual in a cave.

The date 9 Ahau appears in both paintings as well. As a *k'atun* ending, 9 Ahau recurs every 256 years: during the Classic period on 8.13.0.0.0, 9 Ahau 3 Zac (A.D. 297), and 9.6.0.0.0, 9 Ahau 3 Uayeb (A.D. 554). The earlier date accords better with early traits found on the figures: for example, their legs do not overlap and contours describe flat forms. The clover shape of the "Ahau" glyph is also an early trait (Stone 1989b).

However, the earlier of the two dates makes this scene so precocious that caution must be maintained. At 8.13.0.0.0, 9 Ahau 3 Zac (A.D. 297), these paintings would constitute the earliest record of a *k'atun* ending in Mesoamerica. Mathews's (1985: Table 3) list of Early Classic dates on Maya monuments notes the earliest *k'atun* ending a full sixty years later on 8.16.0.0.0 (Uaxactun Stela 19). The scene would also be precocious at 8.13.0.0.0 for having the

earliest example of a Cauac Monster in Maya art rendered with standard iconography. Tate (1982: 33) places the earliest Cauac Monster more than a hundred years later at 9.2.0.0.0 (ca. A.D. 460). Thompson, however, seems to have accepted the early date in placing the Joloniel paintings at A.D. 300 (Thompson 1975: xxxvi).

FIG. 4-91. Giant Ahau Altar, Caracol. Adapted from Beetz and Satterthwaite 1981: fig. 26b.

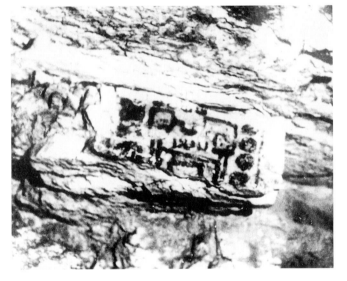

FIG. 4-92. Cauac Monster combined with 9 Ahau, Joloniel. Photograph by Gertrude Duby Blom.

FIG. 4-93. Cauac Monster combined with 9 Ahau, Joloniel. Adapted from photograph by Gertrude Duby Blom.

The Joloniel inscriptions. The inscriptions of Joloniel fall into two chronologically distinct style groups. One uses thick painted borders around texts, and rendering is done in a heavy, cursive, and rather sloppy line (fig. 4-94). The other group does not use borders, and the line is stiffer and more carefully controlled (figs. 4-95, 4-96). The latter are clearly earlier and would seem to be contemporary with the pictorial scenes; this is confirmed by the 9 Ahau date leading off one of the texts (fig. 4-96).

One of the early texts (fig. 4-95) commences with a seating verb prefixed by the third-person possessive pronoun

u- (at A1). The form of the "seating" verb, which still resembles the torso and legs of a seated figure and has a *u*-element infix, is closest to the "seating" glyphs on the Leiden Plaque (Schele and Miller 1986:121, pl. 33). The Leiden Plaque has one of the earliest Long Count dates in Maya inscriptions at 8.14.3.12.1. This provides some justification for the 8.13.0.0.0 placement of the 9 Ahau *k'atun* ending featured in the Joloniel paintings. The remaining glyphs, however, do not appear to be as early; rather, they compare with the style of glyphs on early Cycle 9 texts from such sites as Tikal (e.g., Stela 31).

The "seating" verb at Joloniel is followed by a compound that has a crossed-bands main sign, a T23 **na** subfix, and possibly phonetic **o** as a superfix (at B1). While this could potentially indicate the seating of a *haab* position, such as Zip, it more likely that this is the name of the protagonist. A similar compound (at B5) appears in the other text in the middle of a nominal phrase that includes a reference to God K (at A5) and an old god with a hank of hair that falls in front of his face (at A6; fig. 4-96). The protagonist's

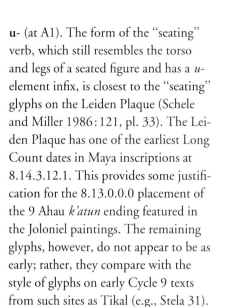

FIG. 4-94. Cursive inscription, Joloniel. Adapted from photograph by Gertrude Duby Blom and drawing by Riese 1981.

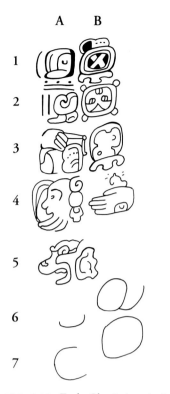

A   B

1
2
3
4
5
6
7

FIG. 4-95. Early Classic inscription commencing with seating glyph, Joloniel. Adapted from photograph by Gertrude Duby Blom and drawing by Riese 1981.

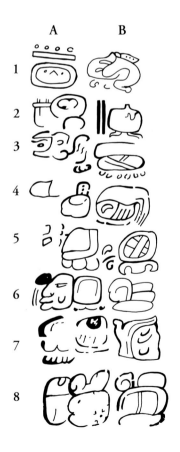

A   B

1
2
3
4
5
6
7
8

FIG. 4-96. Early Classic inscription commencing with 9 Ahau, Joloniel. Adapted from photograph by Gertrude Duby Blom and drawing by Riese 1981.

name probably reads something like **o-tan**, and the text with the seating glyph refers to the accession of a ruler by that name.

The Distance Number following the accession counts ten days and thirteen *winals*, a total of 270 days, and leads to a period ending, as indicated by the pointing finger over a "cycle" compound at A3 (fig. 4-95). That period ending could be the 9 Ahau date, mentioned no less than three times in scenes and inscriptions.

The inscriptions dating to a later period occur in two groups: one large panel with four rows of glyphs (Riese 1981) and a series of single-column short phrases (fig. 4-94). Three of these phrases begin with **u-** third-person pronouns (T11). One of these (and perhaps significantly the last) is **u-ts'ib** "he writes" or "his writing," which may be followed by the name of the scribe (Stuart 1987). Another of these verbal phrases commences with the "scattering hand." The name of the protagonist should follow; it appears to consist of an "Imix" glyph compounded with the head of a spider monkey.

The early Joloniel inscriptions mention the accession of a ruler from a presently unidentified site and refer to the completion of a 9 Ahau period ending. The pictorial scenes treat related events. Illuminated by torchlight in a cave, two lords celebrate a *k'atun* anniversary that occurred only 270 days after the ruler's accession. The ruler may be one of the attendant figures. As to dating the scene and the early inscriptions, a compromise solution is to settle on a ten *tun* anniversary rather than the expected *k'atun* ending. One candidate is the *lahuntun* 8.19.10.0.0, 9 Ahau 3 Muan

(A.D. 426), which is early enough to account for the style but not so early as to raise a number of other problems already mentioned. Even at A.D. 426 the Joloniel paintings would be extremely early for this region of Chiapas, earlier than any Classic art at Palenque, for example. Joloniel seems to have been a cave utilized by the Maya nobility for some of the earliest *k'atun* rituals yet recorded in the Maya area. These paintings also support the idea that Classic Maya accession rituals may have included ceremonies in caves, as argued by Bassie-Sweet (1991). Moreover, Korelstein (1989) has proposed that a glyphic collocation found on several monuments from Palenque, reading **k'uk'-te-wits**, may refer to Joloniel as a pilgrimage shrine, which she suggests was utilized by the Classic Palencanos. She notes that the town of Tumbala, where Joloniel is located, is today called K'uk' Wits and that the cave is an old and venerated place of pilgrimage.

Yaleltsemen, Chiapas

The first mention in print of Yaleltsemen, a cave located about eight kilometers west of Bachajon, appears in Thompson's (1975:xxxvi) synthesis of Maya cave art. He does not mention the cave by name but relates the story of its discovery by Marianne Slocum in 1963 and provides a photograph and interpretation of the figure. In their regional survey of the Tonina area, Becquelin and Baudez (1982:2:601) include a description and photograph (1982:3:1231, fig. 40d) of the painting in addition to identifying the cave's name. My data derive from these two sources.

Yaleltsemen lies in a picturesque setting: the entrance is notched into a sheer cliff; a waterfall above cascades into a pool. The entrance leads to a narrow tunnel where a shaft three meters deep connects with a large boulder-strewn room. About thirty meters into the room is an open area flanked on

Images from the Underworld

FIG. 4-97. Figure and text from Yaleltse-men. Bottom of figure's leg formed by edge of rock (shown with dashed line). Adapted from photograph by Pierre Becquelin.

one side by a prismatic boulder about four and one-half meters long. On this smooth-surfaced limestone block is a painting of a figure, measuring sixty-four centimeters high, and a row of hieroglyphs 1.32 meters long, each glyph standing about eleven centimeters high. The style is unequivocally Late Classic eighth-century Maya (fig. 4-97; Plate 7).

Thompson identifies the figure as the young maize god. One could point to the high forehead as a trait of the tonsured maize god (Taube 1985), but otherwise the figure lacks his definitive characteristics. In fact, the figure looks more like a fully mortal noble. His high status is suggested by the beaded necklace and ear ornament (now smeared). He strikes an unusual seated pose with legs crossed in an oblique angle, while his body leans to the right. It looks as though he is gesturing toward another figure or leaning on an invisible object, making it appear that some part of this scene to the left has been destroyed. However, there is so little room between the figure and the end of the block that more imagery could not be accommodated to the left. The ease with which the artist has rendered this complex pose recalls the graceful figural style of Palenque. Given the location of Yaleltsemen in the western Maya region, a stylistic affiliation with Palenque is not at all surprising.

Actun Dzib (Actun Tz'iib), Belize

Actun Dzib is located in the Toledo District of Belize, a few kilometers from the Kekchi village of Blue Creek. The story of the cave's discovery in 1983 was relayed in a letter from Rosemary Ulrich, then working in the Toledo District for the Summer Institute of Linguistics, to the prime minister of Belize, George Price. She stated that Nicolas Teul, a young Kekchi man from Blue Creek, spotted "writing" on the walls of a cave while on a hunting expedition. A student visiting the area, Mark Richard, heard the story and hired a guide to relocate the cave. He also photographed the wall art and reported the cave to officials. The cave apparently had no local name, so Ulrich christened it Actun Tz'iib (now Dzib), "cave with writing." That same year the Belize department of archaeology sent out a reconaissance team to map the cave, carry out limited excavations, and record the paintings. Since 1988 Actun Dzib has been under investigation by Gary Rex Walters as part of a survey of cave archaeology in the Toledo District. I visited Actun Dzib in 1989.

Actun Dzib is entered by a small opening in a cliff face, perhaps ten meters wide, which accesses the single corridor extending for about one hundred meters (see Appendix A, fig. A-2). With a level dirt floor occasionally obstructed by fallen rocks, the corridor is easy to negotiate. At the outset, passage side walls are almost perfectly vertical, making the corridor look something like a mine shaft. The walls are formed from an eroded limestone with curtainlike faceted surfaces. The cave paintings occur twenty-five meters back from the entrance on smooth portions of these vertical walls. Though a precise count is difficult, there are about seventy-five drawings at Actun Dzib. The pigment consists of a dark substance, possibly a dark brown clay or charcoal or a mixture of both. Though the paintings have not been damaged by vandalism, they have been affected by moisture, and runny paint is common.

Walters (1988) divides the corpus into three panels. Panels 1 and 2 are stylistically identical and could have been produced by the same artist or group of artists. These paintings rely on a distinct formal vocabulary combining straight lines, dots, spirals, and circles. The paintings are not sloppily composed. In fact, Actun Dzib contains the finest schematic paintings in the corpus of Maya cave painting. Panel 1 comprises the group of paintings on the north side of the passage wall covering the lower edge of an overhang (fig. 4-98). In Panel 1 are several splayed zoomorphs, creatures whose arms and legs consist of two opposing U's (fig. 4-99). In one of these a solid circle between

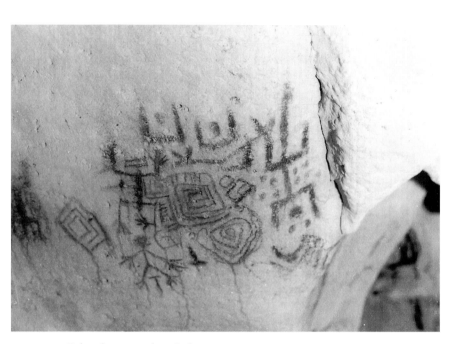

FIG. 4-98. Panel 1, Actun Dzib. After Walters 1988.

one of the U's may be a head, and the extension between the legs, a tail. This creature looks something like a lizard. Several other paintings show the U with the circle, as though just the arms and head of the "lizard" are indicated. One of these quadrupeds with splayed toes and fat body can be identified as a frog or toad. For reasons unknown, each of the four splayed zoomorphs is slightly different. Beneath one is a schematic human figure with a T-form appearing between his legs. Another common design in Panel 1 is the spiral; some form a diamond, while others have their long sides parallel to the ground (fig. 4-100). The largest spiral measures thirty centimeters across.

Panel 2 is found on the south passage wall across from Panel 1 (fig. 4-101), and they share many of the same motifs. There is at least one splayed quadruped. The T-form occurs with even greater frequency in Panel 2 and appears both as a T and an inverted T. Inverted T's (but with enlarged horizontal elements) also appear in clusters on the wall of a cave in the Sierra de Tamaulipas (MacNeish 1958:fig. 45-1). Spirals are also present in Panel 2. Another curious form consists of a series of crooked parallel lines that attach to the body of an insectlike creature (fig. 4-102). The crooked parallel lines, patterned with dots, also occur in Panel 1.

FIG. 4-99. Splayed zoomorph, spirals, and other motifs, Panel 1, Actun Dzib.

Panel 2 also presents a comblike motif, consisting of a bar and usually six vertical lines always pointing upward (fig. 4-103). To the left of Panel 1 is the modern drawing of a heart and cross.

Panel 3, situated on the south wall closer to the entrance, consists of a single painting discovered during Walters's survey of Actun Dzib (fig. 4-104). The painting is of an entirely different character than Panels 1 and 2 and, though crudely drawn, uses conventions of the Greater Classic style.

Unfortunately, the painting is indistinct, which, as noted by Walters (1988), may be due to the deposition of a film of calcite. The individual depicted has exaggerated features: a thick nose and lips and oversized teeth. The eye is also disproportionately large. Small beads are attached to the lower rim of the eye. The manner of drawing the eye with a straight upper lid and a semicircle forming the lower edge, as well as the large attached beads, recall graphic conventions in the Madrid Co-

Images from the Underworld

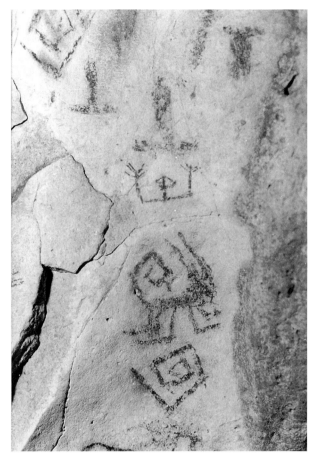

FIG. 4-100. Spiral, quadruped, anthropomorph, and inverted T, Panel 1, Actun Dzib.

dex, suggesting a Late Postclassic date for the painting. However, Walters (personal communication, 1990) has found that Postclassic utilization of caves in this region is virtually nonexistent, so the resemblance may be fortuitous. The figure in Panel 3 raises both arms and one leg, a sure signal that he is dancing. Some lines near the left foot look clawlike, but they are too faint to be reliable. The figure seems to be some kind of grotesque dance performer.

As noted earlier, Actun Dzib contains one of the most important collections of schematic cave art in the Maya area. The careful repetition of forms is consistent with a codified symbol system. Yet this style of cave painting appears to be a local phenomenon; it is not known from any other Maya cave. The inventory of motifs shows some striking parallels with rock art of the American Southwest, where we also find the T-shaped form, the comb design, the splay-legged zoomorph, spirals, and parallel crooked lines (e.g., Schaafsma 1980:figs. 31, 53–54, 96). However, the similarities must be considered fortuitous, as there is no demonstrable link between these two areas.

FIG. 4-101. Panel 2, Actun Dzib. After Walters 1988.

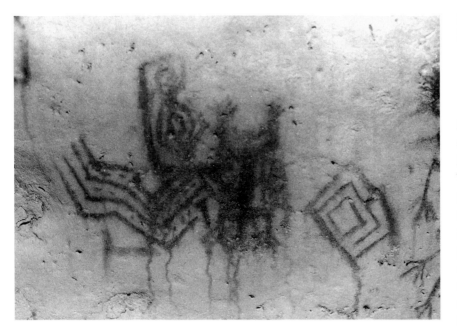

FIG. 4-102. Parallel crooked lines, Panel 2, Actun Dzib.

One possible source of the designs at Actun Dzib is textiles. Morris's (1985) inventory of textile motifs utilized by modern Tzotzil and Tzeltal weavers of highland Chiapas, but also depicted on textiles illustrated in Classic monuments at Yaxchilan, includes elements that recall the Actun Dzib material: zigzag parallel lines, sometimes associated with dots, diamond patterns with interior dots, schematic toads, and other forms reminiscent of the Actun Dzib collection (fig. 4-105a). It is conceivable that the cave motifs derive from a popular tradition of textile decoration, but as James Brady has pointed out to me (personal communication, 1991), some of these motifs also occur on pottery (fig. 4-105b). The Actun Dzib pictorial vocabulary, then, may represent something widespread in the popular arts (thus appearing appropriately enough in a cave) but less important in elite art. As Morris's study shows, too, these motifs are not just decorative but are imbued with symbolic significance.

The ceramic collection from Actun Dzib points to utilization during the Early and Late Classic periods (Gary Rex Walters, personal communication,

1990), and it seems likely that all the paintings date within this time frame. Given the ceramic associations, Panel 3 might date to the Early Classic period. The figure in Panel 3 shares traits with one that appears on a number of basal-flanged Early Classic bowls found at Uaxactun (Smith 1955: figs. 3e and 28, no. 9) and Eduardo Quiroz Cave (Pendergast 1971: fig. 7b). The figure always assumes a prone "swimming" position. The hands appear to be tied together, a typical way of showing captives in the Early Classic. Interestingly, a polychrome sherd with this same motif was found at Actun Dzib (Gary Rex Walters, personal communication, 1989). The figure painted on basal-flanged bowls is slightly grotesque, with a bulbous nose and protruding lips, sometimes with the upper row of teeth showing, facial features that recall the figure in Panel 3.

Roberto's Cave, Belize

Not far from Laguna Village in the Toledo District is Roberto's Cave, discovered and surveyed by Gary Rex Walters in 1988. Roberto's Cave is one of a number of small caves in a bluff over-

looking an immense valley. The cave really consists of a thirty-meter semicircular tunnel through the limestone bluff. There are six rudimentary paintings on the passage walls, many very fragmentary, and all are located fairly high up on the wall out of normal reach. The paintings, all in a blackish pigment, do not appear to have been vandalized, but they have succumbed to natural erosional processes from dripping water. One painting shows an insect about eleven centimeters high (fig. 4-106), and another looks like the body of a serpent with saddle patterns (fig. 4-107). Another, thirteen centimeters high, possibly drawn with charcoal, consists of a circle with spokes. Several other paintings at Roberto's Cave show human figures. The better-preserved of the two is a figure with one arm extended and the other on the hip in what appears to be a dancing pose (fig. 4-108). The ceramic collection from Roberto's Cave and other caves in this area is predominantly Late Classic (Gary Rex Walters, personal communication, 1990), one possible date for the paintings.

Bladen 2 Cave, Belize

The newest addition to the corpus of painted caves in the Maya Lowlands is situated on the Bladen branch of the Monkey River and was discovered by Peter Dunham (personal communication, 1993) in 1993. The cave is the easternmost in a complex of caves designated "Bladen 2" and extends for about thirty meters through a deposit of brecciated limestone. Four linear, black paintings, ranging from 6–16 cm in height, occur at a depth of twenty meters into the cave. They cluster above a

FIG. 4-103. Comblike design, Panel 2, Actun Dzib.

FIG. 4-104. Panel 3, Actun Dzib.

FIG. 4-105. Various motifs: *a,* designs used by highland Chiapas weavers, adapted from Morris 1985; *b,* stylized toad on Protoclassic pottery, Naj Tunich, adapted from Brady 1989: fig. 5.11.

FIG. 4-106. Insect, Roberto's Cave.

FIG. 4-107. Partial serpent, Roberto's Cave.

FIG. 4-108. Dancing figure, Roberto's Cave.

low natural arch, situated at approximately eye level. Each painting was executed on a smooth clast cemented into the brecciated limestone wall. The technique of framing paintings within smooth clasts also occurs at Naj Tunich (e.g., see fig. 5-34), though Bladen 2 is distinct in having four such paintings grouped together. Two of the paintings feature deity heads. One has a sunken mouth and pointed chin and wears a headdress with a frontal serpent and feather crest; in light of the aged features, this entity may represent God N (fig. 4-109). The other head may sport a death collar. Another painting depicts an ophidian supernatural, and a fourth shows a group of obscure motifs stacked vertically. An intriguing archaeological feature of the cave consists of stone slabs found lying about on the floor. In other caves of this region such slabs usually support inverted *ollas* and other offerings (Peter Dunham personal communication, 1993). No offerings were found in this case, most likely as a result of disturbance, possibly recent disturbance by looters. The Bladen 2 Cave is located equidistant, some 4–5 kilometers from each, between two sites known as Quebrada de Oro and RHS.

FIG. 4-109. Deity head from Bladen 2 Cave. Adapted from photograph by Peter Dunham.

FIG. 4-110. Two monkeys and three other animals, Bombil Pec. Adapted from photograph by Patricia Carot in Gatica 1980.

Bombil Pec, Guatemala

Bombil Pec, the only highland Guatemalan cave reported to date with paintings, was investigated in the late 1970s by Patricia Carot (1982). Bombil Pec is located in the state of Alta Verapaz, forty kilometers east of Coban, near Chisec. The paintings are found in an inaccessible part of the cave, requiring one to negotiate two narrow chimneys, each about fifty centimeters in diameter. In a room beneath this narrow opening are five black-line paintings of animals, each measuring about twenty centimeters in length (fig. 4-110). Two of the paintings grouped together are clearly monkeys. Another two with long tails and short ears may be felines. One is too indistinct to identify. The presence of a pair of nearly identical monkeys recalls an episode from the Popol Vuh concerning a pair of monkey brothers. The Hero Twins turned their annoying stepbrothers, Hun Chuen and Hun Batz, into monkeys by tricking them into climbing a tree and loosening their loincloth belts, which magically become monkey tails. In spite of their noisome ways, Hun Batz and Hun Chuen were remembered as great artisans and scribes (Coe 1977).

Santo Domingo, Guatemala

The newly discovered Santo Domingo Cave is located in southeastern Peten within a half-day's walk of the great cave painting site of Naj Tunich. Santo Domingo was first reported to authorities in July of 1988. IDEAH monument inspector Dacio Castellano and guard Bernabé Pop spent one day visiting the cave and informed me (I was working at Naj Tunich at the time) that the cave contained a hieroglyphic inscription. Unfortunately, our group lacked time to investigate the report. The new cave was named Santo Domingo after the closest settlement, located about five kilometers away. James and Sandra Brady carried out the first reconnaissance of Santo Domingo in 1989. The description of the site stems from their survey (Brady and Fahsen 1991).

Entered by way of a sinkhole, the Santo Domingo entrance is impressive; the ceiling rises up to fifty meters. From the entrance, a scramble down boulder debris leads to the wetter tunnel system, which has rimstone dams and other active formations. Brady and Fahsen note that in an alcove on top of a flowstone ledge, dense quantities of charcoal were found in addition to smoke-blackened stalactites, probably the remains of ceremonial fires. A few Classic pottery sherds were also found.

The Santo Domingo paintings are located "in a fissure in the western wall of the tunnel, not far from the entrance" (Brady and Fahsen 1991:53). One wall has the remains of a large painting sixty-three centimeters high, situated at about eye level but now obscured by calcite deposits. The most important painting is found on the northern wall of the fissure, also at eye level. The painting consists of two columns of glyphs (fig. 4-111). The glyphs are quite large, ranging from eight to fifteen centimeters in height. The style of the Santo Domingo inscription is Late

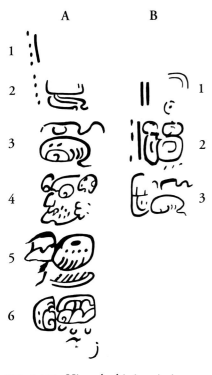

FIG. 4-111. Hieroglyphic inscription from Santo Domingo. Adapted from photographs by James Brady.

FIG. 4-112. Figure with shield, San Miguel. Adapted from photograph by Otis Imboden.

Classic, contemporary with the Naj Tunich texts. The inscriptions of these two caves share many traits, such as the use of a black pigment and the general character of line and details. The reading order of the Santo Domingo inscription in single columns is also like many texts at Naj Tunich. They also share the use of the compound seen at A6. This glyph (with several variations) occurs eighteen times at Naj Tunich.

The Santo Domingo text opens with a Calendar Round date that, because of its condition, is not reconstructable. Based on the *haab* coefficient of four (and assuming a standard Lowland Year Bearer system), the *tsolk'in* day must be either Imix, Cimi, Chuen, or Cib. The month sign has a T116 "tail," which means it could be Yaxkin, Muan, or Xul. Therefore, the Calendar Round date is 9 (Imix, Cimi, Chuen, or Cib) 4 (Yaxk'in, Muan, or Xul).

Brady and Fahsen identify the verb at A3 as *buts* "smoke" and note its repetition at B3. They suggest that the verb alludes to ritual burning, perhaps of copal. Their interpretation, I believe, is incorrect and is based on an inaccurate drawing of the glyph. The name of the protagonist of the first event appears at A4. Here we see an aged rendition of an anthropomorphic jaguar deity (note his snaggle tooth and pointed chin). At A5 he carries the title **ah bak** (T229.501: 25): *ah* "he of" is a male agentive prefix, and *bak* means "bone" but can also mean "captive" (Stuart 1985). The Cordemex Dictionary (Barrera Vásquez 1980:27) defines the phrase *ah bak* as an animal weak in the bones or a child. The aged jaguar deity, perhaps "weak in the bones," can be identified as one of the two "Paddler Gods" (Stuart 1988). They are a pair of old deities, one identified by a stingray spine piercing his nose and the other, the one found at Santo Domingo, by his jaguar attributes. The compound at A6, read **yitah** "his/her companion" by Barbara

MacLeod (see Ch. 7), may have named the Old Jaguar Paddler as the companion of the individual mentioned in the nominal phrase following the **yitah** compound. It is most unfortunate that the name of that entity is no longer present.

The second column of hieroglyphs is badly eroded. The prefix at B3 is the Posterior Event Indicator (T679), preceding what Brady and Fahsen propose to be the same verb as that at A3. B1–B2 appears to be another Calendar Round. Though badly preserved, the Santo Domingo text can be tied definitively to supernatural events involving the Old Jaguar Paddler.

San Miguel, Guatemala

Prehispanic cave art is found in two caves near the archaeological site of San Miguel, located about twenty-four kilometers west of Poptun, Peten. The caves, also housing human skeletal remains and ceramics, were reported to authorities in 1985 by Alfonso Tito Sandoval Segura. In 1988 Miguel Orrego and Otis Imboden carried out a preliminary survey. A more thorough reconnaissance was undertaken by Juan Antonio Siller, whose published report (1989) supplies much of the following information. One of the two caves, known as Cueva de las Ofrendas (also called El Ceibo) owing to its collection of ceramics, is reported to have handprints as well as human skeletal remains (Grube 1989). The other, more interesting cave—from the point of view of cave art—is the so-called Cueva de las Pinturas. This cave has on its walls and ceiling an unspecified number of line drawings in charcoal of human and animal figures, plantlike forms, and geometrical designs, few of which have been published (Siller 1989: figs. 7, 8). One of the human figures shows a costumed figure carrying a shield and weapon (fig. 4-112). Another has arms that cleverly create the outlines of a face (fig. 4-113). In light of the extreme remoteness of the area and lack of post-conquest settlements, it is likely that all of Santo Domingo's cave art is prehispanic. Noteworthy, too, is the prehispanic habitational site near the caves (ibid.: fig. 2). Furthermore, Cueva de las Pinturas lies in a hillside directly overlooking the arroyo of San Miguel.

Cave of Pusila, Guatemala

Michel Siffre (1979) mentions a cave near the village of Pusila, Guatemala (not to be confused with Pusilha, Belize), decorated with petroglyphs and paintings. Pusila is located about ten kilometers east of the Peten highway, just south of San Luis. Siffre's map (p. 79) shows about 150 meters of passageway in the cave. A crude sculpted head is carved near the entrance. One section of wall has a number of drawings, which include a profile face and a near-complete seated figure with folded arms (fig. 4-114). The style of these two drawings points toward a Late Classic date for the entire group. Other drawings consist of meandering lines that do not seem to describe any natural forms (ibid.: fig. 42). One curious group of nonfigurative paintings consists of concentric circles (somewhat like a bull's-eye) with patterned sections or loops around the perimeter (fig. 4-115). The published photograph shows at least five of these forms on the wall, so they must have conveyed some meaning that is now lost to us (ibid.: figs. 47, 48). The Pusila cave also has a collection of positive and negative handprints as well as a child's footprint (ibid.: figs. 40, 41, 46). All of these images utilize black pigment, which in some cases looks like charcoal. The Pusila drawings could well be contemporary with Naj Tunich, which lies only ten kilometers to the northwest. The quality of the drawings is not at all comparable, however; those of Naj Tunich are far superior.

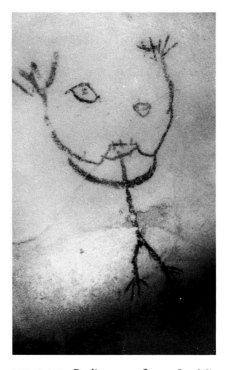

FIG. 4-113. Rudimentary figure, San Miguel. Photograph by Otis Imboden, courtesy of the National Geographic Society.

Caves near Machaquila, Guatemala

Near the town of Machaquila, north of Poptun on the Peten highway, Michel Siffre and his colleagues found two caves with paintings. One cave contains two panels of brownish-red handprints. One well-preserved group has about twenty imprints, while the other is badly effaced due to water damage (Siffre 1979: 138, figs. 67, 68). Other handprints appear in scattered parts of the cave (ibid.: figs. 69, 73). The second cave, located about one hundred meters from the first, is said to have about thirty red dots painted on the wall (ibid.: 139, fig. 75).

FIG. 4-114. Seated Late Classic figure, Cave of Pusila. Adapted from Siffre 1979: fig. 43.

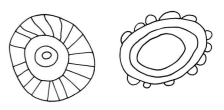

FIG. 4-115. Concentric circles, Cave of Pusila. Adapted from Siffre 1979: fig. 47.

5

Naj Tunich: An Introduction to the Site and Its Art

Location and Discovery

Flanking the Maya Mountains is a rugged karst landscape where a number of important cave-related discoveries have been made over the past two decades. One came to light in the mid-1980s when a group of cave explorers, led by Thomas Miller, discovered a major cave system in the heart of Belize's Vaca Plateau. Part of a single hydrological network formed by the Chiquibul River and its affluents, the caves total fifty kilometers in length, with individual caves measuring up to eighteen kilometers. Passage volumes are of an astounding size, averaging some thirty or forty meters in width (one room measures 150 × 350 meters). Though this is the longest cave system in Central America and one of the largest by volume in the world (Thomas Miller, personal communication, 1987), it was virtually unknown prior to the 1980s.

This heavily karstified region flanking the Maya Mountains, one of the

world's great repositories of caves, is home to one of the most interesting archaeological cave sites in the New World: the cave now called Naj Tunich (G. Stuart 1981; Stone 1982; Brady and Stone 1986). Lying at an elevation of six hundred meters, Naj Tunich is carved into the limestone hills of southeastern Peten, Guatemala (fig. 5-1). The cave is located in the municipality of Poptun, Peten, about one kilometer west of the Belizean border.[1] This area has seen dramatic changes, having gone from wilderness to a frontier settlement of Kekchi and ladino farmers, all in the space of a few years. The Guatemalan government established a national park around the cave where hunting and farming are prohibited; but beyond this, where lush forest covered the hillsides in recent memory, villages and maize fields have firmly taken root.

Naj Tunich lies east of the two largest towns along the southern stretch of the Peten highway: Poptun and San Luis. The cave is situated between the headwaters of two rivers. North of Naj Tunich is the source of the Mopan River, which joins the Belize River far to the north. To the south are the headwaters of the Río Blanco, which, via the Moho River, empties into the Gulf of Honduras.

The cave can be reached from the west by way of a trail that starts in Poptun and passes through the settlement of Tanjoc. About thirty kilometers long and negotiable only on foot or mule, this route takes anywhere from six to ten hours, depending mainly on the weather. An alternate route that permits use of a motorized vehicle begins at Chacte, a town on the Peten highway south of San Luis. From Chacte a dirt road runs northeast for about ten kilometers until it meets a rougher dirt road, which heads in a more northerly direction and hugs the course of the Río Blanco. The intersection of these two roads is known as El Cruce, consisting of little more than a small *tienda*. The northward road connects El Cruce and La Compuerta, one of the new villages established at the edge of the Naj Tunich archaeological zone. This road, which crosses the Río Blanco at several turns, is best tackled in a four-wheel-drive vehicle during the dry season, as rain quickly turns the hilly road into a mire of ankle-deep mud. The Río Blanco also becomes impassable even for four-wheel-drive vehicles during the rainy season.

The story of the discovery of Naj Tunich has been told on several occasions (G. Stuart 1981; Stone 1982:94; Brady 1989:72–77), but it deserves a few more words here. While out on a hunting expedition in 1979, Bernabé Pop discovered Naj Tunich, having, as the story goes, followed his hunting dogs into the entrance. The cave was within the boundaries of his father Emilio's *finca*. In 1979 Emilio Pop's *finca* was extremely isolated, the closest community being Tanjoc, several hours away on foot. A friend of the family, a muleteer and former *chiclero* by trade (known only to me as Ricardo), visited the Pops' farm and learned of Bernabé's discovery of a cave full of paintings. The muleteer happened to know an American couple, Michael and Carole DeVine, who ran a farm, Finca Ixobel, near Poptun. In discussing the possibility of bringing tourists to the cave with the muleteer, the DeVines got wind of Naj Tunich. They visited it in the summer of 1980, confirmed the report of paintings, and eventually alerted the appropriate authorities. Even though the Pops had knowledge of Naj Tunich in 1979, the discovery date is usually placed in 1980, the year the cave became known to the outside world.

By August of 1980 a team of spelunkers had mapped Naj Tunich (Witte and Garza 1981), and the paintings were photographed by Jacques Van Kirk. Some of these photographs appeared in an article in *Prensa Libre*, which is the first published account of Naj Tunich (Rodas 1980). An early visitor, Pierre Ventur, a linguist of Mayan languages from Yale, gave the cave its name: *nah tunich* means "stone house" in Mopan and is also a Mopan expression for "cave." At the time he visited the cave, Ventur was working on Mopan, which is still spoken in the environs of San Luis. As will be seen in Chapter 7, the word *mo'pan* appears in the cave's hieroglyphic texts and may have been a regional toponym prevalent in this area during the Classic period.

Early in 1981, under the aegis of the National Geographic Society, George Stuart and William Garrett led an expedition to Naj Tunich that resulted in a widely read story appearing in *National Geographic* (G. Stuart 1981). At the same time David Stuart (1981) began an ongoing study of the cave's inscriptions. Since 1981 Naj Tunich has been under archaeological investigation by James Brady and Sandra Villagrán de

PLATE 1. Painting 1, Juxtlahuaca. Photograph by Eldon Leiter.

PLATE 2. Right-hand figure in Drawing 1, Actun Ch'on. Photograph by Matthias Strecker.

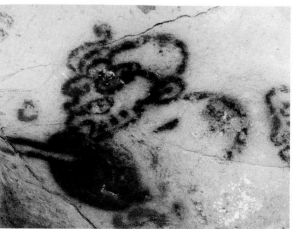

PLATE 3. Death demon with torch, Acum. Photograph by Matthias Strecker.

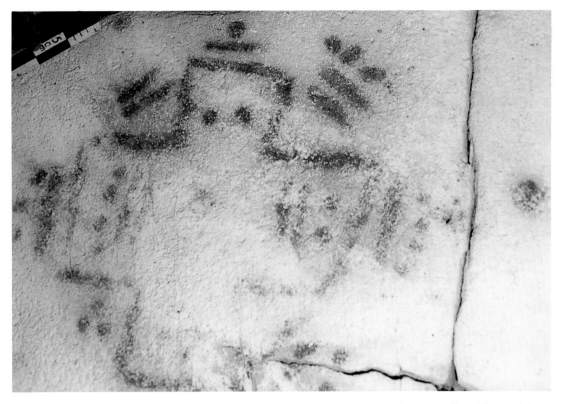

PLATE 4. "Kan cross" with bar and dot numerals, Tixkuytun. Photograph by Alfredo Barrera Rubio.

PLATE 5. Deer with forked blue line touching nose, Tixkuytun. Photograph by Alfredo Barrera Rubio.

PLATE 6. Lord of the Katun, Drawing 35, Dzibichen.

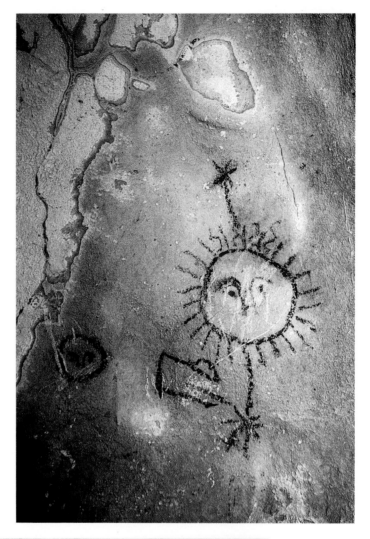

PLATE 7. Human figure, Yaleltsemen.
Photograph by Pierre Becquelin.

PLATE 8. Entrance hall as seen from the Balcony, Naj Tunich. Photograph by Chip and Jennifer Clark.

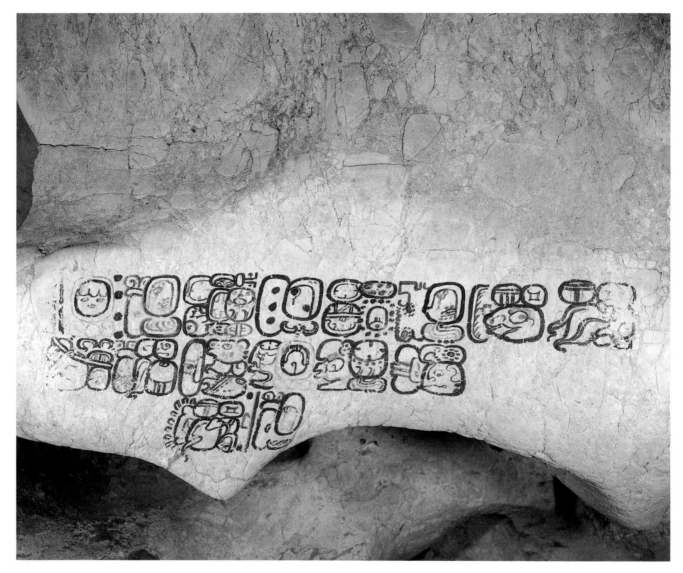

PLATE 9. Drawing 82, Naj Tunich. Photograph by Chip and Jennifer Clark.

PLATE 10. Drawing 68, Naj Tunich.
Photograph by Chip and Jennifer Clark.

PLATE 11. Drawing 51, Naj Tunich.
Photograph by Chip and Jennifer Clark.

PLATE 12. Drawing 18, Naj Tunich.
Photograph by Chip and Jennifer Clark.

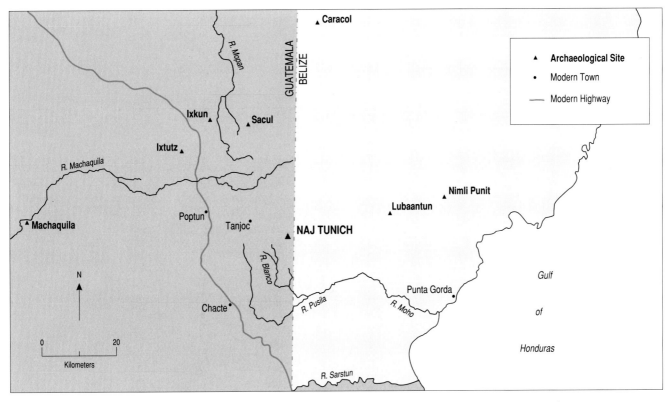

FIG. 5-1. Naj Tunich region.

Brady (Brady 1989), and I have been conducting a study of the cave's collection of paintings (A. Stone 1982; 1983b; 1985b; 1989c).

A Brief Tour through Naj Tunich

Naj Tunich is entered by way of a sinkhole that leads into an impressive entrance hall (fig. 5-2). Carpeted by hundreds of stalactites, the entrance hall ceiling rises about thirty meters above the cave floor (Plate 8). The floor is level and consists of clay deposited by ebbing floodwater during the cave's remote history. This floor is usually damp to wet, depending on the season, as groundwater seepage through the overburden eventually makes its way through this area. During the rainy season, springs flow through fractures in the wall opposite the entrance, providing a temporary source of water. A massive stalagmite dominates the entrance hall, blocking some of the available light. The light that does enter the cave

is reflected off foliage filling the sinkhole (except during the dry season), unfortunately lending a greenish cast to photographs of the entrance.

To enter the cave the visitor must negotiate a hill-size "breakdown" (a heap of rocks from a collapsed ceiling). This breakdown, like no other in a Maya cave, is fitted with stone walls forming irregular terraces that may have helped control access to the interior (fig. 5-3).

The top of the breakdown, an artificially leveled platform, has been dubbed "the Balcony." The most intensely utilized area in the cave (Brady and Stone 1986), the Balcony revealed the densest concentration of artifacts in addition to seven structures, ranging from simple pits to four-sided masonry enclosures that Brady (1989: Ch. 4) proposes are tombs (fig. 5-4; see *T* symbol in fig. 5-2). Artifacts include an important collection of Protoclassic ceramics that reflect the Balcony's peak period of utilization, though Early Classic and

Late Classic building activity was carried out on a smaller scale (Brady 1987; 1989: 397–398). The Maya's extensive use of the Balcony is not surprising, given that it is the most accommodating space in Naj Tunich, receiving some natural light and remaining absolutely dry year round. It also affords an impressive view of the entrance hall (Plate 8).

The tunnel system proper can be accessed only by descending the Balcony breakdown. This route leads through a bottleneck where authorities have installed an iron gate (see "gate" in fig. 5-2). The climb down is precipitous (a handline is provided part way down) and leads into a chamber at the base of a magnificent flowstone pool filled by a spring in the passage wall (fig. 5-5). When Naj Tunich was first discovered, this antechamber to the pool was littered with broken pottery. A precarious crawl on a ledge that skirts the pool leads to the spacious Main Passage,

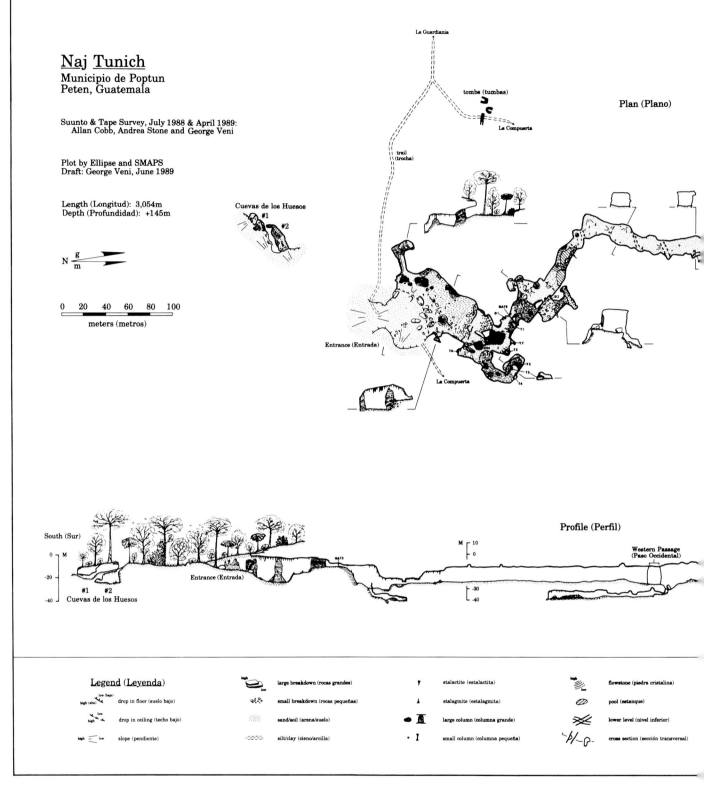

FIG. 5-2. Plan and profile map of Naj Tunich. Survey by Allan Cobb, Andrea Stone, and George Veni. Drafted by George Veni.

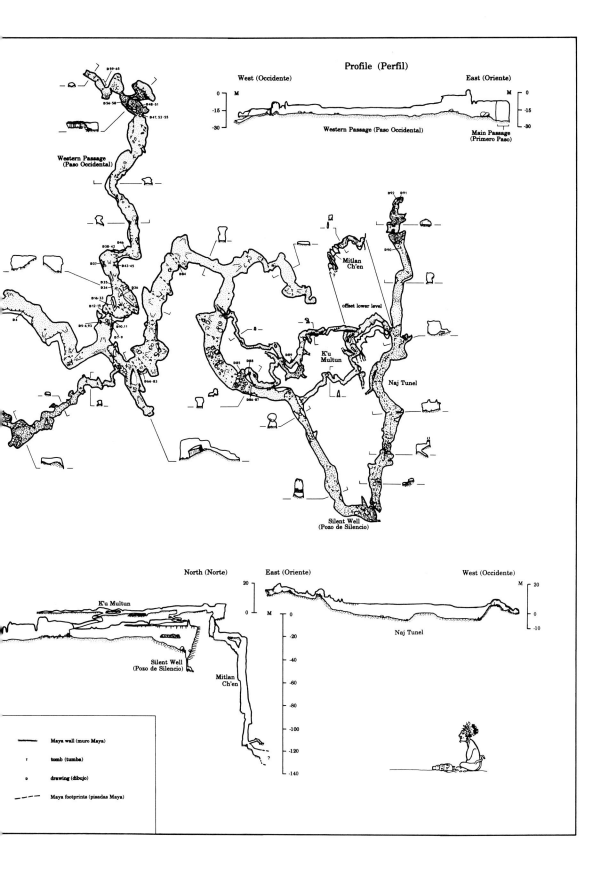

Profile (Perfil)

West (Occidente)

East (Oriente)

Western Passage (Paso Occidental)

Main Passage
(Primero Paso)

Western Passage
(Paso Occidental)

Mitlan
Ch'en

offset lower level

K'u
Multun

Naj Tunel

Silent Well
(Pozo de Silencio)

North (Norte)

East (Oriente)

West (Occidente)

K'u Multun

Naj Tunel

Silent Well
(Pozo de Silencio)

Mitlan
Ch'en

Maya wall (muro Maya)

tomb (tumba)

drawing (dibujo)

Maya footprints (pisadas Maya)

An Introduction to the Site and Its Art

which averages fifteen meters in width. The Main Passage continues north to the Silent Well. The beginning of the Main Passage is an easy trek over a rolling, solid packed dirt floor flanked by gently scalloped limestone walls (fig. 5-6). Large sections of limestone are covered by a rough, brown gypsum crust (fig. 5-7). It was in this kind of commodious setting that the Maya did most of their painting.

After about three hundred meters the Western Passage bifurcates from the Main Passage (fig. 5-9). The Western Passage is the most important area of painting at Naj Tunich. Toward the end is a section formed by calcite deposits. One decorated chamber here has been dubbed the Crystal Room (figs. 5-8, 5-9). Beyond the Western Passage junction the Main Passage twists and turns its way north. This section of the Main Passage, called the North Passage, is clogged with breakdown debris and consequently is more difficult to traverse. The North Passage terminates in a feature called the Silent Well, a sixteen-

FIG. 5-4. Structure 2, Naj Tunich. Photograph by Chip and Jennifer Clark.

Images from the Underworld

FIG. 5-5. Flowstone pool near the beginning of the Main Passage, Naj Tunich. Photograph by Chip and Jennifer Clark.

meter-deep fracture with mud and water at the bottom (fig. 5-9).

The North Passage is networked by an upper-level maze, called K'u Multun, which was thoroughly explored by the Maya in Classic times and, as we shall presently see, decorated with paintings. K'u Multun can be loosely translated as "Sacred Pile of Stones," named after a stone altar found there. The back of K'u Multun overlooks a deep pit that we call Mitlan Ch'en (Underworld Cave). This pit has been surveyed by George Veni and Allan Cobb up to a depth of 180 meters, making it one of the deepest vertical elevations in a cave in Central America (see profile on fig. 5-2). A rope descent down Mitlan Ch'en leads to a part of the cave called Naj Tunel (fig. 2-3). Naj Tunel lies at the level of the North Passage and is actually an extension of it, but the connection is blocked off at the Silent Well (fig. 5-9). Naj Tunel is the most

FIG. 5-6. Main Passage, Naj Tunich. Photograph by Chip and Jennifer Clark.

FIG. 5-7. Typical area in the Main Passage, Naj Tunich. Photograph by Chip and Jennifer Clark.

inaccessible part of Naj Tunich with archaeological materials. Cave painting is also found there.

Any description of Naj Tunich demands superlatives. The cave has commanding dimensions: the length is now calculated at three kilometers and will probably be extended with deeper surveys into Mitlan Ch'en. The quantity of man-made construction in the entrance is substantial, the artifact collection, one of the best ever found in a Maya cave. As though this were not enough, Naj Tunich contains what may well be the finest collection of aboriginal American cave art known (fig. 5-10; see also Chapter 8). In addition to many remarkable figurative paintings, the cave houses hieroglyphic inscriptions—about five hundred hieroglyphs in over forty texts. Among the most impressive paintings in the cave, the texts are an important addition to the corpus of Maya inscriptions.

Hieroglyphic dates indicate that the paintings were created in the period A.D. 692–771, from about Katun 13 to

FIG. 5-8. Crystal Room, Naj Tunich. Photograph by George Veni.

Images from the Underworld

Katun 17 in the Maya Long Count. This was a time when art flourished across the Maya Lowlands. Sites closest to Naj Tunich—Lubaantun, Nim Li Punit, and Pusilha in Belize and Ixkun, Ixtutz, and Sacul in Guatemala—were also active at this time. Indeed, epigraphic and archaeological evidence indicates that Naj Tunich was a major pilgrimage cave for southeastern Peten. The cave's inscriptions have Emblem Glyphs from the regional sites of Ixtutz, Ixkun, and Sacul; references to more distant sites like Caracol are also present. Furthermore, Brady (1989:413) notes that the quantity of construction on the Balcony, the massive terrace walls and structures, points toward large-scale utilization of the cave consonant with its proposed function as a major pilgrimage center. The analysis of the cave's ceramics by neutron activation, which is currently ongoing, will perhaps refine our understanding of Naj Tunich as a sacred cave attracting pilgrims from great distances.

Technological Overview of Naj Tunich Art

Though the fame of Naj Tunich rests on its paintings, other techniques of producing cave art—namely, petroglyphs, drawings, and handprints—are also found there. In the present study all of these technologically distinct images are cataloged under a single rubric, "drawing." Thus far, ninety-four such "drawing units" have been recorded at Naj Tunich. A photograph of each drawing unit appears in Chapter 8 and can be consulted by the reader when drawing numbers are mentioned in the following discussion.

Petroglyphs and Their Production

The petroglyphs of Naj Tunich pale in light of the paintings; yet several are distinguished as the only stylistically datable Late Classic petroglyphs reported from a cave in the Maya area. Eight

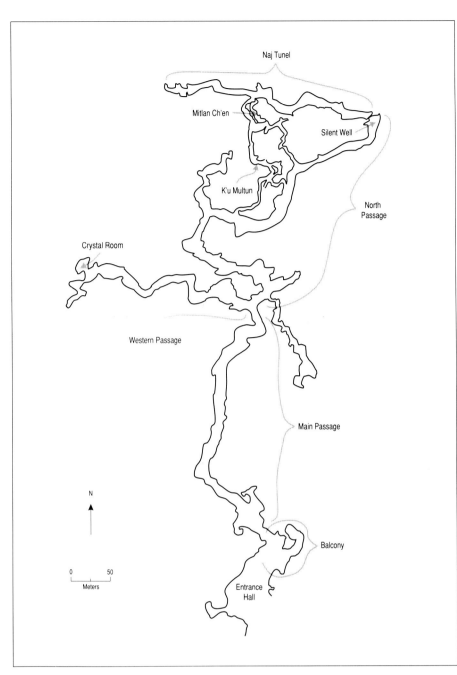

FIG. 5-9. Areas of Naj Tunich mentioned in the text.

petroglyphs, registered in five drawing units, have been discovered at Naj Tunich: Drawings 2, 53, 56, 57, 58, and 89. The undatable and unidentifiable Drawing 2, found just after the climb down the Balcony breakdown, consists of curved lines engraved on a darkly stained limestone wall (fig. 5-11). The light-colored lines are the result of scratching through the dark surface.

The other, far more interesting petroglyphs are lightly incised into precipitated calcite formations (generically called "flowstone"). Most are scratched into a single flowstone wall at the end of the Western Passage. The calcite crust, when scratched, produces a light line that is unfortunately difficult to see except in extreme raking light. Three of these petroglyphs are clearly Late Clas-

FIG. 5-10. Group of paintings, Naj Tunich. Photograph by Allan Cobb.

FIG. 5-11. Crude petroglyph, Drawing 2, Naj Tunich.

FIG. 5-12. Petroglyph of T584 "Ben," Drawing 58, Naj Tunich.

sic: Drawings 53, 57, and 58. Drawing 58 represents a hieroglyph corresponding to the day Ben in the Maya calendar (fig. 5-12). Drawing 57 is a long-billed bird (fig. 5-13). Drawing 53 is a beautiful profile face, typically Late Classic with an aquiline nose, almond eye, and a receding chin (fig. 5-14). Three more faces engraved nearby, in various stages of completion, seem to be imitations of this face.

One petroglyph is found in K'u Multun: Drawing 89 shows a series of lines scratched on a stalactite that seem to form a rudimentary face (fig. 5-15). A line of loops in charcoal frames the top of the petroglyph. Given the archaeological context of K'u Multun, this petroglyph may also be Late Classic.

Handprints and Their Production

A dozen or so positive handprints are found at Naj Tunich. Handprints are

FIG. 5-13. Petroglyph of a long-billed bird, Drawing 57, Naj Tunich.

Images from the Underworld

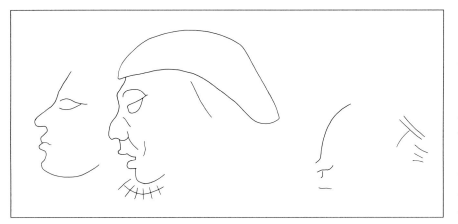

FIG. 5-14. Incised faces on calcite, Drawing 53, Naj Tunich.

FIG. 5-15. Incised lines making crude face, with charcoal loops above, Drawing 89, Naj Tunich.

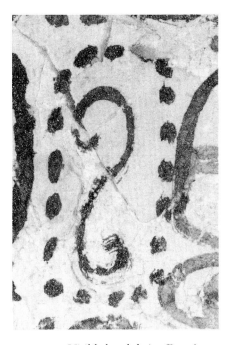

FIG. 5-16. Visible brush hairs, Drawing 34, Naj Tunich.

not as important here as they are in some Yucatecan caves, such as Loltun and Acum. The Naj Tunich handprints are registered in four drawing units: Drawings 1, 14, 86, and 93. Most are in isolated or obscure locations away from major paintings. The single handprint in Drawing 1, for example, is found in an alcove on the Balcony. Drawing 93, consisting of several imprints of a hand and forearm, is isolated at the edge of a large rock. Drawings 14 and 86 are more closely associated with figurative paintings, though Drawing 14, a group of three overlapping handprints, is found in a rather obscure location at ground level. Drawing 86, a group of about six handprints, rests at eye level at the edge of a wall. These latter handprints use a yellowish-brown mud similar to the composition of the cave floor. The other handprints utilize a dark brown coloring material that also resembles the floor sediments in their respective areas.

Paintings and Their Production

The paintings and drawings of Naj Tunich are the largest facet of the cave's collection of art. They comprise eighty-five of the ninety-four drawing units registered. From a technological standpoint the paintings are not uniform. Some made with sticks of charcoal really qualify as drawings. The greater

part of this collection, however, was painted with a brush and liquid paint. The use of a brush is evident in delicate variations in line width and direction, as well as in the fine details. Interestingly, the Naj Tunich painters rarely reveal the individual hairs of the brush. The ends of lines are usually blunt and the line itself a solid course of paint, indicating that the brush tip was kept en masse. Only rarely are individual brush hairs evident (fig. 5-16).

The composition of paint employed by the Naj Tunich calligraphers is not yet known, though visual inspection permits some observations.[2] Certainly, the same paint recipe was not employed throughout the cave, even after one accounts for paint density and wall surface, both of which can influence color. The most common type of paint is, in thick densities, close to an ink black (Plate 9). Some of the darkest paint occurs in Drawings 23, 34, 72, 82, and 83. Even in thin densities this paint looks black to brown. The paint has a dull matte finish, due in part to the gritty texture of the limestone. Other paintings with a yellowish-brown hue are found at the end of the Western Passage (Drawings 59–65); they employ a thin, delicate line and a dilute mixture of a warm-toned paint. Drawing 88 also uses a yellowish-brown paint. What seems likely is that the painters exploited handy clay resources to prepare the paint, as suggested by the fact that color variation in floor clays often corresponds to color variation of paints. The identification of binders used with the colorants still awaits laboratory testing.

The preservation and to some extent the aesthetic character of the paintings was shaped by the three surfaces on which the Maya painted: brecciated limestone, calcite, and gypsum. The principal painting surface is brecciated limestone—that is, crushed, recemented limestone. At Naj Tunich this cream-colored limestone is mottled with patches of pink and orange, forming a handsome foil for the dark calligraphy (Plate 10). The mosaic pattern of limestone inclusions also influenced where the Maya placed paintings. Unfortunately, the gritty surface of the brecciated limestone affords the paint a tenuous grip on the wall (see Appendix A).

There are eleven paintings on calcite (Drawings 47, 48, 49, 50, 51, 52, 54, 89, 90, 91, and 92), their distribution corresponding to the distribution of flowstone in the cave: the Crystal Room and calcified areas in K'u Multun and Naj Tunel. The rough calcite provided a surface with better tooth than the slicker limestone, although it did not permit the fluid line and detail of the latter (Plate 11). However, the preservation of paint on calcite is superior to the limestone. Gypsum was used as a painting surface on only two occasions: in Drawings 3 and 88. As the cave's gypsum deposits are spalling off the wall, gypsum provided the most unstable painting surface, well illustrated by the fragmentary Drawing 3.

The paintings of Naj Tunich have suffered irreparable damage, some of which predates the discovery of the cave. One curious type of defacement, which appears to be prehispanic, consists of "claw marks." The paintings are marred by groups of five parallel lines that tend to splay out at the end as an animal claw would if dragged over a hard surface. The "claw marks" have an average width of one to two centimeters, though they vary greatly in length. The longest one observed measures eighteen centimeters, streaked across the beautiful hieroglyphic text of Drawing 82 (fig. 5-17). These marks do not occur just on paintings, though they are more obvious here; some unpainted walls are covered with dozens of these marks. The marks seem to lie at eye level and above and are found in widely separated areas of the cave, throughout most of the Western Passage and into the North Passage.

Given these facts, it seemed logical to me at the outset that the marks were the work of bats. What other creature could roam the length of the cave and reach high spots on the wall? At least, these were my original thoughts. Bat experts soon convinced me that the marks were not made by bats, which apparently do not drag their claws across the wall, even when hunting insects.[3] It also seems unlikely that the marks are the result of a lost animal clawing the wall, as there is too much variability in the height, direction, and location of the marks for this to seem even a possibility. Once animals are eliminated, the only reasonable conclusion is that the marks are the result of human defacement of the paintings, and this is especially obvious when they form regular patterns, such as the cross-hatched scratches on the rubber ball depicted in Drawing 21 (fig. 5-18). That some person or persons took a tiny five-pronged instrument or perhaps a real animal paw and wandered through the cave on a clawing rampage is evidenced by hundreds of "claw marks" on the walls of Naj Tunich, though it is difficult to imagine why anyone would expend such an effort.

Though the "claw marks" may seem like a wanton act of vandalism (though a ritual motivation cannot be ruled out), the worst damage to the paintings postdates the cave's modern discovery. In late 1980 and early 1981 tourists and other visitors smeared paintings, whether inadvertently or intentionally, by merely touching them, testimony to the extreme fragility of Naj Tunich wall art. The gouged arm of the ballplayer in Drawing 21, however, is evidence of deliberate defacement. In March of 1981 looters attempted to remove one of the paintings on a calcite column in the Crystal Room (Plate 11). This early

FIG. 5-17. "Claw" marks on Drawing 82, Naj Tunich.

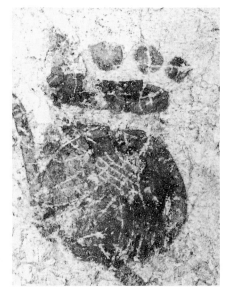

FIG. 5-18. Crosshatched scratches on Drawing 21, Naj Tunich.

phase of damage was addressed by George Stuart (1981) in the *National Geographic* article. Guards placed at the site in 1981 helped curb the initial rash of vandalism, though the smearing of paintings continued (e.g., fig. 5-19; see also Drawing 12).

In late July or early August of 1989, much to the dismay of the archaeological community, an incident of reckless

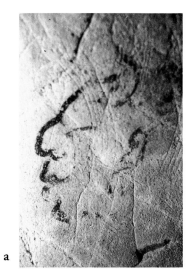
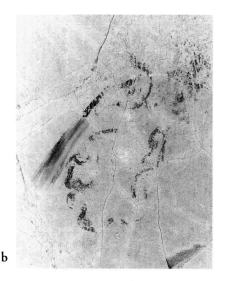

a   b

FIG. 5-19. Drawing 86: *a,* before 1986 (note "claw" marks), photograph by James Brady; *b,* in 1988, photograph by Chip and Jennifer Clark.

FIG. 5-20. Aftermath of 1989 vandalism, detail of Drawing 82. Photograph by Allan Cobb.

destruction, unprecedented, perhaps, in the annals of Maya archaeology, occurred at Naj Tunich. Some unknown person or persons broke through the protective gate, apparently with the premeditated intention of ruining the paintings, and they accomplished their heinous goal all too well. The damage, assessed by James and Sandra Brady (1989; Brady 1990; 1991a), proved to

be extensive: twenty-three paintings were virtually completely destroyed (for identification of damaged paintings, see catalog entries in Chapter 8). The perpetrators accomplished much of the destruction by running their fingers through the damp paint, easily obliterating the fragile surface (fig. 5-20). They also threw a projectile at one painting, dislodging a chunk of the wall (Drawing 34), and rubbed mud on one of the paintings on calcite, which resisted smearing (Drawing 52). Selected for destruction were some of the finest paintings at Naj Tunich. The motivation for the attack and the identity of the perpetrators remains a mystery; however, the immensity of the loss is all too clear. Unlike a shattered sculpture or torn canvas, the damage to the Naj Tunich paintings is wholly irreparable; these rare survivals of aboriginal American cave art are lost forever.

Style

The art of Naj Tunich did not come into being through the efforts of one individual or to commemorate a related series of events, as did the murals of Bonampak, another example of Classic Maya wall painting. Like graffiti, these cave paintings are a disparate collection of images sharing a single wall support. They were executed by many artists working at different times. That different painters contributed to their production is evident in stylistic variation which, on the other hand, does not reflect major chronological breaks; that is, from a broad chronological perspective the paintings are relatively homogeneous. Hieroglyphic dates suggest that they were produced over a period of about eighty years, though there remain serious problems with calculating absolute dates for the texts (see Chapter 7). Based on style alone, a shorter timespan would be equally feasible.

The Naj Tunich artists were clearly professional painters; they may have

Artist 1: Drawings 21, 22, and 23

The likelihood that these three paintings are by the same artist is supported by idiosyncracies of facial features. In Drawings 21 and 22, the facial contours are virtually identical, and a wavy line appears above the eye (fig. 5-22a and b). In addition, the upper lid is formed by a strongly curved line. The proportions and slope of the neck are identical in both figures. Scale, line quality, and paint density are also so similar that both figures may have been painted at the same time. Two head variants in Drawing 23 (at B3 and C4) permit comparison with the faces in Drawings 21 and 22. The upper eyelid has the same wavy contour, and the head form at C4 has the additional wavy line above the eye (fig. 5-22c).

Artist 2: Drawings 28, 30, and 66

An unmistakable style group is represented by these three inscriptions. All of the glyphs found in the short text, Drawing 30, occur in the other two texts, and they show many points of comparison (cf. Drawing 30 with Drawing 28, A12–A17, and Drawing 66, K1–N1).

Similarities can be seen in the form of the "sky" glyph, T561, where the vertical lines in the "wing" touch the bottom of the cartouche (fig. 5-23a and c). T23 phonetic complementation to T561 "sky" has the same contour in all three texts and a large central dot in Drawings 28 and 66 (fig. 5-23c and d). The **bakab** collocation in Drawing 28 (at A10 and B7) and Drawing 66 (at E1 and I1) are virtually identical.

Though painted by the same artist, these three texts are not all found within a circumscribed area. While Drawing 30 is around the corner from Drawing 28, separated only by Drawing 29 (figs. 5-29, 5-37), Drawing 66 is located in an entirely different area of the cave, in the North Passage Group

FIG. 5-22. Comparison of heads in Artist 1 group, Naj Tunich: *a,* Drawing 21; *b,* Drawing 22; *c,* Drawing 23, C4.

FIG. 5-23. Comparison of sky glyphs in Artist 2 group, Naj Tunich: *a,* Drawing 30, A2; *b,* Drawing 28, A6; *c,* Drawing 66, E2.

(fig. 5-33). Drawings 28 and 66 have Calendar Round dates that are only 290 days apart.

Artist 3: Drawings 37 and 52

Drawings 37 and 52 appear to have been painted by the same individual. The opening Calendar Round dates and the use of the "Glyph D" verb link the two inscriptions. A glyph-by-glyph comparison of the calendrical statements shows them to be virtually identical. In addition, the opening Calendar Round dates are only three days apart. Drawing 52 is about 130 meters farther down the Western Passage than Drawing 37.

Artist 4: Drawings 34 and 65

Drawings 34 and 65 were probably painted by the same hand, as suggested by the use of parallel glyphic phrases and their unique details (fig. 5-24). The dates in both texts are also of a type in which the *haab* coefficient is off by a factor of one from the standard system of dates. Drawing 65 is about 160 meters farther down the Western Passage from Drawing 34.

Artist 5: Drawings 11, 67, and 87

These figurative paintings show many comparable elements. The faces all have a shallow jaw, thin, projecting lips, and a stiff, blunt nose (fig. 5-25). The back contour of the left-hand figure in Drawings 67 and 87 is straight and curves at a near right angle into the buttocks and leg line. The contours of the figure in Drawing 11 resemble the right-hand figure in Drawing 87. These three paintings are found in widely separated areas of the cave.

Artist 6: Drawings 18, 72, and 83

Drawings 72 and 83 are located in the same painting group in the North Passage. Each represents a seated figure, and their faces are quite similar, particularly the treatment of the lips and

a   b

FIG. 5-24. Comparison of parallel glyphic phrases in Artist 4 group, Naj Tunich: *a,* Drawing 34, B1–B3; *b,* Drawing 65, C2–C4.

chin (fig. 5-26b and c). The upper lip, for instance, is formed by the intersection of two nearly perpendicular lines. The angles and proportions of the lower lip and chin are also similar on both figures, as is the contour of the neck, shoulder, back, and thigh.

An argument can be made for including Drawing 18 in this group. The right-hand figure in Drawing 18 has a sweeping eye form quite close to that of Drawing 72 (fig. 26a and b). The strong lines of the nose and forehead are also comparable, though the mouth is different. Note, too, that both Drawing 83 and the right-hand figure in Drawing 18 have a line extending from the bridge of the nose to the crown of the head.

Artist 7: Drawings 68, 69, 70, and 76, possibly 71 and 19

Drawings 68, 69, and 70 can be compared on the basis of their texts. In Drawing 68 at A5 and Drawing 69 at A4 the configuration of the *kab* glyph,

T526, is identical, from the eccentric shape of the cartouche to internal details. Both texts also have nearly identical bat head variants (Drawing 68, A2; Drawing 69, A1). At B5 in Drawing 70 is a "sky" glyph (T561:23), which favorably compares with the "sky" collocation in Drawing 68, A1.

Since Drawing 68 includes figures, other figurative paintings can be linked to the texts. Drawing 76 compares favorably to the right-hand figure in Drawing 68. In both, the lines of the buttocks can be seen through the diaphanous loincloth. Both figures also have a gentle curve to the chest and abdomen that is divided into two separate sections. Though clearly not as well crafted, it seems possible that Drawing 71 is linked to this group. Most important is the flattening of the back of the thigh, also found in Drawing 76.

Furthermore, there are many interesting correspondences in costume between the work of Artist 6 and Artist 7. Three figures wear a necklace consisting

Images from the Underworld

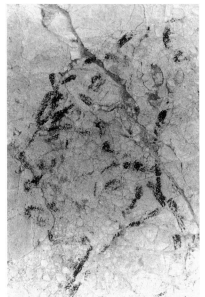

a

b

c

FIG. 5-25. Comparison of heads in Artist 5 group, Naj Tunich: *a,* Drawing 11; *b,* Drawing 87; *c,* Drawing 67.

of a cord tied at the nape of the neck, indicated by one or two loops. In Drawings 72 and 76 a large bead hangs from the cord. Both figures also wear similar cloth hats tied by a band knotted at the front (fig. 5-27). This type of cap is also like the one worn by the right-hand figure in Drawing 18. Hence, it is possible that Artist 6 and Artist 7 are the same individual. At the least they are two painters working in a closely related style. This may explain why Drawing 19, a hieroglyphic text situated near Drawing 18, seems related to both groups of paintings. One head variant of Drawing 19 (B2) uses a crisp line characterizing figures in the Artist 6 group. Drawing 19 is also comparable to the inscriptions in the Artist 7 group. For example, the "sky" glyph at B2 in Drawing 19 is similar to the one at B5 in Drawing 70.

Artist 8: Drawings 27, 39, and 40

Unfortunately, Drawing 39 is in poor condition, but owing to its proximity to

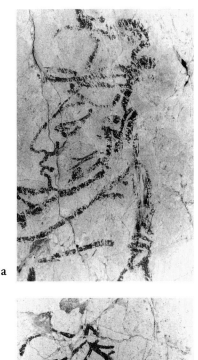

a

c

b

FIG. 5-26. Comparison of heads in Artist 6 group, Naj Tunich: *a,* Drawing 18; *b,* Drawing 72; *c,* Drawing 83.

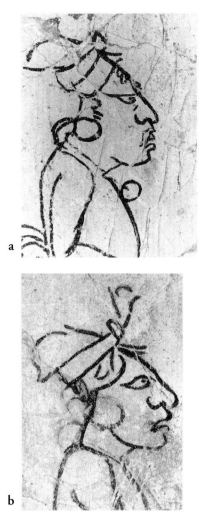

a

b

FIG. 5-27. Comparison of heads in Artist 7 group, Naj Tunich: *a,* Drawing 72; *b,* Drawing 76.

Drawing 40 (they are painted one above the other in the same limestone clast) and the stiff treatment of figures, I suspect that they were painted by the same hand. Drawing 27, like Drawing 40, shows a procession of figures playing musical instruments. They share many specific traits: short forehead, bulbous nose, and narrow eyes. Moreover, in both paintings cloth caps are worn particularly low on the forehead.

Artist 9: Drawings 60, 61, 62, and 63

Drawings 60, 61, 62, and 63 are tiny figures or faces painted with a fine, fluid line. In Drawings 61 and 63 the torsos of the figures are shown frontally, while the lower part of the body is in profile; the angle of the shoulders is virtually identical. The small heads in Drawings 60 and 62 can be linked with this group by the bump on the bridge of the nose. Thus Artist 9 created four images within a circumscribed area.

Artist 10: Drawings 25 and 49

Certain idiosyncracies in these two texts suggest that Drawings 25 and 49 were painted by the same hand: for instance, the grapheme T229 is rendered in nearly identical fashion (fig. 5-28). In Drawing 49 the cartouche for T502 (at A1b) has a peak in the left lower corner, also seen in Drawing 25 (e.g., at A1, A2b, B1, B4, and B8). Also comparable is the configuration of T17 (Drawing 25 at B1 and Drawing 49 at B2) and the "perforated **lu**" (Drawing 25 at B3 and Drawing 49 at A4). The latter forms part of the Sacul Emblem Glyph, suggesting that the same artist from Sacul painted both texts.

As this discussion demonstrates, an individual painter's work could appear in widely separated areas of the cave. One can also get some sense of artistic temperament. Among the best and boldest painters at Naj Tunich are Artist 6 and Artist 7 who, as noted earlier, may be the same individual. Their work is freely painted with a graceful, energetic line. These artists chose to paint most often in the middle of walls, and their work appears in the two most important painting groups. The work of Artist 1, on the other hand, is more static and serene, the quality of line heavier and blunter. Though the scale is small, Artist 1's work conveys a sense of timeless monumentality. It is confined to a single depression in the cave wall.

Other painters are remarkable for their bravado. Artist 5 chose some of the most unusual locations for his work.

For example, Drawing 11, the largest figure at Naj Tunich, rests over three meters above the cave floor in an alcove with a shallow, steep ledge (fig. 5-39). I know from personal experience how precarious it is to stay perched on the ledge; while sketching the figure, I slipped off and, with great discomfort, hit the ground. Drawing 87, a work of the same artist, is located deep in the North Passage (fig. 5-9). Although other innovative artists worked at Naj Tunich, only a single painting can be attributed to them, so they have not been included in this discussion of artists' hands. The creator of Drawing 20, for example, must be credited for his conceptual daring.

We can assume rather safely that the Naj Tunich artists were all male. To support this statement, I would cite the fact that all known illustrations of painters and scribes in Maya art are male, and Maya lore concerning artisan deities agrees with this (Coe 1977). Moreover, Maya inscriptions that name scribes and artists (Stuart 1987) mention male painters exclusively. Furthermore, there are prohibitions against women entering sacred caves among certain Maya populations, and this may have also been the case at Naj Tunich.

These male cave artists were probably part of larger parties of pilgrims, which may have included shamans, nobles, and other attendants. We can only speculate how certain artists were chosen to accompany these cave expeditions, but, no doubt, they were artists of reputation, as the paintings themselves attest. Some artists may have been the presiding shaman or a noble visitor to the cave. Stuart (1987:7), for instance, has proposed that the nominal phrase comprising Drawing 30, also seen in Drawings 28 and 66, identifies a Naj Tunich scribe (Artist 2). Hence, we know the name of one Naj Tunich painter and also have an associated Emblem Glyph, though the site to which

it refers has not yet been identified. Another scribe is mentioned in Drawing 88.

Calendar Round dates in different texts painted by the same hand show certain consistencies. They are always of the same type in terms of which "alignment set" they follow, as this varies at Naj Tunich (see Chapter 7, Table 2). For example, Artist 2 and Artist 3 use the Type III set (standard system) for each of the two inscriptions they painted, while Artist 4's two inscriptions employ the Type II set. In addition, the dates for each artist are sequential in the date list, even though the texts are in widely separated areas of the cave (see Chapter 7, Table 3). Those for Artist 2 are 181 days apart and for Artist 3, 3 days apart. Only the dates of Artist 4 are more than one *tun* apart; they span the period 5.3.2, or 2,402 days. In any case, it is certain that painters returned to Naj Tunich on more than one occasion.

Spatial and Topographic Considerations
Painting Groups
Most paintings at Naj Tunich cluster in intermittent groups within the first one hundred meters of the Western Passage and then, after a long break, at the end of the passage (fig. 5-29). The first group occupies both sides of a narrow corridor (fig. 5-30). There is no evidence that any two paintings in this group are the work of the same artist. The corridor leads directly into a room where the far wall (turning sharply at Drawing 28) displays the greatest concentration of paintings found anywhere in the cave (fig. 5-31). One artist is responsible for several paintings in this group, such as Drawings 21, 22, and 23 (Artist 1) and Drawings 28 and 30 (Artist 2). Another painting group in the Western Passage is found in the Crystal Room, a calcified chamber where four paintings appear on col-

umns (fig. 5-32). Outside the Western Passage, the only other important painting group occurs at the beginning of the North Passage, henceforth called the North Passage Group (fig. 5-33).

Isolated paintings also occur at Naj Tunich (fig. 5-9): in the Main Passage before reaching the bifurcation (Drawings 2–4), in the Western Passage (Drawings 34, 35, and 36) and the North Passage (Drawings 84–87), and in K'u Multun and Naj Tunel (Drawings 88–92). In addition, the Balcony has a single hieroglyphic text painted on a column (Drawing 94). Most isolated paintings are hieroglyphic texts. Only one major figurative painting, Drawing 87, occurs outside of a group context.

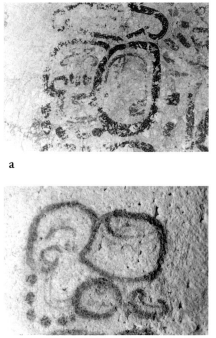

a

b

FIG. 5-28. Comparison of glyphs in Artist 10 group, Naj Tunich: *a*, Drawing 25, A8; *b*, Drawing 49, A1.

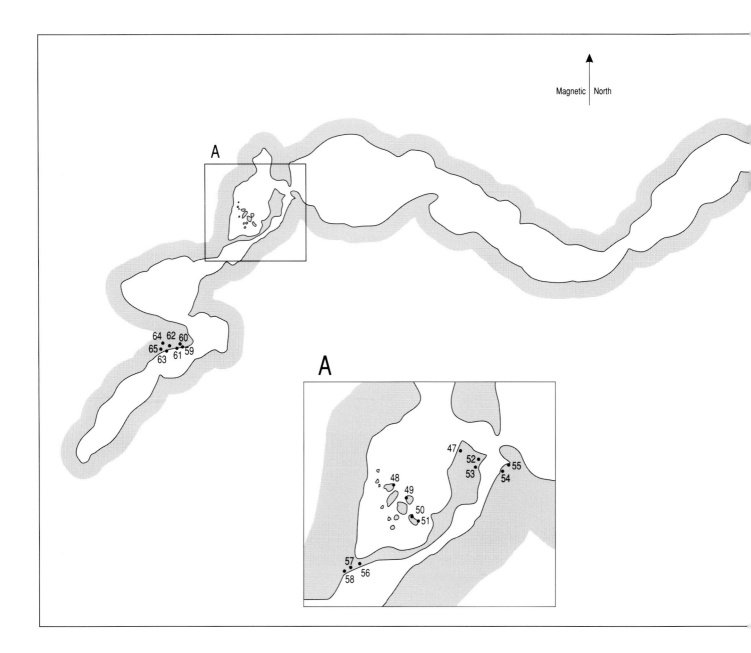

Paintings Composed around Natural Cave Features

Cave artists commonly exploit textures, colors, contours, and protrusions naturally occurring on any cave wall. Paleolithic painters, for instance, made liberal use of wall bulges to impart greater three-dimensionality to painted animals (e.g., Ucko and Rosenfeld 1967: figs. 4, 13; Leroi-Gourhan 1982: 10–11); they also sought out convex and concave walls and painted them with specific classes of animals (Bahn and Vertut 1988: 176). In terms of the creative process, the cave affords conditions that are more easily exploited than changed, and the organic shapes seen in the walls, like patterns formed by clouds, stimulate visual thinking. At Naj Tunich as well, wall fractures, crags, textures, and colors were embraced by the Maya artist, who was keenly attuned to the aesthetic possibilities of his physical environment and who integrated images with cave topography in various ways.

Using smooth limestone clasts as image boundaries. Brecciated limestone at Naj Tunich is inset with smooth clasts that painters utilized as frames. The most striking example of this is Drawings 39 and 40 (fig. 5-34). A natural medial ridge separates the two scenes composed within a single limestone block. Sometimes the boundaries of these clasts form the contours of an image, as in Drawing 55, where the outline of a painted face coincides with the boundaries of a circular chunk of calcite.

Compositions echoing rock forms or fractures. Images at Naj Tunich sometimes echo the shape of their rock sup-

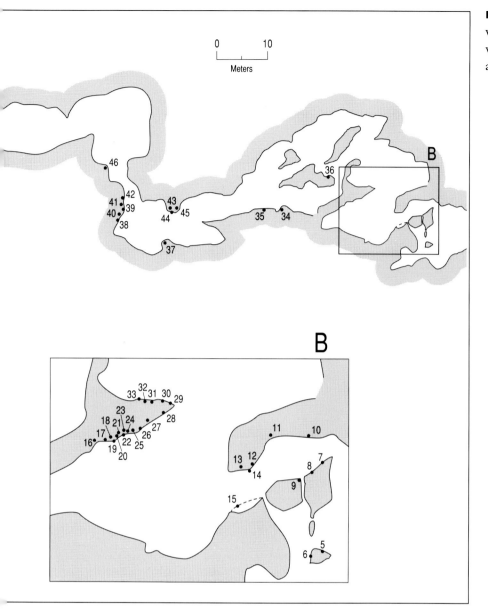

FIG. 5-29. Plan of the Western Passage with painting locations, Naj Tunich. Surveyed by Mark Johnson, Andrea Stone, and Elizabeth Williamson.

port. For example, Drawing 82 complements the shape of an overhang by dropping two glyphs into a third row (fig. 5-35). The size of the glyphs was also expanded to fill the natural frame; these glyphs, measuring eleven centimeters in height, are the largest in the cave.

The composition of Drawing 5 also echoes the frame created by its rock support. The painting depicts a stepped structure that forms a triangular composition and fits perfectly into the triangular profile of the rock (fig. 5-36). In another case, Drawings 28 and 29 are positioned at one edge of a sharp bend in the wall (fig. 5-37). The vertical attenuation of the glyph columns, not seen in other long Naj Tunich texts, resonates, deliberately in my estimation, with the edge of the wall. Finally, one figure was composed within the boundaries of a wall fracture: Drawing 22, a small figure seated in front of a shell, fits perfectly into the frame created by linear fissures in the wall.

FIG. 5-30. Painted corridor, Drawings 7–14, Naj Tunich: *a,* south wall; *b,* north wall.

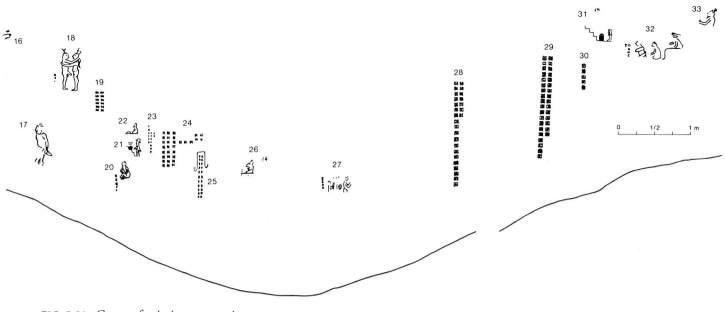

FIG. 5-31. Group of paintings on curving wall, Drawings 16–33, Naj Tunich. Wall bends at break.

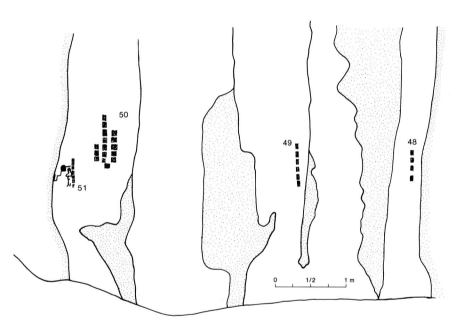

FIG. 5-32. Painted columns in the Crystal Room, Naj Tunich.

Using wall depressions or alcoves as image boundaries. Wall depressions, which form smooth, concave pockets of space, were used as painting surfaces at Naj Tunich. Paintings in one group are situated in a series of these pockets (fig. 5-38). One Naj Tunich painting, Drawing 11, sits squarely in an alcove well above the cave floor (fig. 5-39).

Paintings on speleothems. Precipitated calcite offered interesting shapes and

textures that attracted Maya painters, and they selected unusual speleothems as painting supports, such as the columns in the Crystal Room, as mentioned earlier.

One of the most unusual paintings in the cave, Drawing 90, is painted at the pinnacle of a stalagmite 2.4 meters high in the remote Naj Tunel (fig. 5-40). Drawing 90 may be the most inaccessible hieroglyphic text ever created by

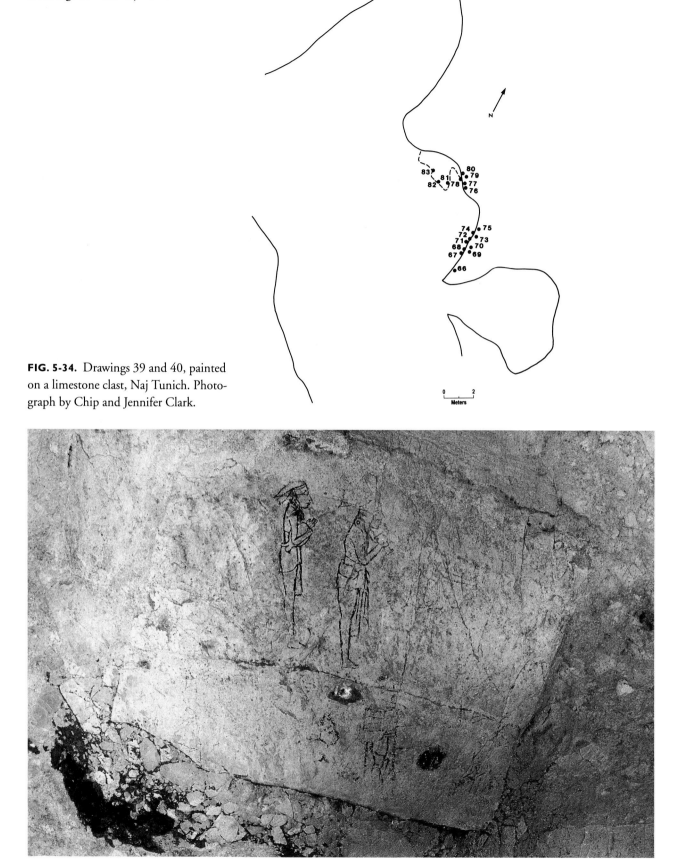

FIG. 5-33. Plan of North Passage Group, Drawings 66–83, Naj Tunich.

FIG. 5-34. Drawings 39 and 40, painted on a limestone clast, Naj Tunich. Photograph by Chip and Jennifer Clark.

Images from the Underworld

FIG. 5-35. Composition and spatial context of Drawing 82, Naj Tunich.

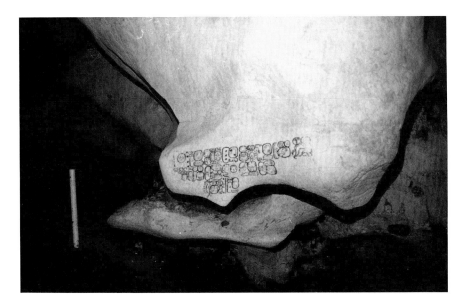

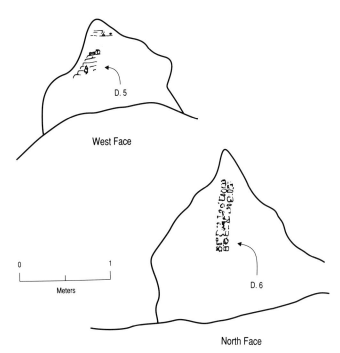

West Face

0   1
Meters

North Face

FIG. 5-36. Composition and spatial context of Drawing 5, Naj Tunich.

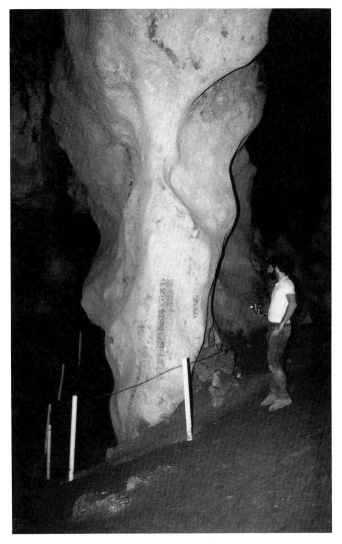

FIG. 5-37. Long texts following narrow wall edge, Drawings 28 and 29, Naj Tunich.

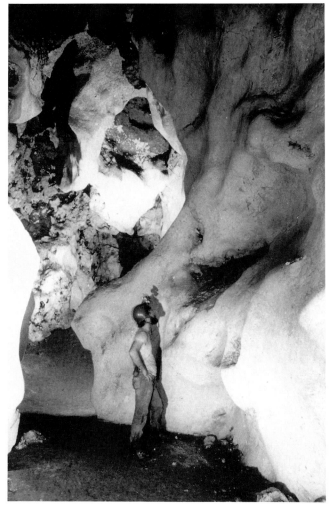

FIG. 5-38. *Upper left:* Paintings in pockets of wall space, Drawings 17, 18, and 19, Naj Tunich.

FIG. 5-39. *Upper right:* Niche with Drawing 11, Naj Tunich. Photograph by Chip and Jennifer Clark.

FIG. 5-40. Painted text on stalagmite in Naj Tunel, Naj Tunich.

Images from the Underworld

the ancient Maya. The painting consists of two hieroglyphs that may actually refer to the position or shape of the stalagmite (fig. 7-34). Standing almost like a signpost, the stalagmite lies at the base of a slope leading to a beautiful calcified chamber (fig. 5-41). Artifacts found in the chamber consist of a stone box made of stalactite fragments and a gadrooned jar (Brady et al. 1992:78, fig. 3). The chamber leads to a narrower passage where two drawings (Drawings 91 and 92) each incorporate stalactites with a schematic face.

Spatial-Topographical Relationships

The Naj Tunich artists chose aesthetically pleasing limestone and calcite concretions as painting surfaces. They also painted in front of areas with level floors, which not only made their job easier but also provided a place for people to congregate. It is not difficult to imagine groups of people standing in front of some painted walls (fig. 5-42). The Maya also seem to have preferred painting in areas that felt intimate and enclosed, much like a room.

The distribution of hieroglyphic inscriptions suggests other motivated choices for the selection of painting areas. Texts often occur at thresholds or sharp bends in the wall—that is, in key transitional spaces. For example, Drawing 52 is located on the right wall of an entryway that leads to the end of the Western Passage (fig. 5-29). This entrance clearly marks a transitional zone between a spacious limestone passage and a more constricted area of flowstone. Likewise, Drawing 88 is strategically located at an entryway into the K'u Multun maze passage (fig. 5-2). This area is also transitional between the lower North Passage and the upper-level maze. Another threshold marker is Drawing 84, a deteriorated inscription accompanied by a jovial, though now badly smeared face. The text is found on the right wall of a spectacular natural

FIG. 5-41. Stalagmite (in shadow at person's left) standing as a gateway to an upper-level room, Naj Tunel, Naj Tunich. Photograph by George Veni.

arch that gives the impression of an enormous gateway (fig. 5-43).

Edges of walls that mark boundaries are usually occupied by an inscription at Naj Tunich. Drawings 28, 29, and 30 mark such a sharp bend in the wall (fig. 5-37). Hieroglyphic texts also seem to bracket the beginning and ending of

painting groups. For example, the area bounding the North Passage Group has an inscription at both sides (fig. 5-42). The last painting in the Western Passage is the longest inscription at Naj Tunich (Drawing 65). In fact, the most extensive texts in the cave are these boundary-marking paintings. I would interpret this pattern in terms of the ritual utilization of the cave; that is, inscriptions attest the visits of pilgrims at transitional or dramatic geological features, where they would be most obvious to the passerby. These are exactly the kinds of places where handprints might be expected; but at Naj Tunich the preferred mode of recording such personal testimonials was in the form of texts.

Archaeological Associations

With few exceptions, which will be noted below, the Naj Tunich paintings had no artifactual associations. According to Brady (1989:80), the entire western branch of the cave (Operation I), where the vast majority of the paintings are located, was virtually devoid of artifacts. This fact is important in trying to reconstruct activities that may have been associated with paintings.

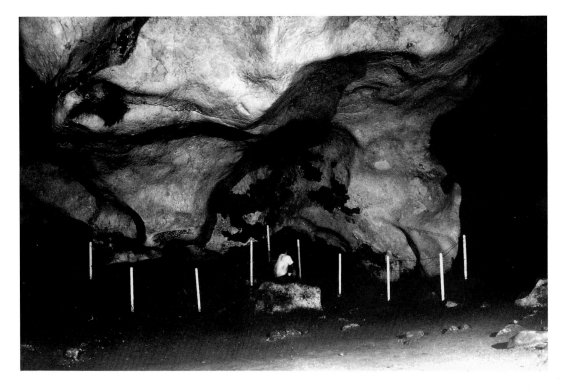

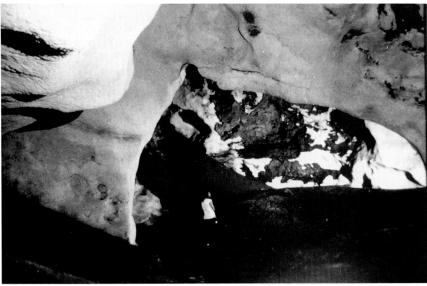

FIG. 5-42. Flat area in front of Drawings 66–83, Naj Tunich. Photograph by Allan Cobb.

FIG. 5-43. Natural arch, Naj Tunich. Drawing 84 is on right wall.

Images from the Underworld

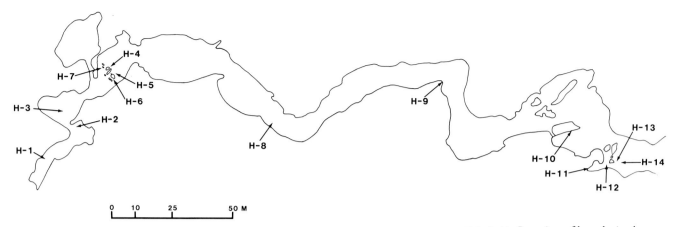

FIG. 5-44. Location of hearths in the Western Passage, Naj Tunich.

Artifacts lying at the base of walls beneath paintings in the Western Passage were found only at the beginning, where the Western Passage intersects the Main Passage. They consist mainly of pottery sherds that might have been deposited there after their use in another part of the cave (ibid.: 82); hence their pertinence to the paintings is questionable.[4] Apart from this, only one other ceramic lot was found in the Western Passage: Lot 3, Operation I, found against a side wall in the middle of the Western Passage, consists of forty-one body sherds from several utilitarian vessels (ibid.: 81). It appears that the breakage or deposition of pottery, evidence of which is abundant in the front and rear of the cave, was not part of the ritual activity associated with the Western Passage.

Hearths and Paintings

Though ceramic associations are virtually nil, paintings occur near hearths and smaller accumulations of charcoal. It was therefore deemed useful to survey the distribution of hearths in the Western Passage (fig. 5-44). However, no hard evidence exists for contemporaneity between hearths and paintings, for the charcoal was not radiometrically assayed; but with the likelihood of contamination, this might not have proven useful.

Large hearths occur directly beneath paintings in only one area, the Crystal Room (H-4–H-7), where calcite columns are ringed by a dense layer of charcoal. While hearth activity was extensive in the Crystal Room and seems to have extended over a period of time, no pottery was found. Two hieroglyphic texts, Drawings 48 and 49, are found on columns with a thick layer of charcoal lying at the base. The other two paintings in the Crystal Room, Drawings 50 and 51, which are actually more elaborate, are not associated with charcoal. However, they are painted on a column close to a side wall where the floor slopes sharply, an awkward area even for standing and certainly not suited for any kind of activity.

Hearths in the Western Passage cluster at the beginning (H-11–H-14) and end (H-1–H-7) of the passage, thereby bracketing all of its three hundred meters. Only two areas of burning were noted in the central section. One of these, H-9, is a small pile of charcoal set in a pocket-sized wall depression. It recalls a type of ceremonial burning that I observed in the largest of the artificial caves of Utatlan, Guatemala (Brady 1991b), where similar depressions excavated in the soft ash contain small piles of charcoal, the remains of burning copal. These small niches served as makeshift personal altars and suggest some-

thing like a station in a ritual circuit. The other hearth in the central section of the Western Passage, H-8, abuts a vertical stone in the middle of the passage.

In the Western Passage only one of the paintings on limestone, Drawing 26, has what might be considered a pile of charcoal at its base. However, the pile is small, and the adjacent wall is free of smoke stain. Charcoal was also found on the floor beneath paintings in the North Passage Group, associated with Drawings 68, 80, and 82. In the case of Drawings 80 and 82, the charcoal was pushed well under an overhang. Paintings at the end of the North Passage, Drawings 86 and 87, also have small piles of charcoal at the base of the wall.

The distribution of hearths in the Western Passage shows a concentration of hearth activity at the beginning and at the end. This is also the pattern for the cave as a whole, which has the greatest number of hearths at the beginning, on the Balcony, and at the end of the North Passage (Brady 1989). Furthermore, the beginning of the Western Passage, where hearths are concentrated, might be seen as marking the bifurcation of two branches of the cave.

This spatial distribution of hearths recalls patterns of hearth activity documented among the Highland Maya.

Based on observed patterns of Quiche ritual, Duncan Earle (personal communication, 1986) suggests that worshippers marking stations of a ritual circuit through a cave would probably stop and burn incense at the beginning and end of the passage as well as at passage junctions. Tedlock (1983:350) describes a similar pattern in Quiche pilgrimages to the main cave shrine of Utatlan: "The shamans penetrate the tunnel, which extends into the center of the ruins, only after having burnt copal in the entrance and asking permission from Mundo, the god of the earth, to enter. Later in agreement with the *chuchkajaw* [daykeeper] of the nearby town which initiated the pilgrimage, one enters until the bifurcation of the tunnel is reached, where copal and candles are burnt, again asking permission to enter" (my translation).

The distribution of hearths in the Western Passage of Naj Tunich and throughout the cave as a whole has striking parallels with the Quiche pattern. Evidence of burning is greatest at the beginning and terminus of the cave itself or any section thereof. The lack of artifacts in the Western Passage indicates that hearth activity there did not include the breakage of pottery or the deposition of nonperishable items.

Apart from the Crystal Room, paintings in the Western Passage reveal few associations with ground fires. Whatever activities occurred amid the painting groups seem to have relied only on torches for illumination, and flecks of charcoal are found throughout the Western Passage (and throughout the cave). The North Passage Group shows more evidence of ground fires, which may indicate some differences in ritual activity in this area.

Drawing 88 and the Altar

The archaeological picture becomes much clearer in the case of Drawing 88, where there is unassailable proof that

rituals were performed in the presence of cave paintings. The discovery of Drawing 88 was made by project geologist George Veni on our 1988 expedition. In the course of exploring the cave for final mapping, he found a small opening about eight meters up on the north wall toward the end of the North Passage (fig. 5-2). The wall is not easily scaled and the entrance is a narrow squeeze, perhaps explaining why this area had escaped modern detection. Indeed, Veni had discovered the maze passage now called K'u Multun, which, all evidence indicates, had lain undisturbed since around A.D. 800.

About fifty meters south of the above-mentioned entry point, the maze again intersects the North Passage. Though the opening is larger here, it can be seen from the North Passage only by descending a steep breakdown, something which had been overlooked in previous exploration. In addition, to enter K'u Multun via this larger entrance requires a rope or ladder. The difficulty in making the ascent must have discouraged

casual intruders. This is fortunate, as next to the entrance sits one of the most remarkable archaeological assemblages found in any Maya cave: a stone structure, which appears to have functioned as an altar, accompanied by votive offerings, and a painted inscription (fig. 5-45).

The altar consists of a meter-high heap of rocks shoved up against the wall (fig. 5-46). A flat rock lay at the top of the pile, though nothing was found on it. Propped up by this mass of rocks is a vertical stone seventy centimeters high. The vertical rock bends and tapers nearly to a point over which the Maya had hung two *olla* rims, each about fifteen centimeters in diameter, the upper one, red, and the lower, black. The stones comprising the altar were in all likelihood laboriously hauled up from the North Passage.

That the Maya performed ceremonies at this altar is evidenced by eight piles of charcoal found in interstices and depressions within the mass of rocks. Most of the burning took place

FIG. 5-45. Stone altar topped by *olla* rims, Naj Tunich. Text is painted on adjacent wall. Drawing by Jennifer Clark.

FIG. 5-46. The altar, Naj Tunich. Note spalling gypsum near text. Photograph by Chip and Jennifer Clark.

toward the top of the heap. The front surface of the tapered vertical stone was smoke-blackened from a fire set behind a small rock resting on the top of the rock pile. A piece of unworked jade was found in a crevice toward the top of the pile, and behind it, a few pieces of charcoal.[5] Charcoal was also spread over the floor behind the altar, following the line of the wall. On the floor near the altar lay sherds from two broken ceramic vessels. One, a Late Classic basal-ridged, polychrome plate, had been deliberately smashed next to the altar (fig. 5-47).

Behind the altar is a painted inscription, Drawing 88. The text has one Calendar Round date, 8 Ahau 8 Uo, which places it at 9.13.0.0.0, ca. A.D. 692 (fig. 7-3). This date accords with the style of the smashed plate. All available evidence points to the idea that a ceremony was performed at the altar that included smashing the plate, painting the inscription, and burning small fires on the altar. Furthermore, it seems probable that the altar was constructed for this particular occasion. The altar assemblage is remarkable in preserving the undisturbed remains of an ancient cave ritual in direct association with a cave painting, something rare, I suspect, in the annals of world cave archaeology. We are fortunate that these materials were ever discovered since the Maya had them so well hidden, but that is precisely why they were found intact.

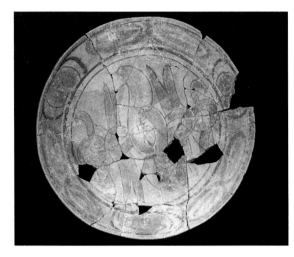

FIG. 5-47. Smashed basal-ridged plate (reconstructed) found next to altar, Naj Tunich. Photograph by James Brady.

One noteworthy feature of the altar is its marked vertical thrust, a trait seen in other cave altars of the eastern Peten–western Belize zone. An altarlike structure was found in 1984 in Actun Kabal, one of the large Chiquibul caves. Situated on a ledge overlooking a deep gorge, this limestone construction has two "rabbit ears" and a ring of stones that meet at a large flat rock (fig. 5-48). The previously mentioned altarlike

stone box found in Naj Tunel, with its six stalactites set on the surface, also has vertical elements (Brady et al. 1992: fig. 3).

The vertical thrust of these altars must be significant, as the ancient Maya attached notions of sanctity and status to verticality, evident even in the form of Maya temples and stelae. In addition, Maya art usually associates the highest figure in a composition with the highest rank or with supernatural status. Modern ethnographies show that verticality still signals high status among the Maya. For example, William Hanks (personal communication, 1989) notes that the Maya of Oxkutzcab associate vertically elevated piles of stone with notions of sacredness. Whereas stones marking land boundaries, which are not considered sacred, would be heaped in a low pile, those marking a sacred location would have greater height. Thus, the vertical stone of the Naj Tunich altar might be understood as a marker of sacred space; the *olla* rims placed at the summit certainly emphasize the altar's vertical thrust.

The archaeological context of Drawing 88 is wholly distinct from that of other paintings at Naj Tunich. First, it seems clear that Drawing 88 was deliberately hidden, something not true of paintings in the main tunnel system. Unique to Drawing 88, too, is the archaeological assemblage—the altar, the votive offerings, and evidence of multiple small fires. Other Naj Tunich paintings have no associated artifacts, although some show evidence of burning in the immediate vicinity. These differences point to varying ritual contexts for the paintings. Since Drawing 88 contains historical information, it is quite possible that the motivation of this altar ceremony will eventually come to light.

FIG. 5-48. Stone construction in Actun Kabal, Belize.

Images from the Underworld

6

Images from Naj Tunich

Ritual lies at the heart of the figurative paintings of Naj Tunich, just as it does for the greater part of Maya narrative art (Kubler 1969:29). However, the cave paintings preserve fragments of Classic Maya ritual rarely open to such direct scrutiny, intimate aspects of cave ritual as practiced over a thousand years ago in southeastern Peten. This was a time when Maya cave ritual was an event of high drama, when it moved to the rhythms of music, dance, and the cries of human sacrifice.

The paintings of Naj Tunich include over forty human figures, as well as a few anthropomorphic deities, and twenty-two complete or partial human heads. In contrast—and certainly out of character for Maya art—the faunal and floral worlds are hardly represented. Only one painting and one petroglyph portray an animal: a peccary in Drawing 8 and a bird scratched into calcite in Drawing 57. As human protagonists dominate the imagery of Naj Tunich, it is essential to understand their purpose and

their relationship, if there is one, with the hieroglyphic inscriptions. What can be said about the social context in which they act? Is social rank evident among the cave figures, as it is, say, in monumental art?

Costume

In the absence of a conjoined text, one way to determine the social status of figures in Maya art is through their costumes and accessories. Maya art, especially monumental sculpture, lavishes great attention on costumes and regalia. Figures typically wear all manner of finery: feathers, jade, animal skins, and so on, usually combined with symbols that establish a contextual, even spatial, framework (fig. 6-1). At Naj Tunich, however, costumes are typically plain, and symbolic appurtenances are relatively rare; but the spare appearance of the cave figures must be understood as a part of the paintings' message. That this is so can be seen in the very uniformity of this simple costume, for the Naj

Tunich figures are garbed in a remarkably similar fashion.

One way that their costume is consistent is that none of the figures wear any kind of footwear, nor do they wear anklets. Their body covering is limited to two basic garments: the loincloth and the hipcloth (fig. 6-2). The loincloth is wrapped around the waist and passed between the legs; the ends of the loincloth hang from the back. This most basic of all male attire, called *ex* in Yucatec and *maxtlatl* in Nahuatl, is the only clothing worn by many of the figures (Drawings 22, 67, 76, 68).

A hipcloth sometimes covers the loincloth. The hipcloth is a square cloth folded into a triangle or rectangle and then secured around the body (Anawalt 1981:177). On seated figures, the hipcloth is indicated by a curving line on the thigh. Some figures also wear a wide sash or belt wrapped around the waist.

These garments are also consistent in having little ornamental embellishment, with few exceptions among the forty-odd figures. For instance, one headdress flap has interior lines, which probably represent a woven pattern (Drawing 5). The jagged end of one belt may be an ornamental fringe (Drawing 72). In two other cases the lines of the loincloth can be seen through the hipcloth, suggestive of a diaphanous fabric, such as a gauze weave (Drawings 68 and 76). Apart from these modest embellishments, the figures are garbed in plain cloth.

The uniformity of costume also extends to the headdress. This usually consists of a cloth headwrap that comes in several varieties. In one case the figure's bound hair projects through the upper opening (fig. 6-3a). Many of the cloth headwraps stand erect, as though made from a stiffened material, usually secured by a cloth band or cord (fig. 6-3b). Other cloth headwraps are decorated with a tassel (fig. 6-3c). In still other cases the upper end of the headwrap forms one or more long flaps that hang

down (fig. 6-3d). One of the more elaborate cloth headwraps is seen in Drawing 22. The cloth appears to be pleated and is tied by a thick, twisted cord knotted at the front (fig. 6-3e). The top has a shaggy fringe made of down or fur. One other cloth cap at Naj Tunich is also topped by a fringe (fig. 6-3f). Considering the variety of materials that can adorn Maya headdresses—flowers, jade, wood—and the many different forms they can take, these cloth headwraps, for all their differences, represent a fairly uniform type of costuming.

A few figures wear no covering on their heads at all (Drawings 18, 20, and 26). In two cases the hair is drawn on top of the head. In another, the hair is loose and stands on end. In terms of their activities, these are among the most unusual figures in the cave, as will be seen later. Clearly, the uncovered head signals some unusual social status at Naj Tunich.

The Naj Tunich figures wear a modest amount of jewelry; the most common ornament is the circular earflare. One elaborate version has a tubular bead stuck through the center (fig. 6-9). Another type of ear ornament is a piece of cloth pulled through the pierced earlobe (fig. 6-4a). The cloth ear ornament is associated with sacrificial rites, both of captives and lords (Schele 1984:21), as well as with certain deity depictions. Unfortunately, ear ornaments are often hastily painted and can be difficult to identify.

A few figures wear necklaces. One type consists of a simple band, sometimes fitting tightly around the neck (fig. 6-4b). Three figures wear a cord with a single bead pendant (fig. 6-4c), and one has several beads at the end of the cord (fig. 6-4c). One figure wears a completely beaded necklace (fig. 6-4d). Most of the Naj Tunich figures wear no necklace at all. Only two figures wear wristlets. Drawing 17 shows the only example of the wide wristlet commonly

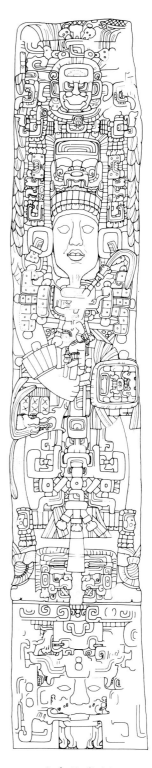

FIG. 6-1. Stela E, Quirigua, north.

Images from the Underworld

worn by the nobility on stelae. A thin wristband is worn by the figure in Drawing 26.

This modest array of jewelry invites comparison with actual jewelry recovered at Naj Tunich. Some close comparisons can be found among the earflares. Both jade and ceramic circular earflares were collected in the cave (Brady 1989:292, 260), as were perforated pendants and beads. One jade "drooping-mouth" pendant was found at the end of the North Passage (ibid.: 290). Perforated seeds, shells, and animal teeth were also recovered and could have come from necklaces. On the whole, the archaeology reveals a greater variety of jewelry than what is portrayed in the paintings. The fancy jewelry found in the cave seems to have been brought there as votive offerings. The jade "drooping-mouth" pendant, for instance, was found with a pile of pottery sherds in an area that revealed evidence of burning, and the pendant itself

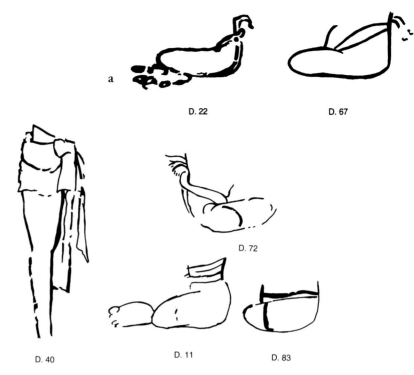

FIG. 6-2. Loincloths and hipcloths on Naj Tunich figures: *a,* loincloth only; *b,* loincloth and hipcloth.

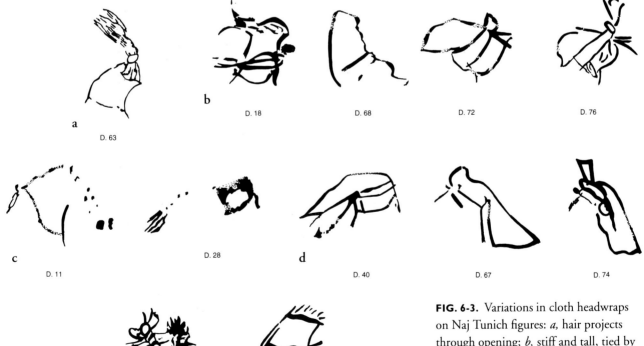

FIG. 6-3. Variations in cloth headwraps on Naj Tunich figures: *a,* hair projects through opening; *b,* stiff and tall, tied by a band; *c,* with beaded tassel; *d,* with hanging flaps; *e,* pleated and tied by twisted cord; *f,* with fringe and beads.

Images from Naj Tunich

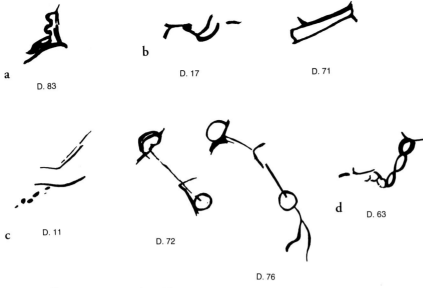

a
D. 83

b
D. 17

D. 71

c
D. 11

D. 72

d
D. 63

D. 76

FIG. 6-4. Ear ornaments and necklaces on Naj Tunich figures: *a,* cloth ear ornament; *b,* simple collar; *c,* round pendant on cord; *d,* beaded necklace.

FIG. 6-5. Quiche man from Chichicastenango wearing a *tzute de cabeza.* Photograph by Margot Blum Schevill.

appears to have been burnt (ibid.:84). Hence, while the jewelry worn by individuals portrayed in the paintings is modest, fine pieces of jewelry were left in the cave as offerings.

Based on this evidence, the typical cave figure might be characterized thus: he is unshod and wears an undecorated loincloth and hipcloth, circular earflares, and a cloth headwrap tied by a band. Variations in costume show little evidence of rank distinction among figures. In Drawing 63, the figure's jewelry is more elaborate than most, and he appears to sit on a cushion (fig. 6-9). These may be the signs of a high-ranking person; yet this is one of the smallest figures in the cave, at nine centimeters in height. In Drawing 27 the front figure in a group of three is larger, suggesting status distinctions within the group (fig. 6-23). But the overwhelming impression left by variations in costume is that of *downplaying* divisions in social rank.

The cloth headwrap, however, may convey information about social status,

as it does among certain contemporary Maya groups. Cakchiquel and Quiche Maya use the *tzute de cabeza,* a rectangular piece of cloth tied around the head, as part of male ceremonial attire (fig. 6-5). Even the manner in which it is tied indicates rank (Mayén de Castellanos 1986:102). In Solola the *tzute de cabeza* is worn by high-status officials, such as the *alcalde* and *regidor.* At Naj Tunich, on the other hand, the cloth headwrap seems to be a general form of ceremonial attire.

In classic Maya art cloth headwraps do not foster an image of authority. They are usually worn by a second tier of court officials or performers, often congregated in groups. Indeed, the cloth headwrap seems closely allied with ritual performance. For example, one group of opossum musicians wears a cloth headwrap, circular earflare, and a cord tied tightly around the neck (fig. 6-6), a costume paralleling that of the Naj Tunich figures. Even the neck cord is worn by several figures at

Naj Tunich, one of whom is a masked dancer (fig. 6-24).

The cloth headwrap, sometimes in net form, is also worn by the old God N in his role as world bearer or in one of his many other guises (fig. 6-7). God N, as Taube (1989a) observes, is closely related to ritual performance. His salacious antics are the subject of many painted vases and modeled figurines (figs. 6-29, 6-30). In most cases, God N is unshod and wears only a loincloth and cloth cap. His costume recalls the typical costume depicted in the cave.

This spare costume also recalls figures from a series of panels found at Rancho San Diego in Yucatan (Barrera Rubio and Taube 1987). These remarkable sculptures depict what might best be described as a Maya bacchanalia. The participants' inebriated state, giving rise to ecstatic dancing and fighting, was apparently induced by an alcoholic enema. One of the figures, using a gourd to give himself an enema, is dressed much like a Naj Tunich pro-

Images from the Underworld

FIG. 6-6. Opossum musicians. From Taube 1989a: fig. 24.1.

FIG. 6-7. God N wearing cloth headwrap, House of the Bacabs, Copan. Adapted from Webster 1989: fig. 13.

FIG. 6-8. Man giving himself an enema, Rancho San Diego relief. From Barrera Rubio and Taube 1987: fig. 9.

tagonist; he is unshod and wears a loincloth and a cloth cap tied by a band (fig. 6-8). Cloth caps are also worn by figures undergoing auto-sacrifice. A Jaina figurine shows a lord with a high cloth hat piercing his penis with a sharpened bone (Schele and Miller 1986: pl. 69). Captives also wear cloth headwraps, as seen in the Fort Worth Panel (Schele 1984: fig. 11).

It seems likely that the cloth headwrap marks an individual as a co-participant in ritual activity and has the dual connotations of ritual performance and group membership. Cloth headwraps unite individuals as equal members of a group, facilitating the temporary breakdown of rank that divided people in the normal course of community life. This "uniform condition," a shedding of everyday social status, characterizes the liminal state in rites of passage (Turner 1977: 95). Indeed, cloth headwraps seem to be associated with liminality.

The Ritual Content

The paintings of Naj Tunich depict some types of ritual performance that are readily identified. For example, in Drawing 63 a figure sits in front of a vessel from which plumes of smoke rise (fig. 6-9). The vessel appears to be a flat-bottomed ceramic dish with a heavy rim, a type of vessel commonly used at Naj Tunich for burning incense (Brady 1989: 212–218). Specialized incense burners, on the other hand, comprise a small percentage of the Naj Tunich ceramic collection. Drawing 63 may show a high-status person, suggested by his throne and beaded necklace, tossing lumps of copal into a ceramic dish.

As burning incense is customary in Maya ritual—cave ritual as well, as we know archaeologically and from modern practices—Drawing 63 underscores the suggestion that the paintings portray actions that took place in the cave. Moreover, the cave paintings do not de-

FIG. 6-9. Drawing 63, Naj Tunich.

FIG. 6-10. Drawing 5, Naj Tunich.

pict an architectural setting that would place scenes in any other location. Only six of the Naj Tunich paintings have architectural elements; four of these treat the ballgame and may therefore allude to the "cave as ballcourt" theme (Drawings 21, 31, 39, and 51). The action in Drawing 5, another painting with architecture, takes place on a series of steps (fig. 6-10), which comparable scenes on vases suggest to be a palace. In Drawing 32 one of three figures sits in a canoelike object, but the form is too faded to identify.

Apart from this, most of the cave paintings define space by a groundline, which could easily represent the cave floor; others make no reference to a spatial setting. As a result, the scenes have an acontextual appearance that is heightened by the absence of symbols on costumes. I would suggest, however, that the cave setting mitigated the need for symbols to establish context (Stone 1989b). Generally, Maya art relies on skybands, water lilies, Cauac Monsters, and other kinds of spatial frames to establish the sacred setting of a narrative (e.g., Schele and Miller 1986:45–47). These motifs are absent at Naj Tunich precisely because the figures already inhabit the sacred space of a real cave. Similarly, the paintings lack frames that would separate them from the cave wall, even though frames are a common feature of Maya vase and mural painting. The only framing devices employed by the cave painters are natural wall features, so the connection between figures and topography is strengthened, as is the sense of a shared spatial setting for paintings occupying the same wall.

Rites of Passage

The overriding theme of the Naj Tunich paintings might be characterized as "ritual as a lived experience." This idea is powerfully communicated in a series of figures occupying a continuous wall surface in the Western Passage (fig. 6-11). One figure in Drawing 17 seems to freeze a moment in the course of some traumatic event, though to our eyes, an ambiguous one. Twisting sharply to the right, this standing male figure assumes one of the most dynamic poses seen in the cave (fig. 6-12). Unfortunately, details are poorly preserved, but the figure's twisting motion conveys important information.

Contorted or awkward postures in Maya art in general reference the antithesis of the normative (ideal) state of placid composure—that is, they signal an emotionally charged state. They are typical of captives who are being apprehended, restrained, or tortured or elites undergoing traumatic auto-sacrificial

Images from the Underworld

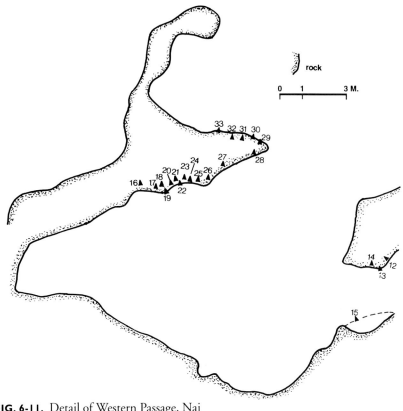

FIG. 6-11. Detail of Western Passage, Naj Tunich.

FIG. 6-12. Drawing 17, Naj Tunich.

rites; for example, the Orator and Scribe tablets from Palenque depict elite auto-sacrifice and show especially complex poses for protagonists of monumental sculpture (fig. 6-20). Some of the most aggressive poses in Maya stone sculpture are seen on the Rancho San Diego reliefs, where raw emotions, unleashed by an intoxicating brew, run high (fig. 6-18).

Agitated poses express a range of human emotion: pain, disgrace, pleasure, and drunkenness. Context determines which of these is represented. In public sculpture, typified by the stela, emotional display was denigrating and was therefore relegated to captives (fig. 6-13). But in private art energetic poses could convey the trauma of rites of passage, precisely the case with Drawing 17 from Naj Tunich.

With hands gathered near his groin, the figure holds a long tubular object. Because of its position, this object might be interpreted as his penis; how-

ever, the identification is far from certain. The object does not resemble typical Maya renditions of phalli, which usually differentiate the glans. Naturally, if it were a penis, this scene might portray masturbation, as has been suggested (Strecker 1987). There are at least two other figures in Maya art shown ejaculating that can be compared with Drawing 17. One appears on a vase from Cahal Pech, Belize (fig. 6-14). The figure in question is an old God N–like character. He assumes an awkward kneeling pose with his chest arched and head thrown back. His penis takes the typical wrenchlike form in which the glans and urethral opening are exaggerated. The semen is shown as multiple lines of dots, a typical way of showing streams of liquid in Classic Maya art. On page 37b of the Dresden Codex (fig. 6-15) is a depiction of Chac ejaculating a stream of semen with a bird head at the end (in the codices fluid is also shown as a volute with hooked projections). At Naj Tunich, however, the proposed "phallus" does not resemble either of the two versions cited above, and there appears to be something like a handle at the base. Nor does the small line at the end of the object look much like a stream of liquid according to Classic Maya conventions.

The object might also be interpreted as a bloodletter, as it is directed toward the groin area. Granted, this object does not resemble typical Maya bloodletters either, which are usually slender, needle-like affairs. Nonetheless, it still seems that auto-sacrifice or, less likely, onanism are the most reasonable interpretations of the figure's action, though it may never be known which of the two is actually portrayed. In either case, the figure appears gripped with tension and engages in some action that involves his genital area. He looks away, facing to his right, the same direction that other figures in this group face. Patches of paint on his nose, mouth, and chin re-

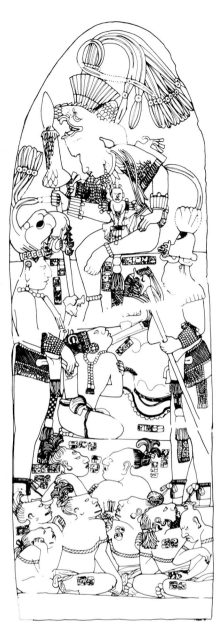

FIG. 6-13. Postures of lords (top) and captives (bottom), Stela 12, Piedras Negras. From Schele and Miller 1986: fig. 5.8.

FIG. 6-14. Figure on vase from Cahal Pech, Belize.

call Landa's observations that during ritual fasting Maya men covered themselves with soot (Tozzer 1941:152, 161, 165).

Drawing 20 lies near Drawing 17 and was found in better condition, although it is one of the unfortunate paintings to have been destroyed in 1989 (fig. 6-16). Drawing 20 also freezes one personal moment in a ritual drama. The figure is nude, which is unusual for a protagonist of Maya art, as, once again, nude males are usually captives. A nude main actor signals an extraordinary social context for the event portrayed, a fact made more evident by the figure's erect phallus. Unlike Drawing 17, the phallus can be securely identified by both the glans and urethral opening.

The figure strikes an awkward pose, one knee up and one down, conveniently hiding his hands, which are buried in his lap. The artist has painted the figure at an oblique angle to the wall, even attempting a three-quarter view of the face. The nostril and eye closest to the viewer are larger, conveying the impression that the face is receding in space. Given that three-quarter views are hardly ever employed for Maya figures, this oblique angle would have been perceived as spatially disruptive, just as a twisting torso or flailing arms would interject a feeling of chaos. Hence, a highly charged emotional state is again visualized through pose but is expressed more through the figure's orientation to the plane of the wall than in the configuration of his limbs.

The unsettling feeling brought on by the nudity and skewed angle is heightened by the figure's unkempt hair, standing erect in spikelike clumps. Like dynamic poses, loose, stringy hair expresses strong emotions and the loss of social standing. On the one hand,

FIG. 6-15. Dresden 37b. Adapted from Villacorta and Villacorta 1976.

Images from the Underworld

unkempt, loose locks reflect a lack of personal grooming and social respectability; therefore, this trait is commonly bestowed on captives in Maya art (fig. 6-17). One of the drunken revelers on the Rancho San Diego panels with wild flowing hair shows how loose hair signals the breakdown of social mores (fig. 6-18). An unkempt appearance also had its place in Maya ritual. Landa states that during Uayeb rites, people suspended their normal grooming habits, fearing that it would bring about some calamity, and he specifically mentions that they did not comb their hair (Tozzer 1941:166). According to López de Cogolludo (1867:1:312), Yucatecan priests wore long hair smeared with sacrificial blood, a hideous hairstyle also worn by Aztec priests. In general, unkempt hair in Maya art has associations with the transgression of social norms, whether seen in a demoralized war captive or a ritual actor in a liminal state.

It is possible that the figure in Drawing 20 is engaged in an auto-erotic act since his hands are located at the base of his penis. Most extant illustrations of drawing blood from the penis in Maya art show that this was done from the glans (Joralemon 1974: fig. 10; Schele and Miller 1986:pl. 69). A broken ceramic phallus found at Naj Tunich also has a "cut mark" on the glans (Brady 1989:255 and fig. 6.2c). Barbara MacLeod (personal communication, 1990) has pointed out, though, that at Chichen Itza the large phallus depicted in the North Temple relief of the Great Ballcourt has two spines piercing the base of the penis (Marquina 1964: photo 440). So the location of the figure's hands in Drawing 20 may not preclude the possibility that he is letting blood or mutilating his penis. It

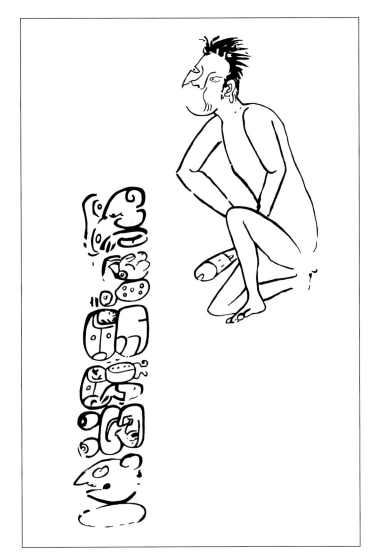

FIG. 6-16. Drawing 20, Naj Tunich.

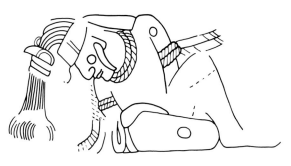

FIG. 6-17. Captive with long hair, Altar 10, Tikal. Adapted from Jones and Satterthwaite 1982: fig. 34b.

FIG. 6-18. Intoxicated man with loose hair, Rancho San Diego relief. From Barrera Rubio and Taube 1987: fig. 14.

is noteworthy that the phallus has linear markings that give it a glyphlike appearance. They might be marks from penile mutilation or might have symbolic significance.

Virtually nothing is known about ritual masturbation in Maya culture, but the extent to which it did exist would not have been easily detected by outsiders, especially not by the inquiring minds of Spanish priests. As mentioned earlier, there are depictions of men ejaculating in Maya art, suggesting that such rites did exist. Furthermore, what Maya cave ritual may have been like in ancient times in the most private of ceremonies is only hinted at in the archaeological record. The Naj Tunich paintings confront us with the possibility that onanism may have had a place in cave ritual.

Far more tame in its allusion to ritual action is Drawing 26 (fig. 6-19), a fragmentary painting of a seated figure. Gazing upward, he draws his right hand toward his open mouth. This gesture recalls the portrait of Chaacal, one of the last rulers of Palenque, from the Tablet of the Orator (fig. 6-20). Schele (1984: 29–30) notes that a speech line is drawn from Chaacal's mouth to the adjacent

column of glyphs, suggesting that the gesture may be one of speaking. The Naj Tunich figure may also be singing or speaking. His open mouth certainly infuses the scene with a kind of tension. The figure's scraggly beard and hair enhance the feeling of a nonnormative context. This figure, too, appears to be an engaged ritual participant.

One of the paintings in the North Passage Group, Drawing 76, shows a figure who appears to be gazing upward (fig. 6-21). His right hand rests near his groin, suggesting sacrificial or autoerotic manipulation of his genitals. Unfortunately, the painting has flaked off in this critical area, so his actions remain obscure; but he, too, may have been involved in some private ritual performance.

Musicians and Dancers

Counted among the ritual performers at Naj Tunich are musicians and dancers. There are two groups of musicians, each with three members, a number common to musicians and dancers on painted vases (fig. 6-6). In Drawing 40 the central figure holds a ceramic drum (fig. 6-22). It has a bulbous body of the "lamp-glass" type and a long, narrow base of the "pedestal-vase" type (Hammond 1972: 127). Behind him another musician is beating a drum that looks like a gourd or *olla*.

In the more fragmentary Drawing 27, the central figure appears to be beating a drum made from a turtle carapace, called *boxel ak* in Yucatec, usually beaten with a deer antler (fig. 6-23). The rear figure holds a rattle. The front figure, much larger than the rest, may be an important official like the *hol pop* described by López de Cogolludo (1867: 1: 300). A kind of expert in public performance, the *hol pop* was an instructor of song and dance and also guardian of the musical instruments.

Unlike the musicians, who play in groups, the dancers perform solo. They

FIG. 6-20. Tablet of the Orator, Palenque. From Schele 1984: fig. 17.

FIG. 6-21. Drawing 76, Naj Tunich.

FIG. 6-19. Drawing 26, Naj Tunich.

Images from the Underworld

FIG. 6-22. Drawing 40, Naj Tunich.

can be identified by their stylized gestures, palms forward and knees bent with one leg raised. The most elaborately costumed dancer, seen in Drawing 71, is the only masked figure at Naj Tunich (fig. 6-24). He wears both a bat face mask and deer headdress and carries what appears to be a rattle. The cord choker, as mentioned earlier, is a costume of ritual performers. The other dancers at Naj Tunich are less complex. Indeed, Drawing 33 shows only the upper portion of the figure, but the raised palm is a sure indication that he is a dancer (fig. 6-25). His oversized "beard" may be part of his costume. The last dancer, seen in Drawing 61, is a delicate figure with one palm forward and the other on the waist, a typical dancing pose (fig. 6-26). The three dancers also share one curious trait, a wavy line, either near the raised palm (Drawings 33 and 61) or near the headdress (Drawing 71). The function of this line is presently unclear.

FIG. 6-23. Drawing 27, Naj Tunich.

FIG. 6-24. Drawing 71, Naj Tunich.

The most common form of human sacrifice portrayed in Classic Maya art is decapitation (Schele 1984:9), the subject of Drawing 11 (fig. 6-27). That humans were sacrificed at Naj Tunich is also suggested by the archaeology. Brady's (1989: Ch. 8) analysis of nineteen human skeletons from the cave indicates that eight of these individuals, including several children, were probably sacrificed. Though none are definitely known to have been decapitated, it remains a possibility.

In Drawing 11 a seated figure holds a severed head, recognizable as such by the loose hair painted in broad streaks and the sketchy profile. A painted vase in the Pearlman collection shows a costumed performer holding a severed head, and here, too, the hair hangs loose (Coe 1982: no. 2). Loose hair demeans the status of the victim, appropriate enough, say, for a war captive. The associated two-glyph text, a God K portrait glyph and a *tsolk'in* date of 13 Ahau (the coefficient sits to the right of the day sign, but this kind of reversal is known from other texts) lends insight into the occasion for the decapitation. Surely 13 Ahau refers to the *k'atun* ending 9.17.0.0.0 13 Ahau 18 Cumku (Stone 1989b). Furthermore, painted below this scene in Drawing 12 is the

FIG. 6-25. Drawing 33, Naj Tunich.

FIG. 6-26. Drawing 61, Naj Tunich.

date 8 Lamat (one of the dots has eroded; fig. 7-4); 8 Lamat occurs just eight days after 13 Ahau on the important *haab* position, the first of Pop, a New Year's day.[1]

Text and image suggest that a ritual decapitation was performed at Naj Tunich as part of a *k'atun* anniversary celebration, an event that occurred only three days before the beginning of the Uayeb and eight days before the New Year. This brings to mind Bricker and

FIG. 6-27. Drawing 11, Naj Tunich.

Bill's (1989) discussion of several almanacs from the Madrid Codex (Madrid 54–55, Madrid 101–102) that feature a human decapitation and the enshrouding of the victim in cloth. The codex shows a bound captive with an axe near his neck and another headless figure. The authors argue that the beheadings are part of Uayeb rites preceding a Cauac year, and they compare certain details to Landa's description of this ceremony. Landa states that a skull, the body of a dead man, and a vulture were placed atop the image of Ek u Uayeyab and all were carried in procession to meet the statue of Uac Mitun Ahau, a Yucatecan death god (Tozzer 1941:147).

Since the date 13 Ahau and the beheading would have occurred just before the Uayeb, this scene forms an intriguing, if not precise, parallel with the Uayeb decapitation ritual. Furthermore, since 13 Ahau completes the *k'atun* cycle, as we know from the Chilam Balams, one could argue that on Katun 17 there was a convergence of the end of the *k'atun* round and the Uayeb–New Year rites. This fact certainly would not have slipped by the Maya and may have inspired particularly elaborate celebrations.

FIG. 6-28. Drawing 18, Naj Tunich.

FIG. 6-29. Jaina figurine showing a buxom woman and old man with deer headdress embracing. Courtesy of Dumbarton Oaks Research Library and Collections, Washington, D.C.

Drawing 18 and Ritual Performance

The theme of ritual performance emerges in a rather unusual guise in Drawing 18, the most graphic depiction of sexual intercourse left us by the ancient Maya (fig. 6-28; Plate 12). Elsewhere I have discussed how this painting falls into a well-known genre in which a decrepit or otherwise unattractive man paws at a voluptuous maiden (Stone 1985b). Depictions of this sort are found on painted vases and modeled in ceramic figurines (see Pendergast 1981–1982; Kubler 1984b; Taube 1989a). Figurines sometimes show the couple locked in embrace, with the withered old man sidled up against the maiden's generous body and well positioned to fondle a thigh or bosom (fig. 6-29). This aged character with a cloth headwrap is the old God N, also identified with the Bacabs and the Pahuatuns (Thompson 1970b; Coe 1973:15). Vase scenes show the old man with a net head tie, a shell pendant, a thick cotton necklace, and other attributes of God N (fig. 6-30). On vases God N emerges from the mouth of a coiling snake as he lunges at the breasts of the demure maiden (Robicsek and Hales 1981; vessels 8–12). For all of his onerous duties, such as atlantean world bearer, God N was the Maya's stereotypical lecherous old man.

Following Thompson's (1939) lead on the Moon Goddess in Mesoamerica and her licentious ways, I earlier proposed that the female partner in Drawing 18 was the Maya Moon Goddess (Stone 1985b). The Moon Goddess, like other Maya deities, has symbolic ties to caves, making her identification here particularly appropriate. She is the patronness of the month called *ch'en* in Yucatec, a word (or one of its cognates) meaning "cave" or "well" in a number of Mayan languages. Her abode is also a cave. One phrase for the new moon, found in the Vienna dictionary, is *binan u tu ch'en* "the moon gone to her well [cave]" (Thompson 1960:236).

In his study of ritual humor in Maya art, Karl Taube (1989a) sheds new light on the theme of the lecherous old man and voluptuous maiden, which must be taken into account in addressing Drawing 18. Taube has shown that Maya art preserves remarkably faithful renditions

FIG. 6-30. Painted vase showing God N grabbing the bosom of a beautiful maiden. From Taube 1989a: fig. 24.17.

of public performance. Ritual dance performers have certain accoutrements, such as dance fans and rattles; they sometimes dance in the company of musicians.

Taube has shown, too, that the old man and maiden are often portrayed as ritual performers; for example, one member of the couple may hold a dance fan. A painted vase also depicts them in a stylized dancing pose, while the old man holds a dance fan (fig. 6-31). The old man is sometimes replaced by a monkeylike performer whom Taube correlates with an entity called the "*pa* character," so named after his portrait glyph, a netted face, which in the Mayan writing system has the phonetic value **pa**. The "*pa* character" usually wears a netted costume, and, like God N, he is decidedly unattractive, conceived with grotesque or zoomorphic deformations; sometimes, for example, he has a hideously enlarged nose or chin, and at other times, simian attributes. His substitution for God N in the old man–young woman theme returns to the idea of public performance, for the "*pa* character" is, above all, a ritual performer.

That this unlikely liaison between a feeble or grotesque man and a lovely maiden is related to public entertainment is vividly illustrated on a vase in a private collection (fig. 6-32). Here the woman dances with a freakish man who prods a phallic nose mask in her direction, while two musicians beat out a dance rhythm (ibid.: 370). The grotesque nose is one more variant of the theme of the unattractive male (though here it has humorous, erotic overtones), comparable to the facial disfigurement of the "*pa* character" or God N's withered looks. It is important to note that the gender of the female figure is indicated by her long skirt (*pik*) and long tresses. Her loose locks of hair probably allude to her sexual availability. An examination of her chest clearly shows that breasts are lacking, which is not at

FIG. 6-31. Painted vase showing old man and young woman dancing. From Taube 1989a: fig. 24.12a.

FIG. 6-32. Painted vase showing bawdy dance. From Taube 1989a: fig. 24.14.

FIG. 6-33. Painted vase showing woman with long tresses and without breasts, possibly indicating a female impersonator. From Robicsek 1978: fig. 228.

Images from the Underworld

all typical of women shown nude from the waist up in Maya art. Another vase with a related scene also shows a woman with multiple locks of hair hanging loosely, though ornamented with pieces of down or cotton (fig. 6-33). She is also nude from the waist up and lacks breasts.

The absence of breasts on many of these dancing women underscores the fact that we are witnessing a performance, as it is traditional among the Maya that men act out female roles in public performance. As might be expected, these performances are usually amusing and baudy satires. Bricker (1973:215) notes that female impersonation is one of the three most important categories of ritual humor among the modern Tzotzil Maya of highland Chiapas. These modern performances often comment on women's deviant behavior, recalling the seductive charm of the Classic female impersonators. For the Yucatec Maya, Taube (1989a:354) cites Starr's description of a Xtol dance performed in Mérida in 1901 in which female impersonators with exaggerated breasts dance with male performers in erotic jest. It is easy to imagine why such antics would be both titillating and humorous. The pairing of a voluptuous seductress, parodied by a man, and a feeble or grotesque man pawing the maiden would make amusing public entertainment almost anywhere.

Returning to Drawing 18, we might note how differently the figures are treated (fig. 6-28). Though not particularly aged, the male is thoroughly unidealized: he has thin limbs and an awkward bulge in his belly and the middle of his back. This is precisely how God N's physique is treated when he is shown nude (cf. Robicsek and Hales 1981: vessel 2). In Drawing 18 the male's face is unattractive: the wide mouth is sharp and angular and his eye lacks definition. His thin cap of hair,

gathered in a ponytail, stands on end, not even dignified by a head covering. Though the face lacks such traits of old age as wrinkles and a snaggle tooth, it is sly and awkward, and therefore falls into the "God N–*pa* character" genre.

Quite the contrary, the partner of this unseemly character is wholly appealing. An elegant, upswept eye and graceful facial markings give her a dignified countenance. The queue of hair trailing down her back is a conventional sign of female gender. Her solid physique, though admirable, is not particularly feminine, and she, too, has no sign of breasts. She wears the cloth headwrap worn by male figures at Naj Tunich. In addition, fragments of paint near the waist and thigh suggest that this figure was wearing a hipcloth. The paint in the groin area may be part of a front cloth flap. The hipcloth is a male garment.

Given that the context of ritual performance pervades the old man–young woman theme, it is reasonable to propose that the masculine characteristics of this figure have a basis in female impersonation, albeit the only female costuming is the queue of hair. In all other respects the figure is dressed in the typical costume of male ritualists at Naj Tunich. Similarly, Bricker (1973:152) found that it was quite acceptable for Tzotzil female impersonators to retain much of their male attire: "The fact that a female impersonator wears men's sandals, trousers, and hat is unimportant; what counts is that he wear the three basic components of the woman's costume: skirt, blouse, and shawl." The mixing of male and female attire may have made the ensemble that much more comical. Drawing 18 indicates that the queue of hair was the critical signifier of female gender at Naj Tunich. I suspect that the female role was played by a male member of the ritual entourage and little was done to change his appearance except add a lock of

hair, which may have been a piece of fur or fabric.

During the actual performance of this satire in the cave, women were most likely excluded from any form of participation. Secreted away in a vast cavern, an all-male audience might exhibit the good-humored camaraderie one would expect in a gender-restricted group. In such circumstances, it is expected that sexual humor would be more biting and blatant. That the arousal of the God N–like character is so realistically portrayed in Drawing 18, far beyond anything seen on vases or figurines, must be explained by the social dynamics of such a gender-restricted audience and the unique social context fostered by the cave itself. The phallic nose mask and the lascivious pawing of God N on vases and figurines are bawdy but within socially accepted limits. With the absence of public scrutiny in the cave, sexual innuendo gives way to brassy eroticism.

Beneath the humor of this burlesque is social commentary that Taube (1989a; 1988b) links to the contradictory persona of God N. God N is at once a mighty thunder god in the guise of the Mams but also a symbol of the excess and corruption that accrue with unbridled power. God N is often shown getting intoxicated or vomiting after such escapades, lusting after young women, or committing other socially repugnant acts. God N stereotypes, in both his physical appearance and actions, an inversion of social ideals. Taube persuasively argues that this is why God N is linked to renewal ceremonies, such as the New Year, when the theme of social deviance (God N's bailiwick) serves as an entertaining and cathartic experience for the audience as well as an affirmation of societal values. God N appears to have special significance for Classic Maya rites of inversion.

been trained vase painters. Indeed, the cave paintings resemble Maya vase painting in certain respects. The scale of the cave paintings, for instance, tends to be small. Some of the smaller figures at Naj Tunich would fit perfectly on a cylindrical vase. The smallest figure measures nine centimeters high (a seated figure), though the largest ranges up to sixty-six centimeters. In general, the Naj Tunich figurative paintings look delicate and diminutive, in some ways mismatched to the scale of a cave wall but well suited to the confined surface of a vase.

The linear black-on-white style also finds its nearest relative in vase decoration and is especially close to two style groups known as Codex (Robicsek and Hales 1981) and Black and White (Kerr 1989–1990:2:189). Both employ a crisp, delicate black line on a cream or white background (fig. 5-21). This results in a highly readable line, and certainly Codex vases offer some of the most detailed narrative scenes in the corpus of painted Maya vases. It is also tempting to view the cream background of Codex-style vases, which have mostly mythological subject matter, as an allusion to the cave-underworld with its limestone walls. The Naj Tunich paintings, too, are extremely readable and have remarkably fine detail, especially considered in the global context of rock art.

Artists' Hands

One way to identify individual artists in a collection of paintings is to look for shared idiosyncracies. Facial features and anatomy, as well as hieroglyphs, are especially prone to individualized treatment. A comparative analysis of this sort, while useful in the present instance to identify several paintings by the same artist, does have its limitations. First and foremost, paintings must share like elements to even attempt a comparison. If texts lack head variants, for example, little can be done to compare them with figurative paintings. Another limitation is in not knowing the range of styles practiced by a single artist. These drawbacks aside, it can be demonstrated that several artists worked at Naj Tunich who produced more than one painting. Ten such artists are identified below. We can get some sense of the spatial distribution and range of themes of their work. This discussion of artists' hands includes material pertinent to the cave's inscriptions; these matters are treated fully in Chapter 7.

FIG. 5-21. Black and White vase with calligraphic style resembling some Naj Tunich inscriptions, Kerr Vessel 4387. Photograph © Justin Kerr 1989.

Images from the Underworld

Though less clear, it may be that the female is tied to the Moon Goddess complex after all, as she may personify a sexually aggressive woman, an attitude surely frowned upon in Classic Maya society. Thompson's (1939) summary of Moon Goddess lore shows that she takes the initiative in affairs of love. The licentious behavior of the young Moon Goddess may be taken as a stereotype of the wanton young woman. Thus, while God N personifies male sexual excess, the young Moon Goddess fulfills that role for young women.

Though depictions of the maiden look innocent at first blush, there are clues, subtle to our eyes, that she is otherwise. In the vase scenes her multiple loose tresses would seem to signal sexual availability. As discussed earlier, the Maya viewed loose tresses as a sign that normative behavior and social ideals have been suspended. On a worldwide basis, loose hair has frequent associations with the unleashing of the libido (Leach 1958). In one depiction of the maiden (fig. 6-33) the multiple strands of hair are adorned with white balls, an ostentatious hairstyle that may mark this woman as a floozie. The fact that she allows such close contact with men is further evidence of her easy ways. Both Landa and Herrera state that men and women did not dance together, except in one erotic dance called the Naual (Tozzer 1941:128, 218). Thus, in Colonial Yucatan heterosexual dancing had erotic connotations.

Not to be overlooked is the presence of the flower, found frequently adorning the head of the female dancer. Thompson (1939:138–140) and Heyden (1983:105–107) discuss the erotic symbolism of flowers in the Maya area and central Mexico. For the Maya of Yucatan the *Plumeria* (frangipani) seems to have symbolized female eroticism. Thompson (1939:138) points out that the Motul dictionary gives a secondary definition of *nikte*, which

means both flower in general and the *Plumeria* in particular, as "unchastity, carnal vice, and naughtiness of women." On one vase scene the flower is large and has a hummingbird sucking the nectar (fig. 6-32). On another it is smaller and is stuck on the end of a jewel (fig. 6-33). In both instances the male figure wears the same floral headdress, perhaps a symbol of their sexual liaison.

In sum, Drawing 18 is part of a thematic genre, found in many media in Maya art, which caricatures sexually deviant behavior but at the same time conveys deeper levels of social criticism. An appropriate name for this theme might be "the shameless couple," for it appears, *au fond*, that the pair is fornicating in public (this we actually see at Naj Tunich), a cause for censure but also titillation and amusement. This caricature is both entertaining and pedagogical in that it provides a commentary on proper sexual comportment. It is also worth entertaining the idea that renewal ceremonies instigated the kind of performance we see in Drawing 18. Recall that a possible New Year's Day (8 Lamat) is recorded in Drawing 12, just a short walk from Drawing 18.

In light of the masculine characteristics of the female in Drawing 18, the Naj Tunich version seems to draw on the visual language of public performance. That the figures are presented as ritual performers corresponds with other figures in the cave who are also engaged ritual participants.

Ritual Activity: Who and Where

The cave paintings portray facets of ceremonial life in Naj Tunich during the Late Classic period. They include (with varying degrees of certainty) burning copal, blood sacrifice, onanism, solo dance performance, group musical performance, singing, ritual decapitation, and satirical dance performance.

Who are these ritual performers? Are we to understand the figures in Drawing 17 and Drawing 20 as shamans, seeking altered states, or are they members of the nobility, as concerned with documenting their spiritual encounters in a cave as they are interested in recording their public life on stelae? Since costumes downplay rank, there is little concrete evidence to answer this question. However, the inscriptions with their numerous Emblem Glyphs suggest that the cave was visited by high-ranking individuals from regional sites. They are probably the protagonists of at least some of the paintings. Certain of these individuals may also be ritual specialists, shamans or shaman's acolytes, as suggested by certain phrases in the inscriptions.

In the Late Classic period at Naj Tunich, the Western Passage may have been the staging ground for activities portrayed in this section of the cave. The Western Passage is relatively flat and easily negotiated. Even the most cumbersome activities shown in the paintings could have been performed there. Brady (1989: Ch. 10) concludes that certain kinds of ritual activities were delegated to different areas of Naj Tunich. The Balcony, for instance, was a burial site, in addition to staging rites that entailed the deposition of pottery. The Western Passage may have been the setting for group performances. This section of the cave was barren of artifacts, which is problematical in trying to reconstruct its function.

Other figures depicted in the cave seem to play no active role at all, and yet they are dressed in the same fashion as figures engaged in the identifiable actions discussed above. It is reasonable to assume that their social status is fundamentally similar to that of the active figures. These static figures are among the finest in the Naj Tunich corpus. In Drawing 72, for instance, a splendid figure sits cross-legged with his right

FIG. 6-34. Drawing 72, Naj Tunich.

hand resting on his left foot (fig. 6-34). In Drawing 74 a figure is shown kneeling with arms crossed (fig. 6-35). A split-level scene, Drawing 67, shows a static, seated figure and an odd frontal figure whose heavy lower lip and strange anatomy suggest another God N–like character (fig. 6-36). One of the most beautiful figures at Naj Tunich, seen in Drawing 22, sits in front of a conch shell (fig. 6-37). These figures, too, must be participants in cave ritual. The seated figures are perhaps to be understood as withdrawn into a contemplative state.

FIG. 6-35. Drawing 74, Naj Tunich.

FIG. 6-36. Drawing 67, Naj Tunich.

FIG. 6-37. Drawing 22, Naj Tunich.

Human Heads

The human face is a common subject of Maya cave art. Crudely sculpted faces are found in caves throughout the Maya area. Velázquez Morlet and López de la Rosa (1988:94) liken those in Yucatan to representations of cave deities, such as the mischievous *alux*. The human face is also found in Olmec cave painting (Grove 1970: figs. 17, 19). Naj Tunich has some twenty-two profile heads and faces painted and carved on its walls.[2] They vary in style, ranging from beautiful Late Classic profile heads to simple schematic faces. In one case, five Classic-style heads ring the interior of an alcove in the North Passage Group. The head is usually treated as a simple profile, but occasionally head-dresses are added (fig. 6-38). At Naj Tunich these heads seem to represent shorthand versions of the full-figure ritualist. In one case a profile is drawn at the same scale and level as a complete figure (fig. 6-34). One of the heads also sports a fringed cloth headwrap, a type of headdress worn by full-length figures. Three paintings at Naj Tunich present schematic faces (fig. 6-39). Unlike the Classic faces and heads, the schematic faces incorporate natural wall features into the drawing. The Western Passage has one frontal face painted in a calcite clast (Drawing 55). Two faces decorate curtain flowstone formations in the area of the cave called Naj Tunel (Drawings 91 and 92).

Representations of Deities

Deities are rare in the paintings of Naj Tunich, but a few do make an appearance. A solar deity comprises Drawing 62, an incomplete face less than four centimeters high (fig. 6-40). One solar attribute is the large, square eye socket, which is usually filled with the square iris of the squint-eyed Sun God. What looks like a fang is the so-called

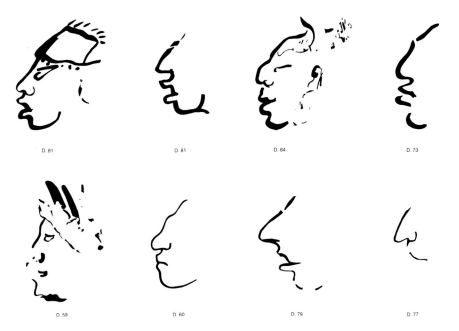

FIG. 6-38. Late Classic profile faces, Naj Tunich.

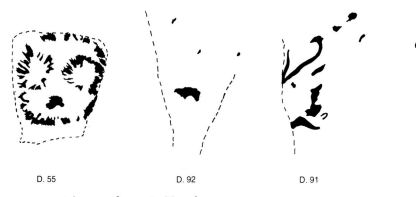

D. 55   D. 92   D. 91

FIG. 6-39. Schematic faces, Naj Tunich.

"*tau* tooth" of the Sun God, the filed, front teeth in the form of a T.

The Hero Twins

Classic versions of Hunahpu and Xbalanque, the Popol Vuh Hero Twins, are also present at Naj Tunich. The Hero Twins are now recognized as having played a major role in Classic mythology and royal symbolism, but their presence at Naj Tunich marks the first time they have been found in a cave. We can thank Michael Coe (1972: 13–14; 1978:59–60) for identifying the Hero Twins in Maya iconography.

FIG. 6-40. Drawing 62, Naj Tunich.

FIG. 6-41. Hunahpu and Xbalanque on Resurrection Vase. Kerr Vessel 1892. Photograph © Justin Kerr 1982.

FIG. 6-42. Names of Hero Twins: *a*, Hunahpu; *b*, Xbalanque.

FIG. 6-43. Drawing 87, Naj Tunich.

He noted a pair of recurring figures on painted vases, one with black body spots and the other with patches of jaguar pelt (fig. 6-41). He christened them the "Headband Gods" after another of their attributes, a cloth head scarf. Coe first suggested that the Headband Gods might be the underworld manifestations of Hunahpu and Xbalanque. His so-called Young Lords, another deity pair with a tonsured hairstyle and zoomorphic headdress, represented them in other guises. Now the Young Lords are known to be the father and uncle of the Hero Twins, Hun Hunahpu and Vukub Hunahpu, as well as maize deities (Taube 1985). The Headband Gods, also known as the Headband Twins (Schele and Miller 1986:51), have been securely linked with Hunahpu and Xbalanque, both thematically and epigraphically (Coe 1989). Especially important is that the name glyph of the spotted figure corresponds closely with the name Hunahpu (fig. 6-42a). It is preceded by the number one, or *hun*, followed by the head variant of Ahau (Schele 1986; Coe 1989:168). Since Hunahpu is the Quiche equivalent of the Lowland day name Ahau, the glyphic phrase **hun ahaw** can be understood as a Lowland version of the name Hunahpu. The glyphic name of Xbalanque is the personified head of the number nine, which includes a "*yax*" glyph set over the bridge of the nose and a patch of jaguar pelt over the lower part of the face (fig. 6-42b).

One of the most important paintings at Naj Tunich is Drawing 87, which shows Hunahpu and Xbalanque seated *en face*, gesturing in such a manner as to appear engaged in an animated dialogue (fig. 6-43). One notable difference is that Xbalanque, the right-hand figure with jaguar-pelt body patches, looks as though his eye is shut. The meaning of this remains unclear, but one possibility is that it refers to his moribund state.

FIG. 6-44. Drawing 21, Naj Tunich.

gun, he handily dispatches the arrogant false sun Vukub Kakix.

In Drawing 21 Hunahpu the hunter is shown in his role as ballplayer. He stands in front of a three-stepped structure, which is the conventional form of ballcourt architecture at Naj Tunich. The ball is superfixed by the number nine. Numerical infixes, usually compounded with other glyphic elements, frequently accompany the rubber ball in Maya ballgame scenes. Their meaning remains obscure. Schele and Miller (1986:255) propose that the number refers to the number of human sacrifices at stake in the game, though this idea remains unsupported. Nine is one of the more common numbers accompanying the ball. This number is especially important in Maya numerology and has long been associated with the underworld in the Maya area and central Mexico (Thompson 1970a:195). The number nine may also refer to Xbalanque, for his personal name is the head variant of the number nine. Could Hunahpu be playing with a ball that was at the same time his brother, Xbalanque?

This painting is located at the deepest point in the cave of any painting in the main passageway and appears by itself on the wall (handprints are found about one meter to the left). This sequestered location may have been a means of putting these gods deep into the underworld.

Another depiction of Hunahpu has been identified by Coe (ibid.:171) in Drawing 21, one of four ballgame scenes found at Naj Tunich (fig. 6-44). Coe's identification stems from the black spots marking the cheek and the woven hat with a short brim. In Maya art this hat is worn by hunters carrying blowguns or spears (fig. 6-45). Coe points to a number of vase images in which Hunahpu wears the woven hat in his guise as blowgunner. That Hunahpu was the archetypical hunter can be seen in his name, as *ahpu* in Quiche means "blowgunner." In the Popol Vuh, Hunahpu uses his blowgun: in one episode, with a shot from his blow-

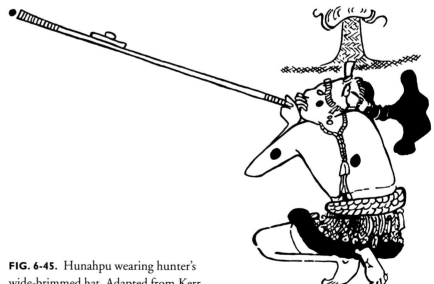

FIG. 6-45. Hunahpu wearing hunter's wide-brimmed hat. Adapted from Kerr 1989:68.

Images from the Underworld

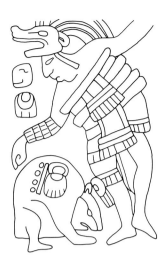

FIG. 6-46. Scene on modeled-carved bottle showing ballplayer and curled-up animal as ball. Adapted from photograph by Linda Schele.

A reverse situation actually occurs in the Popol Vuh, when the head of Hunahpu, severed by a killer bat, is put into play as the ball. In fact, Kowalski (1989) proposes that the La Esperanza ballcourt marker (usually said to be from Chinkultic) depicts a related scene. He identifies the ballplayer as Xbalanque and the ball, which has a youthful head "*ahaw*" infix, as the head of Hunahpu.

In Drawing 21 Hunahpu wears a jaguar-skin skirt, an outfit also worn by ballplayers on the three markers from Copan's Ballcourt II-B (Schele and Miller 1986: fig. 6.11). Schele (1986) has identified the left-hand figure of the second marker as Hunahpu, based on the accompanying text. Thus far, the Copan ballcourt marker and Drawing 21 are the only depictions of Hunahpu as a ballplayer in Classic Maya art. The ballgame is the setting for

much of the drama in the Popol Vuh. It is where divine battle is waged, pitting the story's heroes against the malevolent lords of Xibalba. As mentioned earlier, Hunahpu's severed head is even used to play the ballgame at one point in the story. The head is cleverly recovered with the aid of a rabbit that diverts the Xibalban lords by pretending to be the ball. While they chase the scampering rabbit, Xbalanque restores Hunahpu's head and his life. Schele and Miller (1986:252, pl. 103) show that this "rabbit ruse" was a subject of Maya art. On a small, carved bottle a ballplayer is shown standing over an animal doubled over in the form of a ball (fig. 6-46). At Naj Tunich, Drawing 8 shows an animal, possibly a collared peccary, doubled over, precisely in the manner of the clever rabbit that mimicked the ball (fig. 6-47). Above the peccary a human head of about the same size may be the severed head of Hunahpu.

The inscription in Drawing 23 may contain a reference to Hunahpu, depicted in Drawing 21. These paintings are next to each other on the wall and were painted by the same hand, Artist 1. The name of Hunahpu possibly appears in Drawing 23 in the right-hand column at C4 (fig. 7-6). The number one is the large black spot on the forehead and the personified Ahau has a black spot on the cheek. This version of the name is unusual in that it is preceded by T12, phonetic **ah**, which typically functions as an agentive prefix ("he of"). Here it may provide phonetic complementation to **ahaw**. If this identification of Hunahpu's name is correct, then the text can be understood as mentioning a lord from a site, identified by an Emblem Glyph, as the **yitah** "companion of" Hunahpu, who, as just stated, is portrayed in Drawing 21. Moreover, as Drawings 21, 22, and 23 were painted by the same artist, it is possible that Drawing 22 is a portrait of the lord in question.

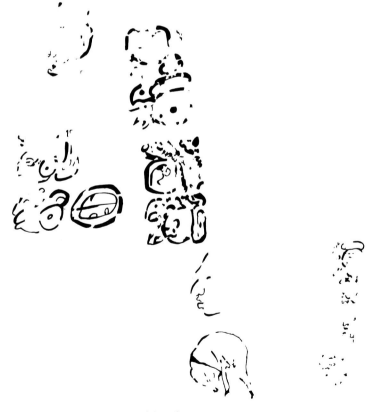

FIG. 6-47. Drawing 8, Naj Tunich.

FIG. 6-48. Drawing 51, Naj Tunich.

FIG. 6-49. Drawing 31, Naj Tunich.

FIG. 6-50. Drawing 39, Naj Tunich.

FIG. 6-51. Drawing 83, Naj Tunich.

Other ballgame scenes at Naj Tunich are poorly preserved and therefore may have had iconographic references that are no longer present, of the sort seen in Drawing 21. Drawing 51, however, is complete and presents a fully mortal ballplayer (fig. 6-48). It is also likely that Drawings 31 and 39 deal with historical rather than mythological references to the ballgame (figs. 6-49, 6-50). There is mounting evidence that the Maya conceived of the ballcourt as an extension of the underworld. Ballcourt markers framed by quatrefoils seem to create symbolic holes that connect the court with this nether realm. Certainly the Popol Vuh shows that the underworld and ballcourts were in some sense synonymous. As mentioned earlier, the Popol Vuh refers to the ballcourt as "Great Abyss [i.e., cave] at Carchah." The ballcourt was Xibalba, inhabited by malevolent underworld gods but also divine heroes. The four ballplayers from

Images from the Underworld

Naj Tunich, the first such figures to be found in a cave, stand as confirmation of the ballcourt's underworld symbolism.

The Dwarf

Drawing 83 is a delightful portrait of a dwarf, looking dignified with his arms folded across his chest (fig. 6-51). The fact that he has a beard and traces of a moustache seems to address his important status. I would propose that this dwarf is not a mere mortal but rather a denizen of the underworld. First of all, his headdress is unusual. Recall that most mortal figures portrayed in the cave wear a cloth headwrap. Indeed, another scene featuring a dwarf shows him wearing a high cloth hat (fig. 6-52). In Drawing 83, however, the dwarf wears a fringed headband, and from the top of his head rises a twisted cord.

There is a widespread belief among Maya (and Mesoamerican) peoples that dwarves, often with meteorological associations, inhabit caves. In Zinacantan it is believed that dwarves live in the subterranean world. When it is transitted by the sun on its nightly journey, the dwarves don mud hats to protect themselves from the heat (Thompson 1970a:347). Among the Quiche Maya of highland Guatemala, the important supernatural dwarf Saki C'oxol inhabits woods and caves. Quiche shamans visit the sacred cave at Utatlan in the hope of encountering Saki C'oxol, for he appears bedecked in silver and will exchange a magical stone for money (Tedlock 1983:350–351).

As the guardian of animals, Saki C'oxol seems to be another version of the Maya earth lord. Such entities control game, rain, and other aspects of subsistence, and they typically live in caves where they are petitioned. I would tentatively propose that Drawing 83 shows one of these important cave-dwelling dwarfs who may have been

FIG. 6-52. Drawing 68, Naj Tunich.

FIG. 6-53. Dwarf drinking from bowl in front of lord wearing rabbit headdress. Kerr Vessel 1453. Photograph © Justin Kerr 1981.

the focus of propitiatory rites at Naj Tunich.

Drawing 68 is another painting that features a dwarf, here in the company of a corpulent lord (fig. 6-52; Plate 10). The lord balances a hemispherical vessel in his right hand, the shape of which recalls a gourd cup (*luch* in Yucatec), fashioned from the *Crescentia Cujete L.* Gourd cups are used today in Yucatan as containers of liquid ritual offerings. This scene closely parallels one on a painted vase from the Ik Emblem Glyph site that shows a dwarf drinking from a hemispherical vessel (fig. 6-53). The headdresses in both scenes have interesting parallels in that the dwarf wears a cloth headwrap and the lord, a long-eared zoomorphic headdress; on the vase this is clearly a rabbit head. In the vase scene, the dwarf raises the bowl to his lips with both hands. This suggests that the lord in Drawing 68, who balances the *luch* in one hand, is not about to drink but is passing the vessel to the other figure. The dwarf's reaching gesture confirms that a transfer is taking place. Furthermore, when the Maya show the transfer of some object in a scene, it is usually depicted in the hands of the person passing it. The short text between the two figures ends with the Ixtutz Emblem Glyph. This is the only figurative scene from Naj Tunich with a conjoined text in which an Emblem Glyph appears. The scene, then, may portray two persons from Ixtutz, though it is not yet clear to whom the nominal phrase refers.

This painting, as well as others discussed earlier, demonstrate that the paintings of Naj Tunich have thematic correspondences with Maya vase painting. The palace scene in Drawing 5, depictions of the Hero Twins, and Drawing 68, the dwarf and lord, resonate with the pictorial repertory of vase painters.

The cave's figurative paintings are largely concerned with ritual performance, not as pomp and circumstance, but as lived experience. They are a testimonial to the acts of piety and quests for communion with the spirits who inhabit the cave. The consistently plain costumes worn by the cave figures suggests a downplaying of rank distinctions, perhaps in accord with the liminal state in which ritualists found themselves at Naj Tunich. The figurative paintings might be described as quasi-narrative; but some (e.g., Drawings 17, 20, 22, 63, and 76) focus so tightly on the protagonist himself that they communicate as much about his existential condition as the details of a story. Achieving a delicate balance between action and introspection, these paintings are among the most interesting in the cave. Whether they portray noble pilgrims or shamans cannot be said with certainty, though the cave's rich archaeology would suggest the former. But some of the noble pilgrims may themselves have been the presiding shamans.

The figurative paintings also convey the idea of the cave as a Xibalba-like domain, identified with the sacred ballcourt in the interior of the earth. Appropriately, the Hero Twins are represented on two occasions. The Hero Twins' adventures may have been recounted in the cave as part of rites addressed to them. The dwarf deity in Drawing 83 echoes the pervasive association of caves with earth-lord cults in the Maya area.

The Naj Tunich paintings are not the first Classic cave paintings to have been discovered in the Maya area. But they show for the first time that Maya cave painting could achieve the sophistication that we have come to expect from some of the best native graphic artists of the New World.

7

The Hieroglyphic Inscriptions of Naj Tunich

by Barbara MacLeod and Andrea Stone

It could be argued that the single most important discovery made at Naj Tunich is the collection of painted hieroglyphic texts. They are scattered throughout the cave, occupying its deepest recesses, at depths of over one-half mile. One inscription can be reached only by a precarious descent on a rope, while another appears in a secret tunnel where broken pottery and other evidence of an ancient ceremony lie strewn across the floor. In certain areas of the cave, texts lie in close proximity to scenes depicting arcane rituals, sometimes involving nude figures in dramatic poses; other figures sit in a relaxed, seemingly meditative state. The overwhelming impression left by all of this, and an assumption in our approach to their decipherment, is that these cave inscriptions came into existence in a highly charged ritual atmosphere.

The cave is home to over forty hieroglyphic texts. Many are fragmentary owing to natural deterioration over the course of more than one thousand years

of existence. Fortunately, twenty-five were found in reasonably good condition or were photographed prior to their destruction in the 1980s. These paintings constitute the largest collection of Maya texts ever found in a cave and one of the largest collections of painted inscriptions to come from a single Maya site. They preserve rare fragments of the Classic Maya's ephemeral mental world and offer unique insights into their utilization of caves as pilgrimage shrines.

Yet, owing to the novel context of cave inscriptions, the texts of Naj Tunich have proven to be an exciting but difficult challenge in decipherment. Though we can make no claim to a final resolution of the problems posed by these cave texts, we have attempted to identify many of the major issues. It is also important in our view to move forward with the task of interpretation and synthesis, even if all of the facts are not currently within our grasp. Hence, we will offer our best explanation of the content of the most important inscriptions in light of the current state of knowledge, keeping in mind that future advances in decipherment may change the picture in unexpected ways.

The following analysis of Naj Tunich's hieroglyphic inscriptions is framed within the current idiom of Maya hieroglyphic decipherment, and it may thus seem arcane to someone who is not an epigrapher. We advise the reader of this and offer a summary of the contents of this chapter for those who may not care to wade into the mire of what admittedly is a complex subject, even for the specialist.

Précis

The cave inscriptions contain two Calendar Round dates marking period endings: 9.13.0.0.0 and 9.17.0.0.0 in the Long Count, falling in A.D. 692 and 771, respectively. These dates provide an anchor for our proposed reconstruction of the remaining Calendar Round dates, which fit roughly into this time span. Many Calendar Round dates do not conform in certain respects to the calendrical system that prevailed in the Maya Lowlands during the Classic period. We suggest that these aberrant Calendar Round dates are the result of some type of ritual manipulation of the calendar, one that presently remains inscrutable.

A number of the inscriptions have parallel clauses that contain one of the most commonly occurring verbs in the cave texts: **ilah** "see"; this verb is often followed by the locative **mo'pan**, which states where the "seeing" event occurred. The name *mo'pan* was in use around the Naj Tunich region during the Classic period, and it survives in the same vicinity today as the name of a river and a Mayan language of the Yucatecan subfamily.

An important glyph in the cave texts is **yitah**, which we interpret as "his companion." This glyph typically links

multiple actors; as many as five occur in any single text. These actors probably represent members of a pilgrimage group, whose names are recorded for posterity on the walls of the cave. Some of these actors may have served specific functions as ritual specialists. One has been identified as a scribe, and certain titles suggest that others were ritual practitioners or shamans.

We have also considered the possibility that some of these actors are supernaturals, perhaps deified ancestors. This idea is suggested by titles that allude to meteorological concepts, such as clouds and lightning. There is an ancient and widespread belief in the Maya area that cave-dwelling ancestors and deities manifest themselves in the guise of these atmospheric forces. But it is also significant that some present-day Maya shamans take their titles from atmospheric phenomena, and Maya kings had titles such as *chak* "thunderbolt" and *muyal* "cloud."

References to the supernatural at Naj Tunich are also suggested in the presence of such compounds as **na-ho-chan**, which in monumental texts denotes a supernatural locale, usually associated with the Paddler Gods. However, its function in the cave is ambiguous.

Two other verbs in the cave texts, **huli** "he arrived" and **pakxi** "he returned," appear to be associated with the comings and goings of noble pilgrims at the cave. Historical persons are clearly mentioned in some of the inscriptions and are linked with glyphs that tie them to regional surface sites around Naj Tunich, such as Sacul, Ixkun, Ixtutz, and Caracol. The Emblem Glyphs and other connections with monumental texts provide important evidence of intersite relations in southeastern Peten. The texts also suggest cooperative ventures among neighboring polities in the utilization of Naj Tunich as a holy shrine. Naj Tunich may have served, then, as a vehicle of regional political cohesion during the Late Classic.

Conventions for Dates and Transcriptions

Our correlation of hieroglyphic dates with the Gregorian calendar follows the so-called "11.16" or "GMT" (Goodman-Martínez-Thompson) correlation (Thompson 1927). We have adopted the 584,285 correlation constant, which has been supported by Lounsbury (1983); however, the two-day difference between it and the alternate 584,283 is not critical for any of the arguments presented below.

It may be helpful to clarify our usage of the terms "grapheme," "collocation," and "glyph." Graphemes make up the affixes and main signs of the writing system and are the smallest coherent unit that can stand independently. A cluster of graphemes, usually occupying a single glyph block, forms a collocation. A "glyph" generally has a more fluid meaning and can refer to a grapheme (e.g., Bricker 1986:1) or to a collocation, such as an Emblem Glyph.

Hieroglyphic transcriptions are written in the standard "*T*-number" (*T* for Thompson) format based on *A Catalog of Maya Hieroglyphs* (Thompson 1962). Transliterations of hieroglyphic signs that denote their syllabic or logographic value are written in boldface type. Mayan language references, from grammars, dictionaries, texts, and other sources, are written in italic type. Glyphs that are presently undeciphered but have an identifiable pictorial referent are written in standard type in English with a descriptive phrase, such as "headband bird."

To locate individual glyph blocks, it is customary to use a grid system in which columns and rows are identified, respectively, by a letter and number; these are provided in the accompanying illustrations. The reader should be forewarned, however, that the texts of Naj

Tunich generally do not follow the pattern of most monumental inscriptions, in which glyphs read down in paired columns. The prevalent reading order in the cave texts is straight down in single columns from left to right, though there are exceptions to this. A quick way to determine the reading order for most texts is to check whether the initial Calendar Round date reads down a column or across a row, though certain inscriptions, such as Drawings 65, 82, and 88, are more elusive. The reading order for any text should be kept in mind when a section of text is referred to by the grid system.

Hieroglyphic Dates
Period-ending Dates

Like so much of the cave's art and archaeology, the hieroglyphic dates of Naj Tunich are something of an anomaly. There are twenty dates in the form of a Calendar Round (CR).[1] The cave's inscriptions do not record a single Long Count date, which presents obvious problems in trying to establish absolute dates.

In the absence of a Long Count date, the Maya could also lock a CR date into linear time by introducing CR dates that fall on period endings. Owing to long intervals between recurrence, period-ending CR dates mark what are for all practical purposes unique stations in the Long Count. Thompson (1960:184) notes that any particular CR date falls on a *k'atun* ending only once in 375,000 years. While a *tun*-ending CR date will recur after a mere millennium, this still makes for a unique occurrence during the roughly six-hundred-year period when Classic Lowland inscriptions were produced.

Naj Tunich has two period-ending CR dates that provide potential anchors for an absolute time frame. One of these, 3 Ahau 3 Mol, is found in two texts in the Western Passage: Drawings 37 and 52. Drawing 37 opens with the

CR date 11 Eb 10 Pax. A Distance Number (DN) of 2.10.8, or 928 days, is added to arrive at 3 Ahau 3 Mol (fig. 7-1). As 3 Ahau 3 Mol must refer to 9.15.10.0.0 (in A.D. 741), 11 Eb 10 Pax can be securely placed at 9.15.7.7.12. Likewise, Drawing 52 commences with a CR date only three days later than that of Drawing 37, 1 Men 13 Pax (9.15.7.7.15), and introduces a DN just three days less to arrive again at 3 Ahau 3 Mol (fig. 7-2).

Between 1981 and 1988, 3 Ahau 3 Mol (9.15.0.0.0) was the only period-ending CR date known from Naj Tunich, providing one probable basis for the resolution of CR dates. However, in 1988 Drawing 88 was discovered with its new period-ending CR date: 8 Ahau 8 Uo (9.13.0.0.0), falling in A.D. 692 (Drawing 88, G4–5, fig. 7-3). It is worth mentioning, though it is probably coincidental, that each of the two period-ending CR dates from Naj Tunich has the same *tsolk'in* and *haab* coefficient.

Preceding the 8 Ahau 8 Uo period ending in Drawing 88 is a DN of 3.13 (seventy-three days), which counts back to 13 Manik Seating of Kayab (9.12.19.14.7), a date not recorded in the text. The DN and the date (at G3) are linked by the collocation T1.?:502, which strongly resembles T1:44:502 **u-to-ma** or **ut-om**, a verb meaning "it will happen" (see note 5). This verb also ties a DN to a period-ending CR date on the fragmentary Monument 157 from Copan (Schele and Grube 1988). It should be noted that 9.13.0.0.0 falls over two *k'atun*s before the earliest date in the sequence, using 3 Ahau 3 Mol as an anchor. Hence, an 8 Ahau 8 Uo anchor would push the Naj Tunich CR dates back by one whole Calendar Round (except those explicitly tied to 3 Ahau 3 Mol).

It cannot be resolved beyond doubt whether 3 Ahau 3 Mol or 8 Ahau 8 Uo is the correct anchor date, but current

FIG. 7-1. Drawing 37, Naj Tunich.

FIG. 7-2. Drawing 52, Naj Tunich. Drawing by Barbara MacLeod.

evidence tends to favor the former (9.15.10.0.0), at least for inscriptions in the main tunnel system. First, the location of Drawing 88 dissociates it from the other paintings (see Chapter 5). Second, one of the Western Passage paintings, Drawing 11, has a short text that mentions the *tsolk'in* date 13 Ahau. Since this date recurs every 260 days, it is logical to assume that the Maya had in mind some highly noteworthy 13 Ahau, such as one marking a period ending. 13 Ahau falls on the *k'atun* ending 9.17.0.0.0 (13 Ahau 18 Cumku), which is closer to the 3 Ahau 3 Mol than the 8 Ahau 8 Uo period ending. Finally, it might be noted that the texts of Naj Tunich show certain af-

finities with texts of nearby sites, such as Sacul, Ixtutz, and Ixkun, as will be discussed in greater detail below. The dates of these texts range from K'atun 16 to K'atun 18, a fact that also points toward the placement of the Naj Tunich CR dates after 9.15.10.0.0. But, in the end, for most of the CR dates in the cave, there is no sure way to tie them to any Long Count anchor.

Multiple-Base Calendar Round Dates

Once an anchor date has been established, problems of an even more puzzling nature confront the investigator. The CR dates of Naj Tunich present a situation unique in the corpus of Maya inscriptions with regard to the

Images from the Underworld

FIG. 7-3. Drawing 88, Naj Tunich.

alignment of month coefficients and day names. This alignment should be invariant because of simple arithmetic: the twenty days of the *tsolk'in* factor into the 365-day *haab* eighteen times, leaving a remainder of five. Since five divides evenly into twenty (four times), this means that any day in the 365-day year (represented by a month and a coefficient of seating to nineteen) can occur only on one of four days. These mathematical conditions result in five possible sets of month coefficients and corresponding day names. They are listed in Table 2. The right-hand column notes the CR dates at Naj Tunich that fall into any of the given sets.

For the moment, we will set aside the question of Year Bearers and consider only the five possible alignments of day names and month coefficients listed in Table 2. These will be called "alignment sets" rather than Year Bearer sets in order to disentangle the two issues, at least for the time being. Once a CR date is recorded in a text, it becomes obvious which of the five alignment sets it follows. With an important exception noted below, Maya inscriptions are highly uniform in their use of the Type III set, though "aberrant" dates appear at a number of sites in isolated instances. The only other set in widespread use is Type IV, so-called "Puuc-style dating." The Type IV set was first thought to occur only in Late Postclassic and Colonial Yucatecan calendrics; however, Proskouriakoff and Thompson (1947) demonstrated its widespread appearance during the Classic period in Campeche and western Yucatan at such sites as Edzna, Xcalumkin, and Uxmal. The earliest inscription from this area with a Type IV date is Stela 18 from Edzna, dating to 9.12.0.0.0. Interestingly, Puuc-style dating occurs at sites that also use the Type III alignment set, which was standard for most of the Maya Lowlands. One unusual monument even contains dates in both systems.[2] Puuc-style dates also appear in several stela inscriptions from Yaxchilan that Proskouriakoff and Thompson suggest were influenced by the northern Maya area. Mathews (1977) proposes that Puuc-style dating could reflect a situation in which the *tsolk'in* and *haab* days began at different times. If the *tsolk'in* day began at sunset and the *haab*, at sunrise, then a night event would see a *tsolk'in* position advance one day over the *haab* station until the following sunrise. Indeed, in Puuc-style dates the *haab* coefficient is one day shy of what the standard system dictates. Therefore, Mathews posits that some Puuc-style dates may refer to events that took place during the night.

Fully attested CR dates are known from only two sources: hieroglyphic inscriptions and ethnohistorical documents. Maya hieroglyphic inscriptions and their Preclassic antecedents provide the only recorded CR dates in the entire corpus of Mesoamerican writing. Though we suppose that the solar and divinatory calendars were maintained as an interlocking system in most Mesoamerican societies, they were recorded as such only in writing systems that kept the Long Count. Central Mexican writing, for instance, records only 260-day stations, even when naming a solar year.

The second source of explicit CR dates, ethnohistorical documents, also comes from the Maya area.[3] CR dates are found in Colonial Yucatecan chronicles, such as the Books of Chilam Balam, the Chronicle of Oxkutzcab, and in Landa's *Relación* (Thompson 1960:124–125). These attested CR dates make it clear which alignment set was in use in Colonial Yucatan. Though there are some inconsistencies, the prevailing Colonial pattern is Type IV, matching Puuc-style dating. Thus, the only alignment sets in widespread use in Mesoamerica that are *explicitly* recorded are Types III and IV.

However, once a set of Year Bearers has been identified, then the alignment set theoretically should become implicit. The Year Bearers consist of the set of four days that begin the solar year, called in Yucatec the *ah kuch haab* "bearer of the year." The Year Bearer was extremely important for Mesoamerican communities in providing a mechanism of annual prognostication. It was an augury of the upcoming year's fortunes to the extent that the solar year was often named by its Year Bearer. Since a complete Year Bearer cycle also took fifty-two vague years, the Calendar Round itself was conceived as a sequence of fifty-two Year Bearers and recorded thus, especially in central Mexico. Year Bearer sets are known for many Mesoamerican societies that failed to record complete CR dates. For example, it is well known that many highland Guatemalan peoples, such as the Quiche, have the set of Year Bearers called Manik, Eb, Caban, and Ik in Yucatec or Quej, E, Noh, and Ik in Quiche. If their New Year's day were to fall on the first of the month (meaning here the month position with a coefficient of one), then it is easy enough to identify their alignment set—it must be Type II.

The disagreement arises over which day of the month marked the day on which the Year Bearer fell, as the month did not necessarily begin on the first day, as we might expect. Maya CR dates show that there was a day within any given month whose coefficient is the seating glyph (T644), and this day *precedes* the day with a coefficient of one. The question is this: was the Year Bearer named for the seating day or the first of the month? For example, in the above-cited case of the Quiche, the alignment set would be Type III, not Type II, if the seating day were considered the New Year's day. Early opinion on this matter is perhaps typified by Morley (1915), who interpreted the

glyph we now read as "seating" as a zero day (though the sign for zero never substitutes for seating) and confidently asserted that this was the day on which the Classic Maya celebrated the New Year. Accordingly, he listed the Classic Maya Year Bearer set as Manik, Eb, Caban, and Ik—that is, the same as the Highland pattern.

Thompson (1960:119–121) crafted the argument most widely adhered to today—that the first of the month named the Year Bearer. He showed that in certain CR dates the month name is preceded by a T128:548 ("end of month") collocation, and in fewer cases it is accompanied by a Long Count date. The Long Count date dictates that the T128:548 collocation plus month sign must be equivalent to the twentieth day of the current month as well as identical with the seating day of the following month. This suggested to Thompson that the seating day was conceptually equivalent to the last day of the previous month. Though Thompson correctly interpreted the T644 "spectacle glyph" as "seating" based on context, he thought that it might have the secondary meaning "entrance of," implying that the month had not fully arrived. So this "zero" day in Thompson's thinking was actually a transitional time, whereas the first of the month marked the bona fide arrival of the New Year.

Within the Thompsonian framework, the Classic Maya Year Bearers are Akbal, Lamat, Ben, and Edznab, the set most widely accepted today (e.g., Satterthwaite 1965:Table 3). Note, however, that the alignment set does not change for the Classic Maya in choosing whether the New Year fell on the zero day or the first day of the month, but rather only the four days that constitute the Year Bearer. However, in calendars where we have only Year Bearer sets and no explicit CR dates, such as among the Highland Maya, this choice between

Images from the Underworld

TABLE 2. Day Name–Month Coefficient Sets and Naj Tunich Calendar Rounds in Each Set

	Month Coefficients	Day Names	Drawing	Calendar Round
I	1, 6, 11, 16	Imix, Cimi, Chuen, Cib	82	13 Ix 4 Zac
	2, 7, 12, 17	Manik, Eb, Caban, Ik	25	1 Chicchan End of Mol?
	3, 8, 13, 18	Akbal, Lamat, Ben, Edznab	70	8 Kan 4 Muan
	4, 9, 14, 19	Kan, Muluc, Ix, Cauac		
	5, 10, 15, 0	Chicchan, Oc, Men, Ahau		
II	1, 6, 11, 16	Manik, Eb, Caban, Ik	19	8 Chicchan 4 Zac
	2, 7, 12, 17	Akbal, Lamat, Ben, Edznab	23	4 Ik 6 Kankin
	3, 8, 13, 18	Kan, Muluc, Ix, Cauac	34	8 Men 9 Kayab
	4, 9, 14, 19	Chicchan, Oc, Men, Ahau	65	10 Manik 16 Cumku
	5, 10, 15, 0	Cimi, Chuen, Cib, Imix	65	13 Kan 18 Kayab
III	1, 6, 11, 16	Akbal, Lamat, Ben, Edznab	37	11 Eb 10 Pax
	2, 7, 12, 17	Kan, Muluc, Ix, Cauac	52	1 Men 13 Pax
	3, 8, 13, 18	Chicchan, Oc, Men, Ahau	37	3 Ahau 3 Mol
	4, 9, 14, 19	Cimi, Chuen, Cib, Imix	52	3 Ahau 3 Mol
	5, 10, 15, 0	Manik, Eb, Caban, Ik	66	12 Kan 2 Muan
			28	11 Chicchan 18 Zec
			24	12 Ik 5 Mol
			29	6 Akbal 16 Xul
			88	8 Ahau 8 Uo
IV	1, 6, 11, 16	Kan, Muluc, Ix, Cauac		
	2, 7, 12, 17	Chicchan, Oc, Men, Ahau		
	3, 8, 13, 18	Cimi, Chuen, Cib, Imix		
	4, 9, 14, 19	Manik, Eb, Caban, Ik		
	5, 10, 15, 0	Akbal, Lamat, Ben, Edznab		
V	1, 6, 11, 16	Chicchan, Oc, Men, Ahau	82	4 Cib 7 Zac
	2, 7, 12, 17	Cimi, Chuen, Cib, Imix		
	3, 8, 13, 18	Manik, Eb, Caban, Ik		
	4, 9, 14, 19	Akbal, Lamat, Ben, Edznab		
	5, 10, 15, 0	Kan, Muluc, Ix, Cauac		

the zero day and first day as the New Year determines the alignment set to which it belongs.

Thus to know with certainty the alignment set and which group of days functioned as Year Bearers, it is necessary to have recorded at least one CR date and some explicit reference to the Year Bearers. It is interesting that few such instances exist in all of Mesoameri-can calendrics where both pieces of information are known. In fact, the only place where both are stated explicitly is in Late Postclassic and Colonial Yucatan. The Madrid Codex has a set of New Year pages (Madrid 34–37) that clearly designate Kan, Muluc, Ix, and Cauac as the Year Bearer set, as well as at least one CR date (e.g., Madrid 85b, 5 Zac 2 Edznab) that is of the Type IV pattern. In Colonial Yucatan the Year Bearers are well known and there are also a number of attested CR dates. Landa's manuscript even includes a table that positions a Year Bearer on the first of Pop (Tozzer 1941:151 n. 748). This unequivocal alignment of the Year Bearer with the first day of the month supports Thompson's thesis that the New Year was celebrated in Classic times on this day as well.

The Year Bearer set is not known with certainty for the Classic Maya, as the New Year day was not marked in such a way as to make its identity transparent, at least according to present knowledge. Taube (1988b:195, 201–203) has pointed out known hieroglyphic references to both the seating of Pop and the first of Pop (following Thompson, he considers the seating of Pop to be the last day of Uayeb). These few occurrences do not lead to a certain identification of either day as the New Year. The Dresden Codex would seem to solve this problem for a Type III alignment set, as it contains both CR dates and a set of four New Year pages in which each page corresponds to one Year Bearer (Dresden 25–28). The Year Bearer for each section is repeated in the left margin of the page. As though in stubborn resistance to a resolution of this problem, the day sign for both the seating and the first of the month are listed in the margin. It may be that New Year ceremonies extended over both days. That fact alone does not tell us which day was the Year Bearer. In this study we will follow the view that the first day of the month was the day that named the Year Bearer. This is what Thompson (1960:124) called the "standard system"—the Type III set with Akbal, Lamat, Ben, and Edznab as Year Bearers.

At Naj Tunich, one inscription provides a modicum of support for Thompson's position. Drawing 12 presents a *tsolk'in* date consisting of a bar and two dots preceding the day Lamat (fig. 7-4). The medial position of the upper dot strongly suggests that a third dot was present, yielding a coefficient of eight. In Drawing 11, located on the same wall above Drawing 12, is a reference to 13 Ahau, which can be reconstructed as 9.17.0.0.0 (fig. 6-27). The next Lamat station after this 13 Ahau is 8 Lamat 1 Pop (9.17.0.0.8). This may be a reference to a New Year's day following on the heels of a *k'atun* ending. Naturally it could only be the New Year if this were to fall on the first of Pop. In addition, Drawing 58 at Naj Tunich is a petroglyph of the day sign Ben (fig. 5-12), also one of the Year Bearers in the standard system.

From the CR dates at Naj Tunich in Table 2, it can be seen that most follow the standard system (Type III). A group of five dates in four paintings also falls into Type II, three dates fall into Type I, and one date, into Type V. Accepting the formula that the first day of the year marked the Year Bearer, then the Type II dates at Naj Tunich could be said to follow the Highland pattern. Noting this Highland connection, Christopher Jones (n.d.) cautiously proposed that peoples with different Year Bearer sets may have utilized Naj Tunich as a shrine, thereby accounting for the calendrical inconsistencies. This multiethnic explanation fits the notion of Naj Tunich as a pilgrimage center, attracting people from far-flung areas. We might ask, then, whether or not the two predominant patterns (Type III and Type II) indicate that distinct ethnic groups, one

with Lowland and one with Highland affiliations, were writing in the cave.

Such an idea must be approached with caution, as southern Lowland Maya writing is consistent in its use of the standard system, even though there are rare occurrences of nonstandard dates. The Type II set is used, for example, in a single date in the following cases:

1. Nim Li Punit Stela 2: 1 Ix 13 Pax
2. Fort Worth Panel: 5 Ix 8 Zac
3. "Site Q" panel in private collection: 1 Cauac 8 Uo

What is distinct in the case of Naj Tunich is that there are five Type II dates, probably more than at any other site. Yet the idea that this date pattern stems from a group of Highland-oriented people whose writing is in all other respects like that of those who use the standard system seems unlikely. First, apart from Puuc-style dating (Type IV), there is no prehispanic evidence for the regional use of a different alignment set anywhere in the Maya Lowlands. For example, with the Naj Tunich Type II dates we might expect to find at least one corresponding surface site (or perhaps a group of painted vases) that also uses the Type II set with consistency. Nothing of this sort has ever been found. Aberrant dates appear on painted pottery, but they show no systematic patterns suggesting a different alignment set either at one site or regionally.

Another factor militating against this position is the presence of Type I dates in the cave. This alignment set is not known to have been used anywhere in Mesoamerica. Furthermore, Drawing 82 has dates in two different systems (Types I and V). To explain this in terms of regional differences in alignment sets would strain the limits of reason. One other argument against the multiethnic theory can be mustered in examining Drawing 82, whose first CR

FIG. 7-4. Drawing 12, Naj Tunich.

date, 13 Ix 4 Zac, is a Type I date. Stephen Houston (letter to Nikolai Grube, 1991) has identified the subject of this clause as an individual from Caracol; yet Caracol monuments use the Type III system of dates. Hence in this instance there is no correspondence between the alignment set of a surface site and aberrant dates in the cave, as would seem fitting to support the multiethnic explanation. The same argument obtains in examining Drawing 23, which commences with a Type II CR date (4 Ik 6 Kankin). The associated clause ends with an Emblem Glyph, discussed below, which may well refer to a site, presently unidentified, in southeastern Peten. In other Naj Tunich texts this same Emblem Glyph occurs in conjunction with Type III dates (e.g., Drawings 28 and 66). Once again, the cave texts fail to correlate the variation in alignment sets with geographical locale, as can be determined by Emblem Glyphs.

Another interpretation of this curious manipulation of dates is that it has ritual motivation. Hieroglyphic dates at Naj Tunich might have been tampered with by shamans and scribes because of their unique ritual context. Tampering with the calendar is certainly suggested by Drawing 82, with its two different day name–month coefficient patterns. It remains to be seen whether associated verbal compounds will ever help illuminate the specific context in which this tampering took place.

Images from the Underworld

TABLE 3. Calendar Round Dates and Long Count Stations by Type

Drawing	Calendar Round	Long Count	Year A.D.
Type III (Standard System)			
88	(13 Manik Seating Kayab)	9.12.19.14.7	Jan. 5, 692
88	8 Ahau 8 Uo	9.13.0.0.0	Mar. 18, 692
37	11 Eb 10 Pax	9.15.7.7.12	Dec. 15, 738
52	1 Men 13 Pax	9.15.7.7.15	Dec. 18. 738
37;52	3 Ahau 3 Mol	9.15.10.0.0	Jun. 30, 741
66	12 Kan 2 Muan	9.16.3.10.4	Nov. 13, 754
28	11 Chicchan 18 Zec	9.16.4.1.5	May 13, 755
24	12 Ik 5 Mol	9.16.10.5.2	Jun. 27, 761
11	13 Ahau (18 Cumku)	9.17.0.0.0	Jan. 24, 771
12	8 Lamat (1 Pop)	9.17.0.0.8	Feb. 1, 771
29	6 Akbal 16 Xul	9.17.0.6.3	May 27, 771
Nonstandard			
Type I			
25	1 Chicchan End of Mol?	9.16.12.6.5	Jul. 10, 763
70	8 Kan 4 Muan	9.15.19.9.4	Nov. 14, 750
82	13 Ix 4 Zac	9.15.13.3.14	Aug. 27, 744
Type II			
23	4 Ik 6 Kankin	9.15.6.5.2	Oct. 31, 737
19	8 Chicchan 4 Zac	9.15.7.2.5	Aug. 30, 738
65	7 Chicchan 19 Pax	9.15.8.8.5	Dec. 23, 739
65	13 Kan 18 Kayab	9.15.8.9.4	Jan. 11, 740
34	8 Men 9 Kayab	9.15.12.9.15	Jan. 1, 744
65	10 Manik 16 Cumku	9.15.13.11.7	Jan. 27, 745
Type V			
82	4 Cib 7 Zac	9.16.16.9.16	Aug. 29, 745
Eroded/illegible			
35	13 ?? 14 Muan		
88	2 ?? 5 Mac		

Long Count Stations

Table 3 lists all of the CR dates from Naj Tunich and their suggested Long Count positions. Certain assumptions underlie this chronology. First, we assume that the aberrant dates vary from the standard system in terms of their *haab* coefficient, as in the manner of Puuc-style dates. Second, we use the criterion of closest proximity to 9.15.10.0.0 as a determination of floating CR dates. However, there is one ex-

ception. The date 6 Akbal 16 Xul in Drawing 29 should be placed accordingly at 9.14.7.11.3 (June 9, 719); however, owing to the dates of other texts in this area of the cave, we have chosen a station one CR later. Another problematical date is that found in Drawing 25, where the *haab* coefficient is not clear. As it is not in bar-and-dot form and does not appear to be a head variant, it should represent either a "seating" or "end of month" coefficient; therefore the date could be either

TABLE 4. Gregorian Correlation of Dates and
Associated Events

Drawing	Long Count	Date A.D.	Event
A. Paintings in the western section of the Western Passage			
37	9.15.7.7.12	Dec. 15, 738	**hu-li**
52	9.15.7.7.15	Dec. 18, 738	**hu-li**
65*	9.15.8.8.5	Dec. 23, 739	**pi-ba-ya**
65*	9.15.8.9.4	Jan. 11, 740	**i-la-ha**
34*	9.15.12.9.15	Jan. 1, 744	**hu-li**
65*	9.15.13.11.7	Jan. 27, 745	**pa-ka-xa**
B. Paintings along one wall in the eastern section of the Western Passage			
23*	9.15.6.5.2	Oct. 31, 737	**il-ya**
19*	9.15.7.2.5	Aug. 30, 738	**pa-ka-xi**
28	9.16.4.1.5	May 13, 755	**yi-il-hi**
24	9.16.10.5.2	June 27, 761	**il-ya**
25*	9.16.12.6.5?	July 10, 763?	**il-ah**
29	9.17.0.6.3	May 27, 771	**yi-il-?**
C. Paintings in the North Passage Group			
70*	9.15.19.9.4	Nov. 14, 750	**il-a-ha**
66	9.16.3.10.4	Nov. 13, 754	**il-a-ha**
82*	9.15.13.3.14	Aug. 27, 744	**fire-bearer**
82*	9.16.16.9.16	Aug. 29, 767	**?**

* = nonstandard date

1 Chicchan Seating of Mol or 1 Chicchan End of Mol (i.e., Seating of Ch'en). Since the coefficient resembles the T128:548 collocation more than a seating glyph, we have listed the latter possibility in Table 3.

The above reconstruction spans the period between 9.12.19.14.7 (Drawing 88) and 9.17.0.6.3 (Drawing 29), a period of 4.0.9.16, or seventy-nine years (A.D. 692–771). This proposed sequence represents a likely scenario but is ultimately hypothetical, owing to the absence of Long Count anchors for the majority of dates in the cave. A number of other reconstructions within a Late Classic time frame are feasible. What may one day clarify the chronology is the discovery of related texts with firm dates from surface sites.

When correlated with the Gregorian calendar, as in Table 4, the proposed Long Count dates show some interesting patterns. The dates appear to cluster seasonally by their location and to a lesser extent by their associated verbs.

A seasonal repetition of events centering on distinct areas of the cave is suggested by the data in Table 4. The Group A dates fall between December 15 and January 27. In three instances where the event is the "Glyph D" verb, now known to be *hul-i* "he arrived," the dates fall within a more confined period—between December 15 and January 1, about a week on either side of the winter solstice. The Group B dates, located in texts along one wall at the beginning of the Western Passage, are less consistent, though three fall between

	DATE (CR)	YILAH	
D. 28	A1　　A2	A3	
D. 66	A1　　A2	B1	C1
D. 30			
D. 25	A1　　A2	A3	

May 13 and June 27, close to the onset of the rainy season and the summer solstice. Paintings in Group C, the North Passage Group, show a pattern of returning to the same point in the tropical year. The dates in Drawings 66 and 70 are exactly four years apart minus one day. The two dates in Drawing 82, though they use different alignment sets, are twenty-three years apart plus two days.

Parallel Clauses

The hieroglyphic texts of Naj Tunich are characterized by numerous parallel clauses and repetition of certain collocations. Stone (1983b) and Johnston (n.d.) have outlined some of these patterns in earlier discussions. They would appear to hold an important key to decipherment, as their recurrence in the cave indicates a sharply tuned consensus. Since the Maya were seldom inclined to write prolifically on cave walls, it would seem that these recurring patterns will ultimately shed light on their motives.

There are four texts that have strong connections in terms of parallel construction. Drawings 28, 66, and 25, opening with (y)ilah mo'pan, are long texts with multiple clauses, while Drawing 30 is a five-glyph nominal phrase (fig. 7-5). It is important to note that Drawings 28, 30, and 66 were painted by the same scribe, Artist 2, while Drawing 25 was painted by Artist 10 (see Chapter 4). Several other texts, Drawings 23, 24, and 29 (figs. 7-6, 7-7, 7-8), also open with (y)ilah mo'pan,

but share less of the nominal pattern. In addition, i-ilah mo'pan appears as a later clause in Drawing 65, H4–H5 (fig. 7-9), and is followed by a unique nominal phrase. These related texts were painted by a number of different scribes, none of whom can be identified as Artist 2 or Artist 10.

The multiple-clause texts begin with CR dates. Those in Drawings 28 and 66 are Type III (standard) dates, while that in Drawing 25 employs a Type I date, though with an admittedly ambiguous *haab* coefficient.

The **ilah** Verb and Its Linguistic Implications

The dates are followed by a verb whose main sign is an eye with sight lines emanating from it, deciphered indepen-

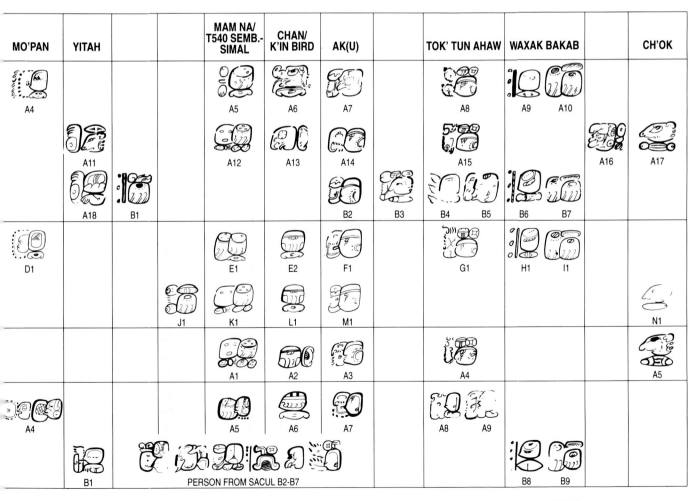

FIG. 7-5. Parallel clauses.

dently by Stuart (1987:25–26) and Houston (1989:39) as **il(ah)** "see." In its various occurrences in monumental texts as well as at the cave, this verb may have suffixed **hi** (Drawing 28, A3, fig. 7-10) as identified by Stuart (1987) or T181 **ha** (Drawing 25, A3, fig. 7-11), and in some cases an **a** syllable intervenes, as in Drawings 66, A2, and 70, B1 (figs. 7-12, 7-13). Fully phonetic spellings also occur, as in Drawing 65, H4 (fig. 7-9). In the cave examples as well as on the monuments, a T17 **yi** (Stuart 1987) prefix may appear, although this seems much more common on the monuments. In the eight examples of the verb at Naj Tunich, only two have prefixed **yi**, and there is no evidence of conflation of the "eye" logograph with **yi**. One example from Drawing 65, H4 (fig. 7-9), has an **i** (T679) prefix, which suggests an **ilah(i)** reading in all cases where **yi** is not prefixed.

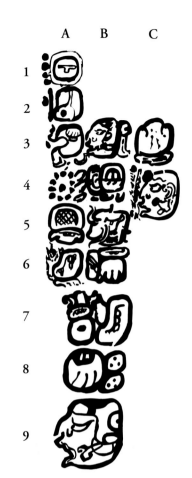

FIG. 7-6. Drawing 23, Naj Tunich.

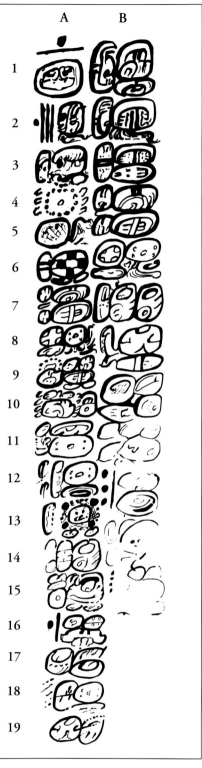

FIG. 7-8. Drawing 29, Naj Tunich. Drawing by Barbara MacLeod.

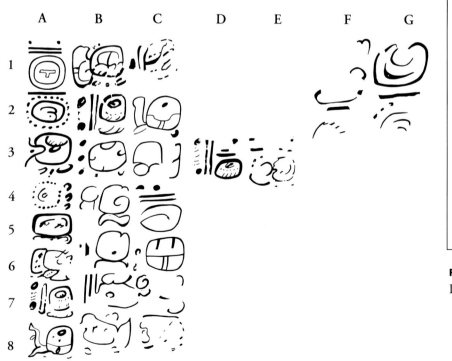

FIG. 7-7. Drawing 24, Naj Tunich.

Images from the Underworld

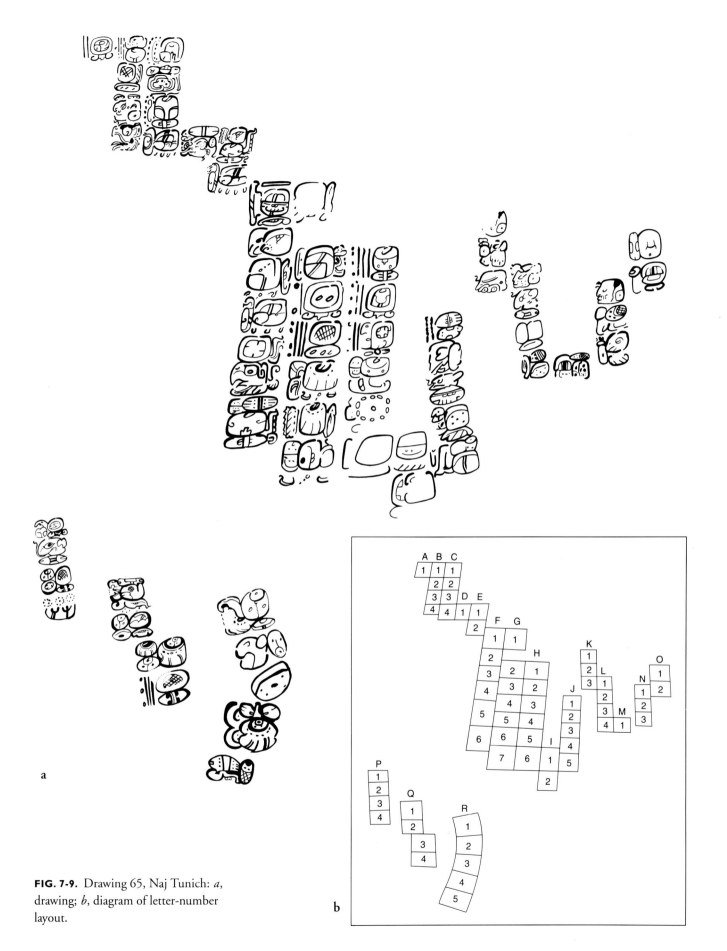

FIG. 7-9. Drawing 65, Naj Tunich: *a*, drawing; *b*, diagram of letter-number layout.

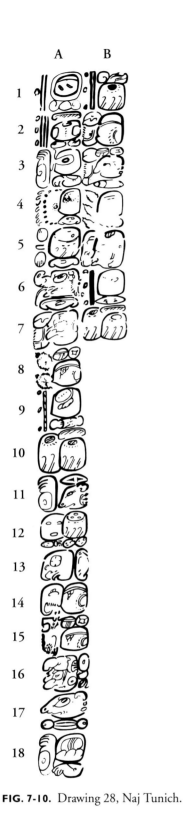

FIG. 7-10. Drawing 28, Naj Tunich.

The verb **ilah** (unmarked or marked with **i-**) is best understood as a Cholan passive verb *il-ah* "it was seen." The grammatical subject (the person or thing seen) follows either immediately or later in the sentence. Where **yi** is prefixed in the cave texts, the reading may become *y-il-ah* "it is seen"; eastern Cholan languages (Cholti and Chorti) have an *-ah* passivizer for both present and past tense, and only the presence or absence of a pronominal prefix distinguishes them.[4]

Alternatively, the forms with the **yi** prefix may be transitive, with a translation "he saw **mo'pan** . . . name." Many examples from the monuments, such as that of Piedras Negras Lintel 3, J1, or those of the Middle Panel of the Temple of the Inscriptions at Palenque, C3

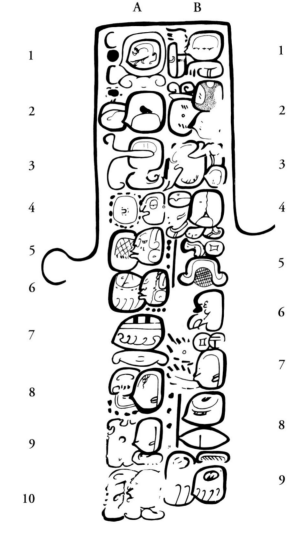

FIG. 7-11. Drawing 25, Naj Tunich.

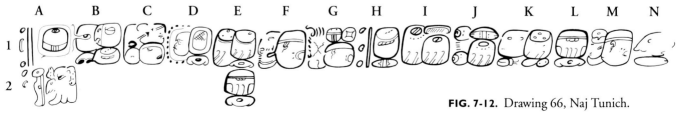

FIG. 7-12. Drawing 66, Naj Tunich.

Images from the Underworld

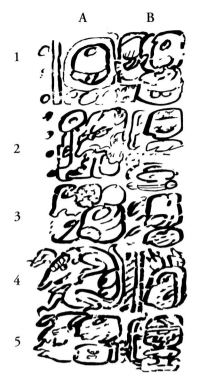

A   B

1

2

3

4

5

FIG. 7-13. Drawing 70, Naj Tunich.

and H2, appear in context to be transitive completives rather than passive incompletives. In Cholan *il* has an irregular *-a* transitive suffix, and in Yucatecan languages all completive transitives take an *-ah* suffix. Thus the interpretation of the **yilah** form as transitive is ambiguous vis-à-vis language identity, and we must assume that the Palenque examples are Cholan. Because verb morphology is language-specific and not easily borrowed, in our view the probable passive constructions employing this verb in the cave present the strongest evidence that Cholan speakers painted at least some of the major texts at Naj Tunich.

In the discussion that follows, Yucatecan sources are often cited as justification for various readings. The presence of many useful reflexes in Yucatec is more an artifact of conquest-period lexicography than a true picture of "the most closely related language(s)." The **balam** spelling for "jaguar" and the **pax-xa** spelling for the month Pax at Naj Tu-

nich (D. Stuart 1981; 1987) are neutral as evidence, since *p'ahram* is "jaguar" in Chorti (with *barum* in Lacandon) and the distribution of Classic Lowland month names is poorly known.

mo'pan: A Local Toponym

In the repetitive clause the **ilah** verb is usually followed by a variously spelled sequence reading **mo-o-pa-na** (fig. 7-5, also figs. 7-6–7-8, 7-12); one exception can be found in Drawing 70 (fig. 7-13, see **ilah** at B1). The main sign is T583 **mo** (Lounsbury 1973:102–103), and it is sometimes enclosed by columns of loops; this bracketing sign appears from other contexts to be phonetic **o** (Linda Schele, personal communication, 1988). In Drawings 25, A3, and 66, D1 (fig. 7-5), a head replaces the **o** bracket, pointing to probable equivalence. The whole suggests **mo'-pan**, which here (immediately following a transitive verb whose subject follows later) should be a toponym. This is commensurate with the broader usage of toponyms in the writing system (Stuart and Houston 1994). Furthermore, the obvious Mopan as a name for a southern group of Yucatecan Maya as well as for the western branch of the Belize River demonstrates that the name exists in the immediate area of the cave. Colonial sources describe the chief settlement of the Mopan "nation" as a town called Mopan (Villagutierre Soto-Mayor 1983:179; Cano 1984:11), which Thompson (1977:5) places at modern-day San Luis. The antiquity of the name Mopan for the river is more obscure, but both San Luis and the headwaters of the Mopan River are within fifteen kilometers of Naj Tunich. Given the linguistic issue raised in the preceding discussion, we may only speculate that **mo'pan* was a Classic regional name that survived into postconquest times and was adopted by Yucatecan speakers (the Mopan Maya) when they moved into former Cholan (or mixed)

territory. Many stones must be left unturned here for the present.

As a toponym, **mo'pan** goes with **ilah**: "he was/is seen at **mo'pan** . . . name," or perhaps in two cases "he saw **mo'pan** . . . name." In Drawing 66, C1 (fig. 7-12), **ik'-?-kab** compounds with **mo'pan**. We propose that **ik'-?-kab** "black-?-earth" is a metaphor for the cave, which the text specifies as lying within the broader precinct known as **mo'pan**. Less probably, **mo'pan** may refer to the cave, with **ik'-?-kab mo'pan** forming a couplet. Drawing 19, A4b, presents another descriptive metaphor for the cave: **ik'-way-nal** (fig. 7-14). The *cenote* or dragon-maw glyph (T769), forming the main sign of this collocation, has been read by MacLeod (n.d.) as **way** "world of dreams and death." This same collocation has also been identified as a "black hole" (Stuart and Houston 1994:71). In one pottery text (fig. 7-15) both underworld toponyms occur.

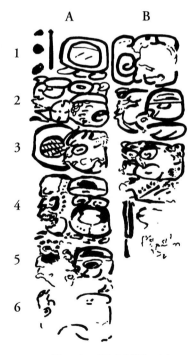

A   B

1

2

3

4

5

6

FIG. 7-14. Drawing 19, Naj Tunich. Drawing by Barbara MacLeod.

The Hieroglyphic Inscriptions of Naj Tunich

FIG. 7-15. *ik'-way* and *ik'-?-kab* toponyms on Kerr Vessel 1440. Adapted from Kerr 1989–1990:1:83.

Components of the Nominal Phrase with Parallel Passages

mam na or mam-na chan

The next segment of the repetitive clause reads **ma-ma-na**, or in one case **ma-na-ma** (fig. 7-5), following Grube's (1987) identification of T142 as **mV**, probably **ma**. We assume that **ma-ma-na** and **ma-na-ma** represent alternate spellings of the same linguistic segment, probably **mam na**. It seems significant that Artist 2 is responsible for the three occurrences of **ma-ma-na**, while Artist 10 painted the sole example of **ma-na-ma**. These variant spellings, then, could be attributed to linguistic idiosyncracies of individual scribes.

A "sky" logograph consistently follows this collocation; in one case the standard form of the "sky" glyph is replaced by the square-nosed serpent with a **na** suffix (Drawing 28, A6). If the cave texts are Cholan, then this might read **chan** "sky." Because **mam na** does not occur without **chan**, they may form a unit, with the whole reading **mam-na-chan**.

In three texts **mam-na** opens the nominal phrase that follows **(y)-ilah mo'pan**. The remainder of the nominal contains a series of glyphs occurring in other nominal phrases: **chan ak(u) tok'-tun-(ni)-ahaw** in various configurations; sometimes other glyphs follow (fig. 7-5). There are several other texts or clauses wherein a variant of this nominal phrase appears, including the third clause in Drawing 65, with **ak** at F2 located between other unique elements

(fig. 7-9). In Drawing 23, A6–B3 (fig. 7-6), **tok'-tun ahaw** follows **ilah mo'pan**. However, **ilah mo'pan** is followed by a distinct nominal sequence in Drawing 24 ending in **ah-bak-wits** at A7–A8 (fig. 7-7) and in Drawing 29 by another lengthy, distinct appellative between A6 and A12 (fig. 7-8).

Who or what is the subject of **(y)-ilah mo'pan**? Given the esoteric setting of the cave and the depiction of arcane rituals in the vicinity of the texts in question, one might speculate that the protagonists of the texts were mortal beings who came with compelling ritual obligations.

It may be significant that the name **mam-?-na-chan** is recorded on the Palenque Sarcophagus Lid in a phrase following the name of the recently deceased king Pacal (fig. 7-16). The text mentions that Pacal is in the "generations of" and subject here to the "action of" *mam-?-na-chan*, who is not a known Palencano ruler. The nature of the Sarcophagus Lid text—a list of Pacal's royal ancestors and their dates of death—suggests that this individual or entity facilitates Pacal's death and transition into the succession of deceased ancestors. A connection with ancestors might be suggested with the translation of *mam-na* as "grandfather-mother," a compound noun that could describe a class of ancestors (Nicholas Hopkins, personal communication, 1991). Comparable expressions for ancestors can be found in some Mayan languages. Among the Tzotzil, *totilme'iletik* "fathers and mothers" is a name for the ancestral gods (Vogt 1969:298). But the Quiche term *chuch-k-ahaw* "mother-father" refers to a shaman and to the head of a local patrilineage—both flesh-and-blood individuals (Tedlock 1982:47). We suggest that the cave's *mam-na-chan* may introduce a ritual practitioner whose title derives from his access to the spirit world.

T540 semblant-si-mal: A Scribe's Name

In three cases (Drawings 28, A12; 30, A1; and 66, K1; figs 7-5, 7-10, 7-17) the repeating nominal phrase opens with a T540 semblant. The rest of the collocation consists of T57 **si** plus T502:178 **mal**. In a second clause in Drawing 66, K1, this opens the nominal phrase designated by Stuart (1987:6–7) as a scribal signature because it follows **u-ts'ib** "his writing." The rest of the "signature" reads **chan ak tok'-tun ahaw ch'ok**. Stuart's identification of this individual as a scribe finds confirmation in the fact that the three texts containing the T540 semblant compound were all painted by the same hand, Artist 2.

As with **mam na**, a sky glyph usually follows the T540 semblant compound, except in Drawing 28, where a **k'in-bird-na** glyph substitutes for "sky" at A13 (fig. 7-5). This may somehow be equivalent to "sky," but it also recalls the **k'in**-bird sequence in the third clause of Drawing 65. Both of these may therefore read **k'in-kun** "sorcerer, diviner," employing recent suggestions by Grube (personal communication, 1991) concerning a **ku** reading for the bird and a **ne** reading for the "curl and comb" element on the bird head in Drawing 65. In Yucatec *ah-k'in* is "diviner" and *kun* is "cast spells" (Barrera Vásquez 1980:352, 401). Alternatively, **k'in kun** might be a sky metaphor or literally "sunseat," since **kun** is also "seat" in Yucatec.

The T540 semblant is problematic here. It does not look sufficiently like canonical T539 "jaguar spotted *ahaw*" to permit an unequivocal **way** "sorcerer" reading (Houston and Stuart 1989; Grube, letter to Stephen Houston and David Stuart, 1989), but that is possible and would be appropriate. The **si** suffix might then suggest *wayas*, a Yucatec-derived form also known from pottery texts. The sign is not clearly crosshatched, as in T540, but rather vaguely blotched on the right. Similar signs on Madrid 102c (Fox and Justeson 1984:65) and in a Primary Standard Sequence on Kerr Vessel 3743 (fig. 7-18) suggest a **na** reading for this sign without crosshatching. We have also considered an **e** reading, interpolating from Landa's **e** and its codical variants, plus the three-circle element in the "*uinal* frog" **e** identified by Nikolai Grube (personal communication, 1989) and David Stuart (Stephen Houston, personal communication, 1991). A **na** is not productive here; **e** (with **si**) may suggest *es*, another root meaning "sorcery," but this is a highly tentative suggestion since the T540 semblant may well be T540, an undeciphered sign. In the final analysis, **way** remains the best possibility.

8-IMIX-nal: Another Actor

The nominal phrase in the third clause of Drawing 28 opens with the numeral eight prefixed to T501 with a **nal** superfix (fig. 7-5). This is followed by the repeating portion of the nominal phrase seen with **mam-na** and the T540 semblant compound; however, it lacks **chan**, and a unique glyph intervenes between **ak** and **tok'-tun-ahaw**.

FIG. 7-16. Sarcophagus Lid inscription, Palenque. From Robertson 1983: fig. 170.

The Standard Nominal Phrase

The opening glyphs in nominal phrases we have just surveyed occur in well-defined contexts: **mam-na** always follows the first clause after **ilah mo'pan**; the T540 semblant compound always occurs in subsequent clauses in texts painted by Artist 2, and the nominal phrase consistently ends with the **ch'ok** title. We therefore conclude that the phrase-initial glyphs constitute the distinctive portions of the names of protagonists who otherwise share a string of titles. We now turn to these shared elements in their name, which we call the "standard nominal phrase." As noted above, parts of this phrase may occur independently in distinct nominals in other texts.

The a-ku Sequence

The sequence **a-ku** appears to be identical to the compound now read **ak** at Piedras Negras (Linda Schele, personal

A

FIG. 7-17. Drawing 30, Naj Tunich.

FIG. 7-18. Kerr Vessel 3743. Photograph © Justin Kerr 1987.

communication, 1990) due to its substitution with the turtleshell **ak**. In one case (Drawing 28, fig. 7-5) a bird head replaces T528 **ku** in conformity with the **kun** suggestion above. The owl/T528 **ku** shield alternation has been noted in nominals at Tikal, with a related substitution in G3 of the Lords of the Night (Linda Schele, personal communication, 1990).

tok' tun ahaw

Following **ak** is a compound consisting of a sign with irregular edges and either "Edznab" or "Cauac" markings prefixed to T528 with a T168 **ahaw** superfix, or alternately where an **ahaw** head follows (fig. 7-5). It seems certain that T528 here represents **tun**, since in two instances (Drawing 25 and 28) a somewhat eroded T116 **ni** is present (fig. 7-5). T116 is also present in a version of this compound appearing in Drawing 23, A6–B3, and what may be a related version in Drawing 82, F1.

We identify the first grapheme in the compound as **tok'** "flint" (Barrera Vásquez 1980:805), a suggestion which finds support in the substitution seen in Drawing 28, A8, where the eccentric form is replaced by two ovoid elements with "Edznab" markings (fig. 7-5). This ovoid version of the prefix resembles the **tok'** "flint knife" sign, T257, appearing in the **tok' pakal** collocation (Houston 1983b).

Owing to the presence of T168 or the youthful head **ahaw** (Drawing 25, A9, Drawing 28, B5, and Drawing 23, B3), **tok' tun ahaw** may be an Emblem Glyph. This suggestion was first put forth by Kevin Johnston (n.d.), who proposed that **tok'** substituted for the "water group" prefix, their common semantic ground being "blood." In Yucatec **tok'** means "let blood" as well as "flint" (Barrera Vásquez 1980:805). However, most Naj Tunich Emblem Glyphs lack the "water group" prefix, which is now read as **k'u(l)** "holy"

(Ringle 1988) and which would have no logical connection with **tok'**.

Houston (1986:fig. 9) illustrates two glyphs from unprovenanced vases that he suggests may be examples of the Xultun Emblem Glyph; they resemble **tok' tun ahaw**, although they consistently lack T116 (fig. 7-19). The Xultun Emblems known from monuments at the site are even less similar to **tok' tun ahaw**; they sometimes have an "eccentric Cauac" main sign and none definitively show the "flint" prefix, nor do they have T116 phonetic complementation. Therefore it does not seem warranted at this time to identify **tok' tun ahaw** as the Xultun Emblem Glyph. However, the vase Emblems and **tok' tun ahaw** present stronger parallels and may in fact refer to the same Emblem Glyph. If **tok' tun ahaw** is an Emblem Glyph configuration, which seems likely, it resembles the pattern seen at Machaquila (fig. 7-20), where "28 Bacab" (also found in the cave) comes after the Emblem Glyph (Drawing 28, A8–A10, Drawing 28, B4–B7, and Drawing 66, G1–I1).

The possibility remains, however, that **tok' tun ahaw** is a title rather than a true Emblem Glyph. It has been noted that **tok' tun ahaw** stands as an independent element in Drawing 23, A6–B3,

FIG. 7-20. "28 Bacab" title on Stela 2, Machaquila. Detail from Graham 1967: fig. 44.

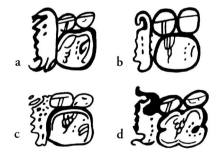

FIG. 7-19. Examples of "*tok'tun*" Emblem Glyphs on vases: *a*, MS 1445; *b*, Robicsek and Hales 1981: Vessel 184; *c*, MS 1446; *d*, Kerr 3743.

FIG. 7-21. Kerr Vessel 1547. Photograph © Justin Kerr 1981.

where syntactically it is the subject of **ilah mo'pan**. If **tok' tun ahaw** were an Emblem Glyph, then this sentence would read "was seen Mopan (by) the lord of the 'tok' tun' polity," with no name specified.

As a descriptive phrase **tok' tun ahaw** shares certain features with the Classic deity called **k'awil**, shown by Stuart (1987:15) to be synonymous with God K. Among other symbolic personae, God K is the god of bloodletting and lineages. As mentioned earlier, *tok'* means "let blood." Although *tok' tunich* is "flint," it may have also meant "bloodletter." In addition, Spero (1987:210, citing Girard 1949) notes that among the Chorti *tok' tun* is the name of the axe wielded by the *ah patnar winikop'* "working men" to beat serpent rain beasts called *chih chan*, thereby producing a rain storm. In Classic iconography God K is the personification of this same genre of rain and lightning axes, usually called the Manikin Scepter (Coggins 1988; Taube 1988b:96).

It was earlier noted that a compound much like **tok'tun ahaw** appears on rim texts of certain unprovenanced polychrome ceramics. It consistently occurs in nominal phrases following the Primary Standard Sequence (PSS), and certain of these post-PSS phrases share other features with the nominal sequences in the cave (for examples, see figs. 7-18 and 7-21). On pottery **ak** also appears in nominal phrases following

FIG. 7-22. Kerr Vessel 3230. Photograph © Justin Kerr 1986.

the PSS (fig. 7-22); in addition, it is seen as a title for historical individuals at Piedras Negras (e.g., Lintel 2; Schele and Miller 1986:pl. 40a, secondary text) and on Arroyo de Piedra Stela 3 at E1 (Houston 1989:fig. 25). As our understanding of the texts on funerary ware deepens, we may confirm that many of these post-PSS titles specify that the owner of the vessel is deceased.

The Rodent Bone Title

The **ch'ok** or Rodent-Bone title, usually taking the form of T758:110, has been noted in the scribe's name, though it also occurs in a short text accompanying a figure in Drawing 20 and in Drawing 65, L2. Houston (1988:132) proposed a reading of **ch'o** for the rodent head T758; the **ko** reading for T110 was provided by Grube and Stu-

art (1987) in a discussion that also outlined contexts for the Rodent-Bone title. MacLeod (1989a), Grube, and Stuart (Nikolai Grube, personal communication, 1988) independently read it as **ch'ok** "youth, offspring" in Cholan (Kaufman and Norman 1984:119). It is very common at Cholan sites and on pottery following the PSS, which is in most cases Cholan (MacLeod 1989b). Both humans and supernaturals carry the title, which in a general sense identifies the individual as a younger member of the lineage. In the cave texts **ch'ok** may convey the idea of secondary status, and we find that the scribe, who is a **ch'ok**, is consistently named second in the sequence of nominals after the **mam na** protagonist.

The "28 Bacab" title consists of the numeral eight prefixed to a full lunar glyph (T683) plus the **ki** suffix (T102); this is followed in a separate glyph block with a phonetic spelling of **bakab** (T501:25:501). Following three examples of the standard nominal phrase (including the "**mam na**" and "**8-imix-nal**" protagonists), as well as one entirely distinct nominal (Drawing 25, fig. 7-5), the "28 Bacab" title also appears in monumental inscriptions with particular frequency at Machaquila (e.g., fig. 7-20). We suggest that the T683:102 sequence that follows the numeral eight may be read as (**h)a-k(i)**, either phonetic complementation to **waxak** "eight" or a -**Vk** (-**ak** in this case) positional participial suffix found in Cholan and Yucatecan languages. The argument is more complex than present space permits, but in brief we propose that **waxak** may be analyzed as **wa'** "standing" (in both Cholan and Yucatecan languages) -**xak** "planted firmly" (Barrera Vásquez 1980:932). Conceivably such a positional compound could take the -**Vk** participial suffix, with the whole reading **wa'-xak-ak bakab** "*bakab* standing firmly." This analysis of **waxak** clarifies a number of otherwise problematic occurrences of the numeral eight, such as that at the end of the text of Copan Stela 6, east, or that closing Quirigua Stela E, west (Maudslay 1889–1902:2:pls. 107, 33). Here *wa'-xak-ak* seems a reasonable attribution for a *bakab*.

The *waxak bakab* title, understood as "*bakab* standing firmly," fits well with our understanding of Bacabs, as evidenced in Maya iconography and ethnohistory. The Bacabs are described by Landa and other Colonial authors as a quadripartite set of gods (Landa calls them "brothers") stationed at the four world directions (Thompson 1970b). As world bearers, the Bacabs are pillar-like supports marking the cardinal directions. Thus, *waxak*, as we interpret it, would be an apt title for a world bearer. The **waxak** title, based on a pun with the numeral eight, also suggests tantalizing connections with the deity known as Vashakmen among the Tzotzil of Zinacantan (Vogt 1969:303–304), a quadripartite world bearer analogous to the Classic and Colonial Bacabs. Like **waxak bakab**, Vashakmen also incorporates the word for eight, *vaxak* in Tzotzil, though *men* presently eludes interpretation, unless it is cognate with Yucatec *men* "do," *ah men* "doer" (shaman). Vashakmen as the name of world bearers among the Tzotzil may have a historical connection to the Classic title **waxak bakab**.

Another context in which to consider the **waxak** title is one in which deities are "stood up" in the process of constituting sacred space. Hanks (1990:339) notes that in the *saantiguar* ceremony, as performed in Oxkutzcab, Yucatan, the officiating shaman invokes deities who are "lowered" into the ritual arena. The boundaries of ritual space are fixed when the deities are "stood up" (*wa'akunta'al*) around the altar. Hence, in Mayan ritual discourse "to stand up" is a trope for positioning deities or offerings in a prescribed (cardinal) order, thereby defining a sacred precinct. The title **waxak** may also refer to the placement of deities through shamanic invocation as a means of constituting a sacred precinct. The presence of this title does not imply that the actors here are deities, however. The Machaquila protagonists employing this title are human.

Other Protagonists at Mo'pan

In Drawing 29 (fig. 7-8), following **y-ilah mo'pan**, a nominal phrase appears that opens with a "checkerboard" shield followed by **ma-yi-ki k'an-bi-ya-ni-?-ahaw nohol**; the last part refers to a "lord of the south"; the rest is at present inscrutable. Two titles follow: **ah-nab**

and a possessed form of this, **y-ah-nabil**, which together suggest perhaps an anointed person or a penitent, depending on the final resolution of this poorly understood title (*nab* is "daub," "anoint" in Yucatec; *nabinah* is "do penance for someone else"). We propose that the **ah nab** performed in some capacity for someone else named **u-pakal k'inich sak-ok**. This nominal phrase ends with a possible Emblem Glyph, followed by **bakab** and **ibin winik**. The **bakab** title has been discussed; **ibin* may be cognate with Chorti *ihp'en* "earth spirit," suggesting either a chthonic supernatural or, more likely, a human who communicates with him.

Part of the first nominal repeats in a subsequent phrase initiated by **y-itah** (Drawing 29, B1). The phrase continues (B2–B8): **y-its'in** "his younger brother" (Stuart 1987:27), which is followed by **ts'i-ts'i-li ma-yi-ki k'an-bi-ya-ni u-chich winik**; **chich winik** may be a reference to a "storyteller," *ah-chich* in Yucatec. Other titles follow, including "**28**" and **ahaw**. A possible Emblem Glyph (eroded) closes the text. Drawing 29 seems to refer to two brothers who "saw Mo'pan." One was the *ah-nab* of an individual who carried the *ibin winik* title and who may or may not have been present. It is possible that Drawing 52 (fig. 7-2) mentions this same "patron"; the preceding nominal is qualified as the **ts'ul** "foreigner" **ah nab** of its'at sak-hok (A7–B8); the latter may be a variation on **sak-ok** noted above in Drawing 29. The **its'at** "sage," "artisan" (Yucatec) reading for the "headband bird" was suggested by Nikolai Grube at the 1991 Maya Meetings at the University of Texas at Austin, and subsequent research has supported this.

The **yitah** Glyph

One of the bones from Burial 116 at Tikal features two gods, seated bow and stern, who take the dead ruler and a bevy of squawking animals on a canoe journey into the underworld. These "Paddlers" were studied by Stuart (1988) and found to be present on many period-ending monuments. Earlier investigations by Mathews (1977) had broken much the same ground, and a recent summary by Schele (1987) outlines the "Paddler" program (see fig. 7-23). Often a glyph spelling **yatih** or **yitah** introduces the Paddlers. Sometimes a double-looped motif appears as the main sign, replacing **ti** or **ta** (fig. 7-23e–g). These Paddler Introductory Glyph variants may follow the opening date on the monument in question; more often they follow a clause in which the ruler is the subject of a period-ending verb.

There is another context wherein **yitah** (but not **yatih**) appears: on monuments between two (rarely more) human nominals who are thus defined as being in some relationship. The question has been raised whether the **yitah** or **yatih** collocation is verbal. Between nominals it is unlikely to be a verb on syntactic grounds; this pattern appears to obtain at Naj Tunich. In all but a few of the Paddler contexts **yitah** or **yatih** may be clearly understood as a possessed noun (*y-itah, *y-atih); the rest are ambiguous but tangential to the present argument. Recently a sibling relationship has been assumed (and in a few cases confirmed by shared parentage) between nominals joined by **yitah**. This interpretation, based on Cholan *ihti'an "sibling" (Kaufman and Norman 1984:121) was reached independently by MacLeod (personal communication to Ruth Krochock, 1987) and Stuart (personal communication to Linda Schele, 1987), and subsequent research by Stuart (in press) and Schele (n.d.) has developed the argument. Because **yitah** links nominals at Naj Tunich, it has been speculated that a sibling or, more loosely, a clan relationship exists here also. However, Terrence

Kaufman (personal communication, 1991) and David Stuart (Ruth Krochock, personal communication, 1991) have expressed subsequent reservations about a cognate relation between *ihti'an and the **yitah** glyph. MacLeod (letter to David Stuart, 1991) has recently reinterpreted **yitah** not as "sibling" but as "friend" or "companion," and we now find that argument to be the best explanation for the cave occurrences.

The first important clue to the meaning of **yitah** and **yatih** was offered by Grube (personal communication, 1989), who noted the entry *at-ey* "be a partner" in Colonial Tzotzil (Laughlin 1988:1:137) as an explanation for the **yatih** form of the Paddler Introductory Glyph. Tzotzil *at "companion" is a reflex of Proto-Mayan *aty/*ety "fellow" (Kaufman and Norman 1984:138), which appears in Yucatecan languages as *et*. This root forms words like *et-taal* "fellow-traveler" and *(y)-etail* "(his) friend" (Barrera Vásquez 1980:974, 161, 158). The latter may be further analyzed as *et-a-il*; -*il* is a suffix frequently marking possessed nouns. The bare stem *eta(h)* permits a reconstruction of *itah "friend" for Cholan, but there is additional evidence in support of this. The Western Cholan conjunction *yit'ok* "with" and the metathesized form *yik'ot* are, judging from Kaufman and Norman's (1984:138) analysis of *et'ok*, the more likely Cholan reflexes of *aty/ety (Kaufman and Norman mention Acalan *yithoc* but not Chol *yit'ok* and *yik'ot*). Further analysis of the conjunction as *y-it-'ok* places the form *it in Cholan (the glottalization of the /t/ in *yit'ok* originates with the prevocalic glottal stop preceding *ok* "foot" in the conjunction). It therefore seems reasonable to propose that *y-itah* meant "his friend," "his companion" in Proto-Cholan and that *y-atih* had a similar meaning in Tzeltalan or in some dialects of Classic Cholan. This suggests that the Paddlers are the "companions"

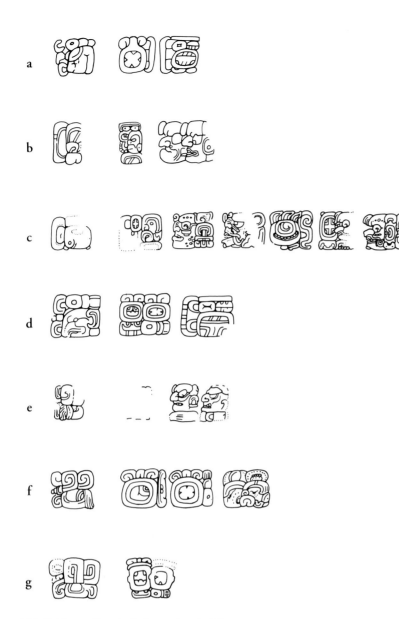

FIG. 7-23. *yatih* and *yitah* associated with Paddler expressions: *a*, Tonina M. 139, adapted from drawing by Linda Schele; *b*, Piedras Negras St. 15, adapted from Schele 1987: fig. 4b; *c*, Dos Pilas St. 8, adapted from drawing by Peter Mathews; *d*, Tonina M. 122, adapted from drawing by Peter Mathews; *e*, Tikal St. 24, adapted from Jones and Satterthwaite 1982: fig. 38c; *f*, Naranjo St. 23, adapted from drawing by Ian Graham; *g*, Tonina M. 110, adapted from drawing by Peter Mathews.

most figures painted in the cave, which, by their simplicity, also seem to downplay rank divisions. Needless to say, the **yitah** glyph is central to our understanding of the cave texts, wherein eighteen instances of its use have thus far been noted.

The texts at Naj Tunich employing the **yitah** glyph are typically complex. Drawing 88 (fig. 7-3) has four **yitah** phrases. It is also of interest that some of the same nominal components that follow **ilah mo'pan** recur after the **yitah** glyph, which opens the next clause in the same text (as with the standard nominal phrase). This repetition may suggest shared titles and kinship, but it does not prove that *y-itah* means "sibling" or "clan member." Where a known "sibling" term, such as *y-its'in* "his younger brother" follows *y-itah* (as in Drawing 29), a "friend" interpretation of the latter makes more sense and avoids the redundancy created by the juxtaposition of two core kin terms.

Other Nominal Phrases with **yitah**

Drawing 88 (fig. 7-3), with its four **yitah** phrases (beginning at A6, D1, E3, and F1), employs nominals that do not repeat in the text. Most have readable or known phonetic components or sequences, but most also elude a full translation. The spatial distribution of the **yitah** phrases—they are physically separated on the wall—makes them appear in fact to be separate texts, each naming a subject.

The first and longest **yitah** phrase in Drawing 88 (A6–C13) contains a PSS-like sequence reading at B9–10, **u-ts'ib yich k'a** ("his writing, its 'page,' the remembrance?"); the T122 **k'a** subfix (MacLeod 1990a) may represent *k'ah* "remembrance" (Wisdom 1950: 499). The word appears in Yucatecan languages also, with -**VI** suffixed; **yich** probably represents the Cholan *u-hich* "its page/writing surface" (MacLeod 1989b).

of the king on period endings and that the protagonists both on the monuments and in the cave who are linked by the **yitah** glyph are simply designated as "friends" or "companions."

From this distance it is difficult to assess the social constraints on this relationship; all evidence points to a degree of formality in that the individuals are co-participants in ritual. At the same time, **yitah** suggests an appearance at least of equal status among protagonists, as this relationship glyph does not establish a political or kin-based rank. The status-leveling function of **yitah** is consonant with the costumes worn by

A similar segment appears in Drawing 51 (fig. 7-24). Here the God N "dedicatory" verb–**yich** sequence at A1–A2 opens a short text that flanks a ballgame scene. MacLeod (1990b) has read the God N verb as **hoy** "it was blessed" and the **yich** PSS nominal as **y-ich** "its page/writing surface" (1989b). Next follows **u-k'a**, recalling the **u-ts'ib yich-k'a** in the first clause of Drawing 88. Drawing 51 might then be read as "his writing (on) its page (the wall), his remembrance . . . name." On Chochola-style carved ceramics an **u-k'ah-Vl** sequence occasionally appears in the PSS, and it is likely that the same root *k'ah* "remember" is represented.

In Drawing 88 the first **yitah** clause ends with something like **ch'ak-ta hu-mam-ahaw** at B13–C13. Presently little of this springs into focus, though *mam* is a widespread word for "grandfather" in Mayan languages and is also the name of an aged mountain-thunder god.

The fifth clause (G1–H6) opens with a Distance Number counted from a date not given, and is followed by a verb, possibly **u-to-ma** (the identification of the superfix as T44 **to** is not certain): **ut-om** "it will happen"[5] and a standard period-ending date (see the preceding discussion of dates). A verb (with a Posterior Event Indicator at G6) reading **ko-ho-yi** (which also appears in Drawing 49, B2; fig. 7-25) is followed by a nominal reading **hu-k'in-ba** or **hu-ba-k'in** (H6). T266, the prefix of the collocation at H6, has recently been read as **hu** by Nikolai Grube (MacLeod 1990b).

The **huli** and **pakxi** Verbs

It has long been known (D. Stuart 1981; Stone 1983b) that a verb identical to one form of Glyph D of the Lunar Series appears three times in the cave: Drawing 34, A3; Drawing 37, A3; and Drawing 52, A4 (figs. 7-26, 7-1, 7-2). Drawing 37 is, unfortunately, too

eroded to analyze. In Drawing 34, A3–A4, the Glyph D verb is followed by the **ik'-?-kab** toponym, which we believe is a reference to the cave. A standard Emblem Glyph that recalls that of Tamarindito follows this, although this identification is doubtful because of the considerable distance between Tamarindito and Naj Tunich.

The clause ends at B2 with a compound featuring a "dotted double scroll" (T632) and a phonetic spelling of **chak**. Nikolai Grube (personal communication, 1990) has demonstrated that this T520:102 collocation substitutes for the zoomorphic head of Chac at Naranjo. A reading of the "dotted double scroll" as logographic **muyal** "cloud" was independently proposed by Stone (personal communication to Barbara MacLeod, 1990) and Houston and Stuart (1990), based on occurrences of -**yal** suffixing and recurrent sky contexts for similar dotted scrolls. The phrase

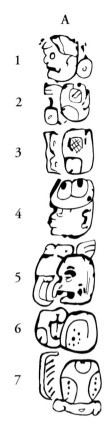

FIG. 7-24. Drawing 51, Naj Tunich.

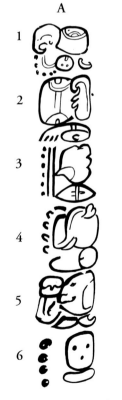

FIG. 7-25. Drawing 49, Naj Tunich.

FIG. 7-26. Drawing 34, Naj Tunich.

muyal chak "cloud *chak*" has obvious atmospheric connotations. We offer the idea that this title may refer to an individual who has the power to converse with rain gods and clouds. Some present-day Maya shamans, such as the Chorti *holchan*, take their titles from atmospheric phenomena; among the Chorti clouds and winds may also be qualified as *holchan* (Fought 1972: 260). In addition, Classic kings employed both *muyal* and *chak* as titles.

In Drawing 34 a **yitah** phrase beginning at B3 ends the text. Apart from Drawing 34, the other occurrence of the Glyph D verb is with a single nominal glyph in Drawing 52 (fig. 7-2 at A4). A complex **yitah** phrase follows.

MacLeod (1990b) has read the Glyph D verb as **hul-i** "he/it arrived"; the reading derives from a phonetic value of **hu** for T45 reached via a study of the God N and T45.843 Step dedicatory verbs. Other evidence, including "arrival" contexts followed by toponyms with humans as subjects, has been documented by both MacLeod and Grube (MacLeod 1990b), and the reading now seems virtually certain.

Stuart (1987) has identified T114 as **xa** and T1048 as **xi**; subsequent observations have strengthened these readings. In his discussion of **xi**, Stuart (pp. 31–33) also mentions, without interpretation, the Naj Tunich texts employing the **pa-ka-xV** verb, where a substitution is seen between **xi** and **xa** (Drawings 48 and 65; see ibid.: fig. 42). It is now possible to analyze this sequence as **pak-xi/pak-xa** and posit its equivalence with Cholti *pak-xi (-el)*, given as "*volver*" "to return" by Morán (1935: 21). The Cholti word may be further analyzed as *pak* "fold" and **xi* "go" (to "fold-go" is to "double back"); both roots appear in Cholan and Yucatecan languages, but *xi* is embedded and not productive. The substitution of **xa** for **xi** may be explained as vowel assimilation conditioned by a preceding

ka (Drawing 65, B2, fig. 7-9). Fought (1972: 24–25; also all text transcriptions), for example, has demonstrated that Chorti is rife with assimilation.

In Drawing 65, B4, the "bird head" nominal subject of **pak-xa** "return" is followed by the same "water scroll" Emblem Glyph seen in Drawing 34. Drawing 48, A1–A3 (fig. 7-27) specifies that an **ahaw** of Sacul (Emblem Glyph at A3), a site quite near the cave, "returned." Here it is certain that a historical person is the subject of **pak-xi**. In Drawing 19 (fig. 7-14) the **pak-xi** verb is followed by the **ik'**-dragon **mawnal** toponym, which was mentioned earlier; this parallels the syntax of Drawing 34 (fig. 7-26) wherein **hul-i** is followed (at A4) by **ik'-?-kab**, the other cave toponym. In Drawing 19 the nominal phrase is rather eroded. A **yitah** phrase ends the text.

In sum, we find these two verbs in five clauses suggesting that historical individuals arrived at or returned to the cave; in two cases a likely cave toponym appears.

The Sacul Connection and Other Historical References

Sacul is a Late Classic site located east of Dolores, Peten, not far from the Belizean border and only about fifteen kilometers north of Naj Tunich. Several texts in the cave mention the Sacul polity, as has been noted by Johnston (n.d.). The texts of Naj Tunich show some obvious similarities in content to the texts of Sacul and the neighboring site of Ixkun.

The Sacul Emblem Glyph (fig. 7-28a) appears in four texts from Naj Tunich in either conflated or extended form (fig. 7-28b–e). In Drawing 25 (fig. 7-11) the nominal, which includes the Sacul Emblem Glyph, follows **yitah** (B1–B4). The preceding nominal, presumably the "companion of" the Sacul individual, is the **mam-na** protagonist discussed earlier, whose name ends

FIG. 7-27. Drawing 48, Naj Tunich.

with the **tok' tun** Emblem Glyph (A6– A10). This text seems to provide evidence of interaction between Sacul and the **tok' tun** polity, an idea also suggested by Drawing 82, which includes references to both Emblem Glyphs.

The Sacul Emblem Glyph appears in somewhat eroded form in Drawing 48 (A3). Reading **pak-xi-ya-ahaw** Sacul-? "returned the lord of Sacul ?," Drawing 48 is a likely candidate for a historical text (fig. 7-27).

Drawing 49 (fig. 7-25), which also features a Sacul **ahaw**, opens with the verb that introduces the Primary Standard Sequence as well as dates and certain other events on stone monuments. It has been read by Schele and Grube (Linda Schele, personal communication, 1991) as *a-tsuki* with a meaning something like "start here" and by MacLeod as *ay* "it existed"; but problems remain with this glyph. The following verb (at A2) is the same **ko-ho-yi** sequence seen at the close of Drawing 88, G6 (fig. 7-3). Next follows what ought to be a personal name; the Sacul Emblem Glyph comes after, and the text closes with **4-na(?)-li(?)**. The key to the text of Drawing 49 is the undeciphered **kohoy** verb, which is structured like an eastern Cholan completive intransitive, but for which we can posit no confident interpretation. The Yuca-

tec entry *koh "letra y escribir"* (Barrera Vásquez 1980:327), rare in the lexical record, may eventually prove useful.

We have in Drawing 82, C3, the most beautiful and complete example of the Sacul Emblem Glyph (fig. 7-28b). Not only is the **pi** suffix clear (see Stuart 1987 on the identification of T177 as **pi**), but T266 **hu** as a prefix indicates that the perforated **lu** main sign is read **hul** "perforate" in many Maya languages. The same configuration is seen in Drawing 49, A4.

Drawing 82 (fig. 7-29) shows interesting parallels with Ixkun Stela 2 (fig. 7-30), which has a full-figure "fire-bearer" (C3), also seen in Drawing 82, where syntactically it functions as a verb (A2). The subject of Drawing 82's "fire-bearer" event is a ruler from Caracol (B2–C1), identified by Houston (letter to Nikolai Grube, 1991). The name appears to be that of Ruler VIII, whose reign is roughly contemporary with Drawing 82 (Houston 1987: fig. 68). The name is written in the cave as **tu-mu-yo-wa k'inich** (on Caracol monuments T184 **ma k'ina** replaces **k'inich**). The subsequent title (C1b) recalls one that was held by Caracol rulers and is the closest thing we have to a Caracol Emblem Glyph. In Drawing 82 T502 **ma** substitutes for the "half-T92" **ma**, typical of the title at Caracol. Grube

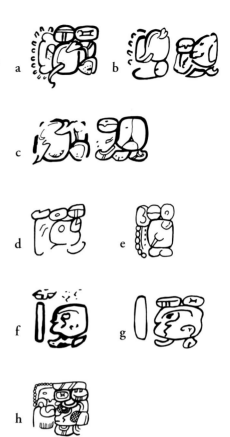

FIG. 7-28. Sacul and Ixtutz Emblem Glyphs: *a*, Stela 1, Sacul; *b*, Drawing 82, Naj Tunich; *c*, Drawing 49, Naj Tunich; *d*, Drawing 25, Naj Tunich; *e*, Drawing 48, Naj Tunich; *f*, Drawing 68, Naj Tunich; *g*, Drawing 69, Naj Tunich; *h*, Stela 4, Ixtutz.

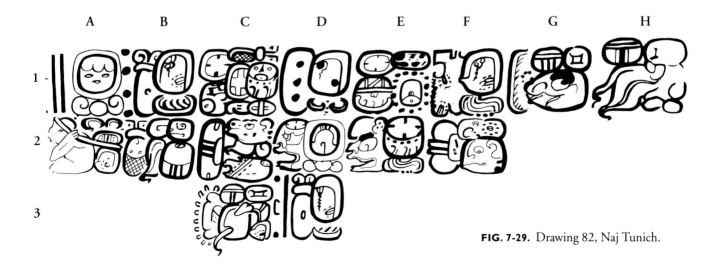

FIG. 7-29. Drawing 82, Naj Tunich.

(1991) notes the same compound in a **yitah** phrase in Drawing 88 (D3), providing tantalizing hints of an association between this important text and the site of Caracol.

After the "fire-bearer" event on Ixkun Stela 2, a later phrase mentions the "agency of Sacul" (C6–D6). This again parallels Drawing 82, where the "fire-bearer" clause is followed by "agency of . . . name . . . Sacul" (D1, C2–C3).[6] In addition to mentioning individuals from Caracol and Sacul, Drawing 82 also records the main sign of the **tok' tun** Emblem Glyph (F1) as well as the "Site Q" (identity and location unknown) Emblem Glyph (G1). Another Emblem Glyph configuration appears at H1 but is too eroded to identify. This text, certainly one of the most important at Naj Tunich, seems to concern various actors from a number of regional sites who co-participated in ritual activities in the cave.

One short text, Drawing 69 (fig. 7-31), is a simple nominal phrase opening with the **ya**-Bat-Jaguar variant of the name Bird Jaguar, possibly *yaxun balam*, as read by Nikolai Grube (personal communication, 1990). The text reads "Bat Jaguar **ch'ok ho-kab ahaw**." The collocation **ho-kab ahaw** also appears in Drawing 68 (figs. 7-28f–g, 6-52). Johnston (n.d.) has identified the **ho-kab** collocation as the Emblem Glyph of Ixtutz, another site in the southeast Peten some thirty kilometers northwest of the cave (fig. 7-28h). A Shield Jaguar of Ucanal appears at C9–C10 on Sacul Stela 1 (fig. 7-32). Surely these names have no connection to the Yaxchilan duo, but the association suggests that they are a nominal pair also in vogue in this region, now defined by Naj Tunich, Sacul, Ixkun, Ixtutz, and Ucanal.

The presence of Emblem Glyphs in certain texts, particularly one representing a polity in the immediate vicinity of the cave, suggests that these texts refer

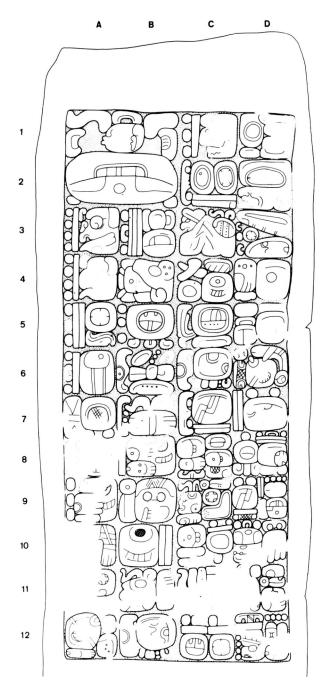

FIG. 7-30. Stela 2, Ixkun. From Graham 1980: fig. 2.141. Courtesy of Ian Graham and the Peabody Museum, Harvard University.

Images from the Underworld

to historical individuals who have come to the cave. In some cases, we are told of their "arrival" and "return." Drawing 34 would seem to be a clearcut example, but here the only component that might be a personal name is **muyal-chak**, which follows the "water scroll" Emblem Glyph. This deviates from the expected formula for a personal name, but may simply refer to a "rainmaker of X polity."

In monumental inscriptions it is common practice to omit the "water group" prefix from the Emblem Glyph of nonlocal individuals (witness, for instance, the oft-mentioned Copan Emblem Glyph at Quirigua). This pattern seems to hold true in the cave where "visitors" from various sites—for example, Sacul, Ixtutz, and the presently unidentified "**tok' tun**" polity—have Emblem Glyphs lacking the "water group" prefix. It is presently unclear why only one Emblem Glyph, the "water scroll" Emblem Glyph, appears in complete form in Drawings 34 and 65. Are the "lords" of this domain native in some sense to the cave?

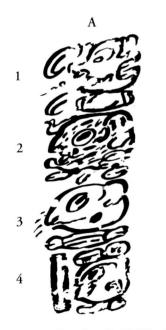

FIG. 7-31. Drawing 69, Naj Tunich.

In Drawing 19, B3, there is a nominal consisting of a jaguar head with a "*pax* emanantion" replacing the lower jaw and a "flint" suffix (fig. 7-14). We have christened this individual Balam Tok' (note a related nominal on Ixtutz Stela 4, B3, fig. 7-33). In Drawing 82, C2, there is a similar nominal but one that includes a **chak** prefix and places the scrolls under a complete animal head. In Drawing 19, B1–B3, the name of Balam Tok' is preceded by **yitah na-chan**. Schele (1989:146–148) observes that **na-chan** is a constant in the name of a supernatural serpent (or "vision serpent") associated with ancestor invocation, but here it may be part of a nominal phrase. An **ilah na-chan** nominal sequence appears in Drawing 70, B1–B2 (fig. 7-13).

Conclusions

One must still wonder why, if the Classic Maya made ritual use of caverns over all the Lowlands, they left detailed written records of their esoteric practices only at Naj Tunich. One explanation might be that texts were painted in other caves, but the vagaries of time and flowing water have obliterated them. This is an unsatisfactory answer, and given the erratic nature of cave weathering, it seems somewhat unlikely. It might also be that records of these rites were not generally kept, that the private nature of cave ritual stood in sharp contrast with the braggadoccio of the elite on public monuments. If so, we may never know why the decision was made to leave an articulate testimonial here (with a lesser but kindred expression at a nearby cave, Santo Domingo) and not elsewhere.

We have suggested that the "language of Naj Tunich" was in many cases Cholan, and not Yucatecan, as has been previously posited (D. Stuart 1981). But in fact, given the interaction between sites in a region that may well have included both Cholans and Yucatecans in Classic

FIG. 7-32. Shield Jaguar of Ucanal, Stela 1, Sacul. Adapted from drawing by Ian Graham.

times, we cannot be certain that only Cholan is represented at the cave. Yucatecan has fewer unequivocal indicators in the writing system. Texts without likely Cholan verbs like passive **ilah** or other markers like **ch'ok** or **yich** are ambiguous—and in the case of the **ch'ok** title, borrowing is certainly possible. The identification of specific painters aids the process of linguistic assignation, provided that at least one text of a given scribe contains a linguistic marker. While it has seemingly become popular to find Cholan everywhere, we have no such agenda. In fact, one short text is suggestive of Yucatecan. This is the text that appears on a stalagmite in Naj Tunel. The two glyphs in Drawing 90 read **chi-li-k'u** (fig. 7-34), a segment that, as Yucatecan *chi'il k'uh* "god's/sacred precinct's mouth," offers several productive lines of interpretation. In Yucatecan *chi'* is "mouth," and the generic "sacrifice" term in Yucatec is *p'a' chi'* "open the mouth"—referring to the nourishing of gods by smearing blood on the mouths of idols (Thompson 1970a:175). Stalagmites are frequently treated as "idols" in both Classic and contemporary Maya cave ritual; here we may have a stalagmite (named in the region of its "mouth") as "the mouth of the god." Alternatively, the stalagmite may represent a portal (or "mouth") debouching onto a more secret area (*k'uh*: "sacred precinct"). The stalagmite, in fact, lies at the base of a slope leading to a room wherein an altarlike construction and a whole vessel were found. These interpretations, if either be correct, point to Yucatecan as the language of this text.

The interaction between individuals of Sacul, Ixkun, and Ucanal as depicted on just two surviving monuments (Sacul Stela 1 and Ixkun Stela 2) indicates that the southeastern Peten was rife with intersite dialogue. The cave texts support the idea of regional interaction. Sacul, Ixtutz, and Caracol are three sites mentioned in the cave texts, and Sacul protagonists are twice linked with individuals from other sites. If **tok' tun ahaw** is a true Emblem Glyph, then it is the most prolific Emblem Glyph at Naj Tunich, occurring with three different protagonists (fig. 7-5) as well as with one unspecified nominal (Drawing 23) and in a more ambiguous context in Drawing 82.

The "water scroll" Emblem Glyph, in Drawings 34 and 65, cannot be identified with a known site at the present time. A "water scroll" Emblem Glyph has been found at Tamarindito (a Petexbatun site), but it seems unrelated to the cave. The "water scroll" Emblem Glyph also appears on Stela 2 of Nim Li Punit, a Late Classic site in southern Belize, not far from Naj Tunich. Since it does not seem to be the local Emblem Glyph (there is a better candidate), it points to an unknown site in the region whose representatives visited both Nim Li Punit and Naj Tunich.

Finally, one example of the so-called "Site Q" Emblem Glyph appears in Drawing 82, G1 (fig. 7-29). This Emblem Glyph is found at more sites in the Maya Lowlands than any other, ranging from Copan in the southeast to Palenque in the northwest. The location of "Site Q" is still uncertain (but it is thought by some epigraphers to be Calakmul), and until this issue is resolved, the significance of its Emblem Glyph in the cave will remain obscure. But Calakmul is far to the north and west of Naj Tunich.

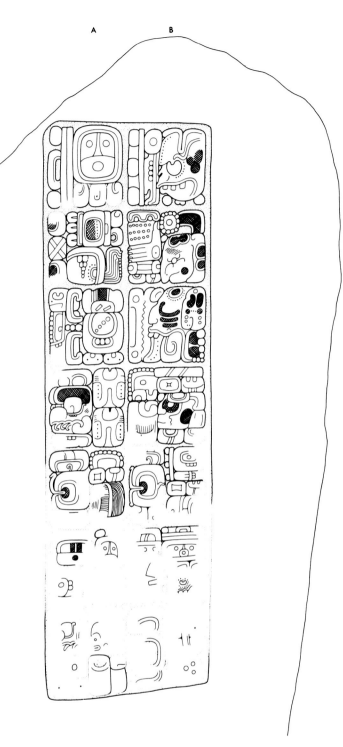

FIG. 7-33. Stela 4, Ixtutz. From Graham 1980: fig. 2.181. Courtesy of Ian Graham and the Peabody Museum, Harvard University.

Images from the Underworld

FIG. 7-34. Drawing 90, Naj Tunich.

When the body of texts and figurative paintings is considered as a whole, a picture emerges of Naj Tunich as a shrine of considerable renown, receiving pilgrims from a number of regional polities. These pilgrimages appear to have been, on occasion, cooperative enterprises, raising the possibility that ritual utilization of the cave helped to secure alliances and foster regional integration. Though evidence exists as to the place of origin of these actors, important questions still remain as to their status. Thus far, only the Caracol ruler can be securely identified as a member of a royal family. Yet the **ahaw** title bestowed on many of the protagonists suggests that the cave texts do concern a nobility. Certainly the archaeology supports this idea.

Some of these individuals may have been the specialists responsible for conducting the ritual proceedings. Certain titles and segments of nominal phrases are suggestive of ritual specialists who may have had varying functions. For instance, the entity "seen at Mopan" or, alternately, one who "saw Mopan," identified as a **mam-na** "grandfather-mother," may have been an officiating shaman. As such, his name always leads off the first clause following **y-ilah mo'pan**. The scribe, on the other hand, always mentioned subsequent to the **mam-na**, carries a title in Drawing 28 interpreted by us as **k'in kun**, which we understand as "diviner," "caster of spells." In Drawing 65, one individual in a series of four is also called a **k'in kun**, followed by **its'in winik** "younger brother person." Such titles may characterize the specialized services performed by one member in a group of ritual practitioners. The **ch'ok** title carried by the scribe may further identify him as an acolyte of the **mam na**.

In discussing Drawing 29 we noted that an individual was called **ah nab**, which may identify him as one doing penance for another. This may repre-sent another kind of ritual office. Both **ah nab** and its possessed form **y-ah-nabil** qualify nominal phrases in two other cave texts, Drawing 52 and Drawing 13. In Drawing 29 the **ah nab** stands in for someone described as an **ibin winik**, which may qualify him as a ritual practitioner with a special relationship to chthonic forces. The **ah nab** of Drawing 52 is also an **its'at** "sage."

There is also a lingering possibility that some of the nominal phrases in the cave texts concern deities or perhaps deified ancestors. This is suggested, for instance, by the presence in one text of the **na-ho-chan** compound (Drawing 65), which, on monuments, usually accompanies the names of the Paddler Gods and is thought to be a celestial toponym. We might recall, too, that the cave of Santo Domingo, near Naj Tunich, has one text that mentions the Jaguar Paddler immediately preceding a **yitah** phrase with an eroded nominal (fig. 4-111). We also noted earlier the presence in two nominal phrases of **na-chan**, an expression associated with "vision serpents" in Maya pottery texts and on one lintel at Yaxchilan (Schele 1989). The presence of such compounds, which are usually associated with supernaturals, leaves open the possibility that deities or ancestors are mentioned on occasion.

In considering the question of ancestor participation, it may be significant that structures on the entrance balcony of Naj Tunich seem to have originally functioned as tombs, most of which had been constructed by the Protoclassic period (Brady 1989). Thus, Naj Tunich had long been a burial site of high-status persons before the paintings came into existence. Some of these interred individuals may have been invoked in the cave rituals.

In conclusion, the historical context of the cave inscriptions is slowly emerging out of obscurity, and it is quite clear, even at this early stage, that Naj

Tunich existed in a politically dynamic atmosphere. The cave was evidently a sacred place of some prestige, certainly regionally and perhaps even beyond. As might be expected, the esoteric component of the texts, the part that addresses their ideological underpinnings, still remains elusive and represents an important area for future inquiry. The figurative paintings, with their depictions of dance, singing, drumming, bloodletting, and meditation on the Hero Twins' adventures, provide direct evidence that ritual motivated the creation of the paintings. The cave images focus on the individual performance of ritual, ritual as a lived experience, and make little reference to contextual detail.

On the other hand, the inscriptions provide historical context—the names of actors, their place of origin—and also describe their actions, though we may not yet fully comprehend the implications of these statements. This historicity takes on added significance when seen against the backdrop of the cave, a sacred site with its own temporal rhythms. The unique character of time and space in the cave surely underlies some of the idiosyncrasies of the texts, such as the unusual configuration of many of the dates. These texts, often situated in transitional and otherwise distinct locations, witness a historical presence, recording for posterity the movement of pilgrims through sacred space. In addressing different aspects of pilgrims' experiences, text and image complement one another. Together they paint a uniquely vivid picture of Maya cave ritual during the Late Classic.

8

A Catalog of Naj Tunich Paintings and Petroglyphs

There has yet to be devised a standard method of cataloging Mesoamerican cave art. For instance, in his Juxtlahuaca study, Gay (1967) uses the descriptive headings "painting" and "drawing," followed by a unique number, whereas Grove (1970) employs this kind of nomenclature only for isolated paintings at Oxtotitlan, which he calls "Mural 1," "Painting 1," and so forth. Those found in groups are given a group or sectional title, such as "A1b." The group classification ("Panel 1" and so on) is used by Strecker (1976) to catalog paintings from Loltun.

Factors such as technique, image size, and distribution must be considered in cataloging cave art. For instance, group labels can pose problems, as when their boundaries are vague. Another problem with group classification is that if all images are not in groups, then isolated paintings must be handled differently, and in my opinion such a mixed classification system is cumbersome.

A recent trend in the nomenclature of Maya stone sculpture has been to avoid functional labels. The catchall heading "monument" is steadily replacing the old system of functional labels, such as "stela," "altar," "zoomorph," and so forth. Even these simple functional distinctions have pitfalls, as when only fragments of a monument survive, leaving functional categories indeterminate. Some functional labels have also proven to be incorrect at a later date ("altar" is a good example).

I found in cataloging the art of Naj Tunich that complications arose when encoding location or technique and that I would be better served by a uniform nomenclature. Classifications based on technique have their own problems. Some cave art combines painting, drawing, and carving. There is one such case at Naj Tunich (Drawing 89); Strecker (1987: fig. 3) reports mixed-media images from Loltun. Distinguishing between a painting and drawing can also be difficult. In order to avoid these problems in cataloging the art of Naj Tunich, I opted for the uniform, minimally descriptive heading "drawing," followed by an identifying number. By employing a single heading and consecutive numbers, I am following established practices in the classification of stone monuments. This type of label has a familiar ring and is easy to remember. Here, the term "drawing" has a neutral meaning attached to it and is applied to all media of cave art at Naj Tunich, whether painted with a brush, drawn with charcoal, or incised. In the catalog particular images that are petroglyphs are identified as such in parentheses.

Determining what constituted a single "drawing" also presented difficulties. Paintings consist of various combinations of figures and text, and sometimes their relationships were unclear. In ambiguous cases, I considered the proximity and style of component parts as well as the productivity of breaking down juxtaposed images into several drawing units. For example, if the drawing was fragmentary to begin with, it often made no appreciable difference whether it was catalogued as one or two drawings. In most cases I opted for simplicity and grouped them together. However, if grouping images under one heading suggested dubious connections, I considered them as separate drawings. No doubt I have separated some images that belong together and lumped others together that are not related; however, I believe these instances are rare and the system is, overall, a good one. Readers may consult the illustrations, as well as plan and profile maps, to judge for themselves. At this point it should be obvious that the official count of paintings and petroglyphs at Naj Tunich, which currently stands at ninety-four, is an approximation based on the determination of drawing units.

At the beginning of each entry in the catalog is the drawing number, which is the official name of the painting or petroglyph. Height and width refer to the maximum dimensions of the entire image as it appears in the corresponding photograph, unless otherwise indicated. Measurements for details of a painting are listed separately. "Distance from Ground Level" refers to the distance between the top of the painting and the ground level immediately below. In cases where the floor sloped or was covered with debris, this distance may be an average or approximation. This measurement provides useful information, indicating whether an image is at eye level, extremely high up on a wall, or close to the floor. It also signals whether the artist needed support to reach the wall and how paintings are spatially related. I found it useful in relocating some of the more obscure paintings. It will be seen that most of the Naj Tunich paintings and petroglyphs are at eye level, between one and two meters above the groundline.

"Description" summarizes salient points concerning the location of the painting—that is, unusual topographic features, wall type, and so on—and offers a description and interpretation of the imagery. Interpretive material covered in other chapters is summarized in the catalog. Discussion of hieroglyphic material is omitted unless it has immediate relevance to the discussion. "Conservation" documents any damage suffered by the painting, mostly from recent vandalism, and also discusses deterioration caused by natural processes when it is deemed noteworthy. When not mentioned, deterioration can be assumed to be the result of natural weathering. The extensive damage suffered in 1989 is briefly mentioned. More details are provided in reports by James and Sandra Brady (Brady and Brady 1989; Brady 1990; Brady 1991a). As I have not witnessed the aftermath myself, my comments remain limited. Additionally, the catalog summarizes the number of figures, hieroglyphs, and profile faces contained in each drawing unit. A note concerning the location of a painting group appears just before the first painting in that group is discussed.

Drawing 1 (fig. 8-1)
Measurements 20 cm h. × 10 cm w.
Distance from Ground Level 1.18 m
Description A single upright positive handprint is found in a natural alcove in the passage leading from the Balcony into the cave. The domed ceiling of the alcove contains several fingerprints. In the adjacent alcove, toward the cave entrance (Operation IV, Lot 7; Brady 1989), there is an amorphous mass of the same brownish-black material that characterizes this handprint and most of the paintings at Naj Tunich.

Drawing 2 (petroglyph; fig. 8-2)
Measurements 21 cm h. × 25 cm w.
Distance from Ground Level 2.30 m
Description The first petroglyph encountered at Naj Tunich is carved on a dark limestone wall that lies above the entrance to a lower-level chamber that contained ceramics, human bones, and other artifacts. The area in front of the petroglyph receives overflow from a large pool of water and is completely inundated at the height of the rainy season. The petroglyph consists of four curving lines, below which are two horizontal bars. It was formed by scratching through a dark stain revealing the underlying limestone.

Drawing 3 (fig. 8-3)
Measurements 15.5 cm h. × 15.5 cm w.
Distance from Ground Level 1.70 m
Hieroglyphs 1
Description The partial outline of a cartouche establishes that Drawing 3 is a hieroglyph, though badly preserved. The cartouche is divided diagonally, and a semicircle is attached to the upper edge. By following the line of the missing contour of the cartouche, one can

FIG. 8-1. Drawing 1. Photograph by Chip and Jennifer Clark.

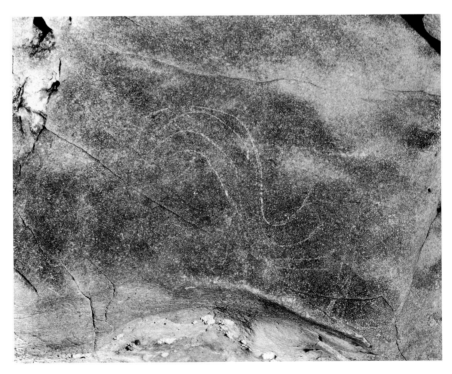

FIG. 8-2. Drawing 2. Photograph by Chip and Jennifer Clark.

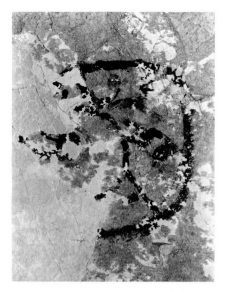

FIG. 8-3. Drawing 3. Photograph by Chip and Jennifer Clark.

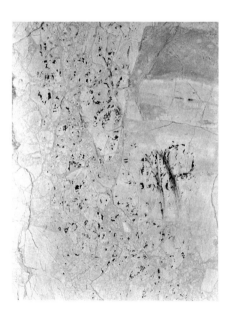

FIG. 8-4. Drawing 4. Photograph by Chip and Jennifer Clark.

see that paint extends beyond the left edge, suggesting that the glyph had some type of prefix.

This painting is located in a recess at a wide point in the tunnel where the walls are encrusted with dark gypsum. The painting is fairly inconspicuous and was discovered only in September of 1981, many months after the discovery of the bulk of the paintings. **Conservation** Paint missing from Drawing 3 is the result of the deterioration of the gypsum crust.

Drawing 4 (fig. 8-4)
Measurements 58 cm h. × 30 cm w.
Distance from Ground Level 1.85 m
Hieroglyphs 3; 18 more probable
Description A badly eroded hieroglyphic text consisting of three or four columns.
Condition The best-preserved glyph at the right (T12.568:534) was smeared sometime after 1986.

Drawing 5 (fig. 8-5)
Measurements 61 cm h. × 48 cm w.
Distance from Ground Level 91 cm
Number of Figures 2; 3 more possible
Description Covering one face of a pyramidal rock are the fragmentary remains of a complex scene that could comprise two distinct paintings, though this is not at all clear due to the painting's poor condition. The best-preserved imagery can be seen in the lower section, where the edge of a stepped platform is plainly visible. Three of the terraces are easily distinguished, though fragmentary lines suggest that there were originally around seven levels. At the lower left a figure wears a circular ear ornament and loincloth, consisting of a waist band and front cloth panels. The headdress with its stiff cloth flaps recalls the headdress of a kneeling figure on Piedras Negras Stela 40 (Morley 1937–1938:5:pl. 135b). To the right, part of a profile face, including the eye,

forehead, and part of the headdress, is visible.

The two figures face one another. The head of the figure at the left tilts upward, and his right arm extends forward; he is possibly kneeling, though this is far from certain. The right-hand figure may be standing, which would explain why his head is taller (about one terrace step higher). A curving line near the left-hand figure's loincloth flap may describe the leg or arm of another figure.

On the top level of the platform rest two objects. One is a bound, layered bundle that has a feathered object lying on its surface. A sacklike bundle lies to the right. The identical juxtaposition of two bundles can also be found on a number of decorated vases (e.g., Robicsek and Hales 1981: fig. 47), showing that the cave painting depicts a conventional theme. Comparative examples on polychrome vases strongly suggest that the layered and tied bundle is a codex, as proposed by Robicsek and Hales. An alternate interpretation is that it represents a layered bundle of cloth. On vases the feathered object that rests on top is not represented in a consistent fashion. Sometimes it is wrapped in cloth and tied. Such an object appears on Piedras Negras Stela 14, where a woman hands it to the enthroned ruler (Maler 1901–1903: pl. 20, 2), and on Piedras Negras Stela 12 (Schele and Miller 1986: fig. 5.8). The wrapped version may be enveloping a bloodletter, suggested by the fact that it is often pointed toward the groin area of male figures. Sometimes, however, the feathers attach directly to a shell (Robicsek and Hales 1981: Vessel 97; Coe 1975: no. 9), and at other times to a glyph (Robicsek and Hales 1981: Vessel 101). Considering its association with what may be a codex and the use of shells as paint containers, the wrapped, feathered object may contain painting implements. Drawing 5 does not pre-

FIG. 8-5. Drawing 5. Photograph by Chip and Jennifer Clark.

serve the area that would identify the type of feathered object attached to the bundle.

Vase scenes which display the two bundles and feathered object usually include an enthroned ruler surrounded by retainers who sometimes hold the flat layered bundle (ibid.: Vessels 95–101). One scene is set in an architectural backdrop, consisting of a long terraced platform, which recalls the Naj Tunich painting (ibid.: fig. 47a). What seems likely is that the lower figures at Naj Tunich are retainers. The upturned

head of the left-hand figure supports this idea, as his gaze may have been directed toward the lord (presumably eroded). The rectilinear forms behind the two bundles could be the remains of the throne room.

The upper section of Drawing 5 does not seem to fit with the scale of the lower scene. At the pinnacle of the rock face is another register with what looks like a figure shown from the waist up, looking downward. This area is so fragmentary, however, that all suggestions must remain tentative.

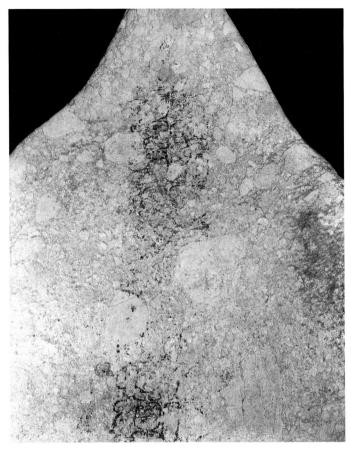

FIG. 8-6. Drawing 6. Photograph by
Chip and Jennifer Clark.

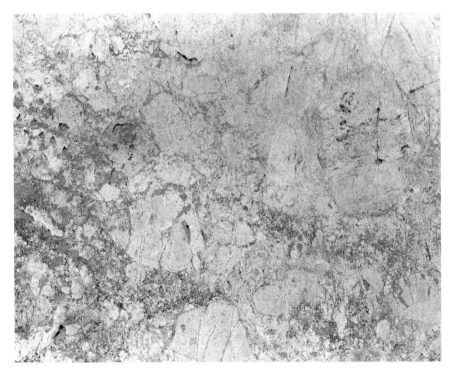

FIG. 8-7. Drawing 7. Photograph by
Chip and Jennifer Clark.

Drawing 6 (fig. 8-6)
Measurements 74 cm h. × 20 cm w.
Distance from Ground Level 1.48 m
Number of Hieroglyphs at least 22 in
the original painting
Description On the north face of the
same pyramidal rock as Drawing 5 is a
two-column text that originally had as
many as twelve rows of glyphs.
Condition Drawing 6 is in poor condition and well illustrates how deterioration of the rock face is associated
with smooth limestone clasts in the
matrix.

Note: Drawings 7–15 are located on
both sides of a narrow corridor where a
visitor would be forced into close contact with the wall. This has led to both
accidental and deliberate damage to this
painting group. A vandal could easily
damage a painting in this area and
quickly exit the cave, something which
apparently happened in the case of
Drawing 12.

Drawing 7 (fig. 8-7)
Measurements 14 cm h. × 10 cm w.
Distance from Ground Level 1.40 m
Number of Hieroglyphs 6
Description Drawing 7 consists of
a hieroglyphic text appearing in two
widely separated columns with three
glyphs each. These glyphs are so badly
conserved that not a single one is
recognizable.

Drawing 8 (fig. 8-8)
Measurements 66 cm h. × 68 cm w.
Distance from Ground Level 2.60 m
Number of Hieroglyphs 19
Number of Figures 1 animal
Number of Profiles 1
Description Drawing 8 is a hieroglyphic text in five columns; it also includes a human profile face and what
may be a peccary bowing down from
the waist. The peccary can be identified
by its cloven hooves and elongated
snout. Possibly the black line near the

Images from the Underworld

neck identifies it as a collared peccary (*Tayassu tajacul*). Collared peccaries get their name from a yellowish-white band encircling their neck. The band here is indicated in black, but the artist could not paint a light band in the monochromatic painting style of Naj Tunich. Collared peccaries actually have alternating bands of light and dark bristles covering their body (Alvarez de Toro 1977:121), though this is rarely depicted in Maya art.

The posture of the peccary recalls scenes on small bottles that show a rabbit bending over in a similar pose at the foot of a ballplayer (Schele and Miller 1986:pl. 103). Schele and Miller (p. 258) interpret this posture in light of a story from the Popol Vuh in which the head of Hunahpu is hung from a calabash tree during a ballgame competition with the Lords of Xibalba, who are bent on destroying Hunahpu and his brother, Xbalanque. A rabbit curls up like a ball to distract the nefarious underworld lords so that Xbalanque can retrieve and reattach the severed head. The Naj Tunich scene shows a peccary rather than a rabbit, but by its juxtaposition with a human head, it evokes the Popol Vuh story. Could the head be that of Hunahpu and the bowing peccary the animal who curled up into a ball to fool the Lords of Xibalba?

The relationship between text and image is vague because of the poor condition of the former. However, in the column of glyphs to the right, a peccary head can be identified, and above that is what appears to be a human head. These two glyphs may be the subject of the verb that precedes them, identifiable as such by T181 verbal suffixing. The column of glyphs to the right are on a smaller scale than those above and to the left, indicating possibly two separate texts.

Conservation An extensive smear of the glyphs of the left-hand group—at A4b, the most badly damaged, and B4—

FIG. 8-8. Drawing 8. Photograph by Chip and Jennifer Clark.

occurred sometime between 1986 and 1988.

Drawing 9 (fig. 8-9)
Measurements 36 cm h. × 17 cm w.
Distance from Ground Level 2.38 m
Number of Hieroglyphs 6
Description Two columns of hieroglyphs are poorly preserved in this text.

Drawing 10 (fig. 8-10)
Measurements 30 cm h. × 33 cm w.
Distance from Ground Level 2.38 m
Number of Hieroglyphs 10
Description This hieroglyphic text appears to have had four glyph columns painted at an oblique angle; interestingly, it follows the line of a shallow fracture in the wall surface.
Conservation This painting was deliberately effaced. All existing photographs of the image show this damage, so it cannot be determined whether the vandalism is modern or ancient. When first discovered, the painting had a pile of three rocks lying directly beneath it,

probably to facilitate reaching the painting, which is rather high. These rocks have now been moved away from the painting to discourage further tampering. The rocks may have helped the painter carry out his task, or they may have been set there by the individual who smeared the painting. I tend to think that the latter is correct, as I have never seen rocks set up by a Maya cave painter to reach a high point on the wall.

Drawing 11 (fig. 8-11)
Measurements 66 cm h. × 86 cm w.
Distance from Ground Level 3.86 m
Description This figure, the largest at Naj Tunich, is painted at the highest point above ground level of any painting. The size of the figure compensates for its greater viewing distance. The painted wall lies directly over a steep ledge, about two meters across, filled with loose dirt. Because of its placement, the figure appears to be sitting in an actual niche. The niche enclosure

FIG. 8-9. Drawing 9. Photograph by Chip and Jennifer Clark.

FIG. 8-10. Drawing 10. Photograph by Chip and Jennifer Clark.

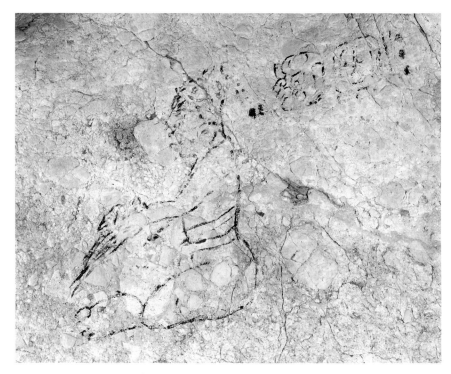

FIG. 8-11. Drawing 11. Photograph by Chip and Jennifer Clark.

with its commanding height and the large scale of the figure convey a sense of importance for this scene.

The figure wears a cap decorated with two beaded tassels, a circular earflare, and a necklace with a small bead pendant. The line across the thigh suggests that he is wearing a hipcloth. In addition, a broad belt wraps around the waist. The bottom of the foot is added to show a cross-legged posture, a feature also of Drawings 22 and 72.

The figure holds what I believe to be a severed head. Ritual decapitation is in keeping with what we know about Maya cave archaeology. Reents-Budet and MacLeod (1986), for instance, report a cave in Belize where the skulls of forty individuals were found cached together. In addition, twelve skulls were found in the Gruta de Xcan (Márquez de Gonzáles, Castillo, and Schmidt 1982:9–10).

Images from the Underworld

a

b

FIG. 8-12. Drawing 12: *a,* before 1988, photograph by James Brady; *b,* after 1988, photograph by Chip and Jennifer Clark.

In Drawing 11 the accompanying text provides a clue as to what precipitated these events. The first glyph shows the head of God K (T1030b) and the second, the *tsolk'in* position 13 Ahau with the coefficient appearing on the right. The placement of the coefficient to the right of the day sign is unusual, but other examples are known, as in a painting from Group G, Tikal (Orrego and Larrios 1983:fig. 11a). Furthermore, the day-sign cartouche and pedestal are unmistakable in the Naj Tunich painting. I have reconstructed the 13 Ahau date as 9.17.0.0.0, 13 Ahau 18 Cumku. To have the head of God K here is most fitting, as he has epigraphic associations with temporal markers, such as the 819-day count.

Drawing 12 (fig. 8-12)
Measurements 10 cm h. × 18 cm w.
Distance from Ground Level 1.46 m
Number of Hieroglyphs 2
Description This short text shows a bar, two dots, and the day sign Lamat. Because of the placement of the dots, it seems certain that the original coefficient was eight. The second glyph lacks a numerical coefficient, suggesting that it was not the *haab* position. I have placed this date at 8 Lamat 1 Pop based on the reconstruction of the 13 Ahau period ending in Drawing 11. The first Lamat position to follow 13 Ahau is 8 Lamat. Furthermore, 8 Lamat 1 Pop is a New Year day, an important day in the Maya ritual calendar.
Conservation Drawing 12 was effaced beyond recognition in early 1988, according to reports relayed by guards. This was a deliberate act of vandalism, although the circumstances under which it occurred remain obscure.

Drawing 13 (fig. 8-13)
Measurements 50 cm h. × 49 cm w.
Distance from Ground Level 1.77 m
Number of Hieroglyphs 16
Description The image consists of a

row of eight hieroglyphs with columns descending at rows D, F, G, and H.

Conservation When first discovered, two hieroglyphs (F1–2) were already smeared. This painting was badly smeared in the 1989 vandalism.

Drawing 14 (fig. 8-14)
Measurements 28 cm h. × 41 cm w.
Distance from Ground Level 69 cm
Description The image consists of positive, overlapping handprints, of which there appear to be at least three. A hollow niche in the rock directly below the handprints could have held small objects, though nothing of this sort was found.

Drawing 15 (fig. 8-15)
Measurements 12 cm h. × 9 cm w.
Distance from Ground Level 1.50 m
Description The remains of a painting are found here, though forms cannot be distinguished.
Conservation All photographs suggest that this painting was smeared before the cave's modern discovery.

Note: Drawings 16–33 form a group. The wall makes a sharp turn after Drawing 28.

Drawing 16 (fig. 8-16)
Measurements 14 cm h. × 9 cm w.
Distance from Ground Level 2.0 m
Description A pointed form is associated with another unidentifiable object.

Drawing 17 (fig. 8-17)
Measurements 65 cm h. × 35 cm w.
Distance from Ground Level 1.24 m
Number of Figures 1
Description A figure stands with his body facing to his left, but turns his head to gaze over his right shoulder. He wears wristlets and a tight collar around his neck. His hair seems to be pulled up in a ponytail, and his head is adorned with what appear to be ribbons and beads. Patches of paint cover his face around the nose, mouth, and chin. A garment line can be seen at the right side of his waist. His hands are drawn to his groin, and he grasps an object that is difficult to identify.

Strecker (1987) suggests that the figure is masturbating, the line projecting from the "penis" being seminal fluid. I hesitate to embrace this explanation largely because the "penis" does not fit with typical Maya depictions of phalli (e.g., Joralemon 1974:figs. 10, 11; Schele and Miller 1986:pls. 69, 84; Actun Ch'on, Drawing 1; Naj Tunich, Drawing 18). The "penis" in Drawing

FIG. 8-13. Drawing 13. Photograph by Chip and Jennifer Clark.

FIG. 8-14. Drawing 14. Photograph by Chip and Jennifer Clark.

Images from the Underworld

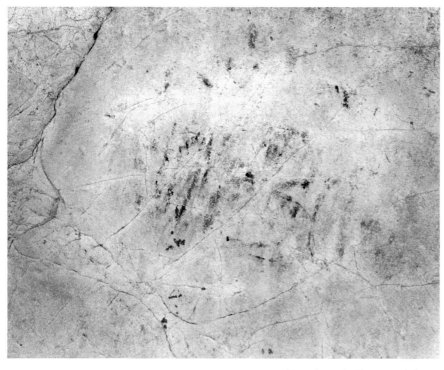

FIG. 8-15. Drawing 15. Photograph by Chip and Jennifer Clark.

17 is rendered in a highly amorphous fashion and has what appears to be a notch at the top and a line dividing the base such that it looks like it has a handle. Furthermore, liquids in Maya art are usually shown as strings of dots and not wavy solid lines. Yet I cannot offer an alternative explanation of the object held in his hands.

The rounded forms below the hands could be the figure's testicles, but, unfortunately, this area is not well preserved; it is possible that they represent part of the costume. Two likely possibilities are that this enigmatic figure is engaged in a rite of drawing blood from the penis or is ejaculating. The tight collar around the neck is found on captives and figures engaged in autosacrifice (Schele and Miller 1986:193) as well as certain types of ritual performers. The contorted pose signals a kind of psychical tension surrounding this figure.

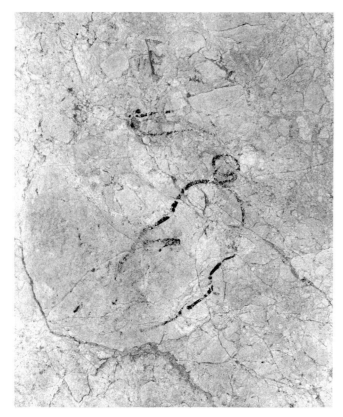

FIG. 8-16. Drawing 16. Photograph by Chip and Jennifer Clark.

FIG. 8-17. Drawing 17. Photograph by Chip and Jennifer Clark.

A Catalog of Naj Tunich Paintings and Petroglyphs

Drawing 18 (fig. 8-18)

Measurements 49 cm h. × 30 cm w.

Distance from Ground Level 1.98 m

Number of Hieroglyphs 5

Number of Figures 2

Description This is one of the most unusual scenes from Naj Tunich. It shows a couple in amorous embrace. The male is nude and ithyphallic. He presses his erect penis against his partner's genital area. She, on the other hand, seems to be wearing a hipcloth, indicated by fragmentary lines across the thigh and waist. There is a stark contrast in the persona of the two figures. Through her idealization and more elaborate costuming, she exudes a noble bearing. He, on the other hand, is slump-shouldered, hump-backed, pot-bellied, and frail, as can be seen in his thin leg. Her body suggests strength and grace, his, weakness and clumsiness. With his iris placed at the back of his eye, he looks sly and impish.

This decrepit character relates to the God N complex. In Maya art God N is frequently portrayed straining the limits of social decorum (Taube 1989a). The sexual content of the Naj Tunich scene ties into typical baudy activities associated with God N. Taube has convincingly argued that these scenes of sexual license have a counterpart in ritual clowning that not only serves to entertain but to reinforce societal values. The idea of ritual performance also helps explain the masculine characteristics of the "female" figure: she has no breasts, and her stout body type seems rather masculine. Since males play female roles in traditional Maya performance, this female figure, indicated by her queue of hair and the manner in which intercourse is portrayed, may actually represent a male performer.

Conservation The testicle of the left-hand figure was smeared sometime after February of 1981. Miraculously, this important painting was spared in the 1989 vandalism.

FIG. 8-18. Drawing 18. Photograph by Chip and Jennifer Clark.

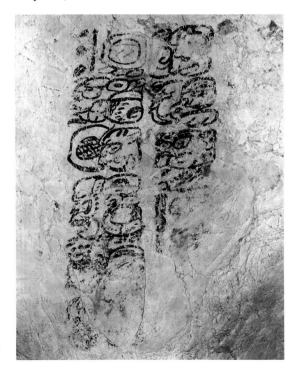

FIG. 8-19. Drawing 19. Photograph by Chip and Jennifer Clark.

Images from the Underworld

Drawing 19 (fig. 8-19)
Measurements 44 cm h. × 22 cm w.
Distance from Ground Level 1.70 m
Number of Hieroglyphs 10
Description Two columns of glyphs read straight down in single columns.
Conservation Smearing of the glyph at A6 is visible in all known photographs of the painting taken since 1980. However, the entire painting was badly smeared in the 1989 vandalism.

Drawing 20 (fig. 8-20)
Measurements figure 30 cm h. × 15 cm w.; text 37 cm h. × 8 cm w.
Distance from Ground Level 1.18 m
Number of Hieroglyphs 6
Number of Figures 1
Description A nude figure in three-quarter view crouches with one knee on the ground. The pose is unusual for the Maya, possibly unique. Considering the lack of precedent for this kind of pose, the artist has handled it well: the left arm is broadened, as it should be, and the legs follow an oblique plane. The artist had some trouble with the left leg, which is drawn nearly in profile. To achieve greater naturalism, this leg would require the most dramatic foreshortening, but that has been avoided by relying on the implied direction of the buttocks and upper thigh.

The face also shows some deft handling of foreshortening. The nose is drawn with some perceptual accuracy. The treatment of the eyes—one in near profile and one near frontal—works reasonably well. The artist ran into trouble with the cheek and jawline, which has become a semicircle. The mouth and part of the jawline have apparently flaked off. A series of curved lines on the left side of the jaw possibly indicates that this is an aged person or maybe the remains of whiskers. The loop under the ear looks like a counterweight for a heavy earflare, though none seems to be worn. Another possibility is that it is a drop of blood, as circlets

FIG. 8-20. Drawing 20. Photograph by Chip and Jennifer Clark.

representing blood are seen behind the ears of some Maya figures (e.g., Schele 1984: fig. 12e).

The unkempt hairstyle, genital display, and oblique orientation of the figure signal his heightened emotional state. It has been suggested that the figure is masturbating (Strecker 1987). This is one possible interpretation, but the scene may also represent a rite of genital mutilation (Stone 1987b).

The six-glyph text is important, given its generous size in relation to the figure. It recalls in a general way captive images from Tikal carved on altars and columns. These figures are nearly nude,

except for a skimpy loincloth, and exhibit animated poses, which often include foreshortening one leg (Jones and Satterthwaite 1982: figs. 30, 32, 62). The altars are accompanied by short texts that lead off with the "general verb" (Schele 1982: 57–58), precisely as we have in the text of Drawing 20.
Conservation There is an area of what may be pigment under the figure's left armpit, which may have resulted from smearing or water seepage. Sections of the text (B2) and the figure (buttocks and foot) are missing where painted on smooth limestone clasts. This painting was destroyed in the vandalism of 1989.

Drawing 21 (fig. 8-21)
Measurements 22 cm h. × 19 cm w.
Distance from Ground Level 1.43 m
Number of Figures 1
Description All of the ballplayers at Naj Tunich are found in architectural settings similar to the three-stepped structure depicted here. The large rubber ball rests on the middle step. Stepped structures are common in Maya ballgame scenes, such as the Hieroglyphic Stairs of Structure 33, Yaxchilan, and on many polychrome ceramics. Schele and Miller (1986:250) discuss what they call the "staircase ritual," in which captives were bound into the form of a ball and rolled down the staircase. Ballcourts in the Maya Lowlands generally lack such steps; their presence in ballgame scenes may, therefore, be explained by the accompanying sacrificial ceremonies. It is also possible that the form of the ballcourt is merely conventional. This is suggested by the fact that the stepped form also appears in the "ballgame" glyph (Houston 1983a). The Naj Tunich ball is superfixed by the number nine. Balls both affixed and infixed with numbers are common in Maya art, though their meaning remains unknown.

Coe (1989:171) has identified the Naj Tunich ballplayer as Hunahpu based on his spotted face and the hunter's hat. The jaguar skin hipcloth is also worn by a ballplayer on the middle marker from Copan's Ballcourt II-B, which Schele (1986) has identified as Hunahpu.

The figure wears typical ballgame attire: a thick waist belt and kneepad. His earflare has a flexible central element that droops down to shoulder level. Baubles are attached to the bridge of his nose.

Conservation The figure's arm was scraped with a sharp implement sometime in March of 1981 (see G. Stuart 1981:233). Crosshatched lines on the ball are the result of scratch marks. The

FIG. 8-21. Drawing 21. Photograph by Chip and Jennifer Clark.

FIG. 8-22. Drawing 22. Photograph by Chip and Jennifer Clark.

Images from the Underworld

figure was virtually destroyed in 1989, though the stepped structure and ball are still intact (see Brady 1991a:114).

Drawing 22 (fig. 8-22)
Measurements 10 cm h. × 20 cm w.
Distance from Ground Level 1.59 m
Description This diminutive, finely painted figure sports a goatee. His head-dress consists of a piece of cloth, secured by a thick, twisted cord tied in a knot on top of his head; short feathers rim the headgear. Though the ear is not clearly painted, one can observe some kind of ornament in this area that hangs straight down. To the right of the ear is a cluster of three knots or bows, again not clearly drawn. Clothing is quite modest here, just a narrow loincloth.

The contained, slumping posture, with arms drawn close to the body, conveys a sense of quiet relaxation. Space is indicated by a groundline that supports the figure and a large shell with characteristic spire and rows of nodules. Though surely exaggerated, the immense size suggests that it is a seashell. Conch shells, shown with spire tops and nodules, are used as trumpets in certain vase scenes (Robicsek and Hales 1981: Vessels 33–37). Spire-topped shells appear in many contexts in Maya art. They function as a shelter for deities; for example, painted vases show a youth pulling God N out of a spire-topped shell (e.g., Coe 1978: no. 10). Spire-topped shells also appear in Maya art as paint containers.
Conservation The shell was smeared early in 1981. The figure was completely destroyed in 1989.

Drawing 23 (fig. 8-23)
Measurements 30 cm h. × 9 cm w.
Distance from Ground Level 1.60 m
Number of Hieroglyphs 15
Description The image consists of three columns of hieroglyphs. To the left of A4 part of a cartouche can be seen. An inexplicable line can also be

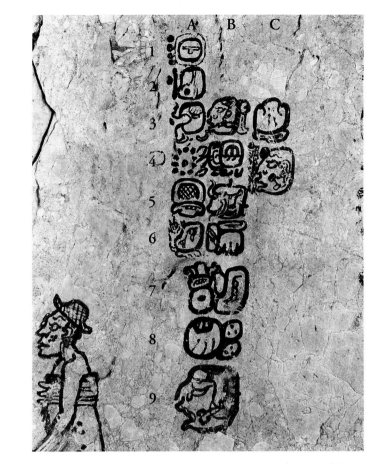

FIG. 8-23. Drawing 23. Photograph by Chip and Jennifer Clark.

seen below A6. Both of these marks appear to be extraneous, as there is no indication, such as flecks of pigment adhering to the wall, that there were more glyphs to the left.
Conservation The bottom glyph was smeared between February and April of 1981. The painting was completely destroyed in 1989.

Drawing 24 (fig. 8-24)
Measurements 53 cm h. × 70 cm w.
Distance from Ground Level 1.60 m
Number of Hieroglyphs 24; 4 more possible
Description The painting consists of seven columns of hieroglyphs.
Conservation The faded appearance of this text seems to be the result of natural weathering. This painting was par-

tially destroyed in 1989, mainly the row of glyphs in column A.

Drawing 25 (fig. 8-25)
Measurements 72 cm h. × 21 cm w.
Distance from Ground Level 1.55 m
Number of Hieroglyphs 19
Description Two columns of glyphs form the image. A line with scrolled ends is painted in thinner pigment around the upper half of the text. Frames are rare among the Naj Tunich texts. The only other example occurs in Drawing 37.
Conservation This painting was partially smeared in 1989.

Drawing 26 (fig. 8-26)
Measurements 19 cm h. × 85 cm w.; figure 16 cm h.

FIG. 8-24. Drawing 24. Photograph by Chip and Jennifer Clark.

FIG. 8-25. Drawing 25. Photograph by Chip and Jennifer Clark.

Distance from Ground Level 1.67 m
Number of Figures 1
Description A lone figure in thin, fragmentary paint sits on a groundline. Head tilted back, he draws his right hand to his open mouth. Scraggly whiskers can be seen around the chin and jawline. His hair is gathered in a short ponytail that hangs over his forehead. He wears a simple costume: a thin wristband and hipcloth. The waist band may be part of a loincloth. A splatter of pigment appears to the right of the figure, and there are extraneous spots of paint below and to the left.

A fruitful comparison can be drawn with the Tablet of the Orator from Palenque, where we have a much better understanding of text and image (fig. 6-20). This figure kneels, has slightly parted lips, and draws his hand to his mouth with the palm turned toward the face, as with the cave figure. Schele (1984) mentions that a line runs from the mouth to the adjacent hieroglyphic text; hence, the figure may be speaking. The figure in Drawing 26 may also be speaking or singing.

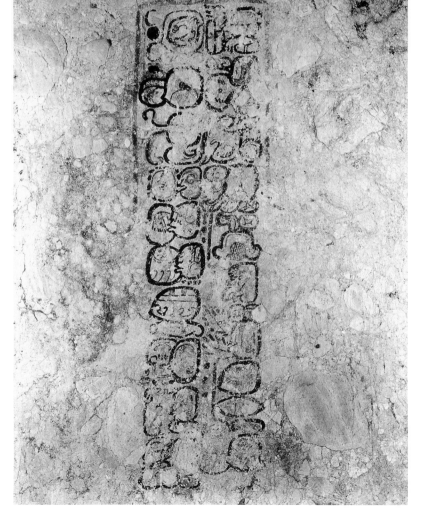

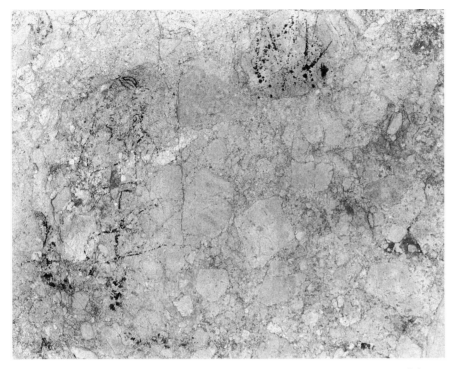

FIG. 8-26. Drawing 26. Photograph by Chip and Jennifer Clark.

FIG. 8-27. Drawing 27. Photograph by Chip and Jennifer Clark.

Drawing 27 (fig. 8-27)
Measurements 18 cm h. × 42 cm w.
Distance from Ground Level 1.42 m
Number of Hieroglyphs 5
Number of Figures 3
Description Three figures stand in procession, accompanied by two texts—one column of five glyphs to the left and, possibly, a row across the top, now destroyed. The front and back figures wear a sphere suspended on a string around the neck. The front figure has a scarf tied around his head. Probably a beaded tassel, like that of the rear figure, trails behind his head (cf. Drawing 11). Remnants of a loincloth are preserved on the front figure. The three figures appear to be a procession of musicians. The rear one holds a bat-shaped object that may be a rattle. The discoidal object held by the central figure is a drum made from a turtle carapace, known as *boxel ak* in Yucatan. Characteristic of a turtle carapace are the concentric rings on the perimeter and crosshatching near the center. Representations of this instrument from the Late Classic show it being struck with a deer antler, sometimes held behind the instrument (e.g., Coe 1975:no. 16). The cave figure could have held an antler in his left hand, which is now missing. According to Landa, however, the natives struck the turtle-shell drum with the palm of the hand (Tozzer 1941:93).

The front figure is so much larger than his companions that he is presumably intended to represent either a more important or mature individual. In Colonial Yucatan one highly respected functionary, called the *hol pop* "head of the mat," was charged with the care of the musical instruments and the instruction in song and dance for community festivities. The large Naj Tunich figure may represent an important group leader, such as the *hol pop*.

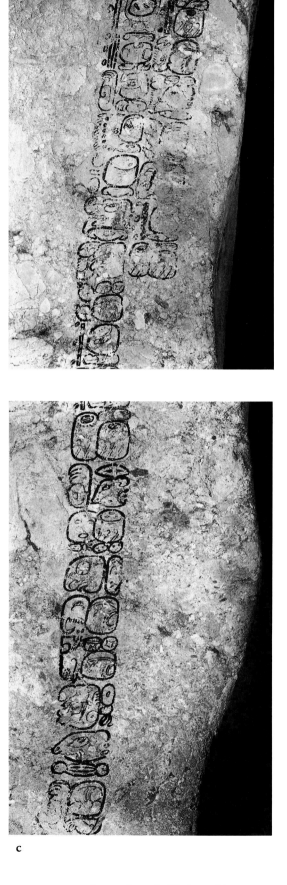

a

FIG. 8-28. Drawing 28: *a*, full; *b*, upper; *c*, lower. Photographs by Chip and Jennifer Clark.

Drawing 28 (fig. 8-28a–c)
Measurements 1.30 m h. × 19 cm w.
Distance from Ground Level 1.90 m
Number of Hieroglyphs 25
Description Consisting of two columns of hieroglyphs, this painting is located at the edge of a wall just before it makes a sharp bend. Around the corner, at equal distance from the wall edge, is another long inscription (Drawing 29), and to the right of that is a short text (Drawing 30). Drawings 28 and 30

c

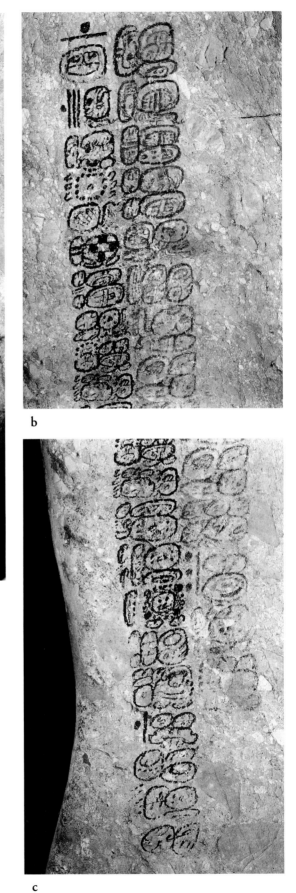

a

FIG. 8-29. Drawing 29: *a,* full; *b,* upper; *c,* lower. Photographs by Chip and Jennifer Clark.

were painted by the same individual. The bend in the wall, where Drawings 28–30 are found, is accompanied by a steep incline in the cave floor, which continues to rise as one reaches the end of this painting group at Drawing 33.

Drawing 29 (fig. 8-29a–c)
Measurements 1.35 m h. × 26 cm w.
Distance from Ground Level 2.0 m
Number of Hieroglyphs 31
Description This hieroglyphic text in

b

c

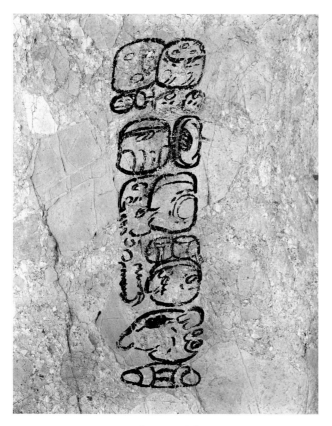

FIG. 8-30. Drawing 30. Photograph by Chip and Jennifer Clark.

FIG. 8-31. Drawing 31. Photograph by Chip and Jennifer Clark.

two columns is the longest painting in the cave. The second column shows a consistent diminution from top to bottom in the amount of paint preserved on the wall. The artist seems to have gradually run out of paint. With weathering over time, the thinner layers of paint have been more severely affected. **Conservation** This painting was badly smeared in 1989.

Drawing 30 (fig. 8-30)
Measurements 33 cm h. × 9 cm w.
Distance from Ground Level 1.71 m
Number of Hieroglyphs 5
Description The drawing consists of a single column of glyphs; 5 cm above is a line 23 cm long that runs to the left.
Conservation Smearing of the third and fourth glyphs occurred between January and February of 1981. The painting was destroyed in 1989.

Drawing 31 (fig. 8-31)
Measurements 33 cm h. × 33 cm w.
Distance from Ground Level 2.17 m
Number of Hieroglyphs 2
Number of Figures 1
Description The fragmentary remains of a ballplayer, ball, and stepped structure comprise Drawing 31. Little of the figure remains; only the kneepad and the front flap of the loincloth are still visible. The ball lies on the groundline, and the player faces both ball and steps. The scene is utterly static, as though freezing a moment before or after play. A hieroglyphic text, now destroyed, framed the top of the scene.

Drawing 32 (fig. 8-32)
Measurements: 35 cm h. × 74 cm w.
Distance from Ground Level 1.56 m
Number of Hieroglyphs 5
Number of Figures 3
Description This curious scene shows three figures, each sitting on a higher groundline than the one in front. The first figure, at left, is drawn at a larger scale than the other two, which is why

his head is nearly at the same level as the second figure. The front figure, who may have sported a beard, folds his arms across his chest and sits cross-legged. He wears an ample loincloth sash that resembles one in Drawing 68. The seated second figure extends his left arm forward. He seems to be wearing a fezlike cap. No other part of his costume has survived.

The middle figure is connected by a groundline to a third individual. The painting becomes quite faded to the right of the second figure but appears to show someone seated in a boxlike object. He extends his right hand forward with wrist up and palm out. This recalls certain carved bones from Tikal (Stuart 1988: fig. 5.17) that show Ruler A sitting in a canoe, grasping the side of the canoe with one hand and raising the

FIG. 8-32. Drawing 32. Photograph by Chip and Jennifer Clark.

other. The Tikal bones have been interpreted as Ruler A's journey into the underworld (Coggins 1975: 476–477). Perhaps Drawing 32 also shows a deceased individual journeying into the underworld.

Drawing 33 (fig. 8-33)
Measurements 19 cm h. × 23 cm w.
Distance from Ground Level 1.90 m
Number of Figures 1
Description A figure shown from the waist up has a prominent, possibly false, beard. His hand is raised, palm out, fingertips upright, a gesture typical of dancing figures in Maya art. In front of his hand is a short wavy line. Drawing 61 also shows a curving line near the hand of a dancing figure.

Drawing 34 (fig. 8-34)
Measurements 31 cm h. × 16 cm w.
Distance from Ground Level 1.47 m
Number of Hieroglyphs 9
Description The drawing consists of two columns of hieroglyphs. Fading can be seen at B4 and B5, clearly due to a thinner mixture of paint.

FIG. 8-33. Drawing 33. Photograph by Chip and Jennifer Clark.

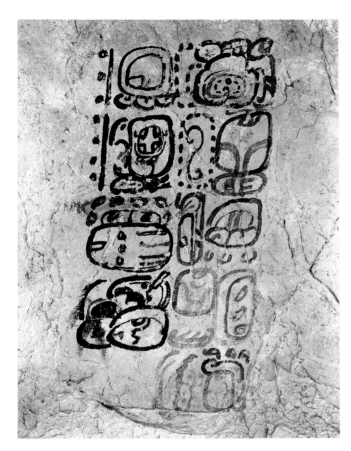

FIG. 8-34. Drawing 34. Photograph by Chip and Jennifer Clark.

FIG. 8-35. Drawing 35. Photograph by Chip and Jennifer Clark.

Conservation Based on early photographs, damage to the glyph at A5 may be quite old. This painting was vandalized in 1989. The glyph at B2 was battered, dislodging a piece of the wall.

Drawing 35 (fig. 8-35)
Measurements 18 cm h. × 16 cm w.
Distance from Ground Level 1.63 m
Number of Hieroglyphs 6
Description The drawings consist of two columns of hieroglyphs. While most of the texts at Naj Tunich read down in straight columns, this text is read across in paired columns.

Drawing 36 (fig. 8-36)
Measurements
    51 cm h. × 7 cm w. (text)
    46 cm h. × 20 cm w. (black area)
Distance from Ground Level 2.30 m
Number of Hieroglyphs 6
Description A solid mass of paint near a column of eroded hieroglyphs is found on the concave surface of a freestanding limestone formation.

FIG. 8-36. Drawing 36. Photograph by Chip and Jennifer Clark.

Images from the Underworld

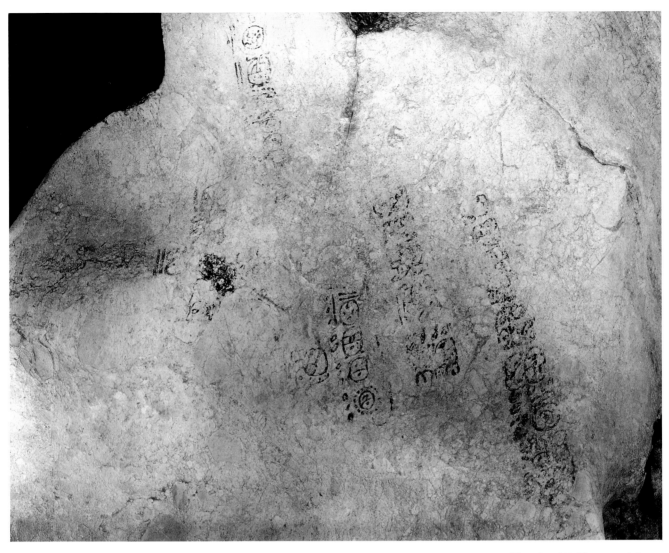

FIG. 8-37. Drawing 37. Photograph by Chip and Jennifer Clark.

Note: Drawings 37–45 are located in an area configured very much like a room. Drawings 37 and 43–45 frame the entry into the room heading west, and Drawings 38–42 mark its end.

Drawing 37 (fig. 8-37)
Measurements 1.55 m h. × 1.20 m w.
Distance from Ground Level 2.0 m
Number of Hieroglyphs 25; 5 more possible
Description A delicate human head, only half of which survives, is juxtaposed with one of the longest hieroglyphic texts in the cave. The head shows curious headgear: a mass of paint resting atop a squarish cap. The text contains the remnants of a framing device—a line to the right of column C—as in Drawing 25.

Conservation The glyphs at C3 (3 Ahau) and F7 were smeared between August of 1980 and February of 1981. The head and adjacent glyphs were later smeared in 1989.

Drawing 38 (fig. 8-38)
Measurements 35 cm h. × 18 cm w.
Distance from Ground Level 1.90 m
Number of Hieroglyphs 10 or more
Description The drawing consists of the fragments of what appears to have been a hieroglyphic text in two columns.

Drawing 39 (fig. 8-39)

Measurements 38 cm h. × 53 cm w.

Distance from Ground Level 1.10 m

Number of Figures 4

Description A ballgame scene is again the subject of a Naj Tunich painting. The ball rests on the second step of a three-stepped structure. The ballplayer stands in profile facing the ball. He wears a massive waist belt and knee guard. His body is framed by an *alfarda* adjacent to one of the steps. The architecture provides a means of positioning figures around the scene. All three figures are kneeling, while the ballplayer looks stalwart, as though dominating the group.

Drawing 40 (fig. 8-40)

Measurements 39 cm h. × 46 cm w.

Distance from Ground Level 1.49 m

Number of Figures 3

Description This musical procession has been dubbed "*los musicos.*" Unlike Drawing 27, the three musicians in Drawing 40 are at identical scale and are similarly dressed in a loincloth/hipcloth assemblage with ample front sashes and headgear of stiffened, folded cloth that sweeps low over the forehead. The left figure has pendant ear ornaments, perhaps of stiffened cloth. The middle figure has circular earflares with an attached cloth strip, as well as a line drawn from the upper lip to the back of the head. This could represent face paint or part of a mask. All that remains of the costume of the right figure are the front panels and sashes of his loincloth/hipcloth assemblage.

Two musical instruments are played. The left figure uses his left hand to beat some sort of drum, either a turtle carapace or a ceramic drum. The object held by the central figure strongly resembles a small ceramic drum. A fragment of such a drum was found in a Chiquibul cave, Actun Kabal. The right figure extends his arm forward and thus

FIG. 8-38. Drawing 38. Photograph by Chip and Jennifer Clark.

FIG. 8-39. Drawing 39. Photograph by Chip and Jennifer Clark.

Images from the Underworld

may have held a rattle, as does the left figure in Drawing 27.

Conservation The ear ornament of the left-hand figure was smeared (G. Stuart 1981:233) between January and February of 1981. The two figures to the left were smeared in 1989.

Drawing 41 (fig. 8-41)
Measurements 24 cm h. × 21 cm w.
Distance from Ground Level 1.64 m
Number of Hieroglyphs 8
Description Three columns of hieroglyphs

Drawing 42 (fig. 8-42)
Measurements 20 cm h. × 6 cm w.
Distance from Ground Level 86 cm
Description The drawing consists of a fragment of what was probably a hieroglyphic text.

FIG. 8-40. Drawing 40. Photograph by Chip and Jennifer Clark.

FIG. 8-41. Drawing 41. Photograph by Chip and Jennifer Clark.

FIG. 8-42. Drawing 42. Photograph by Andrea Stone.

FIG. 8-43. Drawing 43. Photograph by Chip and Jennifer Clark.

FIG. 8-44. Drawing 44. Photograph by Chip and Jennifer Clark.

Drawing 43 (fig. 8-43)
Measurements 23 cm h. × 40 cm w.
Distance from Ground Level 84 cm
Number of Figures 1; 1 more possible
Description This was once a complex scene. Today only part of one figure is identifiable. The figure wears a simple cap that seems to have been filled in with paint. It is probable that the lower right corner had another figure.

Drawing 44 (fig. 8-44)
Measurements 40 cm h. × 20 cm w.
Distance from Ground Level 1.70 m
Number of Hieroglyphs 4
Description A column of four glyphs surrounded by paint fragments suggests that this is part of a larger text.

Drawing 45 (fig. 8-45)
Measurements 22 cm h. × 3 cm w.
Distance from Ground Level 1.73 m
Number of Hieroglyphs 6
Description The drawing consists of a hieroglyphic text, probably in a single column. The text must have been larger.

Drawing 46 (fig. 8-46)
Measurements 54 cm h. × 32 cm w.
Distance from Ground Level 1.85 m
Number of Hieroglyphs 2 probable
Description This appears to have been a hieroglyphic text with glyphs of a relatively large scale. Not pictured here are more painted fragments 34 cm below.

Drawing 47 (fig. 8-47)
Measurements 16 cm h. × 8 cm w.
Distance from Ground Level 1.60 m
Description These lines were scrawled onto a stalactite near the entrance to the Crystal Room with a stick of charcoal. This crude drawing may well be modern.

Note: Drawings 48–51 are found in the Crystal Room, a small chamber decorated with speleothems.

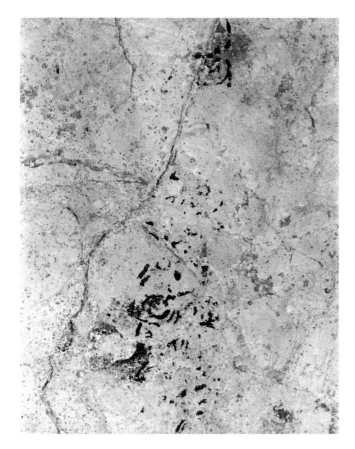

FIG. 8-47. Drawing 47. Photograph by Chip and Jennifer Clark.

FIG. 8-45. *Upper left:* Drawing 45. Photograph by Chip and Jennifer Clark.

FIG. 8-46. *Upper right:* Drawing 46. Photograph by Chip and Jennifer Clark.

Drawing 48 (fig. 8-48)
Measurements 46 cm h. × 15 cm w.
Distance from Ground Level 1.84 m
Number of Hieroglyphs 4
Description The drawing consists of a single column of four glyphs painted on a calcite column; 34 cm below the glyphs are four painted parallel lines (not pictured). The paintings on calcite, such as this, have a much warmer tonality than those on limestone.
Conservation Near the painting are charcoal streaks. The bottom two glyphs have suffered deep chop marks from something like a machete. All of this damage is probably the result of the March 1981 looting attempt (G. Stuart 1981:230–231).

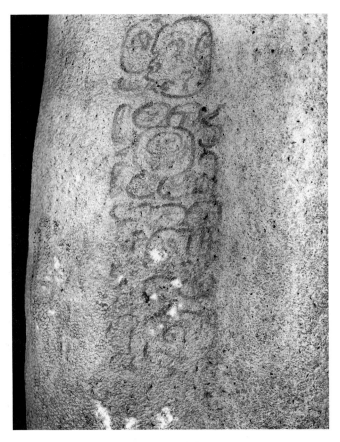

FIG. 8-48. Drawing 48. Photograph by Chip and Jennifer Clark.

FIG. 8-49. Drawing 49. Photograph by Chip and Jennifer Clark.

Drawing 49 (fig. 8-49)
Measurements 61 cm h. × 11 cm w.
Distance from Ground Level 2.45 m
Number of Hieroglyphs 6
Description A single column of hieroglyphs.
Conservation As with Drawing 48, charcoal streaks can be seen on this calcite column.

Drawing 50 (fig. 8-50)
Measurements 81 cm h. × 43 cm w.
Distance from Ground Level 2.12 m
Number of Hieroglyphs 17
Description Three columns of hieroglyphs occupy the same composite calcite shaft as Drawing 51. This is one of the more coarsely painted texts at Naj Tunich, owing partly to the rough calcite surface.
Conservation This painting has been scratched with a sharp implement.

Drawing 51 (fig. 8-51)
Measurements 39 cm h. × 29 cm w.
Distance from Ground Level 1.63 m
Number of Hieroglyphs 7
Number of Figures 2
Description Drawing 51 is the fourth ballgame scene from Naj Tunich. Wearing a heavy belt, the player kneels at the left before a three-stepped structure; on the second step rests an enormous ball. Details of costume and anatomy are generalized, owing to the difficulty of painting on calcite. For instance, the player's hand is shown as a balled fist. Like other Naj Tunich ballgame scenes, action is limited.

The drawing subsumes a figure at the right who may not be part of the ballgame scene, though I have included this figure in the same drawing unit owing to his proximity to the ballplayer. This figure stands on a different groundline and is drawn on a larger scale than the ballplayer. As Maya art is not concerned with creating the illusion of deep space, the two figures cannot possibly be part of the same composition. Based on costume, the right-hand figure does not appear to be a ballplayer, though he stands like the ballplayers in Drawings 31 and 39. He wears a mask or paint on the upper part of his face, a circular earplug, and a wide sash around his waist.

At the extreme right is a single column of hieroglyphs. The back of the adjacent figure is cut off by the text. It seems that the ballplayer and the text were painted first, with the standing figure inserted later. The text may refer to the ballgame scene.
Conservation This painting was the object of an attempted looting in late March of 1981 (G. Stuart 1981:231). Two cuts, ranging from 1 to 1.5 cm

FIG. 8-50. Drawing 50. Photograph by
Chip and Jennifer Clark.

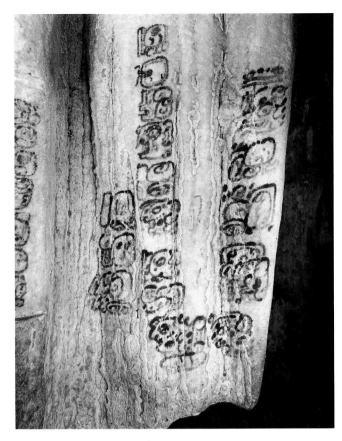

FIG. 8-51. Drawing 51. Photograph by
Chip and Jennifer Clark.

in depth and about 29 cm in length,
are above and below the painting. On
the left side is a shallower cut about
33 cm in length and on the right, a
light scratch. In 1989 the painting was
scratched again by a sharp object.

Note: Drawings 52–55 frame the entry
into a narrow flowstone tunnel that leads
to the end of the Western Passage.

Drawing 52 (fig. 8-52)
Measurements 42 cm h. × 14 cm w.
Distance from Ground Level 2.05 m
Number of Hieroglyphs 16
Description Two columns of hiero-
glyphs are painted on a calcified wall at
the entrance to the last section of the
Western Passage.

FIG. 8-52. Drawing 52. Photograph by
Chip and Jennifer Clark.

Conservation Fresh-looking charcoal marks below the painting seem to be recent. The painting was smeared with mud in 1989.

Drawing 53 (petroglyphs) (fig. 8-53)
Measurements
    18 cm h. × 8 cm w. (Profile 1)
    14 cm h. × 10 cm w. (Profile 2)
    12 cm h. × 4 cm w. (Profile 3)
    5 cm h. × 4 cm w. (Profile 4)
Distance from Ground Level
    1.30 m (Profiles 1 and 2)
    1.75 m (Profile 3)
    1.32 m (Profile 4)
Number of Profiles 4
Description Drawing 53, approached through a narrow flowstone passage, is incised into a smooth, curved flowstone wall. The main image of the drawing is a lovely Late Classic profile of a bearded face with a ballooning hat (Profile 1). Three cruder profiles, in varying states of completion, are carved at the left (not pictured), perhaps in imitation of the finer one. Profile 2 is to the immediate left of Profile 1. Profile 3 is slightly above and 18 centimeters to the left of Profile 2. Profile 4, the least complete—with only part of the forehead—is 23 centimeters below Profile 3.

Drawing 54 (fig. 8-54)
Measurements 4.5 cm h. × 2 cm w.
Distance from Ground Level 1.73 cm
Description These two small vertically aligned circles are painted on a short stalactite.

Drawing 55 (fig. 8-55)
Measurements 8 cm h. × 7 cm w.
Distance from Ground Level 1.50 m
Description A circular patch of light-colored calcite was selected to paint this simple frontal face.

Drawing 56 (petroglyph) (fig. 8-56)
Measurements 10 cm h. × 6 cm w.
Distance from Ground Level 1.60 m
Description This petroglyph is little

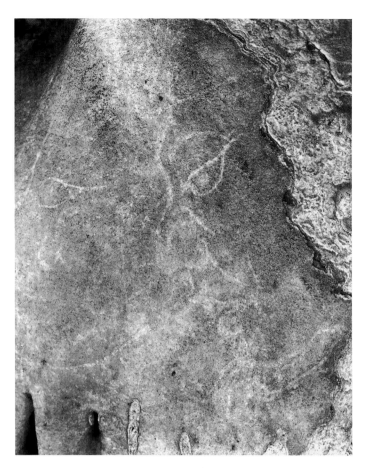

FIG. 8-53. Drawing 53. Photograph by Chip and Jennifer Clark.

more than an odd assortment of lines. To the left are two incised parallel lines 48 centimeters in length (not pictured).

Drawing 57 (petroglyph) (fig. 8-57)
Measurements 13 cm h. × 25 cm w.
Distance from Ground Level 2.24 m
Description The drawing consists of a petroglyph of a bird. The extended beak recalls a raptorial water bird, such as a cormorant or heron, though the wing and body are not correct for these types of birds.

Drawing 58 (petroglyph) (fig. 8-58)
Measurements 13 cm h. × 13 cm w.
Distance from Ground Level 2.0 m
Number of Hieroglyphs 1
Description This petroglyph represents the day sign Ben, one of the Year Bearers in the Maya Lowlands during the

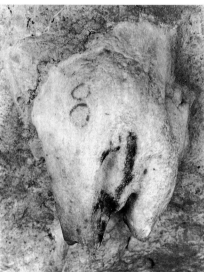

FIG. 8-54. Drawing 54. Photograph by Chip and Jennifer Clark.

Classic period. Its juxtaposition to the bird in Drawing 58 may be meaningful. The Proto-Cholan word *mut* "bird" (Kaufman and Norman 1984:126) was borrowed into Yucatec, where it also has the meaning of "tidings" or "news" (Barrera Vásquez 1980:542). Thompson (1962:164) noted the homophony between "bird" and "tidings" and suggested that certain birds in the Dresden Codex might refer to the prognostication of a time period. Thus, the juxtaposition of a bird with a day sign may refer to the prognostication of that day.

Note: Drawings 59–65 are clustered together on a contiguous wall surface near the end of the Western Passage.

Drawing 59 (fig. 8-59)
Measurements 4 cm h. × 2 cm w.
Distance from Ground Level 75 cm
Number of Profiles 1
Description A profile head wearing a headdress begins the last group of paintings in the Western Passage. As with all paintings in this group, the paint is thin and the color pale. The painting itself is small and the line extremely delicate.

FIG. 8-55. Drawing 55. Photograph by Chip and Jennifer Clark.

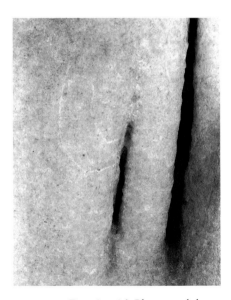

FIG. 8-56. Drawing 56. Photograph by Chip and Jennifer Clark.

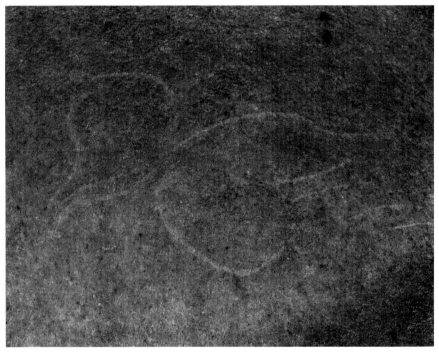

FIG. 8-57. Drawing 57. Photograph by Chip and Jennifer Clark.

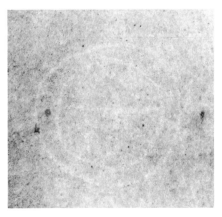

FIG. 8-58. Drawing 58. Photograph by Chip and Jennifer Clark.

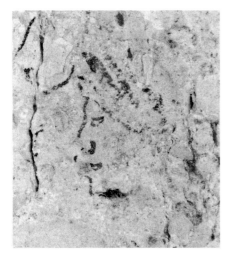

FIG. 8-59. Drawing 59. Photograph by Chip and Jennifer Clark.

FIG. 8-60. Drawing 60. Photograph by Andrea Stone.

FIG. 8-61. Drawing 61. Photograph by Chip and Jennifer Clark.

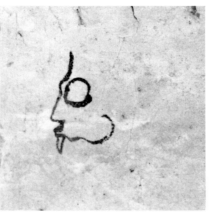

FIG. 8-62. Drawing 62. Photograph by Chip and Jennifer Clark.

Drawing 60 (fig. 8-60)
Measurements 4 cm h. × 2 cm w.
Distance from Ground Level 57 cm
Number of Profiles 1
Description This profile face, lacking eyes, is found close to Drawing 59.

Drawing 61 (fig. 8-61)
Measurements 14 cm h. × 8 cm w.
Distance from Ground Level 61 cm
Number of Figures 1

Description Drawing 61 is a standing male figure whose chest is in a frontal view while his legs are in profile. As only one leg is rendered, the figure looks awkward. Headgear consists of a band tied at the front. The arm positions—one hand forward and one on the hip—is typical of Maya dancing figures. I would identify this figure as a dancer.

Drawing 62 (fig. 8-62)

Measurements 3.5 cm h. × 2 cm w.

Distance from Ground Level 50 cm

Number of Profiles 1

Description Although the head appears incomplete, the paint here is well-preserved, so what remains of the painting represents the original. The profile head has a large eye and front fang. Both of these traits suggest that the head is a solar god or impersonator. About 30 cm above this painting is a similar face in fresh-looking charcoal (not pictured). Like parts of Drawing 53, this seems to be a later imitation of a painting.

Drawing 63 (fig. 8-63)

Measurements 9 cm h. × 10 cm w.

Distance from Ground Level 1.13 m

Number of Figures 1

Description A figure is seated tailor-fashion in front of a heavy-rimmed dish. His chest is shown frontally and his legs, in profile, recalling Drawing 61. The artist is not successful in uniting the torso and legs, so the figure looks awkward. The right hand is smeared, but he clearly gestures forward with his left. His high status is suggested by his relatively fancy costuming and the use of the cushion. Scrolls coming out of the dish suggest that some offering is being burned, most likely copal incense.

Conservation The central portion of the painting is smeared. This is the only painting at the back of the Western Passage to have been vandalized at any time.

Drawing 64 (fig. 8-64)

Measurements 10 cm h. × 20 cm w.

Distance from Ground Level 1.68 cm

Number of Hieroglyphs 3

Description These glyphs are located directly above Drawing 65 and could be part of that text; however, they are painted on a larger scale, are more poorly preserved, and are not integrated into the text; therefore, they have been catalogued separately.

FIG. 8-63. Drawing 63. Photograph by Chip and Jennifer Clark.

FIG. 8-64. Drawing 64. Photograph by Chip and Jennifer Clark.

a

FIG. 8-65. Drawing 65: *a,* full; *b,* detail; *c,* detail; *d,* detail; *e,* detail. Photographs by Chip and Jennifer Clark.

Drawing 65 (fig. 8-65a–e)
Measurements 1.70 m h. × 1.0 m w.
Distance from Ground Level 1.16 m
Number of Hieroglyphs 64
Description This text has the largest number of hieroglyphs of any in the cave. The paint is thin, making the painting difficult to photograph. The text sprawls across the cave wall, making the reading order ambiguous.

b

c

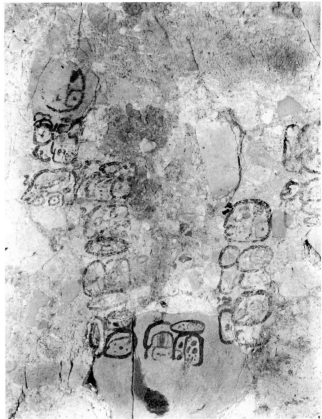

d

e

Note: Drawings 66–83 form a single group along one side of the North Passage just after it bifurcates with the Western Passage.

Drawing 66 (fig. 8-66a–c)
Measurements 14.5 cm h. × 1.22 m w.
Distance from Ground Level 1.27 m
Number of Hieroglyphs 16
Description The drawing consists of two rows of hieroglyphs with fourteen columns.
Conservation Examination of this painting in 1988 indicated that it had suffered considerable paint loss since it was first photographed in 1980. Many of the finer details and crosshatching are no longer visible. Unfortunately, this painting was completely smeared (except the glyph farthest to the right) in 1989.

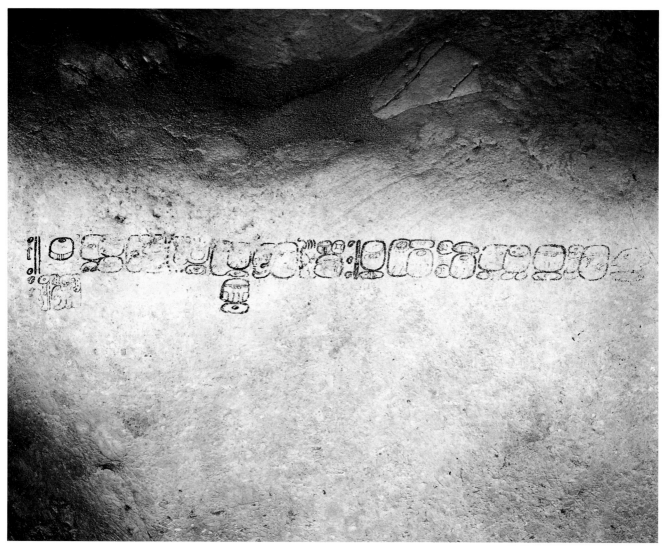

a

Drawing 67 (fig. 8-67)
Measurements 24 cm h. × 31 cm w.
Distance from Ground Level 1.35 m
Number of Figures 2
Description Though the two figures do not appear to be interacting, they are connected by a groundline and so seem to belong to one scene. This is also suggested by their similar scale. Though one figure is seated and one is standing, their heads are at the same level because the seated figure is elevated. The seated figure wears a cloth headdress, circular earflare, and narrow loincloth. The standing figure wears a curious forward-projecting headdress. He has an unflattering physiognomy with a protruding lower lip and hooked nose. His hands are drawn to his abdomen, where we see an abrupt swelling. This at first looks as though he is playing a drum. However, on closer inspection, the swelling appears to be his stomach. Two wavy lines dangling between his legs may be part of a loincloth flap. He seems to be wearing a circular neck pendant filled with black pigment. One of his hands is open and the other, clenched in a fist. This is, indeed, an odd figure, and it is not clear what he represents. He is the only frontal figure among the Naj Tunich paintings.
Conservation The right-hand figure was partially smeared in 1989.

Drawing 68 (fig. 8-68)
Measurements 21 cm h. × 56 cm w.
Distance from Ground Level 1.55 m
Number of Hieroglyphs 5
Number of Figures 2
Description This painting, among the most beautiful at Naj Tunich, features a rotund, seated lord on the right and a corpulent dwarf at the left, gesturing to the lord. The dwarf can be identified by such features as a swollen forehead, pug nose, fat upper lip, and bulging stomach. His pose suggests movement, as though he is reaching toward the lord. He wears a high-topped cloth hat tied by a band, circular earflares, and a string necklace, whose looped tie ends appear

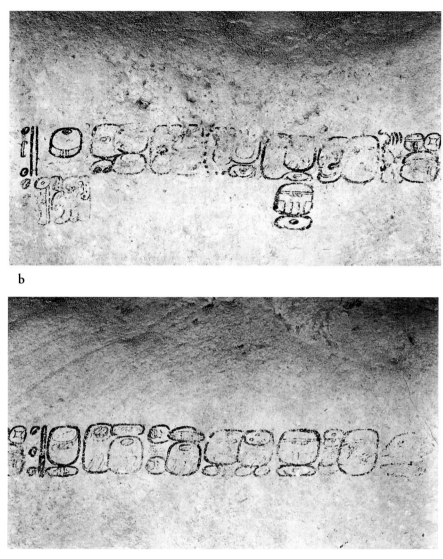

b

c

The lord, seated tailor-fashion, is typical of Maya nobility. He sits taller than his companion and more erect. He has an ample physique that speaks of strength and a lavish diet, and, therefore, power and success. An extension on his headdress recalls a rabbit or deer ear, though this is not certain. In addition, the lord wears a dangling, discoidal ear ornament and a crescentic necklace pendant, perhaps a shell, which is attached to a string looped at the nape of the neck. He wears a billowing loincloth/hipcloth assemblage that is drawn "x-ray" fashion, perhaps indicating a diaphanous material. The parallel curving lines on his cheek normally suggest old age, though this would be incongruent with his idealized presentation. Moreover, the figure's corpulent anatomy is not one typical of an elderly figure. Thus, the lines may represent some type of face paint. The figure holds a bowl in his right hand. It has no rim and is a near-perfect hemisphere. The

FIG. 8-66. Drawing 66: *a,* full; *b,* left; *c,* right. Photographs by Chip and Jennifer Clark.

FIG. 8-67. Drawing 67. Photograph by Chip and Jennifer Clark.

FIG. 8-68. Drawing 68. Photograph by Chip and Jennifer Clark.

FIG. 8-69. Drawing 69. Photograph by Chip and Jennifer Clark.

FIG. 8-70. Drawing 70. Photograph by Chip and Jennifer Clark.

shape is identical to the gourd cup, or *luch*, used in modern Yucatecan ceremonies (Love and Peraza 1984: see photographs). The cup is probably being passed between the two figures.

The last glyph at A4 resembles the Emblem Glyph of Ixtutz. It also occurs in Drawing 69 (A4), which lies adjacent to Drawing 68.

Conservation The right-hand figure was badly smeared in 1989, as were small areas of the dwarf and the text.

Drawing 69 (fig. 8-69)
Measurements 19 cm h. × 6 cm w.
Distance from Ground Level 1.69 m
Number of Hieroglyphs 4
Description The drawing consists of a column of four glyphs.
Conservation Brady and Brady (1989) report that a vandal ran three fingers through this painting in 1989.

Drawing 70 (fig. 8-70)
Measurements 24 cm h. × 12 cm w.
Distance from Ground Level 1.74 m

Number of Hieroglyphs 10
Description The drawing consists of two columns of hieroglyphs.
Conservation The hieroglyphs were partially smeared in 1989.

Drawing 71 (fig. 8-71)
Measurements 32 cm h. × 14 cm w.
Distance from Ground Level 1.60 m
Description Portrayed here is a masked dancer with a deer headdress and bat face mask. The collar around his neck is seen on other ritual performers in Maya art. Garbed in an elaborate loincloth/hipcloth assemblage, the figure raises one leg in a dancing pose and extends both hands forward. In his right hand he holds a rattle, possibly made from a gourd. An irregular line appears in front of the deer headdress but cannot be identified because of poor preservation in this area. Pohl and Pohl (1983) associate this figure, as well as the corpulent lord in Drawing 68, with the deer, which they believe had special significance in the Maya cave ceremony.

Images from the Underworld

FIG. 8-71. Drawing 71. Photograph by Chip and Jennifer Clark.

Drawing 72 (fig. 8-72)
Measurements
    4 cm h. × 3 cm w. (profile)
    14 cm h. × 22 cm w. (figure)
Distance from Ground Level 1.34 m
Number of Figures 1
Number of Profiles 1
Description A seated figure on a groundline wears a high cloth headdress tied by a knotted band, a round ear-flare, and a necklace consisting of a ball suspended on a string, looped and tied at the nape of the neck. The same type of necklace and pendant is also worn by figures in Drawings 27 and 76. A bead-like adornment is seen on the bridge of the nose, and loops, possibly face paint, decorate his forehead. He wears both a loincloth and hipcloth. The figure also sports a thin moustache. The right hand is awkwardly superimposed over the foot.

    To the left is a profile face of similar proportions and style, though the head rests at a slightly lower level than the full figure. This head may not bear any relationship to the figure, but both are rendered in a nearly ink-black paint on an especially light-colored section of limestone. The figure is one of the most vividly painted at Naj Tunich.
Conservation The seated figure was badly smeared in 1989.

Drawing 73 (fig. 8-73)
Measurements 9 cm h. × 3 cm w.
Distance from Ground Level 1.26 m
Number of Profiles 1
Description This profile face lacks eyes. In terms of style, it compares with the right-hand figure in Drawing 67.

FIG. 8-72. Drawing 72. Photograph by Chip and Jennifer Clark.

FIG. 8-73. Drawing 73. Photograph by Chip and Jennifer Clark.

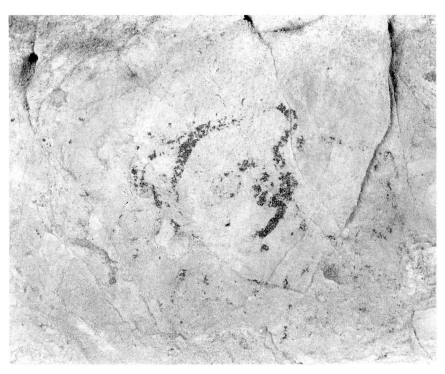

FIG. 8-75. Drawing 75. Photograph by Chip and Jennifer Clark.

FIG. 8-74. Drawing 74. Photograph by Chip and Jennifer Clark.

Drawing 74 (fig. 8-74)
Measurements 14 cm h. × 7 cm w.
Distance from Ground Level 1.20 m
Number of Figures 1
Description This kneeling figure, with arms folded across the chest, wears a circular earflare and cloth headdress. No loincloth is shown; perhaps the figure is nude. The lower half of the face is marked with patches of paint. Artistry is

noticeably lacking in this painting, one of the few poorly painted figures in the Classic style from Naj Tunich.

Drawing 75 (fig. 8-75)
Measurements 7 cm h. × 10 cm w.
Distance from Ground Level 1.35 m
Description The drawing consists of the fragmentary remains of an unidentifiable painting.

Drawing 76 (fig. 8-76)
Measurements 23 cm h. × 7 cm w.
Distance from Ground Level 1.53 m
Number of Figures 1
Description This standing figure is beautifully crafted. The costume reflects the general type prevalent in this group of cave paintings: loincloth, circular earflare, cloth cap tied by a knotted band, and ball pendant strung around the neck. The tie loops of the necklace are clearly visible behind the neck. The figure's now-missing right hand was located near his groin. He may have been engaged in genital bloodletting,

suggested both by the hand position and the hint of emotion in his face, his upcast eyes, and slack jaw.

Note: Drawings 77–81 occupy the curved wall of an alcove.

Drawing 77 (fig. 8-77)
Measurements 3 cm h. × 1 cm w.
Distance from Ground Level 1.02 m
Number of Profiles 1
Description This profile face shows only the nose and upper lip.

Drawing 78 (fig. 8-78)
Measurements 5 cm h. × 10 cm w.
Distance from Ground Level 1.27 m
Description This indistinct form in pale paint shows a lozenge-shaped object with pendant "tail."

Drawing 79 (fig. 8-79)
Measurements 4 cm h. × 3 cm w.
Distance from Ground Level 1.57 m
Description The drawing consists of a profile face lacking eyes.

Images from the Underworld

FIG. 8-76. Drawing 76. Photograph by Chip and Jennifer Clark.

Drawing 80 (fig. 8-80)
Measurements 11 cm h. × 10 cm w.
Distance from Ground Level 1.30 m
Description There are no visible brush strokes in this painting. This nebulous form may have been created by carbonizing the wall with smoke.

Drawing 81 (fig. 8-81a–b)
Measurements
    5 cm h. × 5 cm w. (Profile 1)
    4 cm h. × 5 cm w. (Profile 2)
    6 cm h. × 5 cm w. (Profile 3)
Distance from Ground Level 1.46 m
Description These three profiles, which span a distance of 42 cm, seem related in terms of scale, alignment, and style. The fact that there are three may also be significant, as there are several groupings of three figures among the cave paintings (Drawings 27, 32, and 40). Profile 1, at the right, is the most complete and elaborate. The two left-hand faces are less complete and may be imitations of Profile 1, a practice noted in Drawing 53.

FIG. 8-77. Drawing 77. Photograph by Chip and Jennifer Clark.

FIG. 8-78. Drawing 78. Photograph by Chip and Jennifer Clark.

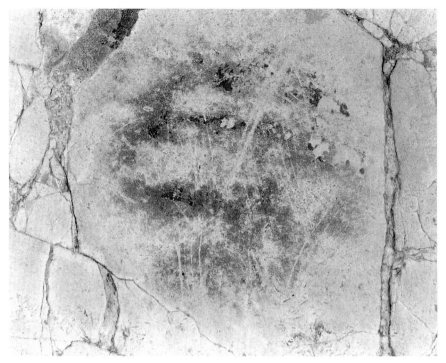

FIG. 8-80. Drawing 80. Photograph by
Chip and Jennifer Clark.

FIG. 8-79. Drawing 79. Photograph by
Chip and Jennifer Clark.

a

b

FIG. 8-81. Drawing 81: *a*, full; *b*, detail
of right-hand head. Photographs by Chip
and Jennifer Clark.

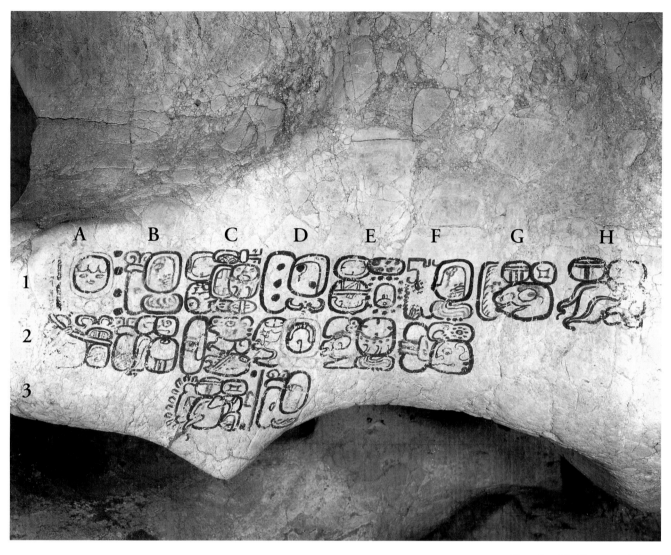

FIG. 8-82. Drawing 82. Photograph by Chip and Jennifer Clark.

Drawing 82 (fig. 8-82)
Measurements 35 cm h. × 1.11 m w.
Distance from Ground Level 1.54 m
Number of Hieroglyphs 16
Description This splendid text is painted on one face of an overhang, under which lie masses of charcoal. The artist adapted the glyph blocks to complement the unusual wall contour by dropping two of the glyphs to fit in a dip. The two rows of glyphs would have been identical in number had this not been done. The artist used two densities of paint to create contrasting tonality. This, in addition to the varying line width, superb calligraphy, and the large size of each glyph (approximately 11 cm), makes Drawing 82 one of the most aesthetically pleasing paintings at Naj Tunich.

Conservation Smudging in the form of a fingerprint can be seen on the cartouche of the glyph at A1 and was noted in 1981. This painting was smeared beyond recognition in 1989 (see fig. 5.20).

Drawing 83 (fig. 8-83)

Measurements 21 cm h. × 10 cm w.

Distance from Ground Level 1.35 m

Number of Figures 1

Description Drawing 83 is painted on a wall that forms one end of the great overhang where we see Drawing 82. The beautifully shaped wall stands out in brilliant white against the blackness of the cave passage. Drawing 83 cannot be viewed in conjunction with any other cave paintings due to its location.

The drawing is another representation of a dwarf. The face of the dwarf is similar to the one in Drawing 68: bulging forehead, pug nose, lantern jaw, and here a protruding lower lip. Some of these traits were noted in Drawing 67. This dwarf wears a strip of cloth around the head, tied at the back. A fringe on the crown and twisted topknot complete the headdress. A strip of cloth dangles from the dwarf's ear. A curving line sweeps across the forehead; this may be face paint. The figure, sporting a moustache and beard, also wears a hipcloth and waist belt.

The dwarf in Drawing 83 conveys a sense of high status with his moustache, beard, and fairly elaborate costume. He might represent a powerful deity petitioned in caves, such as the Quichean dwarf god Saki C'oxol.

Drawing 84 (fig. 8-84)

Measurements 14 cm h. × 31 cm w.
        9 cm h. (profile)

Distance from Ground Level 1.47 m

Number of Hieroglyphs 10; 6 more possible

Number of Profiles 1

Description A lively profile face accompanies a hieroglyphic text of three, or possibly four, columns of glyphs. This painting lies at one side of a magnificent natural arch spanning the North Passage.

Conservation The nose of the profile face was badly smeared between 1982 and 1986.

FIG. 8-83. Drawing 83. Photograph by Chip and Jennifer Clark.

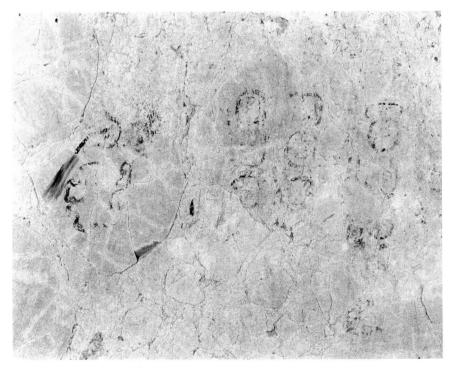

FIG. 8-84. Drawing 84. Photograph by Chip and Jennifer Clark.

Images from the Underworld

FIG. 8-85. Drawing 85. Photograph by Chip and Jennifer Clark.

Drawing 85 (fig. 8-85)
Measurements 7 cm h. × 9 cm w.
Distance from Ground Level 1.89 m
Number of Hieroglyphs 1
Description Here we see a *tun* glyph, T548, surmounted by a faint curving line that may have been part of the *k'atun* superfix, T28. Drawing 85 is located on a wall at the top of a mud-covered hill; 12 m beyond are Drawings 86 and 87.

Drawing 86 (fig. 8-86)
Measurements 40 cm h. × 55 cm w.
Distance from Ground Level 1.76 m
Description Multiple handprints, about six in all, are seen at eye level. Unlike the nearby figurative painting, they are made with ocher-colored mud from the cave floor.

Drawing 87 (fig. 8-87)
Measurements 24 cm h. × 23 cm w.
Distance from Ground Level 1.47 m
Number of Figures 2
Description The two figures illustrated here have hallmark features of the so-called Headband Twins, now known to be the Hero Twins of the Popol Vuh, Hunahpu and Xbalanque (Coe 1973: 13–14; 1978:59–60; 1989). Their hair is tied forward in a ponytail, and they wear a forehead scarf marking their lordly status. The figure on the left, marked by spots on his face, shoulder,

FIG. 8-86. Drawing 86. Photograph by Chip and Jennifer Clark.

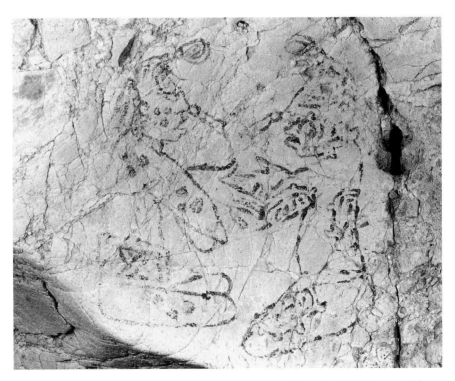

FIG. 8-87. Drawing 87. Photograph by Chip and Jennifer Clark.

arms, and thigh, is Hunahpu. Xbalanque has patches of jaguar pelt on his
face, arm, back, and thigh. Now that
their name glyphs have been identified
in the inscriptions, their identity with
the Popol Vuh twins seems certain (Schele
1986; Schele and Miller 1986:51). The
pair appear together on painted vases
(Robicsek and Hales 1981:Vessels 186,
117, 88) or as individual protagonists
(ibid.:Vessel 109; Coe 1978:no. 8).

Drawing 87 is among the few depictions of deities found in the cave. The
location of this painting, at the deepest
point in the Main Passage of any painting, seems noteworthy in light of the
underworld/Xibalba connection. The
closed eyes of Xbalanque, presumably a
reference to his moribund state, has significance not presently understood.

Note: Drawings 88 and 89 are located
in the K'u Multun maze passage.

Drawing 88 (fig. 8-88a–f)
Measurements 57 cm h. × 54 cm w.
Distance from Ground Level 2.25 m
Number of Hieroglyphs 32
Description This painting was discovered in July of 1988 by George Veni,
who found a connection to an upper-
level maze passage (K'u Multun) a few
meters beyond Drawing 87. The maze
swings around farther south over the
North Passage. Here were found the remains of several smashed plates and a
stone altar with Drawing 88 painted
above.
Conservation The wall in this area is
encrusted with thick sheets of gypsum.
The painting occurs in an area where
the limestone is shedding the gypsum
overlay. Some of the glyphs were painted
over a thin layer of gypsum.

FIG. 8-88. Drawing 88: *a,* full; *b,* detail;
c, detail; *d,* detail; *e,* detail; *f,* detail. Photographs by Chip and Jennifer Clark.

a

b

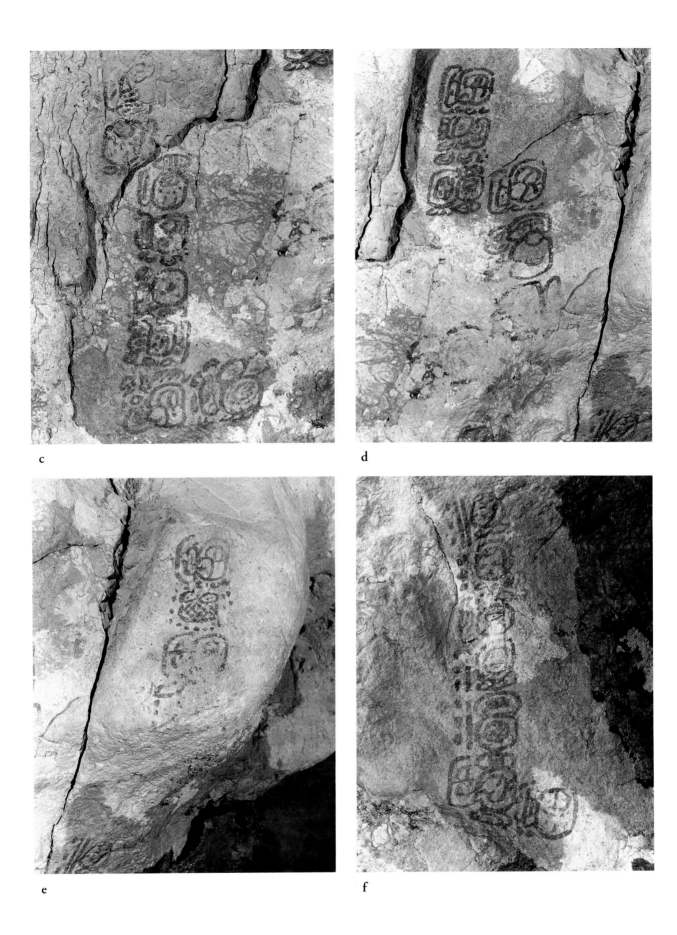

c

d

e

f

Drawing 89 (fig. 8-89)
Measurements 10.9 cm h. × 6 cm w.
Distance from Ground Level 81 cm
Number of Profiles 1
Description Drawing 89 combines both charcoal drawing and scratched lines on a low, short stalactite. Four loops and a wavy line are drawn in charcoal. Scratched lines, partly overlapping the charcoal marks, seem to form a simple face. The drawing is found in the K'u Multun maze.

Note: Drawings 90–93 are located in Naj Tunel, a passage at the rear of K'u Multun that can be reached only by a rope descent down the Mitlan Ch'en pit.

Drawing 90 (fig. 8-90)
Measurements 8.5 cm h. × 5 cm w.
Distance from Ground Level 1.53 m
Number of Hieroglyphs 2
Description One of the most inaccessible texts produced by the Classic Maya, Drawing 90 consists of a vertical column of two glyphs painted at the top of a stalagmite 2.40 m high. The two glyphs may have been drawn with a carbonized stick. To reach this formation is a difficult undertaking, requiring a trip through K'u Multun and down six meters of the Mitlan Ch'en pit, a descent which cannot be free-climbed; the Maya must have descended on a rope. The dangerous nature of this descent is compounded by the fact that the drop continues for over 70 m, so an accident could easily have been fatal. From where the pit communicates with Naj Tunel, one traverses south over a mud floor and encounters the lone text on the formation. No artifacts were found in association with the drawing. Beyond the stalagmite, the mud floor rises to a plateau where the geology changes dramatically. Here one encounters a calcified chamber with stalagmites and flowstone that houses a small altarlike construction and a single whole vessel.

Drawing 91 (fig. 8-91)
Measurements 13 cm h. × 13 cm w.
Distance from Ground Level 1.28 m
Number of Profiles 1
Description A side passage leads off the calcified chamber, described in the comments on Drawing 90, to a smaller, though equally beautiful, chamber. Along one wall is a rudimentary face drawn with charcoal on a flowstone curtain. It appears that the edge of the curtain forms the profile of the face, and black marks represent an eye, hair, and possibly a beard. Since all of the archaeological materials found in this inaccessible section of Naj Tunich are Late Classic in date, it is probable that this crude drawing is from this period as well, demonstrating that Classic and schematic-style paintings can be contemporaneous.

Drawing 92 (fig. 8-92)
Measurements 7 cm h. × 7 cm w.
Distance from Ground Level 1.10 m
Description Drawing 91 is so similar to Drawing 92 that they appear to have been made at the same time, perhaps by the same individual. Located on a similar kind of curtain flowstone and drawn again in charcoal, Drawing 92 represents an extremely simple face, consisting of three dots for the eyes and nose and a wide smudge for the mouth. The facial features are positioned such that the contours of the flowstone form the edge of the face.

Drawing 93 (fig. 8-93)
Measurements 33 cm h. × 31 cm w.
Distance from Ground Level 1.57 m
Description Two positive handprints are unusual in that they include part of the forearm. Due to the recent discovery of this painting (1988), it is not sequential with the other paintings in this section.

FIG. 8-89. Drawing 89. Photograph by Andrea Stone.

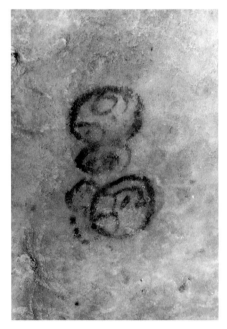

FIG. 8-90. Drawing 90. Photograph by Andrea Stone.

Images from the Underworld

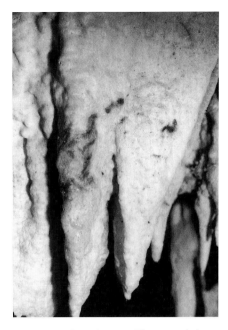

FIG. 8-91. Drawing 91. Photograph by Andrea Stone.

FIG. 8-93. Drawing 93. Photograph by Chip and Jennifer Clark.

FIG. 8-92. Drawing 92. Photograph by Andrea Stone.

Drawing 94 (fig. 8-94)
Measurements 23 cm h. × 9 cm w.
Distance from Ground Level 1.65 m
Number of Hieroglyphs 3
Description This drawing was pointed out by guard Alfonso Tito Sandoval Segura in June of 1989. It is the only example of Naj Tunich wall art found in the Balcony area. The glyphs appear on a large column of curtain flowstone. The thickness of line suggests that the glyphs may have been drawn with a stick of charcoal.
Conservation The drawing is badly weathered, and only the first glyph of this text retains legibility.

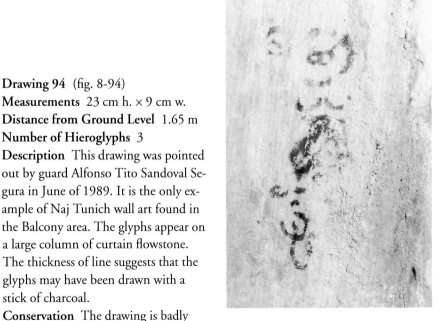

FIG. 8-94. Drawing 94. Photograph by Andrea Stone.

9

Maya Cave Painting: Summary of a Tradition

Twenty-five painted caves have been discussed in the preceding pages. Several others are known to me, but I am reluctant to add them to the official roster until more detailed investigations have been carried out.[1] The twenty-five caves can be broken down as follows: five contain only handprints, ten are what I would consider to be minor sites, and nine are major cave painting sites. The nine important caves are distributed rather unevenly across the Maya Lowlands: five are located in the state of Yucatan, and just one major cave is currently known in Campeche, Chiapas, Belize, and Peten. Yucatan's greater share of painted caves is not surprising in light of the number of dry caves found there, which have relatively easy access to populations with long histories of settlement. Reddell (1977: 219) observes that caves and related karst features occur in all areas of the Yucatan Peninsula except the Eastern Block Fault District.

A Brief History of Maya Cave Painting

Maya cave painting makes an early appearance in the history of Classic Lowland Maya art, although none of the earliest sites with Preclassic architecture—El Mirador, Nakbe, Tikal, and Cerros, for instance—have caves of archaeological significance in the vicinity. The earliest cave paintings, datable by style, appear at the end of the Preclassic at Loltun, Yucatan. This fact is interesting, as during the same period the northern Maya Lowlands lack iconographically elaborated stone monuments and portable objects. The earliest Long Count date known from Yucatan is found on Lintel 1, Structure 3C6, from Oxkintok at 9.2.0.0.0, or A.D. 475 (Mathews 1985: Table 3); only fragmentary sculpture from this period survives there (Proskouriakoff 1950: 155). Yet two Yucatecan caves, Loltun and Caactun, preserve Cycle 8 cave art. What significance can be attributed to the fact that Proto- and Early Classic iconography occurs in Yucatecan caves, while being absent in monumental art? The poor preservation of monumental sculpture in Yucatan may provide the answer, but it also seems possible that Classic iconography, imported from the south, first appeared in caves in the northern Lowlands.

The early style of the art of Joloniel, Chiapas, is equally intriguing. Joloniel lies about fifty kilometers southwest of Palenque. The date of the early group of Joloniel paintings is not firm but certainly ranges between 8.13.0.0.0 and 9.6.0.0.0 (A.D. 297–554). Neither Palenque, Tonina, nor Tortuguero, the three largest sites closest to Joloniel, have hieroglyphic dates before 9.8.0.0.0 (A.D. 593). Indeed, in all of the western Maya Lowlands, dates contemporary with monument erection cannot be placed before 9.3.0.0.0 (A.D. 495). The Houston Panel from Bonampak at 9.3.0.14.3 (A.D. 495), Piedras Negras Lintel 12 at 9.3.19.12.12 (A.D. 514) and Yaxchilan Stela 27 at 9.4.0.0.0 (A.D. 514) are among the earliest monuments from this area (Schele 1991). If the 8.13.0.0.0 placement of the Joloniel paintings proves to be correct, then the cave paintings predate all of the dated Classic art of Chiapas. This may also reflect the vagaries of preservation, but other explanations might be entertained. Did cave art have an important role in early manifestations of Classic art in this region as well?

Late Classic cave painting (possibly Terminal Classic in the Puuc) is the most prolific and widely distributed in the Maya area. A cluster of important painted caves from this period is found in the Sierrita de Ticul, Yucatan: Loltun, Ch'on, Acum, and Tixkuytun. Together they form a regional style of cave painting that can be called the Sierrita de Ticul style. Cave paintings in this style are often large, painted with a broad, firm outline, little detail, and sometimes color infill. They also share

an inventory of motifs that includes large human heads (Acum, Loltun), large, isolated symbols, such as the "Kan cross" and the "mat" symbol (Acum and Tixkuytun), and geometric glyphlike designs that may be affixed with bar and dot numerals (Acum, Ch'on, and Tixkuytun). Another shared element is the animal head, such as the deer heads at Tixkuytun and Acum. The Sierrita de Ticul style also includes a technique of making negative handprints in which the silhouette of the hand forms distinct patterns (Loltun and Acum). The easternmost extension of this handprint technique is at Caactun in central Yucatan. Positive handprints ringed by a circle are also found at several Sierrita de Ticul caves.

The Sierrita de Ticul style now encompasses the area along the Puuc hills between Oxkutzcab and Tekax. That a regional style of cave art, stylistically independent of surface-site art, should exist at all signals regional interaction in terms of cave use. For the Maya, cave art styles would not be expected to spread over a wide area, as cave art is neither portable nor public. Consequently, individual painted caves in the Maya area tend to be idiosyncratic. Actun Dzib in Belize, to mention just one, has a style of cave painting found nowhere else. The Sierrita de Ticul style currently stands alone as a regional style of Maya cave painting.

Late Classic cave paintings in Chiapas and Peten, more than any other group of Maya cave paintings, are comparable to the painting styles of surface sites. Black-line calligraphic paintings, recalling vase painting or linear styles of mural painting, are found at Naj Tunich, Santo Domingo, and Yaleltsemen. They mirror elite art as well in their interest in hieroglyphic writing and fully mortal human protagonists in quasi-narrative scenes, though Drawing 1 from Actun Ch'on, a Sierrita de Ticul cave, also fits into this genre.

The Late Classic Bladen 2 paintings feature supernaturals depicted in a crude, provincial style.

Late Postclassic Maya cave painting, now known with certainty only from Dzibichen, reflects a codical style, featuring static representations of deity and animal figures. In its codical figural style and subject matter, Late Postclassic cave painting echoes Late Postclassic rock art seen in many parts of Mesoamerica which, even more clearly so, echoes codical painting.

Dzibichen, Miramar, and Loltun have Colonial cave art. It also has correspondences with illustrated manuscripts, seen, for example, in the circular (sometimes rayed) faces that are found in Dzibichen and Miramar and that parallel images in Colonial documents, such as the Books of Chilam Balam. Colonial drawings at Dzibichen employ ornamental motifs, such as the guilloche, loops, S-shaped designs, and arabesques, devices which recall decorative embellishments in Colonial art. The Colonial style of cave painting (usually occurring as drawing) also includes scrolls, crosses, and starlike or asterisk designs. The human figure, on the other hand, is treated in a rigid boxlike fashion. "Circle faces" are another hallmark of Colonial cave art; they usually use a continuous line to form one or both brows and the nose, while eyes are simple dots. Two caves (Dzibichen and Miramar) have depictions of Hapsburg eagles.

Maya caves, primarily in Yucatan, where they are accessible to casual visitors, have served as "galleries" for the twentieth-century "artist." Modern drawings mainly consist of signatures, some accompanied by dates going back to the nineteenth century. Other modern cave artists are more ambitious. The walls of Dzibichen are decorated with two bicycles. At Actun Dzib, Belize, a Latin cross and a European-style heart sit alongside a panel of prehispanic drawings. The late settlement of the Toledo District, wherein lies Actun Dzib, makes it likely that the cross and heart are from the twentieth century. An unusual example of modern Maya cave art is found in a cave in western Yucatan whose name is unknown to me, though I have seen it in photographs. This shallow cave has oversized line drawings of Maya deities and glyphs based on a popular version adapted from the Dresden Codex. Such figures decorate rugs, playing cards, books, T-shirts, and all manner of tourist art in Yucatan. They seem to have been recreated in a cave entrance as a roadside attraction for adventure-seeking tourists.

A Bestiary of Maya Cave Painting

Maya cave painting portrays animals with well-known symbolic connections to caves. One of these is the deer. The deer appears in three Yucatecan caves: Dzibichen, Tixkuytun, and possibly Acum. The Dzibichen drawing is the only one that presents the head and body of the deer, and it recalls a petroglyph of a deer from Actun Xch'omil, a cave located five kilometers northwest of Valladolid (Rätsch 1979). The cave Actun Ceh, near Maxcanu, has two petroglyphs that have the rough outlines of a deer head and body, though they seem to be unfinished and the identification is far from certain (ibid.:18, illus. 5). Actun Ceh derives its name from these petroglyphs (*keh* means "deer" in Yucatec). The deer turns up in ritual costuming at Naj Tunich. Drawing 71 shows a dancing figure wearing a deer headdress and bat face mask.

The veneration of a deer head in hunters' ceremonies was widespread among the Maya in days gone by. In 1893 Sapper (1897:269) observed Tzeltal Indians near Zalpaluta, Chiapas, remove the head of a recently killed deer and burn copal in front of it. Sapper's Kekchi companion remarked that his people performed the same ritual and that its purpose was to appease Tzultaca, the Kekchi cave-dwelling earth lord who controlled game animals and other fruits of the earth. Landa (Tozzer 1941:155) describes a hunter's rite celebrated in the month of Zip in which a deer skull was anointed with blue pigment. These deer ceremonies sometimes were held in caves (see Chapter 1, n. 1). Pohl and Pohl (1983) discuss the idea that deer ceremonies related to hunting constituted an important facet of Maya cave ritual in Classic through postconquest times. Sources suggest that the overt purpose of the ceremony was to ask the appropriate deities for forgiveness in killing deer, thereby ensuring the hunter's future success (see Scholes and Adams 1938: 59, 61).

The paintings of deer in Yucatecan caves may relate to this type of hunting ritual. Deer hunting seems to have been an especially important pursuit in Yucatan; in Colonial times Yucatan was called "the land of turkey and deer" (Tozzer 1941:4). Prehispanic works of art from Yucatan frequently show deer in the context of hunting: for example, the Calcehtok Vase (Pohl 1981: fig. 2) and a sculpture from Tabi in the regional INAH museum in Mérida, which shows a deer and two hunters. Pohl (1983:62) makes the interesting observation that young animals may have been deliberately selected for sacrifice. In light of her remark, it is interesting that the Tixkuytun deer has small antlers (Plate 5). Does this painting portray an immature white-tailed deer (*Odocoileus virginianus*) or is it the more delicate brocket deer (*Mazama americana*)?

Included in the bestiary of Maya cave painting are serpents, which also have symbolic ties with caves. Seven serpents are found at Dzibichen. Two are positioned vertically and have a zigzag body, while five are horizontal with their heads to the left and mouths open, showing sharp fangs. In addition, one painting from Roberto's Cave, Belize, has the fragmentary remains of what appears to be a serpent's body.

On the one hand, serpents are a metonym for sacred space of the forest, for the serpent, jaguar, and caiman were the quintessential zoological representatives of the Mesoamerican wilderness. Serpents also have a close relationship in Maya religion with cave-dwelling rain deities who are "owners" of the earth. The serpent may represent lightning, a

companion to storm gods. This is especially suggested by the vertical, zigzag serpent from Dzibichen (fig. 4-72d). Lightning serpents may "stand up" just as lightning "stands up" when it shoots from the earth to the sky. The identification of lightning with serpents is pervasive in Mesoamerican ethnography and iconography (Coggins 1988; Spero 1987; Taube 1986; 1989a). Sometimes the serpent is an assistant to the rain deity. For example, serpents are the servants of Tzultaca, the Kekchi version of this earth and storm deity. Serpents serve as cords for the hammock of Tzultaca and punish moral transgressions on his behalf (Sapper 1897:282). A parallel of this Maya belief is also found among the Popoluca and Nahua people of Veracruz. Here the serpent forms the hammock of a rain and lightning deity (Spero 1987:53).

In Yucatan as well, the rain and lightning god Chac has a close connection with serpents (Taube 1988b:61–62). This is seen in Postclassic codices where God B, long identified as Chac (Schellhas 1904:18), makes repeated appearances with serpents. Sometimes codical serpents have the head of Chac. Spero (1987:216–219) draws an analogy between Chac-related symbolism and the *chih chan* gods, giant horned serpents that control standing water and rain in Chorti mythology (Wisdom 1940:392–397).

The other archetypal beast of the wilderness, the jaguar, appears in Maya cave painting. Two jaguars in a diving position adorn the walls of Dzibichen, and one painting from Bombil Pec may represent a feline. As a nocturnal hunter, the jaguar belongs in the category of nighttime phenomena that also include caves. This is a pan-Mesoamerican belief. The Aztecs, for example, compared the night sky to a spotted jaguar pelt (Brundage 1979:83). Cave-jaguar symbolism can be observed on many levels in Mesoamerican religion.

The visage of the Jaguar God of the Underworld has been found on ceramic vessels in caves of highland Guatemala and Chiapas (Seler 1901; Navarrete and Martínez 1977). The jaguar's solar aspect is evident in its frequent association with the "*k'in*" glyph. It has been proposed that the jaguar represented the sun in its nocturnal aspect (Thompson 1960:134). The idea of the night sun transiting the underworld is another way that the jaguar is linked with caves. The Dzibichen diving jaguars may depict the nocturnal solar descent through the cave-underworld.

Other animals depicted in Maya cave paintings are birds, turtles, and toads or frogs (often difficult to differentiate). Their aquatic symbolism may link them with each other and with caves. Birds are painted at Acum and Dzibichen. The Acum bird (fig. 4-50) is remarkably similar to birds modeled in stucco on the sides of *chultun*s used for water storage in the Puuc area (Barrera Rubio 1985). They, too, have undulating necks and extended bills; they have been identified as ducks with long, stylized necks. The *chultun*s also have modeled representations of turtles, snakes, toads, frogs, and some human figures (ibid.: Table 1). Painted turtles are found at Acum and Dzibichen. The Acum turtle resembles modeled stucco turtles from a chultun at the site of Kom, southwest of Labna (ibid.: fig. 18). A toad or frog can be found among the paintings of Actun Dzib. Barrera Rubio identifies the stucco figures from the *chultun*s as part of a water cult centered around sites in the Puuc.

The monkey is another animal depicted in Maya cave painting. Bombil Pec has a pair of monkeys, and Miramar, a single monkey. The three monkeys show similar traits, such as a potbelly, a raised, curled tail, and upraised arms. These traits also characterize monkeys painted at the Los Monos rock shelter in Chiapas (fig. 4-11b). A

Images from the Underworld

Protoclassic figure from Loltun was earlier noted to have simian features and a taillike curl in front of his chest (fig. 4-27).

Topographic Context Revisited

It has been observed throughout this book that the meaning of Maya cave painting is intimately connected with the multileveled meanings of caves in Maya culture. Caves provided a kind of reference point in the Maya's socio-spatial universe by dint of their disjunctive relationship with the space of mundane social discourse. Cave space was so highly regarded in the Maya belief system that it was recreated in public architecture; artificial caves were even excavated by manual labor.[2] How was Maya cave painting shaped by this powerful, culturally mediated environment?

First, it seems clear that the Maya deliberately placed paintings in remote parts of caves when the opportunity arose. Faced with the choice to paint in an entrance chamber or a deep tunnel, the Maya would usually choose the latter and would sometimes go to more extreme lengths to paint in private areas. Bombil Pec and Yaleltsemen are two caves that require dropping through narrow chimneys to enter lower-level rooms where paintings are found. Paintings at Actun Ch'on are likewise in an obscure side passage. At nearby Acum, the paintings begin about one hundred meters from the entrance after what may have been a small gate. The most dramatic case of the sequestering of Maya cave art occurs at Naj Tunich: paintings in K'u Multun and Naj Tunel are not just hidden but require extraordinary means to reach them.

The sequestered location of Maya cave painting is a function of the cave's role as a remote, pristine, "*suhuy*" environment. The sanctity of space was proportional to its lack of accessibility; hence sequestered paintings were in places with heightened sacred qualities.

No doubt this figured into the ritual function of cave painting, though only Naj Tunich with its hidden painting and associated altar provides indisputable proof of this.

Furthermore, the kind of remote spaces where Maya cave painting is found tells us something about the nature of group participation in making and viewing these images: it must have entailed small groups of people and in some cases have been an utterly private experience. Certain paintings at Tixkuytun are in passages so cramped that it is difficult for one person to comfortably view them. The main scene of Actun Ch'on lies in a space that could not accommodate more than a handful of people. Drawing 88 from Naj Tunich, a hieroglyphic text, suggests that the altar ceremony in K'u Multun was attended by five individuals plus a scribe. No doubt the privacy of these small groups would have had a liberating effect on certain forms of expression: hence the erotica depicted at Naj Tunich and the crudely drawn "vulvas" found at Dzibichen.

Repetition is another characteristic of Maya cave painting of all ilk—from rudimentary to sophisticated. The human handprint is the most oft-repeated form to appear in Maya caves. The handprint seems to be an affirmation of presence—"Kilroy was here"—recorded by a visitor to an exotic place. But, truthfully, we know little about the function of handprints in Maya caves, some of which are quite elaborate, as we have seen. Certain repetitive cave images are later imitations of forms already present on the wall; they are usually incomplete and inferior to the original. The spontaneity evident in such images reveals the personal nature of the cave experience.

But repetition characterizes even the most sophisticated Maya cave paintings. The hieroglyphic inscriptions of Naj Tunich are couched in a kind of formulaic language that might be understood as a litany; they repeatedly refer to such activities as "to see," "to arrive," and "to return," sometimes invoking the same set of protagonists. Here we are on firmer ground in suggesting that repetitive paintings correlate with conventional forms of human behavior: repetition in Maya cave art is linked with the cave's ritual function and the cyclical nature of ritual.

Certainly, the cave represents a true liminal space, a setting for rites of passage revealed as frozen moments of action in the paintings of Naj Tunich. The cave as a liminal, timeless place is a function of its rupture with normative experience. This also has a bearing on certain characteristics of cave art. It was already mentioned that the figurative art of Naj Tunich is devoid for the most part of the symbolic appurtenances that are essential in defining context in Maya art of surface sites. Symbols establishing cosmic settings or alluding to a primordial era would be redundant in the sacred confines of the cave. Not surprisingly, they are absent in cave art.

The lack of frames around virtually all cave paintings has interesting implications in light of ideas put forth by Conkey (1982) regarding image boundaries. She suggests that constructed boundaries reflect degrees of social boundedness. Sundstrom (1990:289) borrows this idea to interpret the loosely structured design fields in the Pecked Abstract style of southern Black Hills rock art in terms of a breakdown of social constraints, presumably encouraged by the ingestion of psychotropic substances. Similarly, the lack of frames in Maya cave art and the casual distribution of images reflect the lack of order and structure inherent in cave space. Disorder is related to the non-normative social context of the cave, to the state of timeless liminality it created for pilgrims. At Naj Tunich, the simple costume worn by the painted figures, downplaying status differences, is testimony to the liminal character of cave space.

Cave Painting and the Built Environment

Ceremonial architecture in the Maya Lowlands was a public theater for spectacular performances by the nobility and a supporting cast of dancers, musicians, and other functionaries. Architecture at all Maya sites served as a backdrop for state rituals, be it heir apparency, the accession of a monarch, a period-ending celebration, or the sacrifice of war captives. These public performances legitimated ruling dynasts by enhancing their prestige and justifying their divine status.

The legitimacy that the elite derived from these rituals hinged on the sanctification of their setting; so it was imperative that the built environment, the theater for public performance, assume the status of sacred space (Stone 1992). The model for the sanctification of public architecture was sacred geography, whose holiness was axiomatic within the Maya's belief system. To the built environment accrued the divine qualities of the forest by the manipulation of sacred symbols: pyramid-temples served as surrogate mountains, and small, enclosed superstructures became surrogate cave shrines. The myriad Cauac Monsters, serpents, jaguars, and other beasts informing Maya iconography completed the fictive forest. Maya kings depicted themselves on stelae as quasi-supernatural beings able to commune with the powerful spirits who resided in the natural wilderness, transformed in the built environment into an architectural wilderness.

Sacred geography was not only replicated in the site center to sanctify elite ritual but also "captured" by the building of architecture around topographic shrines. Perhaps the most remarkable example of this is found not in the Maya area but in central Mexico at Teotihuacan, where a sacred lava tube cave, serving as a pilgrimage shrine for generations, was covered by the largest edifice in Mesoamerica, the Pyramid of the Sun (Heyden 1975). While itself a topographic symbol constituting sacred space in the built environment, the Pyramid of the Sun enclosed a real topographic shrine. Hence, Teotihuacan elites had captured in the urban center two forms of sacred geography: the mountain and the cave. Evidence suggests that Maya elites also "captured" sacred geography by building temples over caves (Brady 1991c).

There was an ongoing dialogue between the wilderness and the built environment among the ancient Maya. Following long-established customs, the peasantry worshiped at real topographic shrines, to seek assistance for pressing needs or to observe rites timed by the calendar.[3] Such folk religious practices infused the topographic symbols of the built environment, the architectural mountains and caves, with deeply personal meaning for the general populace. No doubt this made the religious symbols constructed in elite art that much more effective as propaganda. Put another way, popular ritual practices of the ruled resonated with those of the ruler: the peasantry performed small-scale rituals at real topographic shrines, such as caves, while rulers performed corporate rites at architectural ones. Royalty strengthened the resonance between folk and elite ritual by establishing direct ties with the sacred landscape, by making periodic pilgrimages to important topographic shrines. We know, for instance, that Motecuhzoma II made an annual forty-seven-mile journey to Mount Tlaloc to honor the rain god (Wicke and Horcasitas 1957). While an act of sincere piety, such pilgrimages also had a profoundly political dimension.

Maya cave painting provides evidence of just this kind of elite interaction with topographic shrines. The paintings of Joloniel suggest that a ruler performed a k'atun-ending ritual in a cave, and the inscriptions also mention his accession. K'atun-ending symbolism is likewise the subject of some drawings from Dzibichen, though it is less certain whether the ceremonies were actually performed here. Bassie-Sweet (1991) has argued that caves were used extensively by the Maya elite as places for accession and other royal ceremonies.

Cave paintings from Naj Tunich provide the most detailed picture of elite interaction with a topographic shrine. Naj Tunich may have been something like the "Mount Tlaloc" for certain Maya polities in southeastern Peten. Evidence suggests periodic visits by nobility from Sacul, Ixkun, and Ixtutz, over fifteen kilometers away, as well as from more distant places, such as Caracol. The mechanics of how these polities cooperated in using the cave as a shared pilgrimage center is not yet clear, but this cooperation may have strengthened regional political integration.

Naj Tunich is typical of Classic cave painting and Maya art in general in its essential interest in ritual activity. At Naj Tunich the protagonists of these rites may be the elites of neighboring polities recording their acts of piety for posterity, as they were wont to memorialize themselves in art of the built environment. However, unlike the typical relief sculpture, the cave paintings show little concern with personal glorification. The simple costume—the modest loincloth and cloth headwrap—has already been discussed in terms of its status-leveling function, and there is an absence of nominal tagging texts with most of the figures. Thus, the figures project a sense of humility and anonymity, even though historical persons may be mentioned in nearby texts. Moreover, the texts themselves describe the relationship among the various protagonists as *itah* "companion." The persons sojourning to the cave in groups—which range from two to five, according to the glyphic evidence—held a nonhierarchical "companion" status, perhaps as co-participants in ritual.

It was earlier noted that at Naj Tunich paintings, especially hieroglyphic texts, are often found in key transitional spaces in the cave or on unusual geological formations. As the hieroglyphic texts are the most historically situated paintings, mentioning dates, names, and Emblem Glyphs, we might interpret them as an attempt to register a historical presence at significant geological junctures. Yet in the cave the text's historicity confronts a liminal, timeless, sacred environment. The aberrant Calendar Round dates, so common in the cave's inscriptions, may reflect this meeting of the historical and timeless sacrality. The figurative paintings are more direct expressions of the timeless liminality associated with cave ritual. These paintings usually lack conjoined texts that would directly embed them in some kind of historical matrix. The activities and simple dress of these figures and, perhaps most important, the fact that they usually act in isolation (whereas texts usually mention multiple protagonists) further link the figures with the experiential aspects of cave ritual.

In conclusion, Maya cave painting is a heterogeneous collection of images generated by individuals with vastly different levels of skill, ranging from the ordinary peasant to the professional artist. However, these idiosyncratic qualities, which hint of the unique and personal, are part of its remarkably fresh character. The refined vision of the Naj Tunich paintings puts them in a class apart. Their precisely articulated visual language conveys more to us about the motivation and meaning of Maya cave painting than any other part of the corpus.

Cave painting has much to tell us about the relationship between art and environment among the Maya. The cave influenced the form and content of cave art, at times becoming part of the image, but always acting as a uniquely private setting charged with meaning. Cave painting also sheds light on prehispanic forms of ritual behavior about which little would be known if we depended solely on the archaeological record. These paintings also give us an expanded view of the Maya artist not seen in the glorious temples and sculptures or even the enigmatic scenes on painted vases. Maya cave painting resides in a kind of space considered so powerful that it was emulated in the form of architecture and endlessly repeated in images geared to sustain the nobility. This art speaks to us through the centuries, perhaps as no other, of a pre-Columbian view of the natural environment that also defines the nature of space, religion, and power.

The Geologic Context of Maya Cave Paintings

by George Veni

Since the explorations of Stephens (1841), caves have been known by archaeologists as integral features of Maya religion and culture. There are two primary reasons for the importance of caves to the Maya. First, 69 percent of the Maya region is a karst terrain in which caves abound (fig. A-1). Second, karst terrains generally have little surface water, and survival in such areas requires access to groundwater, which is what caves often provide. As sole sources of life-giving water, caves were attributed both great practical and religious importance by the Maya (Veni 1990a).

To fully grasp the utility of caves as Maya water sources and ceremonial centers, it is important to understand the processes which created those caves and which subsequently preserve and destroy the archaeological materials within them. The following discussion reviews the processes of karst and cave development, examines the origin of certain caves containing Maya paint-

ings, and considers the geologic factors affecting the paintings' preservation and management. Special attention is given to Naj Tunich, the most important Maya cave painting site.

Karst Geology

Karst is the term for a landscape developed by solution of the bedrock and the loss of water to the subsurface, typically via features such as caves and sinkholes. Karst occurs in areas containing soluble rock, such as limestone, dolomite, gypsum, or halite. While all rock is prone to some degree of dissolution, the soluble rocks are those which undergo greater chemical than mechanical erosion.

Worldwide, and especially in the Maya region of Mesoamerica, limestone is the primary karstified rock and is the only such rock examined in this discussion. Limestone is composed chiefly of calcium carbonate, often derived from the deposition of calcium carbonate–shelled sea creatures that have died and accumulated on the sea floor. Compaction and cementation of these shells and other sediments results in their fusion into a solid limestone rock.

Uplift of the limestone above sea level exposes it to erosion by chemical and physical or mechanical processes. Chemical erosion is the most important weathering process in limestone. It begins with rainfall picking up carbon dioxide in the atmosphere, and especially as it soaks into the soil, to form a mild carbonic acid:

$$\underset{\text{(water)}}{H_2O} + \underset{\text{(carbon dioxide)}}{CO_2} \rightarrow$$
$$\underset{\text{(carbonic acid)}}{H_2CO_3} \qquad \text{(eq. 1)}$$

While water alone has little ability to dissolve limestone, when it is thus charged with carbon dioxide, it has the capacity to break up the calcium carbonate (calcite) molecule:

$$\underset{\text{(calcite)}}{CaCO_3} + \underset{\text{(carbonic acid)}}{H_2CO_3} \rightarrow$$
$$\underset{\text{(calcium ion)}}{Ca^{2+}} + \underset{\text{(bicarbonate ion)}}{2HCO_3^-} \qquad \text{(eq. 2)}$$

Limestone is generally a nonporous rock and water cannot easily seep into it. However, stresses during the deposition and uplift of the rock result in fractures into which water can flow. As water enters these fractures, the fractures slowly enlarge due to its corrosive action. When fully saturated with respect to calcite, the water will stop enlarging the fracture until fresh, undersaturated water flows in. The saturation threshold, however, can be increased if the fracture has enlarged to a width of five to ten millimeters, where turbulent flow can occur. At such a time, the rate of the fracture's enlargement increases exponentially due to the water's greater chemical and mechanical erosive capability. The fracture's increased size results in a greater hydraulic transmissivity, which captures flow from other fractures to thus enlarge itself even more. When the solutionally enlarged

fracture becomes large enough for a person to enter, it is called a cave.

Many caves form below the water table in the phreatic zone, where all fractures, pores, caves, and other voids are completely filled with water. When the water table descends below the cave, the cave is then in the air-filled vadose zone. At such times speleothems, such as stalactites and stalagmites, may be deposited, and collapse may occur where the ceiling had been supported by the water's buoyancy. The collapse will raise the ceiling to a higher, arched, and more stable configuration. Occasionally the collapse will continue up to the surface to form a large pit, sometimes referred to as a collapse sinkhole. In the Yucatan, if water is present at the base of these pits or sinkholes, they are called *cenotes*. Solution sinkholes occur when water, flowing down to a cave entrance or enlarged surface fracture, dissolves the bedrock into a funnel around that opening. Sometimes the opening may not be apparent due to sediment or other washed-in debris.

The extent, shapes, and origins of caves can vary depending upon factors such as the thickness and fracturing of the limestone, the presence of insoluble beds, climate, relief, and fluctuations of and location relative to the water table. Yet, in spite of these variables, the fundamental principles of karst water chemistry and flow can be applied to determine the origin of particular caves and their karst features.

Maya Caves and Cave Paintings

The karst of Maya Mesoamerica can be divided into three main groups: the mountainous highlands of Chiapas and western Guatemala; the lowlands of the Yucatan Peninsula; and the limestone surrounding the Maya Mountains in Belize and eastern Guatemala (fig. A-1). Major caves occur in each of these areas, and the types of caves vary significantly,

Images from the Underworld

but each area contains caves with Maya paintings.

Highland Caves

In highland Chiapas, two caves are known to contain Maya paintings: Joloniel and Yaleltsemen. Unfortunately, no maps or detailed descriptions exist on which to base a substantive hypothesis of the caves' origins. Thompson (1975: xxxvi–xxxvii) discusses both caves and provides only a brief description of Yaleltsemen. The uniform shape of Yaleltsemen's entrance tunnel leads him to speculate that it may have been "worked by man." Very smooth and uniform cave walls are not unusual, however, and often indicate development under phreatic conditions.

Both of these highland caves are formed in Cretaceous limestone, which has been severely fractured and folded in the uplift of the mountains of southern Mexico. Deep valleys cut through the limestone mountains, and deep caves form by capturing drainage high in the mountains and releasing it at the valley floors. Caves up in the valley walls, such as those containing the Maya paintings, are often relictual features of older drainage systems, long since abandoned by water as new, deeper flow routes are established. This lack of flooding in these caves is an important factor in their past use by the Maya and in the preservation of their paintings.

Yucatan Caves

The Yucatan Peninsula is a broad, low-relief platform, composed largely of flat-lying Tertiary limestone. Many of the peninsula's longest caves are along its eastern coast and are currently filled with water. Back, Hanshaw, and Van Driel (1984) describe how fluctuations in mean sea level and its reactions with nonsaline groundwater have directly affected the development of the coastline's morphology and its caves.

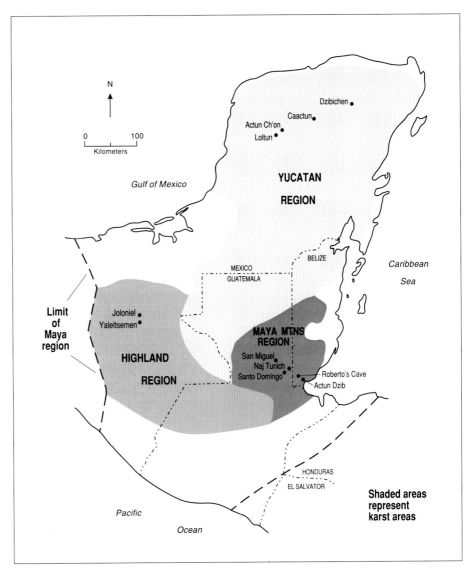

FIG. A-I. Karst areas of Maya Mesoamerica.

Of the nearly one dozen Maya cave painting sites known in the Yucatan Peninsula, only four have been geologically investigated: Actun Ch'on, Caactun, Dzibichen, and Loltun. All four caves are situated far from the seacoast and were created in pre-Maya times when the water table, and possibly relative sea level, was much higher than current levels. None of the caves drain any significant amount of surface water, so their paintings are safe from flooding.

Actun Ch'on is one of the most geologically interesting of the Yucatan's cave painting sites. It shows two different types of development: a collapse chamber and a maze (fig. 4-35). The lower, southwest end of the entrance room is the only intact portion of its precursor, a phreatically formed chamber. Collapse occurred after the water table dropped and when erosion of a hillside intersected the chamber. The ceiling of the original room was located eight meters below the present entrance. Although the present floor is only three meters lower, the original floor is likely several meters lower and now covered by rubble and washed-in sediment. Any off-going passages integrating this chamber with an underground stream system have also been covered by sediment and collapse.

The maze in Actun Ch'on was formed by very slow-moving, possibly ponded waters. Not shown on the map is an estimated two hundred meters of maze, which was explored for more paintings but not surveyed. The end of the maze was not reached. Other extensive maze caves, including the Maya painting and petroglyph site Caactun, also exist in the Yucatan and reflect a period of underground ponded water. With no distinct direction of flow, groundwater dissolved passages along available fractures to create a crisscrossing maze pattern. In the case of both Actun Ch'on and Caactun, it is currently not clear if the water originated from somewhere nearby on the surface, or if the water table rose into the maze level, which may be a more soluble zone of limestone.

For either scenario of maze origin, the paintings in both caves are safe from damage by flowing water. If the water originated on the surface nearby, the inflow points would be small, scattered, and unable to capture and transmit underground large amounts of surface water from semiarid hillsides. If the water rose from deeper in the limestone, the current water table is so far below that its fluctuations will have no impact on the caves.

Loltun (fig. 4-22) was formed seven kilometers south of Actun Ch'on and probably at about the same time. Loltun's greater elevation may signify a higher location along the water table, as its large, smooth-walled passages are indicative of phreatic flow down a gradient, unlike Ch'on, where there was insufficient velocity to create such defined streamways. Like Actun Ch'on, however, the cave is presently far enough above the water table to be unaffected by it, and although more surface water

does enter Loltun, it is not enough to harm the cave paintings.

Dzibichen (fig. 4-65) is the smallest of the four Yucatan cave painting sites discussed here. It is simply a phreatic chamber that has collapsed following the lowering of the water table. The small perennial pool at the cave's lowest point may be at the local water table, which is fairly shallow in that area. The cave's collapsed entrance does not capture any significant amount of surface water, and the water table does not rise high enough to pose a threat to the cave's paintings.

A cave situated next to Dzibichen, known to locals as its *hermano*, or "brother," was not entered for lack of a rope needed to descend its entrance. Like Dzibichen, it is formed by collapse—possibly the same collapse. Exploration of the *hermano* may not yield more paintings, but it should provide a more detailed understanding of the geology of Dzibichen.

Maya Mountain Caves

No caves are found in Belize's Maya Mountains. These mountains are composed of igneous Triassic intrusives and older Paleozoic metasediments, neither of which form karst terrains and caves. However, the region of the Maya Mountains (fig. A-1) contains Cretaceous limestones that were deposited upon and adjacent to these older rocks and extend from Belize into Guatemala. Some of the world's largest known cave passages, as in the Chiquibul Cave System, sit directly adjacent to these nonkarst mountains. These caves were formed by large volumes of tropical floodwaters—chemically aggressive for lack of saturation with respect to limestone—flowing off the Maya Mountains to carve huge tunnels through the karst.

Archaeologic materials have been found in caves of this region, some of which have been disturbed or destroyed

by flooding. In-situ deposits have only been found well above modern flood levels, either on high ledges within flood-prone passages or in older high-level passages and caves that have been long abandoned by floodwaters in favor of lower routes.

Actun Dzib (fig. A-2) and Roberto's Cave (fig. A-3), on the eastern side of the Maya Mountains in Belize, are examples of abandoned cave flow routes. The presence of converging upper and lower passages in Actun Dzib indicates that varying water levels were present as the cave developed. The present lack of flowing water is due to its migration to even lower levels and abandoning the known upper portion of the cave. At Roberto's Cave the drop in water level is even more dramatic, as surface stream erosion cut a valley where a more extensive cave once existed. Roberto's Cave is a small surviving segment of that old cave system. It is situated in a cliff high above the valley floor and water table, and no water flows through it.

There are three other cave painting sites in the Maya Mountains west of the range in Guatemala: San Miguel, Santo Domingo, and Naj Tunich. San Miguel, the farthest of these caves from the Maya Mountains, has not been geologically investigated and is not discussed here.

Santo Domingo is somewhat similar in origin to nearby Naj Tunich. These caves were not formed by massive flooding from the Maya Mountains but instead by slow-moving phreatic waters. The caves' entrances were formed by surface erosion truncating major passages. The lowering of the water table has left the caves high and dry, except for their entrance areas, where water has seeped in to deposit massive speleothems and create pools of water.

The greatest natural threat to the painted text in Santo Domingo is the water seeping down the calcite flowstone deposit on which it is drawn. Although much of the flowstone is dry, some minor damage has occurred where seepage has eroded a portion of the text. Additional minor damage has resulted from seeping water, not by eroding the text but by depositing calcite over it.

Geology of Naj Tunich

The geologic context of the paintings in Naj Tunich is by far the most complex and best studied of all the Maya cave painting sites. Naj Tunich is formed in Cretaceous-age Coban Limestone, a brecciated limestone that was deposited, broken up, and recemented (fig. A-4). The cause and date of the brecciation is not known due to difficult access to the

region and subsequent limited study of the geology. The Coban was later overlain by a suite of clastic silts, clays, and marls of the Cojaj Formation. With the Tertiary-age uplift of the Maya Mountains forty kilometers to the northeast, the bedrock of the Naj Tunich area was uplifted and slightly tilted to dip toward the south, and the Cojaj was eroded off the Coban Limestone.

As the limestone became exposed, karstification began and formed a sinkhole topography to drain water internally through cave conduits. Naj Tunich was one such conduit. Its development, vital to understanding the modern processes affecting the cave paintings, can be divided into 3 distinct stages: phreatic stage, sulfate stage, and modern stage (Veni 1990b).

Stage 1: Phreatic Stage

It is not certain when groundwater first flowed through the Coban Limestone in the vicinity of Naj Tunich; it is likely some water first infiltrated through the overlying sediments. However, when the limestone was eventually exposed to the surface, water began sinking underground in progressively larger volumes as fractures and other zones of weakness were enlarged. As conduits enlarged, they could carry more water and would pirate water from other conduits that were less efficient in groundwater transmission. Eventually a few conduits came to dominate the local hydrology, and they enlarged to become the main passages of Naj Tunich. Figure A-5 shows this first stage of development. While the area above Naj Tunich was covered by the Cojaj's clastic sediments, the cave was being formed by water entering the limestone at a more distant location.

This initial period of cavern development was under phreatic conditions, as evidenced by the cave's smooth passage walls, cuspate corners, and other related morphologic features (fig. 5-6). It was

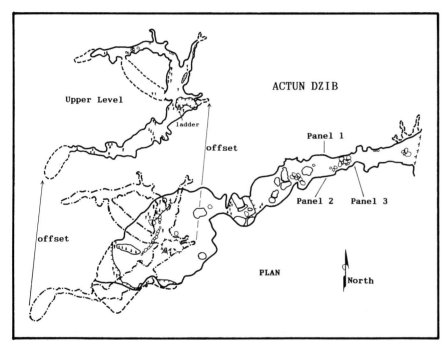

FIG. A-2. Plan of Actun Dzib. No scale given. Adapted from Walters 1988.

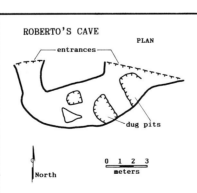

FIG. A-3. Plan of Roberto's Cave. Adapted from Walters 1988.

during this stage that the overall size, character, and layout of the cave's passages were formed. Presently over three kilometers of passages have been mapped in Naj Tunich (fig. 5-2), and more remains to be explored.

Stage 2: Sulfate Stage

Following the phreatic stage, the water table in the area suddenly dropped to a lower level and water flow through Naj Tunich ceased. During this time the area over the cave was still covered by the Cojaj Formation. The Cojaj retarded the downward movement of water and the cave became very dry. Some minor amounts of water, however, slowly migrated through the Cojaj down to the cave (fig. A-6). This water became rich in sulfates derived from oxidation with pyrite in the Cojaj's clastic sediments. When the sulfate ions, carried in solution, reacted with the dry limestone cave walls, they deposited gypsum crystals:

$$\underset{\text{(hydrogen ion)}}{H^+} + \underset{\text{(sulfate ion)}}{SO_4^{2-}} + \underset{\text{(limestone)}}{CaCO_3}$$
$$+ \underset{\text{(water)}}{2H_2O} \rightarrow \underset{\text{(gypsum)}}{CaSO_4 \cdot 2H_2O}$$
$$+ \underset{\text{(bicarbonate ion)}}{HCO_3^-} \qquad \text{(eq. 3)}$$

The gypsum began to form as a crust on the cave walls and ceiling, but it dehydrated and converted to bassanite or possibly anhydrite. These minerals are characterized by the formation of crusts with an internal pitted, spongy texture and case-hardened brown surfaces (Hill and Forti, 1986). The crusts in Naj Tunich attained thicknesses of three or four centimeters.

Stage 3: Modern Stage

The sulfate crusts in Naj Tunich never became very thick because the overlying Cojaj Formation, the sulfate source, was soon eroded away to begin the present stage of the cave's evolution. The now-exposed Coban Limestone began to rapidly form sinkholes to funnel surface

FIG. A-4. Brecciated limestone at Naj Tunich.

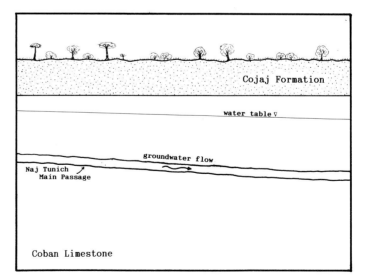

FIG. A-5. Phreatic Stage of Naj Tunich development.

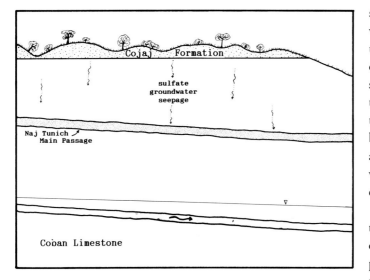

FIG. A-6. Sulfate Stage of Naj Tunich development.

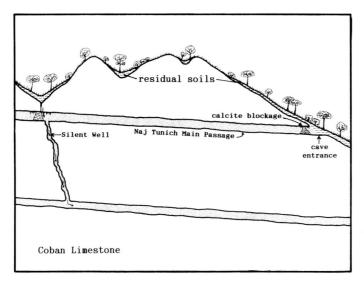

FIG. A-7. Modern Stage of Naj Tunich development.

water underground. Largely horizontal in extent, Naj Tunich was not an important conduit in vertically transmitting that water to the water table.

At stage 3 the cave was intersected by surface drainage in two primary locations: the beginning and end of the cave's Main Passage. The south end of that passage is a large room that was intersected by a downcutting valley to open the cave's only known entrance. Water seeping down through the lime-

stone near the entrance formed a huge wall of stalagmites, stalactites, and columns that coalesced and nearly blocked off the northward extension of the passage and cave. Almost one kilometer to the north, however, the other end of the passage was completely blocked off by such massive speleothem growth, and the pit known as the Silent Well was formed to channel incoming water deeper into the limestone (fig. A-7).

In spite of surface water intersecting the cave at its peripheries, the majority of the cave has remained dry. This is probably due to clays and silts within the overlying soils that were deposited during the erosion of the Cojaj Formation. Yet without the Cojaj, water migrating to the sulfate crusts of the cave walls became undersaturated with respect to sulfate and dissolved the crusts at their contact with the walls. As a result, the crusts have begun to slowly spall off the cave walls, leaving a thin veneer of silt behind. It is on this surface that the Maya executed most of their paintings in Naj Tunich (see figs. 8-3, 8-88).

Geologic Factors in the Deterioration of Maya Cave Paintings

The primary factor in the natural deterioration of the Maya cave paintings is the type of substrate on which the paint was applied. The known Maya cave paintings have been largely well preserved because the Maya selected clean, dry walls and speleothems on which to execute their drawings. The paintings occur on four types of surfaces: calcite speleothems, limestone, limestone clasts, and limestone matrix.

Paintings on calcite speleothems often show the best degree of preservation. The speleothems used were generally inactive (i.e., dry) and had no veneer of silt that could dislodge and take attached paint with it. Their surface textures are rough so the paint adheres well, although the roughness compromises the quality of some of the drawings' details (see fig. 8-50). In Actun Dzib and Santo Domingo, some paintings have suffered slight damage by water seepage on surfaces that were probably dry when the paintings were executed.

With the exception of Naj Tunich and Bladen 2, cave wall paintings were rendered on unbrecciated limestone. Unlike speleothems, dry limestone walls are usually coated with at least a fine silt veneer. The silt is a remnant from the time water coursed through the cave, often carrying silt and other sediments in its flow. Some of the silts are limestone grains that were being chemically eroded from the cave walls. Any paint placed upon either the water-deposited or limestone-grain silt will be removed when those grains fall from the walls (fig. A-8).

The silt grains fall by two primary mechanisms: gravity fall and groundwater seepage. Gravity fall results when the force of gravity overcomes the grain's adhesion to the cave wall. Silt fall by groundwater seepage occurs when minute volumes of water within the rock move toward the cave walls and dislodge the silt. The flow rate can sometimes be so small that the walls can feel dry to the touch. In such cases, without any obvious moisture or discoloration of the wall rock by groundwater, it can be almost impossible to distinguish silt fall by gravity versus that by seepage. Gravity and seepage can also dislodge paint attached directly to the wall, but in most cases this bond is stronger than that of the silt to the wall—especially when the silt is weighted with paint. Regardless of fall by gravity or groundwater, rough-textured walls tend to retain their paint better than very smooth walls.

In Naj Tunich the cave walls are brecciated and offer two types of painting surfaces: limestone clasts (large limestone fragments) and limestone

FIG. A-8. Line of silt on floor fallen from overhang ledge, Naj Tunich. Photograph by Andrea Stone.

matrix (smaller, finer-grained limestone material that fills the spaces between the clasts). The Maya's preferred painting surface was on the limestone clasts. Along the cave walls these clasts were eroded into very smooth drawing surfaces. Clasts one meter in diameter and larger are exposed in the walls throughout Naj Tunich. Maya artists often selected these large clasts on which to compose their scenes or glyphic texts (see fig. 5-34). The smoothness of the clasts' surface, however, did not allow for good adherence to the rock, and gravity has subsequently pulled down some of the silt and attached paint (fig. A-7).

The limestone matrix, the infilling material between the clasts, is a coarser surface to which the paint could more readily adhere. Many of the paintings display sharp differences in the degree of paint preservation where single paint strokes extend over both matrix and clasts. Surprisingly, some such occurrences show poor preservation of the paint on the matrix and good preservation on the clasts. The reason is probably the greater migration of moisture through the porous matrix, which will dislodge the silt grains, matrix grains, and paint from the walls (fig. A-9).

In Naj Tunich, in addition to the wall silts already discussed, the walls are covered with a thin layer of sulfate silt, a residual of the fallen sulfate crusts. Like the other silts, some of these silts have fallen by the force of gravity and some by groundwater seepage. The sulfate silts, however, are more susceptible to chemical erosion by groundwater seepage and would thus fall more readily than neighboring water-lain or limestone silts.

Of all the known cave painting sites, none of the paintings have been affected by floodwaters, perhaps because the Maya avoided flood-prone caves or because flooding may have already destroyed those drawings—but this does not seem likely. Few of the known paintings have been damaged by water flowing down cave walls or speleothems. This testifies to the Maya's meticulous selection in painting sites, so it is not likely they would have selected flood-prone caves

in which to chronicle obviously important events.

Human-Induced Geologic Impact on Maya Cave Paintings

Human activity poses four primary threats to the Maya cave paintings: vandalism, increased atmospheric carbon dioxide, algal growths, and increased groundwater seepage. Of these, only vandalism does not escalate the rate of the natural geologic deterioration of the paintings.

Human traffic in caves, even if regulated and escorted to prevent vandalism, will increase the amount of atmospheric carbon dioxide. Carbon dioxide is naturally exhaled when breathing, and it can react with ambient humidity and moisture on cave walls to produce carbonic acid. This acidified aerosol moisture can thus dissolve the walls' limestone silt and sulfate coatings, augmenting the fall of whatever may be painted on them.

Should any of the cave painting sites be opened for viewing by the general public and electric lights strung, the artificial lighting could produce the algal

growths common in most commercial caves. Such growths would damage the paintings, and cleaning the algae might cause even more destruction. Human respiration in the cave could also stimulate organic growths by increasing the cave's humidity and number of aerosol bacteria.

With most of the known cave painting sites, human respiratory carbon dioxide and bacterial damage should not be a problem. The size of most of the caves precludes visitation in numbers that would cause an adverse impact. The actual number of people that could view the paintings, without causing such damage, will vary with each cave and would have to be determined according to each cave's size, water and rock chemistry, atmospheric carbon dioxide and humidity, and the rate of cave-air circulation with the outside air.

The Yucatan cave paintings benefit from the peninsula's semiarid climate. A wetter climate would result in more water seeping down cave walls and eroding the paintings. In such a climate the peninsula's thin soil covering would do little to retain water, transpire it through the vegetation, and thus prevent much of it from infiltrating into the caves. A related potential problem exists for the cave painting sites in the Maya Mountains. In that area of rain forest, slash and burn agriculture is the commonly employed practice due to its efficiency, low cost, and use of nonmechanized labor. Slash and burn, however, denudes the landscape of the vegetation that keeps soil from being washed away during the region's torrential tropical rains. If the soil and vegetation above the caves in this area are diminished or lost, the water seeping through the limestone may increase and have catastrophic effects on the paintings. Naj Tunich is especially sensitive to the impact of soil and vegetation loss.

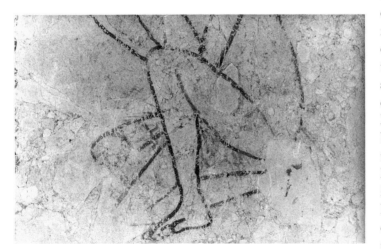

FIG. A-9. Detail of Drawing 20, Naj Tunich. Note sharp difference in paint adhesion at right foot and buttocks area of kneeling figure. Photograph by Chip and Jennifer Clark.

Conclusions

Maya cave painting sites occur in caves of diverse origins and diverse climatic, geologic, and topographic settings. The details of each cave's geology and development provide information on what factors influence the deterioration of the paintings and what management steps are needed in their preservation.

Where possible, cave entrances should be secured to prevent vandalism, but any gating should not interfere with natural airflow through the caves. Geologic studies of these caves, to develop optimal management plans, should include analyses of the limestone, wall silts, seepage and flood waters, overlying soils, and paint pigments. Additionally, minimum two-year studies should be conducted with year-round monitoring of the following parameters: rainfall, cave and surface temperature, cave and surface humidity, cave and surface barometric pressure, cave airflow, cave atmospheric carbon dioxide, cave wall carbon dioxide, and cave wall moisture and groundwater seepage.

By understanding these factors and their interrelationships at each cave, it is then possible to project their impact on the caves' paintings. Effective management strategies can then be developed based on those projections.

Standard Cave Map Symbols

Cave walls	═══════		Cobbles	(symbol)
Upper level	— · — · —		Sand/soil	(symbol)
Lower level	— — — —		Clay	(symbol)
Continues too small	(symbol)		Stalactite	(symbol)
			Stalagmite	(symbol)
Drop in floor	high (symbol) low		Column	(symbol) or (symbol)
Drop in ceiling	high (symbol) low			
Slope	high (symbol) low		Flowstone	high (symbol) low
Large breakdown	(symbol)		Water, with flow	(symbol)
Small breakdown	(symbol)		Cross section (view in direction of arrow)	
Bedrock	(symbol)		(symbol)	

253

Notes

Chapter 1. Introduction

1. The *cura* Pedro Sánchez de Aguilar (1937) provides several accounts from Yucatan of natives caught using caves for ritual activities prohibited by the church. In one case the *cura* himself discovered a cave full of "idols" near Cehac in 1606 (ibid.: 39). He also states that another official (*Beneficiado*) removed idols from a cave in 1605 near the town of Tixotsuc (ibid.: 166). The natives fled into the bush to avoid punishment (*el Castigo*). Testimonies dating to 1562 state that idols and skulls were found in a cave in the province of Mani and sixty idols were found in a cave near Yaxcaba (Scholes and Adams 1938:1:25, 104). The *Relación del Pueblo de Yalcón* also states that some Franciscan friars had removed idols hidden by the natives in their houses and caves (*Relaciones histórico-geográficas de la gobernación de Yucatán* 1983:2: 336). López de Cogolludo (1867:2: 497–498) reports that one Pedro Che, a Maya who worked in the convent of Mani, was out hunting and stumbled upon a cave ritual in progress. Blood of a sacrificed deer had been smeared over idols resting upon an altar while the smell of copal wafted in the air. The incident was relayed to a local Spanish cleric. It is likely that such offenses were punished by whipping and torture to force a confession.

Chapter 2. The Topographic Context of Maya Cave Painting

1. For example, Lothrop (1933:49, 81) calls certain images "pictographs" that are actually carved on boulders at Chuitinamit on the shore of Lake Atitlan.

2. Parietal art can have a limited archaeological context, as when a fallen piece of decorated wall is buried under cultural material, providing a *terminus ante quem* for the rock picture. Sometimes cave art is found in close association with undisturbed cultural remains (see Meighan 1981:81). The difficulty

always is in determining contemporaneity between artifact and image.

3. These specific topographic features are mentioned repeatedly in the ethnohistoric and ethnographic literature as having an important ritual function. For instance, Ximénez (1857:189) remarks of the inhabitants of highland Guatemala: "They made sacrifices in caves and in dark places, and at crossroads, and on the crests of mountains." For the Kekchi, crosses dedicated to the mountain-valley god Tzultaca are found in caves, mountains, and crossroads (Carlson and Eachus 1977:41). According to Villa Rojas (1956:31), sacred landforms among the Mixe consist of "certain caves, hills, natural springs, and rocks of special form." Likewise, Dahlgren (1966:236) notes that the Mixtec guarded their idols and made sacrifices in "temples, hills, and caves."

4. I inquired of Emilio Pop, a Kekchi Maya living near Naj Tunich, why people were coming anew to perform "Christian" ceremonies in the cave entrance. He replied that they worshipped there because of the cave's silence; thus, God could hear them more clearly. This is but one explanation as to why distant places offer better lines of communication with supernatural beings.

5. Anyone who has explored Maya caves knows that the Maya went to great lengths to find remote spots in caves to leave offerings and that they also blocked off access to certain passages, usually with rough-hewn masonry walls. Masonry constrictions are seen, for example, at Eduardo Quiroz Cave (Pendergast 1971), Las Cuevas (Anderson 1962), and Actun Acum (see Chapter 4). Note, too, that the cave underneath the Pyramid of the Sun at Teotihuacan was restricted by a series of barrier walls (Baker et al. 1974). This desire for secrecy and remoteness may reflect the ritual importance of the unsullied, or *suhuy*, environment.

Chapter 3. A Further Exploration of Topographic Context: The Mesoamerican Landscape and the Cave

1. That *oztotl* and *tepetl* were recognized as animate nouns is seen in the fact that they have the plural forms *oztomeh* and *tepemeh*. Only animate nouns are pluralized in Classical Nahuatl.

2. The iconography comprising this earth monster series and the related Cihuacoatl complex has an earlier manifestation at Chichen Itza. This figure, like the central Mexican version, wears a skirt bearing crossed bones and disks and may be partly skeletalized. The figure appears at Chichen Itza on the pilasters of the Lower Temple of the Jaguars and as a reclining figure, often sprouting a plant from its abdomen, appearing in the basal register of many reliefs and wall paintings. Taube (1988b:120) has pointed out that the figure can be identified with Goddess O, best known for her portraits in the Dresden and Madrid Codex (e.g., Dresden 74 and Madrid 10b); but there are at least two Late Classic examples of this old goddess on painted vases (Kerr 1989–1990:1:20; Taube 1988b:fig. 40b). This iconography, then, may have originated in the Maya area, though it receives little attention in the Classic period and makes a resurgence in the Postclassic.

3. For example:

Yucatec
chi': boca
chi' na: puerta de casa (Barrera Vásquez 1980:91,101)

Greater Cholan
ti': mouth (Kaufman and Norman 1984:132)

Ch'ol
ti' na: puerta de la casa (Aulie and de Aulie 1978:174)

Quiche

chi: mouth, lips, entrance, rim, brink, border

u chi haa: door (Edmonson 1965:26)

Cakchiquel

chi ru: *boca, puerta, ventana, agujero, causa, razón, motivo* (Sáenz de Santa María 1940:86)

4. See the famous Tlalocan mural and the now-destroyed mural in the Temple of Agriculture, which show a female goddess penetrated by a cavity in the shape of a spiderlike insect.

5. Nicholson 1971:414. A useful comparison between the Maya God N complex and Tlaloc appears in Klein 1980:175–184.

6. Muñoz Camargo 1892:131, cited in López Austin (1973:64). The latter author brings together a useful discussion of mountains and rain gods among the Aztecs (pp. 61–64).

7. A Kekchi dictionary (Sedat 1955: 81) lists the following entry under *itzam*: "*iztam, nombre de un cerro de Lanquín. Xa'an itzam chanqueb re, rixakil kacua' Xacabyoc xtsululeb Xelaju, Vieja Itzam le dicen, mujer del señor Xacabyoc, cerro de Quezaltenango.*"

8. These terms are by no means applied only to mountains. Vogt (1969: 579) discusses their use as a kind of archetype of hierarchical relationships that linguistically pervades many domains of ritual life in Zinacantan.

9. Heyden (1989:212–213) discusses the tree, another vertical feature of the landscape, as a human metaphor. She notes that the Aztecs called trees at times "our father" or "our prince" and that the tree was a metaphor for the ruler. The ruler-tree metaphor appears in the Maya area as well, where Classic Maya rulers were represented as the world tree (Schele and Miller 1986: 77).

10. Seler (1960:5:461, pl. xlv) found a ceramic jar with a face bearing Tlaloc rings in a cave near Chocoman,

Veracruz. The well-known Maya cave Balankanche revealed a sizable collection of Tlaloc effigy jars (Andrews 1970).

11. Though the Totilme'iletik of Zinacantan live in and are affiliated with mountains, the analogous Me'iltatil, ancestors of the Tzeltal of Pinola, are said to live inside the cave Muk' Naj, located within the mountain Sohktik (Hermitte 1970:33–34). Similarly, the ancestral creator couple of the Kanjobal of Santa Eulalia is said to live inside the sacred cave Yalan Na' (La Farge 1947:127). Any significant distinction between the notion of being inside a mountain versus inside a cave is blurred in the ethnographic literature; the two ideas appear to be functionally synonymous.

12. Naj Tunich was given the name *nah tunich* by Pierre Ventur, who worked among the Mopan of San Luis, Peten.

13. Tedlock (1985:110) translates *xikiri pat*, the name of one of the lords of Xibalba, as "house corner," which would tie in nicely with the notion of the cave as a house. Edmonson (1971: 61), however, translates the same name as "flying noose."

14. Francisco Ximénez elicited interpretations of the twenty days of the sacred calendar from a ritual specialist in the Quiche area. He recorded *casa* "house" for the day Akbal. When Franz Termer attempted to compile a similar list in Santa Rosa Chujuyub, Quiche, the informant gave *casa* for the day Cauac (Termer 1957:120). Both Akbal and Cauac can be associated with caves, the former through its connection to darkness and the latter through its connection to rain. Their responses are interesting in light of the Nahuatl term Calli ("house"), which corresponds with Akbal.

15. The identification of caves with holes is brought out in a Yucatecan folk tale recorded by Redfield and Villa Ro-

jas (1934:333). This tells of a man who watches the Chacs ride out on horses from their cave abode into the sky in order to make it rain. They are said to ride out through circular holes.

16. The practice of heaping stones on shrines occurs in the Kekchi area as well. Deiseldorff (1926:380) states that the Kekchi erect wooden crosses on the roads of mountaintops. They are arrayed with piles of stone and bouquets of flowers and are believed to invigorate the legs. Further light is shed on this by Sapper (1897:271), who comments:

> At the crossing of the roads all the Indians of Guatemala and Chiapas belonging to the tribes of the Maya family, erect crosses, to which the passersby pay their respects in a singular fashion. Usually the Indian who crosses such a pass carries with him a stone, so that stone heaps of considerable size are frequently to be seen at these crosses. It is also common for offerings in the form of flowers or green boughs to be laid before the cross or bound to it, and it is noteworthy that often in the case of widely separated tribes (for example, Choles in Chiapas and Kekchi Indians in Guatemala) the same varieties of flowers are used for this purpose.

17. Girard (1962:197–205) discusses an idol-altar-pit complex in the Chorti area in which two pits are dug in front of a cross shrine and filled with offerings to the earth god and goddess.

18. The following are examples of this motif. In Yalcoba, Yucatan, it is said that since people claim that money is found in caves, the gods must hide their monetary wealth within them (Sosa 1985:424). A tale is told in a Zapotec town, Ixtepeji, about a man who seeks riches from the spirit of the cave. The man labored for six months, whereupon the cave filled with water and spoiled his attempts at acquiring wealth (Kearney 1972:94). A Mixe folk tale tells of two roads in a cave, one leading through a mountain where a treasure

can be found. The other road leads to "*el infierno*" (Miller 1956:159). In another Mixe tale, a lightning deity keeps boxes of money hidden inside a cave (ibid.:262–268, cited in Spero 1987:24). Among the Zoque of Rayón, Chiapas, a horned serpent guards a treasure in a cave (Thomas 1975:234–235, cited in Spero 1987:29). In the Mixteca Alta the cave as an underworld house is called *vehe quihin* "big house." Jansen (1982:255) states, "Vehe quihin is not just a place of infernal beings, but of wealth" [my translation]. Taggart (1983:114) discusses a class of Nahuat folktales that clearly fits into this genre. Men enter the forest and encounter lightning or an earth goddess. They then have some favor granted or gain wealth, and then in some manner lose it. Grigsby (1986) reports a group of seven ritual caves near Tlalxictlan in the highlands of central Mexico. One of the caves is called "the enchanted store" and is a repository of expensive items, such as television sets and canned goods, which are accessible at midnight on the New Year. However, the cave can close and trap people inside until the next year.

19. Thompson (1975:xxvii–xxviii) quotes a passage from Thomas Gage that tells of his exploration of a ritual cave near Mixco, Guatemala, in the seventeenth century in search of a wooden idol. Gage revels in the fact that coins were found under the idol, "that made us search the cave more diligently," whereupon to his delight he found more coins, offerings of fruit, maize and honey, as well as dishes of burnt copal.

20. Typically souls are offered in return for immediate material gain. Payment may also consist of working for the cave deity before and after death. In addition, if petitioning is not carried out correctly, some grave harm may befall the petitioner.

21. The association of caves with wealth and treasure is also part of European folk culture. Jung (1950:117–118), for example, discusses the archetypal myth, widespread in the ancient world, of a dragon guarding a treasure in a cave.

22. Taussig's (1980:Ch. 11) *The Devil and Commodity Fetishism in South America* addresses this very issue. He believes that the devillike attributes of this pre-Columbian mountain deity, who is a possessor of wealth, are a late accretion and reflect the indigenous reaction against the appropriation of resources by nonindigenous governing powers.

23. The western Mixe believe that wind and lightning inhabit caves (Beals 1973:98). Dahlgren (1966:238–239) discusses the worship of rain gods in caves in the Mixteca Alta during the early Colonial period. In one case the idol worshipped in the cave was a stalagmite. Nahua-speaking people around Córdoba, Veracruz, reportedly believe that a dwarflike creature, colored blue and with a hole in the top of his head, inhabits the caves of sacred mountains and brings rain, storms, and lightning (Martínez and Reyes García 1970:544). See also Thompson (1975:xxvi) and Spero (1987).

24. After the discovery of Naj Tunich, a local Kekchi wanted to make a pilgrimage to the cave to pay homage to the maize god (Brady and Stone 1986). Among Nahua speakers of Puyecaco, Veracruz, the maize god, Pilsintsi', also thought of as "the master of seeds," is said to be localized in a cave (Sandstrom 1975:221).

25. In Colonial Yucatan Xibalba was the name of a devillike demon. For example, we find in López de Cogolludo (1867:Book 4, Ch. 7, 310) "*Hablaban con el demonio a quien llamaban Xibilba, que quiere decir el que se desaparece o desvance.*" The Motul Dictionary (1929:920) defines *xibalba* as "*diablo.*"

26. In the Nahuatl-speaking area where the cave of Milpa Alta is located, certain evil spirits dwell within who cause illness and are called *manglinos*, or *nahuatoton* (Ramirez 1913:355). Regarding the Tzeltal of Amatenango del Valle, Nash (1970:11) notes, "Danger is localized in a series of caves which are avoided."

Chapter 4. Maya and Mesoamerican Cave Painting: A Survey of Sites and Images

1. In what they do and do not portray, the tabletop altars and Mural 1 have a complementary relationship. As a throne, the altars would have a real person, presumably the ruler, sit over a portrayal of a person in a cave. On the other hand, Mural 1 portrays a person sitting on an altar, while a real person could enter or emerge from a real cave.

2. Also see the petroglyph Abaj Takalik Monument 1 (Wicke 1971: fig. 24) and a rock painting in red from Aldes Eje Quemado, Amatitlan, Guatemala (see *Mexicon* 1979:1(1):6).

3. One other Olmec-style work, Chalcatzingo Monument 2, has a reclining figure usually portrayed with an erect phallus, derived from a drawing published by Piña Chan (1955). Both Grove (1968:488) and Angulo V. (1987:143) cast doubt on the presence of a phallus in the original carving. This so-called phallus is not distinctly carved and may represent some costuming, or it may have been added at a later date. Both authors admit the possibility that the figure was ithyphallic, but neither believes this to have been the case.

4. See bibliographies on Mexican and Central American rock art in Cera (1976), Strecker (1982a), Pompa y Pompa and Valencia Cruz (1985), Casado López (1987), and Bonor (1989).

5. Ricardo Velázquez Valadez systematically photographed and catalogued the art of Loltun. I have consulted these unpublished materials, which are on file at the Centro Regional de Yucatán del INAH in Mérida.

6. Room designations in Loltun come from the map in Zavala Ruiz et al. (1978).

7. Coe (1966) notes the shared use of the ball and cylinder fringe and the large belt disks on the Dumbarton Oaks pectoral and the Loltun relief. Both also have similarly configured, early versions of the personified Jester God resting above the bead and cylinder band. The Loltun Jester God is plainly visible in an illustration of the relief based on a rubbing by Ricardo Velázquez Valadez (Andrews 1981: fig. 2). The Jester God has an Olmec cast with squarish lips and a pug nose.

8. Puuc-style dating uses the same Year Bearer set as that used in Landa's time: Muluc, Ix, Kan, and Cauac. Proskouriakoff and Thompson (1947) note the earliest occurrence of Puuc-style dating in western Yucatan at 9.12.0.0.0, but its antiquity is unclear since early inscriptions are rare in this region. For further discussion of Puuc-style dating and Year Bearers, see Chapter 7.

9. Sundry materials related to Acum are held in the archives of the Middle American Research Institute, Tulane University. They include two typescript reports, "Actun Acum, Oxkutzcab, informe preliminar" (1980) and "La Cueva Acum, municipio de Oxkutzcab, Yucatán" (1984). Accompanying them are a sketch map of the cave, drawings, photographs, photographic negatives, and slides.

10. Red hematite was also splashed on the walls of the Cueva de la Sangre at Dos Pilas (James Brady, personal communication, 1991).

11. The Hermita Virgen del Pilar in Oxkutzcab, dated 1697, has a Hapsburg eagle over the entrance (Vega Bolaños 1945:487). A crude Hapsburg eagle is incised into a stucco wall at a Colonial church at Kan Xoc near Valladolid. Here a window forms the eagle's body, and a royal crown is incised between the two heads.

12. Riese's (1981) published drawing of this scene shows the left figure grabbing the torch as though he has three arms. The third arm is a misinterpretation of dark wall stains appearing in the photograph.

Chapter 5. Naj Tunich: An Introduction to the Site and Its Art

1. This distance is a close approximation based on a study of contour maps made by George Veni.

2. Preliminary tests on the darker pigment are inconclusive.

3. Merlin Tuttle (personal communication, 1986) of Bat Conservation International and Charles O. Handley (personal communication, 1988) of the Smithsonian Institution, Museum of Natural History, kindly provided this information.

4. Artifacts in association with paintings in the Western Passage were found in the narrow corridor with paintings on both walls, described earlier (fig. 5-30). These materials were collected in Lot 5 of Operation I, which is divided into three sublots (Brady 1989:81–82). Sublot 5A was found directly beneath Drawing 13 and consists of ten sherds of striated pottery, some with appliqué decoration, and four sherds of Late Classic Saxche Orange Polychrome. A polishing stone was also found with this group of material. Against the opposite (south) wall of the corridor is Sublot 5B, which contains three unidentified polychrome sherds, one of which is Early Classic. Also along the south wall is Sublot 5C, containing thirty-two sherds of a utilitarian vessel and a piece of a conch shell.

5. Landa mentions that during Uayeb rites the Maya offered beads to their idols, which they would burn over incense (Tozzer 1941:166). Jade that had been exposed to fire was also discovered in Naj Tunich (Brady 1989: 292). Jewelry cast into the Sacred Cenote at Chichen Itza further testifies to

the Maya's fondness for using jade as a votive offering in topographic shrines.

Chapter 6. Images from Naj Tunich

1. Katun 17 has the third-closest temporal relationship with a New Year of any *k'atun* during the Classic period. The second-closest is 5 Ahau 3 Pop, 8.15.0.0.0, and the closest is 9.6.0.0.0, which occurred during the Uayeb, on 9 Ahau 3 Uayeb. This is one of two *k'atun*s, the other being 9.7.0.0.0, associated with the so-called Hiatus. The dearth of dedicatory monuments on 9.6.0.0.0 might be attributed to its occurrence during the Uayeb, which was generally an inauspicious period for the Maya.

2. See painted Late Classic-style heads in Drawings 8, 37, 59, 60, 72, 73, 77, 79, 81 (which has three), and 84. Drawing 62 is the head of a deity. Painted schematic heads, both frontal and profile, can be seen in Drawings 55, 91, and 92. Drawing 53 is a petroglyph with one beautiful Late Classic face and three cruder ones (one of which was barely begun). Drawing 89 has a few rudimentary scratched lines that resemble a face.

Chapter 7. The Hieroglyphic Inscriptions of Naj Tunich

1. For a comprehensive discussion of the workings of the Maya calendar see Thompson 1960.

2. Mathews (1977) reports that a stela in a private collection from the Piedras Negras region records the Puuc-style date 2 Ix 6 Kankin, but also the Type III period-ending date 10 Ahau 8 Mac. In addition, Type III and Type IV dates occur in the inscriptions of individual Puuc sites. For example, most of the dates from Uxmal employ the standard system, but the ballcourt rings use Puuc-style dating and record the CR dates 6 Ix 17 Pop and 7 Men 18 Pop (Kowalski 1987 : 36).

3. There are in postconquest central Mexican sources correlations of the 260-day cycle and the Christian calendar (a famous example being that Tenochtitlan fell on 1 Coatl, or August 13, 1521 o.s.). These sources also place months in the native calendar within the Christian year. These correlations have provided a basis for reconstructing the relationship between the 260-day and 365-day cycles among specific central Mexican populations (Caso 1971: Tables 4 and 5). But the hypothetical nature of this framework is revealed in such arguments as whether the Year Bearer marked the first day of the year or the last day of the last month before the *nemontemi*, as Caso (p. 346) asserts. Such an argument is not even feasible if the alignment set were truly known. To keep a Calendar Round within the same alignment set, the Year Bearer must move through the 365-day year in increments of five. Thus, the Year Bearer could occur on the first day of the year or the first day of the *nemontemi* but not the last day of the year before the *nemontemi* if the Calendar Round were to stay within the same alignment set. The debate as to which day of the year marked the New Year has different ramifications for Mayanists who would have to change their proposed Year Bearer set in switching positions on this issue. On the other hand, Central Mexican scholars do not propose changing the Year Bearer set; they would therefore have to change their proposed alignment set, as this is not an established fact.

4. For the identification and further discussion of verbal affixes mentioned in this essay see MacLeod 1987.

5. Stephen Houston (personal communication, 1991) notes that David Stuart first proposed this reading, while Schele and Grube (1988) mention contributions by Terrence Kaufman and Ben Leaf.

6. The proposed reading order of the left half of Drawing 82 is A1-B1-A2-B2-C1-D1-C2-C3-D2-D3. The right half is not entirely clear at this time but may continue E1-F1-E2-F2-G1-H1.

Chapter 9. Maya Cave Painting: Summary of a Tradition

1. Caves still awaiting investigation include Cueva de Tres Manos near Akil, Yucatan, which has negative handprints (Lisa Rock, personal communication, 1990); a cave with a black painting of a deer located between Uayma and Tinum, Yucatan (Helga Maria Miram, personal communication, 1991), and some caves with paintings noted by Bonor, also in Yucatan (1989 : 82, Table 3). In addition, Burkitt (1930 : 51) mentions a cave near the ruins of Chipal in Ixil country of highland Guatemala wherein "there is a rude human figure about half a meter high or so, sketched on the face of the rock." Whether "sketched" means "incised" or "drawn" is not clear.

2. The digging of artificial caves is a distinct feature of Maya culture (Brady and Veni 1992). In highland Guatemala artificial caves were dug in the soft volcanic ash usually in relation to ceremonial architecture. The best-known artificial caves are at Utatlan, the ancient Quiche capital, and appear to date from prehispanic times (Brady 1991b).

3. Gary Rex Walters (personal communication, 1989) observes that caves in the Toledo District of Belize with Classic-period utilization reveal evidence of small-scale ritual use, presumably by a local peasantry.

Bibliography

Aguilar Zinser, Carmen. 1974. Enseñanza objetiva teológica del inframundo maya, en la Cueva de Joloniel, en Chiapas. *Excelsior*, August 4.

Alvarez de Toro, Miguel. 1977. *Los mamíferos de Chiapas.* Tuxtla Gutiérrez: Universidad Autónoma de Chiapas.

Anawalt, Patricia Rieff. 1981. *Indian Clothing before Cortes: Mesoamerican Costumes from the Codices.* Norman: University of Oklahoma Press.

Anderson, A. H. 1962. Cave Sites in British Honduras. *Akten des 34 Internationalen Amerikanistenkongresses Wien.* Vienna: Verlag Ernst Berger, Horn.

Anderson, Martha G., and Christine Mullen Kreamer. 1989. *Wild Spirits, Strong Medicine: African Art and the Wilderness.* New York/Seattle/London: Center for African Art/University of Washington Press.

Anderson, James. 1967. The Human Skeletons. In *The Prehistory of the Tehuacan Valley* (ed. Douglas S.

Byers), 1:91–113. Austin: University of Texas Press.

Andrews, E. Wyllys IV. 1970. *Balankanche, Throne of the Tiger Priest.* MARI Pub. 32. New Orleans: MARI, Tulane University.

———. 1975. Explorations in the Gruta de Chac, Yucatan, Mexico. In *Archaeological Investigations on the Yucatan Peninsula*, pp. 1–21. MARI Pub. 31. New Orleans: MARI, Tulane University.

Andrews, Anthony P. 1981. El Guerrero de Loltún: Comentario analítico. *Boletín de la Escuela de Ciencias Antropológicas de la Universidad de Yucatán* 8–9(48–49):36–50.

Angulo V., Jorge. 1987. The Chalcatzingo Reliefs: An Iconographic Analysis. In Grove 1987, pp. 132–158.

Apostolides, Alex. 1987. Chalcatzingo Painted Art. In Grove 1987, pp. 171–199.

Arnold, Dean. 1971. Ethnomineralogy of Ticul, Yucatan Potters: Etics and

Emics. *American Antiquity* 36(1): 20–40.

Aulie, H. Wilbur, and Evelyn W. de Aulie. 1978. *Diccionario ch'ol-español; español-ch'ol.* Mexico City: Instituto Lingüístico de Verano.

Back, William, Bruce B. Hanshaw, and J. Nicholas Van Driel. 1984. Role of Groundwater in Shaping the Eastern Coastline of the Yucatan Peninsula, Mexico. In *Groundwater as a Geomorphic Agent* (ed. R. G. LaFleur), pp. 282–293. Binghamton Symposium in Geomorphology, International Series 13. Boston: Allen and Unwin.

Bahn, Paul G. 1978. Water Mythology and the Distribution of Palaeolithic Parietal Art. *Proceedings of the Prehistoric Society* 44: 125–134.

———. 1992. Where's the Beef? The Myth of Hunting Magic in Palaeolithic Art. In *Rock Art and Prehistory* (ed. Paul Bahn and Andrée Rosenfeld), pp. 1–13. Oxbow Monograph 10. Oxford: Oxbow Books.

———, and Jean Vertut. 1988. *Images of the Ice Age.* London: Windward.

Baird, Ellen Taylor. 1989. Stars and War at Cacaxtla. In *Mesoamerica after the Decline of Teotihuacan: A.D. 700–900* (ed. Richard Diehl and Janet Berlo), pp. 105–122. Washington: Dumbarton Oaks.

Baker, George T., III, Hugh Harleston, Jr., Alfonso Rangel, Matthew Wallrath, Manuel Gaitán, and Alfonso Morales. 1974. *The Subterranean System of the Sun Pyramid at Teotihuacan: A Physical Description and Hypothetical Reconstruction.* Mexico City: Uac-Kan.

Bardawil, Lawrence. 1976. The Principal Bird Deity in Maya Art—An Iconographic Study in Form and Meaning. In *Second Palenque Round Table, 1974* (ed. Merle Greene Robertson), pp. 195–209. Palenque Round Table Series 3. Pebble Beach: Robert Louis Stevenson School.

Barrera Rubio, Alfredo. 1985. The Rain Cult of the Puuc Area. In *Fourth Palenque Round Table, 1980* (ed. Elizabeth P. Benson), pp. 249–260. Palenque Round Table Series 4. San Francisco: Pre-Columbian Art Research Institute.

———, and Karl A. Taube. 1987. Los relieves de San Diego: Nuevas perspectivas. *Boletín de la Escuela de Ciencias Antropológicas de la Universidad de Yucatán*, 14(83): 3–18.

Barrera Vásquez, Alfredo, ed. 1980. *Diccionario maya Cordemex: Maya-español, español-maya.* Mérida: Ediciones Cordemex.

Bassie-Sweet, Karen. 1991. *From the Mouth of the Dark Cave: Commemorative Sculpture of the Late Classic Maya.* Norman: University of Oklahoma Press.

Bastante Gutiérrez, Oscar. 1982. Algunas cuevas en Teotihuacan. In *Memoria del Proyecto Arqueológico Teotihuacan 80–82*, pp. 341–354. Colección Científica 132. Mexico City: INAH.

Beals, Ralph. 1973. *Ethnology of the Western Mixe.* New York: Cooper Square Publication.

Becquelin, Pierre, and Claude F. Baudez. 1982. *Tonina: Une cité maya du Chiapas (Mexique).* Vol. 2. Mexico City: Centre d'Etudes Mexicaines et Centraméricaines.

Beetz, Carl P., and Linton Satterthwaite. 1981. *The Monuments and Inscriptions of Caracol, Belize.* University Museum Monograph 45. Philadelphia: University Museum, University of Pennsylvania.

Beltrán de Santa Rosa María, Pedro. 1746. *Arte del idioma maya reducido a sucintas reglas, y semilexicon yucateco.* Mexico City.

Berjonneau, Gérald, and Jean-Louis Sonnery, eds. 1985. *Rediscovered Masterpieces of Mesoamerica: Mexico-Guatemala-Honduras.* Boulogne: Editions Arts 135.

Berlo, Janet Catherine. 1983. Conceptual Categories for the Study of Texts and Images in Mesoamerica. In *Text and Image in Pre-Columbian Art: Essays on the Interrelationship of the Verbal and Visual Arts* (ed. Janet C. Berlo), pp. 1–39. BAR International Series 180. Oxford: British Archaeological Reports.

Blaffer, Sarah C. 1972. *The Black-man of Zinacantan.* Austin: University of Texas Press.

Bonavia, Duccio. 1985. *Mural Painting of Ancient Peru.* Bloomington: Indiana University Press.

Bonor Villarejo, Juan Luis. 1987. Exploraciones en las grutas de Calcehtok y Oxkintok, Yucatán. *Mayab* 3: 24–31.

———. 1989. *Las cuevas mayas: Simbolismo y ritual.* Madrid: Universidad Complutense de Madrid.

Bowditch, Charles P. 1910. *The Numerations, Calendar Systems, and Astronomical Knowledge of the Maya.* Cambridge, Mass.

Bowles, John H. 1974. Notes on a Floral Form Represented in Maya Art and Its Iconographic Implications. In *First Palenque Round Table, 1973* (ed. Merle Greene Robertson), pp. 121–128. Palenque Round Table Series 1. Pebble Beach: Robert Louis Stevenson School.

Brady, James E. 1987. A Re-evaluation of Protoclassic Orange Wares. In *Maya Ceramics: Papers from the 1985 Maya Ceramic Conference* (ed. Prudence M. Rice and Robert J. Sharer), pp. 469–477. BAR International Series 345. Oxford: British Archaeological Reports.

———. 1988. The Sexual Connotation of Caves in Mesoamerican Ideology. *Mexicon* 1(93): 51–55.

———. 1989. An Investigation of Maya Ritual Cave Use with Special Reference to Naj Tunich, Peten, Guatemala. Ph.D. diss., University of California, Los Angeles.

———. 1990. Report on Recent Damage to the Inscriptions of Naj Tunich. *Mexicon* 12(1): 5–6.

———. 1991a. New Vandalism at Naj Tunich Cave. *National Geographic Research and Exploration* 7(1): 114–115.

———. 1991b. Caves and Cosmovision at Utatlan. *California Anthropologist* 18(1): 1–9.

———. 1991c. The Petexbatun Regional Cave Survey: Ritual and Sacred Geography. Paper presented at the 47th International Congress of Americanists. New Orleans.

———, and Andrea Stone. 1986. Naj Tunich: Entrance to the Maya Underworld. *Archaeology* 39(6): 18–25.

———, and Federico Fahsen. 1991. The Discovery of a New Maya Cave Painting Site in Guatemala. *Explorers Journal* 69(2): 52–55.

———, and Sandra Villagrán de Brady. 1989. Reconocimiento de los daños causados recientemente a las inscripiones de la cueva de Naj Tunich. Report presented to the IDEAH, August 30, 1989. Typescript.

———, and George Veni. 1992. Manmade and Pseudo-Karst Caves: The Implications of Subsurface Features within Maya Centers. *Geoarchaeology* 7(2): 149–167.

———, George Veni, Andrea Stone, and Allan Cobb. 1992. Explorations in the New Branch of Naj Tunich: Implications for Interpretation. *Mexicon* 14(4): 74–81.

Brainerd, George. 1958. *The Archaeological Ceramics of Yucatan.* Anthropological Records 19. University of California: Berkeley/Los Angeles.

Breuil, Véronique. 1986. Registro de las cuevas de la región de Xcochcax: Informe de trabajo de la temporada 1986. Typescript.

Bricker, Victoria R. 1973. *Ritual Humor in Highland Chiapas.* Austin: University of Texas Press.

———. 1986. *A Grammar of Mayan Hieroglyphs.* MARI Pub. 56. New Orleans: MARI, Tulane University.

———, and Cassandra R. Bill. 1989. Mortuary Practices in the Madrid Codex. Paper presented at the Séptima Mesa Redonda de Palenque, Chiapas.

Broda, Johanna. 1971. Las fiestas aztecas de los dioses de la lluvia. *Revista Española de Antropología Americana* 6: 245–327.

———. 1989. Geography, Climate and the Observation of Nature in Pre-Hispanic Mesoamerica. In *The Imagination of Matter: Religion and Ecology in Mesoamerican Traditions* (ed. David Carrasco), pp. 139–153. BAR International Series 515. Oxford: British Archaeological Reports.

Brundage, Burr Cartwright. 1979. *The Fifth Sun: Aztec Gods, Aztec World.* Austin: University of Texas Press.

Burkhart, Louise M. 1989. *The Slippery Earth: Nahua-Christian Moral Dialogue in Sixteenth-Century Mexico.* Tucson: University of Arizona Press.

Burkitt, Robert. 1930. Explorations in the Highlands of Western Guatemala. *Museum Journal* (University Museum, University of Pennsylvania) 21(1): 41–72.

Byland, Bruce E., and John M. D. Pohl. 1987. The Marriage of Twelve-Wind and Three-Flint at White Hill. *Thesis* 2(1): 10–17.

Cano, Agustin. 1984. *Manche and Peten: The Hazards of Itza Deceit and Barbarity.* Trans. Charles P. Bowditch and Guillermo Rivera. Culver City: Labyrinthos.

Carlson, John. 1981. A Geomantic Model for the Interpretation of Mesoamerican Sites: An Essay in Cross-Cultural Comparison. In *Mesoamerican Sites and World-Views* (ed. Elizabeth P. Benson), pp. 143–211. Washington: Dumbarton Oaks.

Carlson, Ruth, and Francis Eachus. 1977. The Kekchi Spirit World. In *Cognitive Studies of Southern Meso-*

america (ed. Helen L. Neuenswander and Dean E. Arnold), pp. 36–65. Museum of Anthropology Publication 3. Dallas: Summer Institute of Linguistics.

Carmen Leon Cázares, María del, and Mario Humberto Ruz. 1988. *Constituciones diocesanas del obispado de Chiapa, hechas y ordenadas por su señoria ilustrísima, el señor maestro don fray Francisco Nuñez de la Vega.* Mexico City: UNAM.

Carot, Patricia. 1982. L'occupation prehispanique des grottes de L'Alta Verapaz. *Journal de la Société des Americanistes* 68:27–32.

Casado López, María del Pilar. 1987. *Proyecto Atlas de Pictografías y Petrograbados.* Cuaderno de Trabajo 39. Mexico City: INAH.

Caso, Alfonso. 1946. Calendario y escritura de las antiguas culturas de Monte Albán. In *Miguel Othón de Mendízabal: Obras completas.* Vol. 1. Mexico City.

———. 1971. Calendrical Systems of Central Mexico. *HMAI* (ed. Robert Wauchope), 10:333–348. Austin: University of Texas Press.

Cera, Claire. 1976. Peintures rupestres prehispaniques du Mexique. In *Trois ans d'enseignement et de recherches en archéologie mésoaméricaine,* pp. 17–26. Paris: University of Paris.

———. 1977. Evolución de la pintura rupestre prehispánica en Mexico: Problemas de identificación y cronología. In *XV Mesa Redonda de la Sociedad Mexicana de Antropología,* pp. 463–466. Mexico City: Sociedad Mexicana de Antropología.

———. 1980. Hallazgo de pinturas en la Cueva de la Chepa, Chiapas. *Bulletin de la Mission Archéologique et Ethnologique Française au Mexique* 2: 7–12.

Clancy, Flora. 1985. Maya Sculpture. In Gallenkamp and Johnson 1985, pp. 58–70.

Clark, John W. 1965. Art at Cueva

Ahumada Rinconada, Nuevo Leon, Mexico. *Katunob* 5(4):4–6.

Coe, Michael D. 1966. *An Early Stone Pectoral from Southeastern Mexico.* Studies in Pre-Columbian Art and Archaeology 1. Washington: Dumbarton Oaks.

———. 1973. *The Maya Scribe and His World.* New York: Grolier Club.

———. 1975. *Classic Maya Pottery at Dumbarton Oaks.* Washington: Dumbarton Oaks.

———. 1976. Early Steps in the Evolution of Maya Writing. In *Origins of Religious Art and Iconography in Preclassic Mesoamerica* (ed. H. B. Nicholson), pp. 107–122. UCLA Latin American Studies Series 31. Los Angeles: UCLA Latin American Center Publications/Ethnic Arts Council of Los Angeles.

———. 1977. Supernatural Patrons of Maya Scribes and Artists. In *Social Process in Maya Prehistory* (ed. Norman Hammond), pp. 327–347. London/New York: Academic Press.

———. 1978. *Lords of the Underworld.* Princeton: Art Museum, Princeton University.

———. 1981. Religion and the Rise of Mesoamerican States. In *The Transition to Statehood in the New World* (ed. Grant D. Jones and Robert R. Kautz), pp. 157–171. Cambridge, Eng.: Cambridge University Press.

———. 1982. *Old Gods and Young Heroes: The Pearlman Collection of Maya Ceramics.* Jerusalem: Israel Museum, Jerusalem.

———. 1989. The Hero Twins: Myth and Image. In *The Maya Vase Book: A Corpus of Rollout Photographs of Maya Vases* (ed. Justin Kerr), 1: 161–183. New York: Kerr Associates.

———, and Richard A. Diehl. 1980. *In the Land of the Olmec.* 2 vols. Austin: University of Texas Press.

Coggins, Clemency C. 1975. Painting and Drawing Styles at Tikal: An His-

torical and Iconographic Reconstruction. Ph.D. diss., Harvard University.

———. 1988. The Manikin Scepter: Emblem of Lineage. *Estudios de cultura maya* 17:123–158.

Collier, Jane F. 1973. *Law and Social Change in Zinacantan.* Stanford: Stanford University Press.

Conkey, Margaret W. 1982. Boundedness in Art and Society. In *Symbolic and Structural Archaeology* (ed. Ian Hodder), pp. 115–128. Cambridge, Eng.: Cambridge University Press.

Cortez, Constance. 1986. The Principal Bird Deity in Preclassic and Early Classic Maya Art. Master's thesis, University of Texas, Austin.

Craine, Eugene R., and Reginald C. Reindorp, trans. 1979. *The Codex Pérez and the Book of Chilam Balam of Mani.* Norman: University of Oklahoma Press.

Dahlgren, Barbara. 1966. *La Mixteca: Su cultura e historia prehispánicas.* Mexico City: UNAM.

Davis, Whitney. 1984. Representation and Knowledge in the Prehistoric Rock Art of Africa. *African Archaeological Review* 2:7–35.

Diccionario de San Francisco. 1976. Ed. Oscar Michelon. Bibliotheca Linguística Americana 2. Graz: Akademische Druck- und Verlagsanstalt.

Dieseldorff, Erwin P. 1926. El Tzultacá y el Mam, los dioses prominentes de la religión maya. *Anales de la Sociedad de Geografía e Historia* 2(4):378–386.

Drennan, Robert D. 1976. Religion and Social Evolution in Formative Mesoamerica. In *The Early Mesoamerican Village* (ed. Kent V. Flannery), pp. 306–368. New York: Academic Press.

Durán, Diego. 1971. *Book of the Gods and Rites and the Ancient Calendar.* Trans. Fernando Horcasitas and Doris Heyden. Norman: University of Oklahoma Press.

Du Solier, Wilfrido. 1939. Una representación pictórica de Quetzalcoatl en una cueva. *Revista Mexicana de Estudios Antropológicos* 3:129–141.

Eastham, Anne, and Michael Eastham. 1979. The Wall Art of the Franco-Cantabrian Deep Caves. *Art History* 2(4):365–387.

Edmonson, Munro S. 1965. *Quiche-English Dictionary*. MARI Pub. 30. New Orleans: MARI, Tulane University.

———. 1971. *The Book of Counsel: The Popol Vuh of the Quiche Maya of Guatemala*. MARI Pub. 35. New Orleans: MARI, Tulane University.

Eliade, Mircea. 1959. *The Sacred and the Profane: The Nature of Religion*. New York: Harcourt, Brace, and World.

Fontenrose, Joseph. 1959. *Python: A Study of Delphic Myth and Its Origins*. Berkeley/Los Angeles: University of California Press.

Fought, John G. 1972. *Chorti (Mayan) Texts 1*. Philadelphia: University of Pennsylvania Press.

Fox, James A., and John S. Justeson. 1984. Polyvalence in Mayan Hieroglyphic Writing. In *Phoneticism in Mayan Hieroglyphic Writing* (ed. John S. Justeson and Lyle Campbell), pp. 17–166. Pub. 9. Albany: Institute for Mesoamerican Studies, State University of New York at Albany.

Gallenkamp, Charles, and Regina Elise Johnson, eds. 1985. *Maya: Treasures of an Ancient Civilization*. New York: Harry N. Abrams.

Gann, Thomas. 1926. *Ancient Cities and Modern Tribes: Exploration and Adventure in Maya Lands*. New York: Charles Scribner and Sons.

García Bárcena, Joaquín, and Diana Santamaría. 1982. *La Cueva de Santa Marta Ocozocoautla, Chiapas*. Colección Científica 111. Mexico City: INAH.

Garibay K., Angel María. 1965. *Teogonía e historia de los mexicanos: Tres opúsculos del siglo XIV*. Mexico City: Editorial Porrúa.

Gatica Trejo, Ricardo. 1980. El lugar de los ritos mayas amenezado ahora por el hombre. *El Gráfico*, June 29.

Gay, Carlo. 1967. Oldest Cave Paintings of the New World. *Natural History* 76(4):28–35.

———. 1971. *Chalcacingo*. Graz: Akademische Druck- u. Verlagsanstalt.

Gendrop, Paul. 1980. Temples, Caves, or Monsters? Notes on Zoomorphic Facades in Pre-Hispanic Architecture. In *Third Palenque Round Table, Part 2* (ed. Merle Greene Robertson), pp. 45–59. Palenque Round Table Series 5. Austin: University of Texas Press.

Girard, Rafael. 1949. *Los chortis ante el problema maya*. 3 vols. Mexico City: Antigua Libreria Robredo.

———. 1962. *Los mayas eternos*. Mexico City: Antigua Libreria Robredo.

González Licón, Ernesto. 1986. *Los mayas de la gruta de Loltún, Yucatán, a través de sus materiales arqueológicos*. Colección Científica. Mexico City: INAH.

———. 1987. Tipología cerámica de la gruta de Loltún, Yucatán. In *Memorias del Primer Coloquio Internacional de Mayistas*, pp. 165–173. Mexico City: UNAM.

Gossen, Gary H. 1974. *Chamulas in the World of the Sun*. Cambridge, Mass.: Harvard University Press.

Graham, Elizabeth, Logan McNatt, and Mark A. Gutchen. 1980. Excavations in Footprint Cave, Caves Branch, Belize. *Journal of Field Archaeology* 7(2):153–172.

Graham, Ian. 1967. *Archaeological Explorations in El Peten, Guatemala*. MARI Pub. 33. New Orleans: MARI, Tulane University.

Graham, Ian. 1980. *Corpus of Maya Hieroglyphic Inscriptions*. Vol. 2, pt. 3. Cambridge, Mass.: Peabody Museum of Archaeology and Ethnology, Harvard University.

Grant, Campbell. 1967. *Rock Art of the American Indian.* New York: Promontory Press.

Griaule, Marcel. 1934. Rites rélatifs aux peintures rupestres dans le Soudan français. *Comptes Rendus Sommaires des Séances de la Société de Biogéographie* 95:65–68.

Griffin, Gillet G. 1981. Olmec Forms and Materials Found in Central Guerrero. In *The Olmec and Their Neighbors* (ed. Elizabeth P. Benson), pp. 209–222. Washington: Dumbarton Oaks.

———. 1982. Una representación olmeca de arquitectura en las pinturas rupestres de Juxtlahuaca. In *Las representaciones de arquitectura en la arqueología de América* (ed. Daniel Schávelzon), pp. 44–46. Mexico City: UNAM.

Grigsby, Thomas L. 1986. The Survival of a Cave Cult in Central Mexico. *Journal of Latin American Lore* 12(2): 161–180.

Grove, David C. 1967. Juxtlahuaca Cave (Guerrero) Revisited. *Katunob* 6(2):37–40.

———. 1968. Chalcatzingo, Morelos, Mexico: A Reappraisal of the Olmec Rock Carvings. *American Antiquity* 33(4):486–491.

———. 1969. Olmec Cave Paintings: Discovery from Guerrero, Mexico. *Science* 164(3878):421–423.

———. 1970. *The Olmec Paintings of Oxtotitlan Cave, Guerrero, Mexico.* Studies in Pre-Columbian Art and Archaeology 6. Washington: Dumbarton Oaks.

———. 1973. Olmec Altars and Myths. *Archaeology* 26:128–135.

———, ed. 1987. *Ancient Chacatzingo.* Austin: University of Texas Press.

———. 1989. Olmec: What's in a Name. In *Regional Perspectives on the Olmec* (ed. Robert J. Sharer and David C. Grove), pp. 8–14. Cambridge, Mass.: School of American Research/Cambridge University Press.

———, and Jorge Angulo V. 1987. A Catalog and Description of Chalcatzingo's Monuments. In Grove 1987, pp. 114–131.

Grube, Nikolai. 1987. Notes on the Reading of Affix T142. *Research Reports on Ancient Maya Writing* 4. Washington: Center for Maya Research.

———. 1989. Archaeological Investigations in the Southern Peten. *Mexicon* 11(3):44–45.

———. 1991. Epigraphic Research at Caracol, Belize. Typescript.

———, and David Stuart. 1987. Observations on T110 as the Syllable *ko. Research Reports on Ancient Maya Writing* 8. Washington: Center for Maya Research.

Guiteras-Holmes, Calixta. 1961. *Perils of the Soul: The World View of a Tzotzil Indian.* New York: Free Press of Glencoe, Inc.

Gussinyer, Jordi. 1976. Pinturas rupestres de Chiapas: El abrigo Juy-Juy. *Revista Autónoma de Chiapas* 1(2): 79–94.

———. 1980. Les pintures rupestres de l'abric de "Los Monos" de Chiapas. *Boletín Americanista* 22(30): 125–155.

Haberland, Wolfgang. 1972. The Cave of the Holy Ghost. *Archaeology* 25(4):286–291.

Hammond, Norman. 1972. Classic Maya Music, Part I: Maya Drums. *Archaeology* 25(2):125–131.

Hanks, William F. 1984. Sanctification, Structure, and Experience in a Yucatec Ritual Event. *Journal of American Folklore* 97(384):131–166.

———. 1990. *Referential Practice: Language and Lived Space among the Maya.* Chicago: University of Chicago Press.

———, and Don S. Rice, eds. 1989. *Word and Image in Maya Culture: Explorations in Language, Writing, and Representation.* Salt Lake City: University of Utah Press.

Hansen, Richard D. 1991. The Road to Nakbe. *Natural History,* May, pp. 8–14.

Hatt, Robert T., Harvey I. Fisher, Dave A. Langebartel, and George W. Brainerd. 1953. *Faunal and Archaeological Researches in Yucatan Caves.* Bulletin 33. Bloomfield Hills: Cranbrook Institute of Science.

Heizer, Robert F., and Martin A. Baumhoff. 1962. *Prehistoric Rock Art of Nevada and Eastern California.* Berkeley: University of California Press.

Hermitte, Esther M., 1970. *Poder sobrenatural y control social.* Ediciones Especiales 57. Mexico City: Instituto Indigenista Interamericano.

Heyden, Doris. 1975. The Cave underneath the Pyramid of the Sun at Teotihuacan. *American Antiquity* 40(2): 131–147.

———. 1976. Los ritos de paso en las cuevas. *Boletín INAH,* época 2, 19: 17–26.

———. 1981. Caves, Gods, and Myths: World-View and Planning in Teotihuacan. In *Mesoamerican Sites and World-Views* (ed. Elizabeth P. Benson), pp. 1–35. Washington: Dumbarton Oaks.

———. 1983. *Mitología y simbolismo de la flora en el México prehispánico.* Mexico City: UNAM.

———. 1989. The Skin and Hair of Tlaltecuhtli. In *The Imagination of Matter: Religion and Ecology in Mesoamerican Traditions* (ed. David Carrasco), pp. 211–224. BAR International Series 515. Oxford: British Archaeological Reports.

Hill, Carol A., and Paolo Forti. 1986. *Cave Minerals of the World.* Huntsville: National Speleological Society.

Holland, William R. 1963. *Medicina maya en los altos de Chiapas.* Mexico City: Instituto Nacional Indigenista.

Houston, Stephen D. 1983a. Ballgame Glyphs in Classic Maya Texts. In *Recent Contributions to Maya Hieroglyphic Decipherment, vol. 1* (ed. Stephen Houston), pp. 26–30. New Haven: HRAflex.

———. 1983b. A Reading for the Flint-Shield Glyph. In *Recent Contributions to Maya Hieroglyphic Decipherment, I* (ed. Stephen Houston), pp. 13–25. New Haven: HRAflex.

———. 1986. Problematic Emblem Glyphs: Examples from Altar de Sacrificios, El Chorro, Río Azul, and Xultun. *Research Reports on Ancient Maya Writing* 3. Washington: Center for Maya Research.

———. 1987. Notes on Caracol Epigraphy and Its Significance. In *Investigations in the Classic Maya City of Caracol, Belize: 1985–1987* by Arlen F. Chase and Diane Z. Chase, Appendix II. San Francisco: Pre-Columbian Art Research Institute.

———. 1988. The Phonetic Decipherment of Mayan Glyphs. *Antiquity* 62(234): 120–135.

———. 1989. *Reading the Past: Maya Glyphs.* Berkeley/Los Angeles: University of California Press/British Museum.

———, and David Stuart. 1989. The *Way* Glyph: Evidence for "Co-essences" among the Classic Maya. *Research Reports on Ancient Maya Writing* 30. Washington: Center for Maya Research.

———, and David Stuart. 1990. T632 as **Muyal,** "Cloud." Central Tennessean Notes in Maya Epigraphy, no. 1. Nashville.

Hunt, Eva. 1977. *The Transformation of the Hummingbird: The Cultural Roots of a Zinacantecan Mythical Poem.* Ithaca: Cornell University Press.

Jansen, Maarten. 1982. *Huisi Tacu.* 2 vols. No. 24. Amsterdam: Centrum voor Studie en Documentatie van Latijns Amerika.

Jiménez Moreno, Wigberto. 1974. *Primeros Memoriales de Fray Bernardino de Sahagún.* Colección Científica 16. Mexico City: INAH.

Joesink-Mandeville, Leroy V., and Sylvia Meluzin. 1976. Olmec-Maya Relationships: Olmec Influence in Yucatan. In *Origins of Religious Art and Iconography in Preclassic Mesoamerica* (ed. H. B. Nicholson), pp. 87–105. UCLA Latin American Studies Series 31. Los Angeles: UCLA Latin American Center Publications/Ethnic Arts Council of Los Angeles.

Johnston, Kevin. n.d. Variation in Emblem Glyph Prefixion in Classic Maya Inscriptions. Typescript.

Jones, Christopher. n.d. Untitled essay on Naj Tunich. Typescript.

———, and Linton Satterthwaite. 1982. *The Monuments and Inscriptions of Tikal: The Carved Monuments.* Tikal Report 30, Part A. Philadelphia: University Museum, University of Pennsylvania.

Joralemon, Peter D. 1971. *A Study of Olmec Iconography.* Studies in Pre-Columbian Art and Archaeology 7. Washington: Dumbarton Oaks.

———. 1974. Ritual Blood-Sacrifice among the Ancient Maya: Part I. In *Primera Mesa Redonda de Palenque, Part II* (ed. Merle Greene Robertson), pp. 59–75. Palenque Round Table Series 2. Pebble Beach: Robert Louis Stevenson School/Pre-Columbian Art Research.

———. 1976. The Olmec Dragon: A Study in Pre-Columbian Iconography. In *Origins of Religious Art and Iconography in Preclassic Mesoamerica* (ed. H. B. Nicholson), pp. 27–71. UCLA Latin American Studies Series 31. Los Angeles: UCLA Latin American Center Publications/Ethnic Arts Council of Los Angeles.

Jung, Carl G. 1950. Lecture IV. In *The Symbolic Life: Miscellaneous Writings.* Trans. R. F. C. Hull, 18: 102–134. Bollingen Series 20. Princeton: Princeton University Press.

Justeson, John S., William M. Norman,

Lyle Campbell, and Terrence Kaufman. 1985. *The Foreign Impact on Lowland Mayan Language and Script.* MARI Pub. 53. New Orleans: MARI, Tulane University.

Kaufman, Terrence S., and William M. Norman. 1984. An Outline of Proto-Cholan Phonology, Morphology, and Vocabulary. In *Phoneticism in Mayan Hieroglyphic Writing* (ed. John S. Justeson and Lyle Campbell), pp. 77–166. Pub. 9. Albany: Institute for Mesoamerican Studies, State University of New York at Albany.

Kearney, Michael. 1972. *The Winds of Ixtepeji: World View and Society in a Zapotec Town.* New York: Holt, Rinehart, and Winston.

Kehoe, Thomas F. 1990. Corralling Life. In *The Life of Symbols* (ed. Mary LeCron Foster and Lucy Jayne Botscharow), pp. 175–192. Boulder/San Francisco/Oxford: Westview Press.

Kelley, David H. 1976. *Deciphering the Maya Script.* Austin: University of Texas Press.

Kerr, Justin. 1989–1990. *The Maya Vase Book: A Corpus of Rollout Photographs of Maya Vases.* 2 vols. New York: Kerr Associates.

Klein, Cecilia F. 1980. Who Was Tlaloc? *Journal of Latin American Lore* 6(2):155–204.

———. 1988. Rethinking Cihuacoatl: Aztec Political Imagery of the Conquered Woman. In *Smoke and Mist: Mesoamerican Studies in Memory of Thelma D. Sullivan* (ed. J. Kathryn Josserand and Karen Dakin), pp. 237–277. BAR International Series 402. Oxford: British Archaeological Reports.

Knorozov, Yuri V. 1967. *The Writing of the Maya Indians.* Trans. Sophie Coe. Peabody Museum of Archaeology and Ethnology, Russian Translation Series 4. Cambridge, Mass.: Harvard University.

Korelstein, Audrey. 1989. In the Land of the Maya: Tradition and the Structuring of Space. Paper presented at the 88th meeting of the American Anthropological Association. Washington, D.C.

Kowalski, Jeff K. 1987. *The House of the Governor: A Maya Palace at Uxmal, Yucatan, Mexico.* Norman: University of Oklahoma Press.

———. 1989. The Mythological Identity of the Figure on the La Esperanza ("Chinkultic") Ball Court Marker. *Research Reports on Ancient Maya Writing* 27. Washington: Center for Maya Research.

Kubler, George. 1969. *Studies in Classic Maya Iconography.* Memoirs of the Connecticut Academy of Arts and Sciences 18. New Haven: Connecticut Academy of Arts and Sciences.

———. 1972. La evidencia intrínseca y la analogía etnológica en el estudio de las religiones mesoamericanas. In *Religión en Mesoamérica: XII Mesa Redonda.* Mexico City: Sociedad Mexicana de Antropología.

———. 1973. Science and Humanism among Americanists. In *The Iconology of Middle American Sculpture,* pp. 163–167. New York: Metropolitan Museum of Art.

———. 1984a. Renascences and Disjunction in Mesoamerican Art. In *The Collected Works of George Kubler* (ed. Thomas F. Reese), pp. 351–372. New Haven: Yale University Press.

———. 1984b. Ancient American Gods and Their Living Impersonators. *Apollo,* April, pp. 240–246.

———. 1985. Pre-Columbian Pilgrimages in Mesoamerica. In *Fourth Palenque Round Table, 1980* (ed. Merle Greene Robertson and Elizabeth P. Benson), pp. 313–316. Palenque Round Table Series 4. San Francisco: Pre-Columbian Art Research Institute.

La Farge, Oliver. 1947. *Santa Eulalia: The Religion of a Cuchumatan Indian Town.* Chicago: University of Chicago Press.

———, and D. Beyers. 1931. *The Year Bearer's People.* MARI Pub. 3. New Orleans: MARI, Tulane University.

Laughlin, Robert M. 1988. *The Great Tzotzil Dictionary of Santo Domingo Zinacantán.* 3 vols. Smithsonian Contributions to Anthropology 31. Washington: Smithsonian Institution Press.

Leach, E. R. 1958. Magical Hair. *Journal of the Royal Anthropological Institute of Great Britain and Ireland.* 88: 147–164.

Lee, Thomas A., Jr. 1969. Cuevas secas del Río La Venta, Chiapas: Informe preliminar. *Antropología e Historia de Guatemala* 21(1–2):23–37.

———. 1985. *Los códices mayas.* Tuxtla Gutiérrez: Universidad Autónoma de Chiapas.

Leicht, Raymond C. 1972. The Dos Peñas Rock Paintings: A Local Style from the Chilapa Region, Guerrero. *Katunob* 8(1):58–69.

Leroi-Gourhan, André. 1982. *The Dawn of European Art.* Cambridge, Eng.: Cambridge University Press.

Lewis-Williams, J. David. 1981. *Seeing and Believing: Symbolic Meaning in Southern San Rock Paintings.* New York: Academic Press.

López Austin, Alfredo. 1973. *Hombre-dios: Religión y política en el mundo nahuatl.* Mexico City: UNAM, Mexico.

———. 1980. *Cuerpo humano e ideología: Las concepciones de los antiguos nahuas.* Mexico City: UNAM.

López de Cogolludo, Diego. 1867. *Historia de Yucatán.* 2 vols. Mérida: Manuel Aldana Rivas.

Lothrop, Samuel K. 1933. *Atitlan: An Archaeological Study of Ancient Remains on the Borders of Lake Atitlan.* CIW Pub. 444. Washington: Carnegie Institution of Washington.

Love, Bruce, and Eduardo Peraza C. 1984. Wahil Kol: A Yucatec Maya

Agricultural Ceremony. *Estudios de Cultura Maya* 15:251–300.

Lounsbury, Floyd G. 1973. On the Derivation and Reading of the "Ben-Ich" Prefix. In *Mesoamerican Writing Systems* (ed. Elizabeth P. Benson), pp. 99–144. Washington: Dumbarton Oaks.

———. 1983. The Base of the Venus Table of the Dresden Codex and Its Significance for the Calendar-Correlation Problem. In *Calendars in Mesoamerica and Peru: Native American Computations of Time* (ed. Anthony Aveni and Gorden Brotherston), pp. 1–26. BAR International Series 174. Oxford: British Archaeological Reports.

Lynch, B. Mark, and R. Donahue. 1980. A Statistical Analysis of Two Rock-Art Sites in Northwest Kenya. *Journal of Field Archaeology* 7:75–85.

MacLeod, Barbara. 1987. *An Epigrapher's Annotated Index to Cholan and Yucatecan Verb Morphology*. Columbia: University of Missouri Museum of Anthropology.

———. 1989a. The 819-Day-Count: A Soulful Mechanism. In Hanks and Rice 1989, pp. 112–126.

———. 1989b. Writing on a Curved Page: A Reading of the Manik Collocation in the Primary Standard Sequence. *Mexicon* 11(2):27–30.

———. 1990a. Deciphering the Primary Standard Sequence. Ph.D. diss., University of Texas at Austin.

———. 1990b. The God N/Step Set in the Primary Standard Sequence. In *The Maya Vase Book: A Corpus of Rollout Photographs of Maya Vases* (ed. Justin Kerr), 2:331–346. New York: Kerr Associates.

———. n.d. Notes on the Dragon Maw as *way*. Typescript.

———, and Dennis Puleston. 1980. Pathways into Darkness: The Search for the Road to Xibalba. In *Third Palenque Round Table, 1978, Part 1*

(ed. Merle Greene Robertson and Donna Call Jeffers), pp. 71–78. Palenque Round Table Series 4. Palenque/Monterey: Pre-Columbian Art Research Institute/Herald Printers.

MacNeish, Richard S. 1958. *Investigations in the Sierra de Tamaulipas, Mexico*. Transactions of the American Philosophical Society, vol. 48, part 6. Philadelphia: American Philosophical Society.

———. 1972. The Evolution of Community Patterns in the Tehuacán Valley of Mexico and Speculation about the Cultural Processes. In *Man, Settlement, and Urbanism* (ed. Peter J. Ucko, Ruth Tringham, and G. W. Dimbleby), pp. 67–93. London: Duckworth.

———. 1983. Mesoamerica. In *Early Man in the New World* (ed. Richard Shutler, Jr.), pp. 125–135. Beverly Hills: Sage Publications.

Maler, Teobert. 1902–1903. *Researches in the Central Portion of the Usumasintla Valley*. Memoirs of the Peabody Museum of American Archaeology and Ethnology 2. Cambridge, Mass.: Harvard University.

Márquez de González, Lourdes, Antonio Benavides Castillo, and Peter J. Schmidt. 1982. *Exploración en la Gruta de Xcan, Yucatán*. Mérida: Centro Regional del Sureste del INAH.

Marquina, Ignacio. 1964. *Arquitectura prehispánica*. Mexico City: INAH.

Martín Arana, Raul. 1987. Classic and Postclassic Chalcatzingo. In Grove 1987, pp. 387–399.

Martínez, Hildeberto, and Luis Reyes García. 1970. Culto en las cuevas de Cuautlapa en el siglo XVIII. *Comunidad* 5(27):543–551.

Mathews, Peter. 1977. The Inscriptions on the Back of Stela 8, Dos Pilas. Typescript.

———. 1980. Notes on the Dynastic Sequence of Bonampak, Part 1. In *Third Palenque Round Table, Part 2* (ed. Merle Greene Robertson), pp. 60–73. Palenque Round Table Series 5. Austin: University of Texas Press.

———. 1985. Maya Early Classic Monuments and Inscriptions. In *A Consideration of the Early Classic Period in the Maya Lowlands* (ed. Gordon R. Willey and Peter Mathews), pp. 5–54. Pub. 10. Albany: Institute for Mesoamerican Studies, State University of New York at Albany.

Maudslay, Alfred P. 1889–1902. *Biologia Centrali-Americana: Or Contributions to the Knowledge of the Fauna and Flora of Mexico and Central America*. 5 vols. London: F. Ducane Godman and O. Salvin.

Mayén de Castellanos, Guisela. 1986. *Tzute y jerarquía en Sololá*. Guatemala: Museo Ixchel del Traje Indígena de Guatemala.

Mayer, Karl Herbert. 1988. Tikal Ceramics from the Mundo Perdido on Exhibit. *Mexicon* 10(1):3–4.

Meighan, Clement W. 1981. Theory and Practice in the Study of Rock Art. In *The Shape of the Past: Studies in Honor of Franklin D. Murphy* (ed. Giorgio Buccellati and Charles Speroni), pp. 66–91. Los Angeles: University of California Institute of Archaeology.

Mendieta, Geronimo de. 1945. *Historia eclesiástica indiana*. Mexico City: Editorial Salvador Chavez Hayhoe.

Mercer, Henry. [1896] 1975. *The Hill-Caves of Yucatan*. Reprint. Norman: University of Oklahoma Press.

Milbrath, Susan. 1987. Birth Images in Mixteca-Puebla Art. In *The Role of Gender in Precolumbian Art and Architecture* (ed. Virginia E. Miller), pp. 153–178. Lanham: University Press of America.

Miller, Arthur G. 1973. *The Mural Painting of Teotihuacan*. Washington: Dumbarton Oaks.

———. 1977. "Captains of the Itza": Unpublished Mural Evidence from Chichen Itza. In *Social Process in Maya Prehistory: Studies in Honor of Sir Eric Thompson* (ed. Norman Hammond), pp. 197–225. London/ New York: Academic Press.

———. 1982. *On the Edge of the Sea: Mural Painting at Tancah-Tulum, Quintana Roo, Mexico*. Washington: Dumbarton Oaks.

Miller, Mary Ellen. 1986. *The Art of Mesoamerica from Olmec to Aztec*. London: Thames and Hudson.

Miller, Mary Ellen, and Stephen D. Houston. 1988. The Classic Maya Ballgame and Its Architectural Setting. *Res* 14:47–65.

Miller, Virginia E. 1983. A Reexamination of Maya Gestures of Submission. *Journal of Latin American Lore* 9(1):17–38.

———. 1989. Star Warriors at Chichen Itza. In Hanks and Rice 1989, pp. 287–305.

Miller, Walter S. 1956. *Cuentos mixes*. Biblioteca de Folklore Indígena 2. Mexico City: Instituto Nacional Indigenista.

Mora L., Raziel. 1974. Las pinturas rupestres de Atlihuetzían, Tlaxcala (México). *Anales de Antropología* 11: 89–108.

Morán, Francisco. 1935. *Arte y diccionario en lengua choltí*. Publication 9. Baltimore: Maya Society.

Morley, Sylvanus G. 1915. *An Introduction to the Study of the Maya Hieroglyphs*. Bulletin 57. Washington, D.C.: Bureau of American Ethnology.

———. 1937–1938. *The Inscriptions of Peten*. 5 vols. CIW Pub. 437. Washington: Carnegie Institution of Washington.

Morris, Walter F. 1985. Flowers, Saints, and Toads: Ancient and Modern Maya Textile Design Symbolism. *National Geographic Research* 1(winter): 63–78.

Moser, Christopher. 1975. Cueva de Ejutla: ¿Una cueva funeraria posclá-

sica? *Boletín INAH*, época 2, 14:
25–36.

Motolinía, Toribio (de Benavente).
1951. *Motolinia's History of the Indians of New Spain*. Trans. Francis Borgia Steck. Washington: Academy of American Franciscan History.

Motul Dictionary. 1929. *Diccionario de Motul. Maya-español atribuido a Fray Antonio de Ciudad Real y arte de la lengua por Fray Juan Coronel*. Ed. Juan Martínez Hernández. Mérida: Talleres de la Compañia Tipográfica Yucateca.

Muñoz Camargo, Diego. 1892. *Historia de Tlaxcala*. Ed. Alfredo Chavero. Mexico City: Oficina Tip. de la Secretaria de Fomento.

Nash, June. 1970. *In the Eyes of the Ancestors: Belief and Behavior in a Maya Community*. New Haven: Yale University Press.

Navarrete, Carlos. 1960. Archaeological Explorations in the Region of the Frailesca, Chiapas, Mexico. *Papers of the New World Archaeological Foundation* 7, Publication No. 6. Orinda: New World Archaeological Foundation.

———. 1971. Prohibición de la danza del tigre en Tamulte, Tabasco, en 1631. *Tlalocán* 6(4):374–376.

———, and Eduardo Martínez. 1961. Investigaciones arqueológicas en el río Sabinal, Chiapas. *Revista del Instituto de Ciencias y Artes de Chiapas* 2(5):49–83.

———, and Eduardo Martínez. 1977. *Exploraciones arqueológicas en la Cueva de los Andasolos, Chiapas*. Tuxtla Gutiérrez: Universidad Autónoma de Chiapas.

Neuenswander, Helen. 1981. Vestiges of Early Maya Time Concepts in a Contemporary Maya (Cubulco Achi) Community: Implications for Epigraphy. *Estudios de Cultura Maya* 13: 125–164.

Nicholson, H. B. 1962. Notes and News: Middle America. *American Antiquity* 27(4):622.

———. 1971. Religion in Pre-Hispanic Central Mexico. *HMAI* (ed. Robert Wauchope), 10: 395–446. Austin: University of Texas Press.

———. 1976. Preclassic Mesoamerican Iconography from the Perspective of the Postclassic: Problems in Interpretational Analysis. In *Origins of Religious Art and Iconography in Preclassic Mesoamerica* (ed. H. B. Nicholson), pp. 157–175. Los Angeles: UCLA Latin American Center/Ethnic Arts Council.

Nuttall, Zelia. 1926. Official Reports on the Towns of Tequizistlan, Tepechpan, Acolman, and San Juan Teotihuacan Sent by Francisco de Casteneda to His Majesty, Philip II, and the Council of the Indies, in 1580. *Papers of the Peabody Museum of American Archaeology and Ethnology*, vol. 11, no. 2. Cambridge, Mass.: Harvard University.

———. 1975. *The Codex Nuttall: A Picture Manuscript from Ancient Mexico*. New York: Dover.

Ochoa Salas, Lorenzo. 1972. Las pinturas rupestres en la Cueva de la Malinche. *Boletín INAH* 2(5):3–14.

Olavarrieta Marenco, Marcela. 1977. *Magia en los Tuxtlas*. Mexico City: Instituto Nacional Indigenista.

Orrego Corozo, Miguel, and Rudy Larrios Vallalta. 1983. *Reporte de las investigaciones arqueológicas en el Grupo 5E-11, Tikal*. Guatemala City: Instituto de Antropología e Historia de Guatemala.

Palacio, Joseph O. 1977. *Excavation at Hokeb Ha, Belize*. Occasional Publication 3. Belize City: Belize Institute for Social Research and Action.

Panofsky, Erwin. 1960. *Renaissance and Renascences in Western Art*. Stockholm: Almquist and Wiksell.

Parsons, Elsie C. 1936. *Mitla Town of Souls*. Chicago: University of Chicago Press.

Parsons, Lee A. 1983. Altars 9 and 10, Kaminaljuyu, and the Evolution of the Serpent-Winged Deity. In *Civilization in the Americas: Essays in Honor of Gordon Willey* (ed. Richard M. Leventhal and Alan L. Kolata), pp. 145–156. Cambridge, Mass.: University of New Mexico Press/Peabody Museum of Archaeology and Ethnology.

———. 1986. *The Origins of Maya Art: Monumental Stone Sculpture of Kaminaljuyu, Guatemala, and the Southern Pacific Coast*. Studies in Pre-Columbian Art and Archaeology 28. Washington: Dumbarton Oaks.

Pasztory, Esther. 1974. *The Iconography of the Teotihuacan Tlaloc*. Studies in Pre-Columbian Art and Archaeology 15. Washington: Dumbarton Oaks.

———. 1983. *Aztec Art*. New York: Harry N. Abrams.

Pearse, A. S. 1938. *Fauna of the Caves of Yucatan*. CIW Pub. 491. Washington: Carnegie Institution of Washington.

Pendergast, David M. 1971. *Excavations at Eduardo Quiroz Cave, British Honduras (Belize)*. Royal Ontario Museum Art and Archaeology Occasional Paper 21. Toronto: Royal Ontario Museum.

———. 1981–1982. The Old Man and the Moon. *Rotunda* 14(4): 7–12.

Piho, Virve. 1982. Estructuras piramidales en las pinturas rupestres de Achichipilco. In *Las representaciones de arquitectura en la arqueología de América* (ed. Daniel Schávelzon), pp. 374–383. Mexico City: UNAM.

———, and Carlos Hernandez. 1972. Pinturas rupestres aztecas en el Popocatepetl. In *XII Mesa Redonda de la Sociedad Mexicana de Antropología, Religión en Mesoamérica*, pp. 85–90. Mexico City: INAH.

Pijoán, José. 1946. *Summa artis: Histo-*

ria general del arte. 10 vols. Madrid: Espasa-Calpe.

Piña Chan, Román. 1955. *Chalcatzingo, Morelos, México*. Dirección de Monumentos Prehispánicos, Informe 4. Mexico City: INAH.

Pohl, Mary. 1981. Ritual Continuity and Transformation in Mesoamerica: Reconstructing the Ancient Maya Cuch Ceremony. *American Antiquity* 46(3):513–529.

———. 1983. Maya Ritual Faunas: Vertebrate Remains from Burials, Caches, Caves, and Cenotes in the Maya Lowlands. In *Civilization in the Ancient Americas* (ed. Richard M. Leventhal and Alan L. Kolata), pp. 55–103. Cambridge, Mass.: University of New Mexico Press/Peabody Museum of Archaeology and Ethnology.

———, and John D. Pohl. 1983. Ancient Maya Cave Rituals. *Archaeology* 36:28–32, 50–51.

Pompa y Pompa, Antonio, and Daniel J. Valencia Cruz. 1985. *Bibliografía para el estudio del testimonio rupestre en México*. Cuaderno de Trabajo 59. Mexico City: INAH.

Price, Sally. 1989. *Primitive Art in Civilized Places*. Chicago: University of Chicago Press.

Proskouriakoff, Tatiana. 1950. *A Study of Classic Maya Sculpture*. CIW Pub. 593. Washington: Carnegie Institution of Washington.

———, and J. Eric S. Thompson. 1947. Maya Calendar Round Dates such as 9 Ahau 17 Mol. *Notes on Middle American Archaeology and Ethnology* 79. Washington: Carnegie Institution of Washington.

Puleston, Dennis E. 1977. The Art and Archaeology of Hydraulic Agriculture in the Maya Lowlands. In *Social Process in Maya Prehistory* (ed. Norman Hammond), pp. 449–467. London/New York: Academic Press.

Querejazu Lewis, Roy. 1987. Arte parietal y ofrendas en Jatun Potrero. *Sociedad de Investigacion del Art Rupestre de Bolivia Boletín* (La Paz) 1:17–21.

Ramirez Castaneda, Isabel. 1913. El Folk-lore de Milpa Alta, D.F., Mexico. In *Eighteenth International Congress of Americanists 1912*, pp. 352–361. London: Harrison and Sons.

Rands, Robert. 1953. The Water Lily in Maya Art: A Complex of Alleged Asiatic Origin. *Bureau of American Ethnology Bulletin* 151. Washington.

Rätsch, Christian. 1979. Zwei Yukatekische Höhlen mit Felsbildern. *Mexicon* 1(2):17–19.

Reddell, James R. 1977. *A Preliminary Survey of the Caves of the Yucatan Peninsula*. Austin: Speleo Press.

Redfield, Robert, and Alfonso Villa Rojas. 1934. *Chan Kom: A Maya Village*. CIW Pub. 448. Washington: Carnegie Institution of Washington.

Reents-Budet, Dorie, and Barbara MacLeod. 1986. The Archaeology of Petroglyph Cave, Belize. Typescript.

Reilly, F. Kent, III. 1990. Cosmos and Rulership: The Function of Olmec-Style Symbols in Formative Period Mesoamerica. *Visible Language* 24(1):12–37.

Relaciones histórico-geográficas de la gobernación de Yucatán. 1983. 3 vols. Ed. Mercedes de la Garza. Mexico City: UNAM.

Ricketson, Edith Bayles. 1936. Pictographs at Lake Ayarza, Guatemala. *Maya Research* 3(3–4):244–248.

Riese, Berthold. 1981. Maya-Höhlenmalereien in Nord-Chiapas. *Mexicon* 3(4):55–56.

Ringle, William M. 1988. Of Mice and Monkeys: The Value and Meaning of T1016, the God C Hieroglyph. *Research Reports on Ancient Maya Writing* 18. Washington: Center for Maya Research.

Robertson, Merle Greene. 1983. *The Sculpture of Palenque*. Vol. 1. Princeton: Princeton University Press.

Robicsek, Francis. 1978. *The Smoking Gods*. Norman: University of Oklahoma Press.

———, and Donald M. Hales. 1981. *The Maya Book of the Dead: The Ceramic Codex*. Charlottesville: University of Virginia Art Museum.

———, and Donald M. Hales. 1982. *Maya Ceramic Vases from the Late Classic Period: The November Collection of Maya Ceramics*. Charlottesville: University of Virginia Art Museum.

Robina, Ricardo de. 1956. *Estudio preliminar de las ruinas de Hochob, municipio de Hopelchén, Campeche*. Mexico City.

Rodas, Haroldo. 1980. Gruta de las inscripciones, con murales mayas descubierta en Peten, cerca de Belice. *Prensa Libre* (Guatemala City), August 31.

Roys, Ralph L. 1954. *The Maya Katun Prophecies of the Books of Chilam Balam, Series I*. CIW Contribution 57. Washington: Carnegie Institution of Washington.

———. 1966. Native Empires in Yucatan. *Revista Mexicana de Estudios Antropológicos* 20:153–177.

———. 1967. *The Chilam Balam of Chumayel*. Norman: University of Oklahoma Press.

Ruspoli, Mario. 1986. *The Cave of Lascaux: The Final Photographs*. New York: Harry N. Abrams.

Ruz, Mario Humberto. 1982. *Los legítimos hombres: Aproximación antropológica al grupo tojolobal 3*. Mexico City: UNAM, Centro de Estudios Mayas.

Sáenz de Santa María, Carmelo. 1940. *Diccionario cakchiquel-español*. Guatemala City: Tipografía Nacional.

Sahagún, Fray Bernardino de. 1950–1982. *Florentine Codex: General History of the Things of New Spain*. Trans. Arthur O. Anderson and Charles E. Dibble. Santa Fe/Salt Lake City: School of American Research/University of Utah.

———. 1979. *Codice florentino*. 3 vols. Mexico City: Biblioteca Medicea

Laurenziana/Archivo General de la Nación, Secretaria de Gobernación.

Samaniego, Lorenzo, Enrique Vergara, and Henning Bischof. 1985. New Evidence on Cerro Sechin, Casma Valley, Peru. In *Early Ceremonial Architecture in the Andes* (ed. Christopher B. Donnan), pp. 165–190. Washington: Dumbarton Oaks.

Sánchez de Aguilar, Pedro. 1937. *Informe contra idolorum cultores del obispado de Yucatán*. Mérida: E. G. Triay e Hijos.

Sandstrom, Alan R. 1975. Ecology, Economy and the Realm of the Sacred; An Interpretation of Ritual in a Nahua Community. Ph.D. diss., Indiana University.

Sapper, Carl. 1897. *Northern Central America with a Trip to Highland Anahuac: Travels and Studies of the Years 1888–1895*. Trans. A. M. Parker. Brunswick: Friedrich Viewig and Son.

Satterthwaite, Linton. 1965. Calendrics of the Maya Lowlands. In *HMAI* (ed. Robert Wauchope), 3:603–631. Austin: University of Texas Press.

Schaafsma, Polly. 1980. *Indian Rock Art of the Southwest*. Santa Fe: School of American Research.

———. 1985. Form, Content, and Function: Theory and Method in North American Rock Art Studies. In *Advances in Archaeological Method and Theory* (ed. Michael B. Schiffer), 8:237–277. New York: Academic Press.

Schávelzon, Daniel. 1980. Temples, Caves, or Monsters? Notes on Zoomorphic Facades in Pre-Hispanic Architecture. In *Third Palenque Round Table, 1978, Part 2* (ed. Merle Greene Robertson), pp. 151–162. Palenque Round Table Series 5. Austin: University of Texas Press.

Schele, Linda. 1982. *Maya Glyphs: The Verbs*. Austin: University of Texas Press.

———. 1984. Human Sacrifice among the Classic Maya. *Ritual Human Sacrifice in Mesoamerica* (ed. E. H. Boone), pp. 7–48. Washington: Dumbarton Oaks.

———. 1986. The Figures on the Central Ballcourt Marker AIIb at Copan. Copan Note 13. Austin.

———. 1987. New Data on the Paddlers from Butz'-Chan of Copan. Copan Note 29. Austin.

———. 1989. A Brief Note on the Name of the Vision Serpent. In *The Maya Vase Book: A Corpus of Rollout Photographs of Maya Vases*, 1:146–148. New York: Kerr Associates.

———. 1991. An Epigraphic History of the Western Maya Region. *Classic Maya Political History: Hieroglyphic and Archaeological Evidence* (ed. T. Patrick Culbert), pp. 72–101. Cambridge, Eng.: School of American Research/Cambridge University Press.

———. n.d. Brotherhood in Ancient Maya Kingship. Typescript.

———, and Nikolai Grube. 1988. The Future Marker on a Hand Scattering Verb at Copan. Copan Note 42. Austin.

———, and Mary Ellen Miller. 1986. *The Blood of Kings: Dynasty and Ritual in Maya Art*. Fort Worth: Kimbell Art Museum.

Schellhas, Paul. 1904. *Representation of Deities of the Maya Manuscripts*. Papers of the Peabody Museum of Archaeology and Ethnology, vol. 4, no. 1. Cambridge, Mass.: Harvard University.

Schevill, Margot B. 1985. *Evolution in Textile Design from the Highlands of Guatemala*. Occasional Papers 1. Berkeley: Lowie Museum of Anthropology.

Scholes, France V., and Eleanor B. Adams. 1938. *Don Diego Quijada, Alcalde Mayor de Yucatán, 1561–1565*. 2 vols. Mexico City: Editorial Porrúa.

Schultze-Jena, Leonhard. 1946. *La vida y las creencias de los indígenas quichés de Guatemala*. Trans. Antonio Goubaud Carrera and Herbert D. Sapper. Publicaciones Especiales 1. Guatemala City: Instituto Indigenista Nacional.

Sedat, Guillermo S. 1955. *Nuevo diccionario de las lenguas k'ekchí y española*. Chamelco: Instituto Lingüístico de Verano en Guatemala.

Seler, Eduard. 1901. *Die alten Ansiedlungen von Chaculá im Distrikte Nenton des Departments Huehuetenango der Republik Guatemala*. Berlin: Verlag von Dietrich Reimer.

———. 1960. *Gesammelte Abhandlungen zur Amerikanischen Sprach- und Alterthumskunde*. 5 vols. Graz: Akademische Druck- und Verlagsanstalt.

———. 1963. *Comentarios al Codice Borgia*. 3 vols. Mexico City: Fondo de Cultura Económica.

Siffre, Michel. 1979. *A la recherche de l'art des cavernes du pays maya*. Paris: Editions Alain Lefeuvre.

Siller, Juan Antonio. 1989. Viajes de reconocimiento arquitectónico a la región maya: Reciente localización de las cuevas de San Miguel en el Petén, Guatemala. In *Memorias del Segundo Coloquio Internacional de Mayistas*, pp. 167–177. Mexico City: UNAM.

Siméon, Rémi. 1981. *Diccionario de la lengua náhuatl o mexicana*. 2d ed. Mexico City: Siglo Veintiuno.

Smith, Mary Elizabeth. 1973. *Picture Writing from Ancient Southern Mexico: Mixtec Place Signs and Maps*. Norman: University of Oklahoma Press.

Smith, Robert E. 1955. *Ceramic Sequence at Uaxactun, Guatemala*. 2 vols. MARI Pub. 20. New Orleans: MARI, Tulane University.

Sosa, John R. 1985. The Maya Sky, the Maya World: A Symbolic Analysis of Yucatec Maya Cosmology. Ph.D. diss., State University of New York at Albany.

Spero, Joanne M. 1987. Lightning Men and Water Serpents: A Comparison of Mayan and Mixe-Zoquean Beliefs. Master's Thesis, University of Texas at Austin.

Stephens, John Lloyd. 1841. *Incidents of Travel in Central America, Chiapas, and Yucatan*. New York: Harper and Row.

Stirling, Matthew W. 1955. Stone Monuments of the Río Chiquito, Veracruz, Mexico. *Bureau of American Ethnology Bulletin* 157:1–23.

Stone, Andrea J. 1982. Recent Discoveries from Naj Tunich Cave, El Peten, Guatemala. *Mexicon* 4(5–6):93–99.

———. 1983a. The Zoomorphs of Quirigua, Guatemala. Ph.D. diss., University of Texas at Austin.

———. 1983b. Epigraphic Patterns in the Inscriptions of Naj Tunich Cave. In *Recent Contributions to Maya Hieroglyphic Decipherment* (ed. Stephen Houston), 1:83–103. New Haven: HRAflex.

———. 1985a. Variety and Transformation in the Cosmic Monster Theme at Quirigua, Guatemala. In *Fifth Palenque Round Table, 1983* (ed. Virginia Fields), pp. 39–48. Palenque Round Table Series 7. San Francisco: Pre-Columbian Art Research Institute.

———. 1985b. The Moon Goddess at Naj Tunich. *Mexicon* 7(2):23–29.

———. 1987a. Cave Painting in the Maya Area. *Latin American Indian Literatures Journal* 3(1):95–108.

———. 1987b. Commentary. *Mexicon* 9(2):37.

———. 1989a. Actun Ch'on, Oxkutzcab, Yucatán: Una cueva maya con pinturas del clásico tardío. *Boletín de la Escuela de Ciencias Antropológicas de la Universidad de Yucatán* 16(99):24–35.

———. 1989b. The Painted Walls of

Xibalba: Maya Cave Painting as Evidence of Cave Ritual. In Hanks and Rice 1989, pp. 319–335.

———. 1989c. Las pinturas y los petroglifos de Naj Tunich, Petén: Investigaciones recientes. In *Segundo Simposio sobre Investigaciones Arqueológicas de Guatemala*, pp. 239–263. Guatemala City: Ministerio de Cultura y Deportes.

———. 1992. From Ritual in the Landscape to Capture in the Urban Center: The Recreation of Ritual Environments in Mesoamerica. *Journal of Ritual Studies* 6(1):109–132.

Stone, Doris. 1982. Cultural Radiations from the Central and Southern Highlands of Mexico into Costa Rica. In *Aspects of the Mixteca-Puebla Style and Central Mexican Culture in Southern Mesoamerica*, pp. 61–70. MARI Occasional Papers 4. New Orleans: MARI, Tulane University.

Strecker, Matthias. 1976. Pinturas rupestres de la Cueva de Loltún. *Boletín INAH*, época 2, 18:3–8.

———. 1981. Exploraciones arqueológicas de Teobert Maler en cuevas yucatecas. *Boletín de la Escuela de Ciencias Antropológicas de la Universidad de Yucatán* 8–9(48–49):20–31.

———. 1982a. *Rock Art of East Mexico and Central America: An Annotated Bibliography*. 2d ed. Monograph 10. Los Angeles: Institute of Archaeology, University of California.

———. 1982b. Representaciones de manos y pies en el arte rupestre de cuevas de Oxkutzcab, Yucatán. *Boletín de la Escuela de Ciencias Antropológicas de la Universidad de Yucatán* 9(52):47–57.

———. 1984a. Felsmalereien von Chicoasén, Chiapas. *Mexicon* 4(2):21–22.

———. 1984b. Cuevas mayas en el municipio de Oxkutzcab, Yucatán (1): Cuevas Mis y Petroglifos. *Boletín de la Escuela de Ciencias Antropológi-*

cas de la Universidad de Yucatán 12 (68):21–28.

———. 1985. Cuevas mayas en el municipio de Oxkutzcab (2): Cuevas Ehbis, Xcosmil y Cahum. *Boletín de la Escuela de Ciencias Antropológicas de la Universidad de Yucatán* 12(70):16–23.

———. 1987. Representaciones sexuales en el arte rupestre de la región maya. *Mexicon* 9(2):34–37.

Stresser-Pean, Guy. 1990. Pinturas rupestres del Risco de los Monos: Situación del acantilado San Antonio Nogalar. In *El arte rupestre en México* (ed. María del Pilar Casado), pp. 587–610. Mexico City: INAH.

Strömsvik, Gustav. 1956. Exploration of the Cave of Dzab-Na, Tecoh, Yucatan. *Current Reports* 35, pp. 463–470. Washington: Carnegie Institution of Washington.

Stuart, David. 1981. Untitled essay on Naj Tunich. Typescript.

———. 1984. Royal Auto-Sacrifice among the Maya. *Res* 7/8:6–20.

———. 1985. The "Count of Captives" Epithet in Classic Maya Writing. In *Fifth Palenque Round Table, 1983* (ed. Virginia Fields), pp. 97–102. Palenque Round Table Series 7. San Francisco: Pre-Columbian Art Research Institute.

———. 1987. Ten Phonetic Syllables. *Research Reports on Ancient Maya Writing* 14. Washington: Center for Maya Research.

———. 1988. Blood Symbolism in Maya Iconography. In *Maya Iconography* (ed. Elizabeth P. Benson and Gillet G. Griffin), pp. 175–221. Princeton: Princeton University Press.

———. In press. New Decipherments of Maya Kinship Terms. In *The Language of Maya Hieroglyphs*. Santa Barbara: New Scholar.

———, and Stephen D. Houston. 1994. *Classic Maya Place Names*. Dumbarton Oaks Studies in Pre-

Columbian Art and Archaeology 33. Washington: Dumbarton Oaks.

Stuart, George E. 1981. Maya Art Treasures Discovered in Cave. *National Geographic* 160(2):220–235.

Sullivan, Thelma D. 1974. Tlaloc: A New Etymological Interpretation of the God's Name and What It Reveals of His Essence and Nature. *Atti del XL Congresso Internazionale degli Americanisti*, 2:213–219. Rome/Genoa.

Sundstrom, Línea. 1990. *Rock Art of the Southern Black Hills: A Contextual Approach*. New York: Garland Publishing.

Taggart, James M. 1983. *Nahuat Myth and Social Structure*. Austin: University of Texas Press.

Tate, Carolyn. 1982. The Maya Cauac Monster's Formal Development and Dynastic Contexts. In *Pre-Columbian Art History* (ed. Alana Cordy-Collins), pp. 33–54. Palo Alto: Peek Publications.

Taube, Karl A. 1983. The Teotihuacan Spider Woman. *Journal of Latin American Lore* 9(2):107–189.

———. 1985. The Classic Maya Maize God: A Reappraisal. In *Fifth Palenque Round Table, 1983* (ed. Virginia M. Fields), pp. 171–181. Palenque Round Table Series 7. San Francisco: Pre-Columbian Art Research Institute.

———. 1986. The Teotihuacan Cave of Origin. *Res* 12:51–82.

———. 1988a. A Prehispanic Maya Katun Wheel. *Journal of Anthropological Research* 44(2):183–203.

———. 1988b. The Ancient Yucatec New Year Festival: The Liminal Period in Maya Ritual and Cosmology. Ph.D. diss., Yale University.

———. 1989a. Ritual Humor in Classic Maya Religion. In Hanks and Rice 1989, pp. 351–382.

———. 1989b. Itzam Cab Ain: Caimans, Cosmology, and Calendrics in Postclassic Yucatan. *Research Reports*

on *Ancient Maya Writing* 26. Washington: Center for Maya Research.

Taussig, Michael T. 1980. *The Devil and Commodity Fetishism in South America.* Chapel Hill: University of North Carolina Press.

Taylor, Dicey. 1980. The Cauac Monster. In *Third Palenque Round Table, 1978, Part 1* (ed. Merle Greene Robertson and Donna Call Jeffers), pp. 79–90. Palenque Round Table Series 4, Palenque/Monterey: Pre-Columbian Art Research Institute/Herald Printers.

Tedlock, Barbara. 1982. *Time and the Highland Maya.* Albuquerque: University of New Mexico Press.

———. 1983. El C'oxol: Un símbolo de la resistencia quiché a la conquista espiritual. In *Nuevas perspectivas sobre el Popol Vuh* (ed. Robert M. Carmack and Francisco Morales Santos), pp. 343–357. Guatemala City: Editorial Piedra Santa.

Tedlock, Dennis. 1985. *Popol Vuh: The Definitive Edition of the Mayan Book of the Dawn of Life and the Glories of Gods and Kings.* New York: Simon and Schuster.

Termer, Franz. 1957. *Etnología y etnografía de Guatemala.* Guatemala City: Editorial del Ministerio de Educación Pública.

Thomas, Norman D. 1975. Elementos pre-colombinos y temas modernos en el folklore de los zoques de Rayón. In *Los zoques de Chiapas.* Mexico City: Instituto Nacional Indigenista.

Thompson, Edward H. 1897. Cave of Loltun, Yucatan. *Memoirs of the Peabody Museum of American Archaeology and Ethnology,* vol. 1, no. 2. Cambridge, Mass.: Harvard University.

Thompson, J. Eric S. 1927. A Correlation of the Mayan and European Calendars. *Field Museum of Natural History, Anthropological Series* 17(1): 1–22.

———. 1930. *Ethnology of the Mayas of Southern and Central British Hondu-*

ras. Field Museum of Natural History Publication 274, Anthropological Series 17, no. 2.

———. 1939. *The Moon Goddess in Middle America with Notes on Related Deities.* CIW Pub. 509, Contribution 29. Washington, D.C.: Carnegie Institution of Washington.

———. 1959. The Role of Caves in Maya Culture. *Mitteilungen aus dem Museum für Völkerkunde in Hamburg* 25:122–129.

———. 1960. *Maya Hieroglyphic Writing: An Introduction.* Norman: University of Oklahoma Press.

———. 1962. *A Catalog of Maya Hieroglyphs.* Norman: University of Oklahoma Press.

———. 1970a. *Maya History and Religion.* Norman: University of Oklahoma Press.

———. 1970b. The Bacabs: Their Portraits and Their Glyphs. In *Monographs and Papers in Maya Archaeology* (ed. William R. Bullard, Jr.), pp. 469–486. Papers of the Peabody Museum of Archaeology and Ethnology 61. Cambridge, Mass.: Harvard University.

———. 1975. Introduction to *The Hill-Caves of Yucatan* by Henry Mercer, pp. vii–xliv. Norman: University of Oklahoma.

———. 1977. A Proposal for Constituting a Maya Subgroup, Cultural and Linguistic, in the Peten and Adjacent Regions. In *Anthropology and History in Yucatan* (ed. Grant D. Jones), pp. 3–42. Austin: University of Texas Press.

Todorov, Tzvetan. 1984. *The Conquest of America: The Question of the Other.* New York: Harper and Row.

Townsend, Richard F. 1982. Malinalco and Lords of Tenochtitlan. In *The Art and Iconography of Late Post-Classic Central Mexico* (ed. Elizabeth H. Boone), pp. 111–140. Washington: Dumbarton Oaks.

Tozzer, Alfred P. 1941. *Landa's* Rela-

ción de las Cosas de Yucatán. Papers of the Peabody Museum of Archaeology and Ethnology 18. Cambridge, Mass.: Harvard University.

Tuan, Yi-Fu. 1974. *Topophilia: A Study of Environmental Perceptions, Attitudes, and Values.* Englewood Cliffs: Prentice-Hall.

———. 1975. Geopiety: A Theme in Man's Attachment to Nature and to Place. In *Geographies of the Mind* (ed. David Lowenthal and Martyn J. Bowden), pp. 11–39. New York: Oxford University Press.

Turner, Paul R. 1972. *The Highland Chontal.* New York: Holt, Rinehart, and Winston.

Turner, Victor. 1967. Ritual Symbolism, Morality, and Social Structure among the Ndembu. In *The Forest of Symbols: Aspects of Ndembu Ritual,* pp. 48–58. Ithaca: Cornell University Press.

———. 1970. Forms of Symbolic Action: An Introduction. In *Forms of Symbolic Action* (ed. Robert Spencer), pp. 3–25. Seattle/London: American Ethnological Society, University of Washington Press.

———. 1972. The Center Out There: Pilgrim's Goal. *History of Religions* 12:191–230.

———. 1974. Pilgrimages as Social Processes. In *Dramas, Fields and Metaphors: Symbolic Action in Human Society,* pp. 166–230. Ithaca: Cornell University Press.

———. 1977. *The Ritual Process: Structure and Anti-Structure.* Ithaca: Cornell University Press.

Ucko, Peter J., and Andrée Rosenfeld. 1967. *Paleolithic Cave Art.* New York: McGraw-Hill.

Valentine, J. Manson. 1965. The Discovery and Possible Significance of X-Kukican, Ancient Maya Site. Report 1. Tuscaloosa: Alabama Museum of Natural History.

Van Gennep, Arnold. 1960. *The Rites of Passage.* Trans. Monika B. Vizedom

Images from the Underworld

and Gabrielle L. Coffee. Chicago: University of Chicago Press.

Vega Bolaños, Luis. 1945. *Catálogo de construcciones religiosas del estado de Yucatán*. Vol. 2. Mexico City: Talleres Gráficos de la Nación.

Velázquez Morlet, Adriana, and Edmundo Lopéz de la Rosa. 1988. Subproyecto de pictografías y petrograbados. In *Zonas arqueólogicas: Yucatán, Proyecto Atlas Arqueológico Nacional*. Mexico City: INAH.

Velázquez Valadez, Ricardo. 1980. Recent Discoveries in the Cave of Loltun, Yucatán, Mexico. *Mexicon* 2: 53–55.

————. 1981. Etapas de funcionalidad de las grutas de Loltún. In *Memoria del Congreso Interno*, pp. 139–144. Mexico City: INAH.

Veni, George. 1990a. Maya Utilization of Karst Groundwater Resources. *Environmental Geology and Water Sciences* 16(1):63–66.

————. 1990b. Geologic and Management Considerations in the Preservation of the Maya Naj Tunich Paintings, Peten, Guatemala. In *American Indian Rock Art* (ed. Solveig Turpin), 16:49–61. Proceedings of the International Rock Art Conference of the American Rock Art Research Association. Austin: Texas Archaeological Research Laboratory, University of Texas.

Villa Rojas, Alfonso. 1956. Introduction to *Cuentos mixes* by Walter S. Miller, pp. 1–68. Biblioteca de Folklore Indígena 2. Mexico City: Instituto Nacional Indigenista.

Villacorta, Antonio J., and Carlos A. Villacorta. 1976. *Codíces mayas*. Guatemala City: Tipografía Nacional.

Villagra Caleti, Agustín. 1971. Mural Painting in Central Mexico. In *HMAI* (ed. Robert Wauchope), 10: 135–156. Austin: University of Texas Press.

Villagutierre Soto-Mayor, Juan de.

1983. *History of the Province of the Conquest of the Itza*. Trans. Robert D. Wood. Culver City: Labyrinthos.

Villela F., Samuel L. 1989. Nuevo testimonio rupestre olmeca en el oriente de Guerrero. *Arqueología* 2:37–48.

Vogt, Evon Z. 1969. *Zinacantan: A Maya Community in the Highlands of Chiapas*. Cambridge, Mass.: Belknap Press.

————. 1976. *Tortillas for the Gods: A Symbolic Analysis of Zinacanteco Rituals*. Cambridge, Mass: Harvard University Press.

————. 1981. Some Aspects of the Sacred Geography of Highland Chiapas. In *Mesoamerican Sites and World-Views* (ed. Elizabeth P. Benson), pp. 119–138. Washington: Dumbarton Oaks.

von Winning, Hasso. 1949. Shell Designs on Teotihuacan Pottery. *El Mexico Antiguo* 7:126–153.

Walters, Gary Rex. 1988. Maya Ceremonial Caves Project, 1988, Belize, Central America. Typescript.

Webster, David. 1989. The House of the Bacabs: Its Social Context. In *The House of the Bacabs* (ed. David Webster), pp. 5–40. Studies in Pre-Columbian Art and Archaeology 29. Washington: Dumbarton Oaks.

Wellmann, Klaus F. 1979. *A Survey of North American Indian Rock Art*. Graz: Akademische Druck- und Verlagsanstalt.

Whittaker, Arabelle, and Viola Warkentin. 1965. *Chol Texts on the Supernatural*. Mexico City: Summer Institute of Linguistics.

Wicke, Charles R. 1971. *Olmec: An Early Art Style of Pre-Columbian Mexico*. Tucson: University of Arizona Press.

————, and Fernando Horcasitas. 1957. Archaeological Investigations on Mount Tlaloc, Mexico. *Mesoamerican Notes* 5. Mexico City: Mexico City College.

Willey, Gordon R. 1973. Mesoamerican Art and Iconography and the Integrity of the Mesoamerican Ideological System. In *The Iconography of Middle American Sculpture*, pp. 153–162. New York: Metropolitan Museum of Art.

Wisdom, Charles. 1940. *The Chorti Indians of Guatemala.* Chicago: University of Chicago Press.

———. 1950. *Materials on the Chorti Language.* Collection of Manuscripts on Middle American Cultural Anthropology 28. Chicago: University of Chicago Library. Microfilm.

Witte, Karen, and E. Garza. 1981. Naj Tunich: The Writing on the Wall. *National Speleological Society News*, July, pp. 149–151.

Wonham, J. David. 1985. *Lake Pethá and the Lost Murals of Chiapas.* Pre-Columbian Art Research Institute Monograph 2. San Francisco: Pre-Columbian Art Research Institute.

Ximénez, Francisco. 1857. *Las historias del origin de los indios de esta provincia de Guatemala.* Ed. K. Scherzer. Vienna: Academia Imperial de las Ciencias.

Young, M. Jane. 1988. *Signs from the Ancestors: Zuni Cultural Symbolism and Perceptions of Rock Art.* Albuquerque: University of New Mexico Press.

Zavala Ruiz, Roberto, Luis C. Millet, Ricardo Velázquez Valadez, and Roberto MacSwiney. 1978. *Guía de las grutas de Loltún, Oxkutzcab, Yucatán.* Mexico City: INAH.

Index

110, 117, 125, 127, 128, 136, 146, 148, 158, 164, 213, 215, 217, 259n. 4

Naj Tunich petroglyphs: Drawing 2, 107, 187, figs. 5-11, 8-2; Drawing 53, 107, 108, 214, 217, 225, 260n. 2, figs. 5-14, 8-53; Drawing 57, 107, 108, 214, figs. 5-13, 8-57; Drawing 58, 107, 108, 214–215, figs. 5-12, 8-58; Drawing 89, 107, 108, 232, 260n. 2, figs. 5-15, 8-89

Nakbe, 74, 235

Navarrete, Carlos, 3, 52, 54, 87

New Year, 60, 61, 142, 145, 146, 161, 193, 258n. 18, 260n. 1

Nicholson, H. B., 11

Nim Li Punit, 107, 162, 182

Niwan Pukuh, 39

Norman, Will, 175

Nuñez de la Vega, Francisco, 40, 44

Olmecs, 10, 19–20, 22, 28, 37, 73–74; cave art of, 46–51, 148. See also Cacahuaziziqui; Juxtlahuaca; Oxtotitlan

Orrego, Miguel, 4

Oxkintok Lintel 1, 235

Oxtotitlan: paintings of, 47–50, 51, 185, figs. 4-6, 4-7; Mural 1, 20, 258n. 1, fig. 4-4

Paddler Gods, 97, 156, 175, 183

Palenque: and Joloniel, 90, 236; Sarcophagus Lid, 43, 170, fig. 7-16; Tablet of the Orator, 137, 140, 200, fig. 6-20; Temple of the Inscriptions, 168; and Yaleltsemen, 91

Panofsky, Erwin, 11

Parsons, Lee, 58

Pasión de Cristo, 83

Pearse, A. S., 86

Pendergast, David, 3

Perraza, Carlos, 70

Petroglyph Cave, 4

Piedras Negras, 168, 171, 173, 188, 236, 260n. 2, fig. 6-13

Piña Chan, Román, 258n. 3

Pohl, John, 222, 237

Pohl, Mary, 222, 237, 238

Pop, Bernabé, 100

Pop, Emilio, 100, 256n. 4

Popocatepetl rock shelter, 55, fig. 4-19

Primary Standard Sequence, 171, 173, 176, 179

Principal Bird Deity, 72, 74

Proskouriakoff, Tatiana, 58, 159, 160, 259n. 8

Puleston, Dennis, 28, 42

Pusilha, 107

Pusila, Caves of, 54, 98, figs. 4-114, 4-115

Puuc-style dating, 159–160, 162, 259n. 8, 260n. 2

quatrefoil, 23, 36, 37, 152

Quetzalcoatl, 21, 55

Quirigua: ballcourt markers, 36–37, fig. 3-33; inscriptions, 181; Stela E, 174, fig. 6-1; zoomorphs, 4, 22, 43, figs. 3-6, 3-35

Rain gods, 31, 33, 39, 40, 41, 80, 173, 178, 238, 257n. 6, 258n. 23. See also Chac; Chauc; Tlaloc

Rancho San Diego reliefs, 134, 137, 139, figs. 6-8, 6-18

Reddell, James, 86, 235

Redfield, Robert, 17, 257n. 15

Reents-Budet, Dorie, 4, 192

Reilly, Kent, 47

Richard, Mark, 91

Riese, Berthold, 87, 259n. 12

ritual. See cave ritual

Roberto's Cave, 4, 54, 94, 238, 246, figs. 4-106, 4-107, 4-108, A-3

Robicsek, Francis, 188

rock art: African, 10, 12; art historical context of, 10, definition of, 9; ethnographic context of, 10–11, 13; and the internal evidence, 12; Mesoamerican, 45, 120; North American, 10, 11, 12, 13, 93; South American, 13; topographic context of, 12–14

Roys, Ralph, 43, 85

sacred geography: and binary model of space, 7–8, 15–16, 19; and built environment, 240–241; and caves, 16–17; among Nahua, 16; among Olmec, 19–20; origins in Mesoamerica, 18–19; among Tzotzil, 15–16, 17; among Yucatec, 17

Sacul, 156, 158, 178, 179–180, 181, 182, 241

Sahagún, Bernardino de, 31, 32, 34, 36, 40

Saki C'oxol, 40, 153, 228

Sánchez de Aguilar, Pedro, 255n. 1

San Lorenzo: ceramics, 28; Monument 20, 19, 22, fig. 2-6

San Miguel, 97–98, 246, figs. 4-112, 4-113

Santa Marta paintings, 46, 52

Santo Domingo, 96–97, 181, 183, 236, 246, 250, fig. 4-111

Sapper, Karl, 237, 257n. 16

Schaafsma, Polly, 9

Schele, Linda, 150, 175, 179, 181, 191, 198, 200, 260n. 5

Schematic rock art, definition of, 46

Schmidt, Peter, 61

scribe, 90, 96, 117, 165, 170, 181, 183, 239

Seler, Eduard, 36, 257n. 10

serpents, 21, 23, 34, 47, 49, 50, 51, 54, 77, 78, 79, 80, 83–84, 94, 96, 238, 240

shaman, 13, 42, 74, 117, 128, 146, 153, 154, 156, 170, 174, 178

Sierra de Tamaulipas rock paintings, 54, 85–86, 92

Sierrita de Ticul: definition of, 56; style, 236

Siffre, Michel, 98

Siller, Juan Antonio, 97

Slocum, Marianne, 90

Sombreron, 39

Sosa, John, 36, 38

Spero, Joanne, 44, 172

Standard Nominal Phrase, definition of, 171

Starr, Frederick, 145

Stephens, John Lloyd, 243

Stirling, Matthew, 49

Stone, Andrea, 35, 165, 177

Strecker, Matthias, 3, 4, 35, 52, 57, 61, 65, 68, 69, 85, 86, 185, 194

Stuart, David, 24, 100, 117, 166, 170, 171, 173, 175, 177, 178, 260n. 5

Stuart, George, 100, 110

suhuy, 17, 239

Sullivan, Thelma, 34

Sumidero Canyon paintings, 52

sun, 16, 36, 37, 38, 74, 78, 81, 84, 148, 153, 217, 238

Sundstrom, Linnéa, 9, 240